STUDY GUIDE

Davide Hakes

Edward Gamber

Suzanne Iskander
University of Guelph-Humber

The Economics of Money, Banking, and Financial Markets

Fourth Canadian Edition

Frederic S. Mishkin
Columbia University

Apostolos Serletis
University of Calgary

Pearson Canada
Toronto

ISBN 978-0-321-67512-5

Acquisitions Editor: Claudine O'Donnell
Developmental Editor: Christina Lee
Project Manager: Cheryl Jackson
Copy Editor: Susan Bindernagel

8 17

Printed and bound in the United States of America.

Contents

Contents

HOW TO USE THIS STUDY GUIDE

This *Study Guide* will help you learn the concepts in *The Economics of Money, Banking, and Financial Markets.* As you work through each chapter, you will actively review the important definitions, details of financial institutions, and economic principles from your textbook. You will also actively apply the economic models to graphical and numerical problems. This reinforcement of the important textbook ideas will allow you to more quickly master the concepts and will better prepare you for exams.

Each chapter corresponds with your textbook and contains the following learning tools.

- *Chapter Synopsis/Completions:* Each chapter begins with a summary of the chapter. Students complete the key terms from the text in the synopsis. This section is particularly important because a working economic and financial vocabulary is necessary in order for the student to advance through the material.

- *Helpful Hints:* This section provides some additional suggestions and examples to help clarify the more difficult material.

- *Practice Problems and Short-Answer Questions:* Provided are a number of multi-step problems that require numerical, graphical, or written solutions. The problems are based on the larger issues developed in the chapter. Smaller issues are addressed with short-answer questions.

- *Critical Thinking:* This section provides a single multi-step problem that is an application of one of the major issues developed in the chapter.

- *Self-Test:* The self-test section provides fifteen true/false and thirty multiple-choice questions to validate areas of successful learning and to highlight areas needing improvement.

- *Solutions:* Detailed solutions for all problems and questions are provided at the end of the *Study Guide.*

You should experiment with different ways to use this *Study Guide* to better help you learn. Most students should work through each section of the *Study Guide* in order. However, if you feel *very* comfortable with the text material, then you might want to proceed directly to the Self-Test section. If you are happy with your performance, then you can begin the next chapter.

Suzanne Iskander

CHAPTER **1**

Why Study Money, Banking, and Financial Markets?

CHAPTER SYNOPSIS/COMPLETIONS

The study of money, banking, and financial markets is of value because it provides answers to everyday financial questions. Financial institutions in the economy have an impact on how efficiently funds are moved from savers to borrowers. Money and monetary policy influence inflation, interest rates, and aggregate output.

(1) _____ _____ allow funds to move from people with an excess of funds to those with a shortage. In the bond market, firms borrow by issuing (2) _____ (claims on the issuer's income or (3) _____) called bonds. (4) _____ require the issuer to make periodic payments to the purchaser. These payments are known as interest. The (5) _____ _____ is the cost of borrowing expressed as a percent per year. The interest rate is determined in the bond market. Since different interest rates tend to move together, economists often simply refer to "the" interest rate. In the stock market, firms issue securities called (6) _____ _____. Stock represents a share of ownership of the company.

Financial institutions are necessary in order for financial markets to function efficiently. (7) _____ _____ borrow from one group and lend to another. Banks are financial intermediaries that accept deposits and make loans. (8) _____ _____ are major disruptions in financial markets characterized by sharp declines in asset prices and the failure of many firms. Other related financial institutions are insurance companies, mutual funds, finance companies, and investment banks. (9) _____ are still the largest group of financial intermediaries, but the other financial institutions are growing in importance. A recent financial innovation is the delivery of financial services electronically, which is known as (10) _____.

(11) _____, or the money supply, is defined as anything that is generally accepted in payment for goods and services or the repayment of debt. Changes in the money supply have an impact on many economic variables. Money affects the (12) _____ _____, the upward and downward movements in (13) _____ _____. Output is usually measured by GDP. Reductions in the growth rate of the money supply have preceded every period of declining output, known as (14) _____, since the beginning of the twentieth century. Not every reduction in the money supply, however, is followed by a recession. The (15) _____ _____ usually rises during recessions. The money supply also has an effect on the (16) _____ _____

_____ and the (17) _____ _____. There is a positive relationship between (18) _____ and the growth rate of the money supply. Generally, high growth rates of the money supply are associated with high interest rates on long-term bonds, and low growth rates of the money supply with low long-term bond rates, but this relationship is too complex to address here. (19) _____ _____ is the theory that relates changes in the quantity of money to changes in aggregate economic activity and the price level. (20) _____ _____ is the management of money and interest rates. Monetary policy is conducted by a country's (21) _____ _____. The Canadian central bank is known as the (22) _____ _____. (23) _____ _____ involves decisions about government spending and taxation. A (24) _____ _____ is the excess of government expenditures over tax revenues, while a (25) _____ _____ arises when tax revenues exceed government expenditures. Budget deficits may result in a financial crisis, an increase in the growth rate of the money supply, a higher rate of inflation, and higher interest rates.

Financial markets have become increasingly integrated throughout the world. In the (26) _____ _____, currencies of one country are exchanged for currencies of another. The price of one country's currency in terms of another's is known as the (27) _____ _____. An (28) _____ in the Canadian dollar means that it buys more units of a foreign currency. A decline in the exchange rate is associated with a (29) _____ of the Canadian dollar.

This textbook stresses the economic way of thinking by developing a unifying framework for the study of money, banking, and financial markets. It focuses on tools rather than simple facts, so your knowledge will not become obsolete. The analytical framework focuses on changes in one variable at a time, holding all other variables constant.

HELPFUL HINTS

1.   Be prepared to rely on the model of supply and demand. This text, along with most economics texts, uses the model of supply and demand where applicable to illuminate the workings of the market. If you have forgotten the basics of supply and demand analysis, it might be to your advantage to improve your understanding of the model by reading the supply and demand chapter in the introduction of any principles of economics text.

2.   Throughout the text, when dealing with supply and demand in the financial markets, always identify each side of the market as either the borrower or the lender of the funds. For example, in the bond market, the supplier of the bond is the borrower, and the demander of the bond is the lender. Then, after you have solved the analytical problem at hand, you can ask yourself, does this result make sense in term of the borrowers and lenders?

3.   Aggregate income and aggregate output are considered equal because the purchase of final goods and services (output) generates an equivalent value of payments to the factors of production that produced the output (income).

4.   The term "business cycle" mistakenly suggests that the movements in output are smooth and predictable. In reality, business cycles are irregular, unpredictable, and of varying duration. For this reason, business cycles are sometimes referred to as "economic fluctuations," which highlights their unpredictable nature.

EXERCISES

Practice Problems

1.   Suppose you are the Chief Financial Officer (CFO) of a large corporation. For each of the following situations, which of the following financial markets would your company use: the bond market, the stock market, or the foreign exchange market? Explain.
a.   Your company has $100 million that it would like to use to construct a factory in Germany.

_____

_____

b. Your company wishes to borrow $100 million to construct a factory in Canada.

_____

_____

c. Your company wishes to raise $100 million to construct a factory by selling additional shares of ownership in the company. That is, your company wishes to take on new partners.

_____

_____

2. Suppose that you are the head of the central bank of Canada.
a. What is the name of the organization that you direct?

_____

_____

b. Suppose Canada is experiencing a high rate of inflation. Is the money supply likely to be growing slowly or quickly? Explain.

_____

_____

c. If you wished to reduce the rate of inflation, what would you do to the growth rate of the money supply? Explain.

_____

_____

d. What is the likely effect of your anti-inflationary monetary policy on aggregate output and unemployment? Explain.

_____

_____

3. Some of the most important financial markets are discussed briefly in Chapter 1. The statements below refer to three of these markets in Canada: the bond market, the stock market, and the foreign exchange market. Indicate to which of the three markets each statement refers. Let B = bond market, S = stock market, and F = foreign exchange market.

_____ 1. The market where interest rates are determined.

_____ 2. The market where claims on the earnings of corporations are traded.

_____ 3. Individuals trying to decide whether to vacation in British Columbia or France might be influenced by the outcomes in this market.

_____ 4. The most widely followed financial market in Canada.

_____ 5. The prices of Japanese video cassette recorders sold in Canada are affected by trading in this market.

4.   For each of the following cases, indicate whether it represents depreciation or appreciation of Canadian dollar, by writing in the space provided a D for depreciation or an A for appreciation.

_____   1.   Canadian goods become more expensive in other countries.

_____   2.   It becomes cheaper to travel to other countries.

_____   3.   Imported cars become more expensive in Canada.

_____   4.   Canadian exported goods cost less in foreign countries.

_____   5.   Canadians will prefer to buy imported jeans, not Canadian-made jeans.

_____   6.   The value of each euro in terms of a Canadian dollar decreases.

Short-Answer Questions

1.   Suppose that Ford Motor Company of Canada imports a few auto parts from the United States but exports a great number of cars to the United States. Would Ford prefer that the Canadian dollar be strong on the foreign exchange markets (the Canadian dollar buys much foreign currency) or weak? Explain.

_____

_____

2.   Suppose that you are going to travel in Europe for the summer after you graduate from university. Would you prefer that the dollar be strong on the foreign exchange markets or weak? Explain.

_____

_____

3.   In which of the following markets is the interest rate determined—the bond market, stock market, or the foreign exchange market?

_____

_____

4.   Look at the graph in Chapter 1 of your text that shows the exchange rate of the Canadian dollar over the last 37 years. During which year would you think that exporters would have had the greatest difficulty selling their goods overseas? Why?

_____

_____

5.   What are financial intermediaries? Why is a bank considered a financial intermediary? Why do you think an insurance company is also considered a financial intermediary?

_____

6.   In addition to chartered banks, what other institutions are considered to be banks?

_____

7.   Suppose that the economy is in a recession. Just prior to the recession, what likely happened to the growth rate of money? In what direction is aggregate output likely to be moving? Unemployment? Inflation? Long–term bond interest rates?

_____

_____

8. Monetary policy is the management of which two monetary variables? What institution is responsible for monetary policy in Canada?

_____

_____

9. A pawnshop is a retail store that sells used goods such as jewellery, clothing, and electronic equipment. The pawnbroker obtains these used goods from individuals who borrow from the pawnbroker. The pawnbroker promises to return the used goods to the individual once the loan and interest charges are paid. However, if the individual does not bring in the pawn receipt by the agreed date, then the pawnbroker sells the goods. Are pawnbrokers financial intermediaries? How are they similar to banks? In what ways do they differ?

_____

_____

_____

10. On the eve of the Great Depression in 1929, the money supply (M2) in Canada was approximately $2.2 billion. By 1933, the money supply had fallen to $1.9 billion. What do you expect happened to the price level and economic activity in Canada during the period 1929 to 1933?

_____

_____

_____

Critical-Thinking Questions

You are watching a business news report on television with your roommate. The news reporter states that the Bank of Canada is raising interest rates and reducing the growth rate of the money supply in order to reduce the risk of future inflation. Your roommate says, "We need to take a bigger course load next semester and graduate early, because there is always a recession following a reduction in the growth rate of money. If we wait too long, it will be much harder to find a job."

1. Is it true that a recession always follows a reduction in the growth rate of the money supply? Explain.

_____

_____

_____

2. If there is a recession, will it be more difficult to find a job when you graduate? Explain.

_____

_____

_____

3. If the Bank of Canada reduces the growth rate of money, what will likely happen to the inflation rate? Explain.

_____

_____

_____

SELF-TEST

True-False Questions

Circle whether the following statements are true (T) or false (F).

T   F   1.   The interest rate is determined in the stock market.

T   F   2.   An increase in the value of the dollar relative to foreign currency (a strong dollar) means that foreign goods have become less expensive to Canadian residents, and Canadian goods have become more expensive to foreigners.

T   F   3.   Companies are financial intermediaries because they borrow from their depositors and loan those funds to others.

T   F   4.   A financial intermediary is an institution that borrows from people who have saved and then loans those funds to others.

T   F   5.   Banks are the largest financial intermediaries in the Canadian economy.

T   F   6.   Since different interest rates tend to move together, economists often refer to "the" interest rate.

T   F   7.   An increase in the growth rate of money has preceded every recession in Canada since the beginning of the twentieth century.

T   F   8.   A recession is a sudden expansion in Gross Domestic Product.

T   F   9.   An increase in the growth rate of the money supply is associated with an increase in the rate of inflation.

T   F   10.   Monetary policy is the management of fiscal deficits and surpluses.

T   F   11.   Economists frequently talk about "the interest rate" because most interest rates move up and down together.

T   F   12.   The budget deficit is the excess of government tax revenues over government expenditures.

T   F   13.   Some economists express concern that huge government budget deficits cause the money supply to grow more rapidly, causing inflation.

T   F   14.   One can reasonably assume that financial intermediaries would not exist unless they provided services that people valued.

T   F   15.   Economists tend to disregard events in the stock market since stock prices tend to be extremely stable and are therefore of little interest.

Multiple-Choice Questions

Circle the appropriate answer.

1.   The foreign exchange market is where

    a. the interest rate is determined.

    b. the price of one country's currency in terms of another's is determined.

    c. the inflation rate is determined.

    d. bonds are sold.

2.   Stock prices, as measured by the S&P/TSX Composite Index,

    a. have not changed much over time.

    b. have risen smoothly over time.

    c. have been extremely volatile over time.

    d. have declined substantially since they peaked in the mid 1980s.

3.   Which of the following is an example of a debt security that promises to make payments periodically for a specified period of time?

    a. Bond.

    b. Stock.

    c. Financial intermediary.

    d. Foreign exchange.

4. Which of the following is likely to occur if the stock market has been rising quickly?

   a. Consumers are willing to spend more on goods and services.

   b. Firms will increase their investment spending on new equipment.

   c. Firms will sell newly issued stock to raise funds for investment spending.

   d. All of the above.

5. If the dollar becomes weaker on the foreign exchange market (the value of the dollar falls relative to the value of foreign currency), which of the following is true?

   a. A trip to Europe is going to be less expensive in terms of dollars.

   b. Ford will export more cars to Mexico.

   c. A BMW automobile produced in Germany will cost less to import into Canada.

   d. Canadian citizens will import more goods and services from abroad.

6. When a firm issues stock, it

   a. has borrowed from the public.

   b. has taken on additional partners that own part of the assets of the firm and share in the firm's earnings.

   c. has purchased foreign currency.

   d. has agreed to make periodic payments for a specific period of time to the owner of the security.

7. Which of the following is an example of financial intermediation?

   a. A saver makes a deposit in a credit union, and the credit union makes a loan to a member for a new car.

   b. Research in Motion issues a bond that is sold to a retired person.

   c. Research in Motion issues common stock that is sold to a college student.

   d. All of the above are examples of financial intermediation.

8. Which of the following are the largest financial intermediaries in the Canadian economy?

   a. Insurance companies.

   b. Finance companies.

   c. Chartered banks.

   d. Mutual funds.

9. The term "bank" generally includes all of the following institutions except   .

   a. chartered banks.

   b. credit unions.

   c. trust and mortgage loan companies.

   d. finance companies.

10. A decrease in the growth rate of the money supply is most likely to be associated with

   a. a decrease in both aggregate output and the inflation rate.

   b. an increase in both aggregate output and the inflation rate.

   c. a decrease in aggregate output and an increase in the inflation rate.

   d. an increase in aggregate output and a decrease in the inflation rate.

11. If inflation is higher in Canada than in the United States, it is likely that

   a. aggregate output is larger in Canada than in the United States.

   b. the Canadian money supply is growing faster than in the U.S. money supply.

   c. Canada has a larger fiscal deficit.

   d. Canada has higher interest rates.

12. Monetary policy is the management of
    a. budget surpluses and deficits.
    b. government spending and taxation.
    c. the money supply and interest rates.
    d. unemployment and aggregate output.

13. Fiscal policy involves decisions about
    a. the money supply and interest rates.
    b. unemployment and inflation.
    c. government spending and taxation.
    d. the Bank of Canada.

14. Low growth rates in the money supply are most likely to be associated with
    a. a high rate of inflation and high long-term bond rates.
    b. a high rate of inflation and low long-term bond rates.
    c. a low rate of inflation and high long-term bond rates.
    d. a low rate of inflation and low long-term bond rates.

15. An increase in the growth rate of the money supply is most likely to be followed by
    a. a low point in the business cycle.
    b. a recession.
    c. a reduction in inflation.
    d. an increase in inflation.

16. The process of channeling funds from individuals with surplus funds to those desiring additional funds in which the security issued by the borrower is not purchased by the saver is known as
    a. theft.
    b. redistribution.
    c. barter.
    d. financial intermediation.

17. An increase in interest rates is likely to cause spending on houses to
    a. fall.
    b. rise.
    c. rise in the short run if interest rates are expected to fall in the future.
    d. remain unchanged.

18. A _____ is an example of a security, which is a claim on future income or _____.
    a. bond; interest rate
    b. bond; debt
    c. stock; assets
    d. stock; debt

19. Assume that large budget deficits have significant impacts on the level of interest rates. In which market will budget deficits have their biggest impact directly?
    a. The stock market.
    b. The bond market.
    c. The wheat market.
    d. The gold market.

20. An increase in the value of the dollar relative to all foreign currencies means that the price of foreign goods purchased by Canadians
    a. increases.
    b. falls.
    c. remains unchanged.
    d. There is not enough information to answer.

21. Which of the following is most likely to result from a stronger yen?
    a. Canadian goods exported abroad will cost less in Japan, and so Japanese will buy more of them.
    b. Canadian goods exported abroad will cost more in Japan, and so Japanese will buy more of them.
    c. Canadian goods exported abroad will cost more in Japan, and so Japanese will buy fewer of them.
    d. Canadians will purchase more foreign goods.

22. Financial innovation
    a. proceeds at a slow pace.
    b. makes use of computers and the Internet.
    c. demonstrates a lack of creativity.
    d. does not lead to higher profits.

23. Suppose that due to a fear that Canada is about to enter a long period of stagnant growth, stock prices fall by 50% on average. Predict what would happen to spending by consumers.
    a. Spending would probably increase.
    b. Spending would probably fall.
    c. Spending would probably be unaffected.
    d. The change in spending would be ambiguous.

24. An increase in the growth rate of the money supply is most likely to be followed by
    a. a recession.
    b. a decline in economic activity.
    c. inflation.
    d. all of the above.

25. A sharp decrease in the growth rate of the money supply is most likely to be followed by
    a. a decline in economic activity.
    b. an upswing in the business cycle.
    c. inflation.
    d. all of the above.

26. Which of the following are true statements?
    a. Inflation is defined as a continual increase in the money supply.
    b. Inflation is a condition of a continually rising price level.
    c. The inflation rate is measured as the rate of change in the aggregate price level.
    d. Only (b) and (c) of the above are true statements.

27. If France experiences higher inflation than Thailand, then
    a. the percentage change of the price level is greater in France.
    b. the percentage change of the price level is greater in Thailand.
    c. the growth rate of the money supply is likely higher in Thailand.
    d. only (a) and (c) of the above.

28. Monetary policy, which involves the setting of interest rates, is usually conducted by a
    a. commercial bank.
    b. national bank.
    c. central bank.
    d. presidential bank.

29. Budget deficits are important to study in a money and banking class because
    a. budget deficits cause banks to fail.
    b. without budget deficits banks would not exist.
    c. budget deficits may influence the conduct of monetary policy.
    d. of each of the above.

30. Budget deficits can be a concern because they might
    a. ultimately lead to lower inflation.
    b. lead to lower interest rates.
    c. lead to a higher rate of money growth.
    d. cause all of the above to occur.

CHAPTER 2

An Overview of the Financial System

CHAPTER SYNOPSIS/COMPLETIONS

Financial markets (bond and stock markets) and (1) _____ _____ (banks, insurance companies, pension funds) move funds from lender-savers to borrower-spenders.

    (2) _____ _____ channel funds from those who have saved to those who wish to spend more than their income. This movement of funds can be accomplished by direct finance, where borrowers borrow directly from lenders by selling securities to lenders. Securities are also known as financial instruments. This movement of funds improves efficiency by channeling funds to those with productive uses for the funds from those with no investment opportunities, producing an efficient allocation of capital (wealth that is used to produce more wealth). It also allows consumers to better time their purchases.

    Financial markets can be categorized as debt and (3) _____ _____, primary and secondary markets, (4) _____ and (5)_____ _____ _____ markets, and money and (6)_____ _____. In a debt market, the borrower issues a debt instrument in which the borrower agrees to pay interest and principal payments until (7) _____. Alternatively, in an equity market, firms issue stock, which are claims to share the net income and assets of the firm. The owner may also receive (8) _____. (9) _____ _____ are where new issues of a security are sold, often to (10) _____ _____ that underwrite the securities. (11) _____ _____ are where existing issues are resold. Secondary markets can be exchanges, where buyers and sellers meet in a central location, or over the counter where (12) _____ at different locations have an inventory of securities. The (13) _____ _____ is where short-term securities (maturity of less than one year) are traded. The capital market is where longer-term debt and equity instruments are traded.

    The main money market instruments are Government of Canada treasury bills, certificates of deposit, commercial paper, repurchase agreements, and overnight funds. Treasury bills are the most (14) _____ instruments because they are most actively traded and have essentially no default (15) _____. Overnight funds are loans from one bank to another, usually overnight. The interest rate in this market, the (16) _____ _____, is important because it is a measure of the stance of monetary policy. The main capital market instruments are stocks, mortgages, corporate bonds, Government of Canada bonds, Canada Savings Bonds, provincial and (17) _____ _____, government agency securities, and consumer and bank commercial loans. For corporate finance, each year the volume of new issues of bonds exceeds the volume of new issues of stock.

    (18) _____ _____ are sold in a foreign country and are denominated in the currency of the country in which the bonds are sold. (19) _____ are bonds denominated in a currency

other than the country in which it is sold. (20) _____ are dollar-denominated deposits in foreign banks outside the United States or in foreign branches of U.S. banks.

Eurodollars are an important source of funds to Canadian banks. Foreign stock markets have also grown in importance.

A second route by which funds can move from lenders to borrowers is known as indirect finance because an intermediary is between the lenders and the borrowers. A financial intermediary borrows funds from one group and lends to another in a process known as financial intermediation. Financial intermediaries reduce transactions costs, allow for (21) _____ _____, and solve problems caused by (22) _____ _____ and (23) _____ _____. (24)_____ _____ associated with borrowing and lending are reduced because banks exploit (25) _____ _____ _____ when writing loan contracts. This gain in efficiency allows intermediaries to provide liquidity services to their customers.

Risk sharing allows intermediaries to sell assets with less risk than the risk of the assets they purchase, which is known as (26) _____ _____. Risk sharing also allows individuals to diversify their assets.

Financial transactions suffer from asymmetric information because the borrower knows more about the probability of repayment than the lender. Before the transaction, adverse selection may occur because borrowers most unlikely to repay are most eager to borrow. After the transaction, moral hazard may occur if the borrower engages in immoral behavior by using the loan in a way that reduces the probability of repayment. Financial intermediaries screen out bad credit risks to reduce adverse selection, and monitor borrowers to reduce moral hazard.

The primary financial intermediaries are:
- *Depository institutions, or banks:* Chartered banks, trust and mortgage loan companies, credit unions and caissses populaires.
- *Contractual savings institutions:* Life insurance companies, property and casualty insurance companies, and pension funds and government retirement funds.
- *Investment intermediaries:* Finance companies, mutual funds, and money market mutual funds.

The government regulates financial markets for two main reasons: to increase the information available to investors and to ensure the soundness of the financial system. To avoid the problems of asymmetric information, provincial securities commissions require corporations that issue securities to disclose information about their sales, assets, and earnings, and restricts insider trading. To avoid a (27) _____ _____ that could lead to a collapse of financial intermediaries, the government has implemented various types of regulations. Regulations include restrictions on who can set up a financial intermediary, requirements for disclosure of information, restrictions on assets and activities, limits on competition, the requirement that depository institutions maintain minimum levels of capital, and deposit insurance.

HELPFUL HINTS

1.   A financial instrument, such as a corporate bond, is a liability to the firm that issued it and an asset to the person that buys it. Therefore, if the question is asked, "Is a corporate bond an asset or a liability?" the response must be, "to whom?" That is, the same instrument will appear on different sides of the balance sheet for the issuer and the buyer.

2.   When a security is traded in a secondary market, the firm receives no funds. Yet the secondary market is important to the firm because it makes their securities more liquid, making the securities more desirable and raising their price. In addition, the secondary market also sets the price of the security that the issuing firm receives in the primary market should the firm issue additional securities.

3.   The problems of asymmetric information affect a loan transaction both before and after the loan is made. *Before* the loan is made, adverse selection may occur because risky borrowers have the greatest incentive to borrow. *After* the loan has been made, moral hazard occurs if borrowers use the borrowed money in a riskier fashion that was agreed to in the loan contract. To avoid this problem, banks screen and monitor borrowers.

EXERCISES

Practice Problems

1. For each of the following financial transactions, determine whether the transaction represents a case of *direct finance* or a case of *indirect finance*, by writing in the space provided a D for direct finance and an I for indirect finance.

    ___ a. You deposit $10,000 in your savings account at First Bank and Mary Smith borrows $10,000 from First Bank to buy a car.
    ___ b. You purchase stock in RIM through your stockbroker.
    ___ c. You pay your life insurance premiums and your life insurance company makes a mortgage to a homebuyer.
    ___ d. You buy shares in a mutual fund, and the mutual fund buys stock in RIM.
    ___ e. You purchase bonds issued by General Electric through your broker.
    ___ f. You borrow $10,000 from your parents to help pay for college tuition.
    ___ g. You purchase a Canadian government bond in an over-the-counter market.
    ___ h. You pay $1,000 per month into your pension fund. The pension fund purchases stock in Pearson Addison-Wesley Publishing Company.

2. For each of the following financial transactions, determine whether the transaction involves debt or equity markets, primary or secondary markets, exchanges or over-the-counter markets, and money or capital markets.

    a. You buy a Canadian Government Treasury Bill that matures in six months from your broker.

    _____

    b. You buy stock in Microsoft from your broker.

    _____

    c. The investment banking division of First Bank underwrites Microsoft's new issue of stock.

    _____

    d. You buy a bond issued by Hewlett Packard that matures in 20 years from your local bond dealer.

    _____

    e. You buy stock in Ford Motor Company through a discount broker.

    _____

3. The following questions address the soundness of financial intermediaries.

    a. What is a financial panic?

    _____

    b. What are the five types of regulations the government employs in an attempt to ensure the soundness of our financial intermediaries? Explain.

    _____

    _____

4.   Match the regulatory agency to whom it regulates. Remember that some financial institutions are regulated by more than one agency.

Regulatory Agency		Whom It Regulates	
___ 1.	Office of the Superintendent of Financial Institutions Canada (OSFI)	a.	Commercial banks
___ 2.	Quebec Deposit Insurance Board	b.	Organized exchanges
___ 3.	CompCorp	c.	TMLs
___ 4.	Bank of Canada	d.	CUCPs
___ 5.	Canada Deposit Insurance Corporation (CDIC)	e.	Life insurance companies
___ 6.	PACIC	f.	Futures market traders
___ 7.	Ontario Securities Commission (OSC)	g.	P&C insurance companies

5.   List the six types of money market instruments.

    1. _____
    2. _____
    3. _____
    4. _____
    5. _____
    6. _____

Short-Answer Questions

1.   Explain the difference between direct and indirect finance.

    _____
    _____

2.   Explain the differences between debt and equity markets, primary and secondary markets, exchanges and over-the-counter markets, and money and capital markets.

    _____
    _____

3.   Which money market instrument is considered most liquid? Why? Which capital market instrument has the greatest dollar amount outstanding? On an annual basis, which capital market instrument do firms use most to acquire additional capital funds?

    _____
    _____

4. Other things being the same, which of the following instruments are the least risky to own: short-term bonds, long-term bonds, or equities? Why?

    _____

    _____

5. What is the difference between a *foreign bond* and a *Eurobond*? What is the relationship between a Eurobond and European currency known as the euro?

    _____

    _____

6. Suppose that after John receives an auto loan from his credit union, he takes the money to a casino and gambles instead of using the money to buy a car. What type of asymmetric information problem have we witnessed: adverse selection or moral hazard? Explain.

    _____

    _____

7. Name three reasons why a financial intermediary might be able to move funds from lenders to borrowers efficiently.

    _____

    _____

8. What are the main categories of depository institutions? What is their main source of funds (liabilities)? Which category of depository institution is the largest in terms of assets?

    _____

    _____

9. What type of investment intermediary sells shares and buys money market instruments? What is the most unusual feature of these funds?

    _____

    _____

10. Which institutions are subject to Canada Deposit Insurance Corporation (CDIC) regulations, and what is the nature of the regulations?

    _____

    _____

Critical-Thinking Questions

Your grandmother dies and bequeaths to you $10,000. When you receive the cheque, your best friend accompanies you to the bank in which you plan to deposit the money. Once inside the bank, your friend notices that the rate the bank pays on savings deposits is 3% while the rate the bank charges on auto loans is 9%. Your friend suggests, "Why don't you just stand by the door to the auto loan office and offer the next auto loan customer a loan directly from you? You could charge much more than the 3% you would get on your deposit and cut out the middleman."

1. Explain why it would likely be unprofitable for you to make such a loan.

    _____

    _____

2. Why is it more likely that the bank is able to make the loan profitably?

_____

_____

_____

SELF-TEST

True-False Questions

Circle whether the following statements are true (T) or false (F).

T   F   1. When financial markets enable a consumer to buy a refrigerator before she has saved up enough funds to buy it, they are helping to increase economic welfare.

T   F   2. Direct finance does not involve the activities of financial intermediaries.

T   F   3. The difference between a primary and a secondary market is that in a primary market new issues of a security are sold, while in a secondary market previously issued securities are sold.

T   F   4. An over-the-counter market has the characteristic that dealers in securities conduct their trades in one central location.

T   F   5. Financial intermediaries only exist because there are substantial information and transactions costs in the economy.

T   F   6. Liquidity of assets is as important a consideration for contractual savings institutions as it is for depository institutions.

T   F   7. Money market mutual funds to some extent function as depository institutions.

T   F   8. The volume of new corporate bonds issued in Canada is substantially greater than the volume of new stock issues.

T   F   9. The Ontario Securities Commission is the chartering agency for all commercial banks in Ontario.

T   F   10. The primary role of the Ontario Securities Commission is to make sure that adequate and accurate information can be obtained by investors.

T   F   11. An over-the-counter market is less competitive than a market with an organized exchange.

T   F   12. The money market has fewer price fluctuations than the capital market.

T   F   13. A well-functioning financial market has negative effects on the well-being of consumers.

T   F   14. The main disadvantage of owning a corporation's equities rather than its debt is that an equity holder is a residual claimant.

T   F   15. Treasury bills are the most liquid of all the money market instruments because they are the least actively traded.

Multiple-Choice Questions

Circle the appropriate answer.

1. Which of the following cannot be described as indirect finance?
    a. You take out a mortgage from your local bank.
    b. An insurance company lends money to General Motors Corporation.
    c. You borrow $1000 from your best friend.
    d. You buy shares in a mutual fund.
    e. None of the above.

2. Which of the following statements regarding direct finance is false?
   a. An investor with funds lends directly to the borrower in direct finance.
   b. Financial intermediaries are not used in direct finance.
   c. Financial markets are not used in direct finance.
   d. Liabilities are created in direct finance.

3. Which of the following is a short-term financial instrument?
   a. Government of Canada treasury bill.
   b. Share of Air Canada stock.
   c. Municipal bond with a maturity of 2 years.
   d. Residential mortgage.

4. If you want to invest funds for a period greater than one year, you would most likely invest in which market?
   a. A primary market.
   b. A capital market.
   c. A money market.
   d. An over-the-counter market.
   e. None of the above.

5. As compared to capital markets, money markets
   a. are usually more widely traded.
   b. trade debt instruments with shorter terms.
   c. have smaller fluctuations in price.
   d. all of the above.
   e. none of the above.

6. Which of the following statements about the characteristics of debt and equity is true?
   a. They can both be short-term financial instruments.
   b. Bondholders are residual claimants.
   c. The income from bonds is typically more variable than that from equities.
   d. Bonds pay dividends.
   e. None of the above.

7. Which of the following markets in Canada is never set up as an organized exchange?
   a. Stock market.
   b. Corporate bond market.
   c. Canadian government bond market.
   d. Futures market.

8. Which of the following statements regarding equities is true?
   a. Equities often pay dividends.
   b. Equities are debt instruments.
   c. The equity owner is the residual claimant.
   d. Only (a) and (b) of the above.
   e. Only (a) and (c) of the above.

9. A bond denominated in a currency other than that of the country in which it is sold is called a(n)
    a. foreign bond.
    b. Eurobond.
    c. equity bond.
    d. currency bond.

10. If a bond is sold in India but it is denominated in British pounds, then that financial instrument is called
    a. a Eurodollar.
    b. a euro.
    c. a Eurobond.
    d. a Europe.
    e. none of the above.

11. Financial intermediaries promote efficiency and thereby increase people's wealth
    a. by reducing the transaction costs of linking together lenders and borrowers.
    b. to the extent that they help solve problems created by adverse selection and moral hazard.
    c. by providing additional jobs.
    d. because of all of the above.
    e. because of only (a) and (b) of the above.

12. Which of the following can reduce the amount of financial risk for a group of investors?
    a. A credit union.
    b. An insurance company.
    c. An investment bank.
    d. All of the above.
    e. None of the above.

13. Banks engage in asset transformation in order to
    a. decrease their liabilities.
    b. lower transaction costs.
    c. create less risky assets.
    d. provide liquidity services.
    e. none of the above.

14. Typically, lenders have inferior information relative to borrowers about the potential returns and risks associated with any investment project. This difference in information is called _____, and it gives rise to the _____ problem.
    a. asymmetric information; moral hazard
    b. asymmetric information; adverse selection
    c. adverse selection; moral hazard
    d. adverse selection; asymmetric information

15. Contractual savings institutions include
    a. commercial banks and TMLs.
    b. life insurance companies and pension funds.
    c. finance companies and mutual funds.
    d. all of the above.
    e. only (a) and (b) of the above.

16. TMLs and CUCPs
    a. are not depository institutions.
    b. primarily hold business loans as assets.
    c. are not currently regulated by the government.
    d. have become more like banks over time.
    e. none of the above.

17. Which of the following is a depository institution?
    a. Life insurance company.
    b. Credit union.
    c. Pension fund.
    d. Finance company.

18. The primary assets of TMLs and CUCPs are
    a. money market instruments.
    b. corporate bonds and stock.
    c. consumer and business loans.
    d. mortgages.

19. The primary liabilities of TMLs are
    a. bonds.
    b. mortgages.
    c. deposits.
    d. commercial paper.

20. TMLs and CUCPs are regulated by
    a. the Bank of Canada.
    b. the Office of the Superintendent of Financial Institutions Canada (OSFI).
    c. the Canada Deposit Insurance Corporation (CDIC).
    d. all of the above.

21. The Canada Deposit Insurance Corporation (CDIC) was created
    a. in order to provide life insurance to all households.
    b. in order to limit interest rates that are paid on deposits.
    c. in order to protect depositors from bank failure.
    d. only (a) and (b) of the above.
    e. only (b) and (c) of the above.

22. Financial panics generally occur when
    a. depositors cannot determine which banks are sound and which are unsound.
    b. interest rates are too low.
    c. deposit insurance is created.
    d. the government regulates the banking sector.

23. Which of the following is a transaction involving indirect finance?
    a. New shares of stock are issued by a corporation.
    b. One corporation buys a bond issued by another corporation.
    c. A pension fund manager buys a bond in the secondary market.
    d. Both (a) and (b) of the above.

24. Which of the following are the primary liabilities of property and casualty insurance companies?

    a. Stocks and bonds.

    b. Premiums from policies.

    c. Chequing accounts.

    d. All of the above.

25. Lenders usually have inferior information, as compared to borrowers, about potential risks associated with an investment project. The difference in information is known as

    a. relative informational disadvantage.

    b. asymmetric information.

    c. variable information.

    d. caveat venditor.

26. Treasury bills are the _____ liquid of all money market instruments and they have (a) _____ possibility of default.

    a. least; high

    b. least; no

    c. most; high

    d. most; no

27. Which of the following is true?

    a. Treasury bills earn more interest than certificates of deposit.

    b. Treasury bills and certificates of deposit are long term.

    c. Overnight funds are the loans made by the Bank of Canada to other banks.

    d. None of the above.

28. A bond denominated in Euros is called a _____ only if it is sold _____ the countries that have adopted the euro.

    a. Eurobond; outside

    b. Eurobond; inside

    c. foreign bond; outside

    d. foreign bond; inside

29. Chartered banks, TMLs, and CUCPs are regulated by _____ and _____.

    a. the Bank of Canada; the Office of the Superintendent of Financial Institutions Canada

    b. the Bank of Canada; Canada Deposit Insurance Corporation

    c. the Office of the Superintendent of Financial Institutions Canada; Provincial Securities and Exchange Commission

    d. both (b) and (c) of the above

30. All deposits under _____ at member deposit-taking financial institutions are insured by CDIC.

    a. $10 000

    b. $50 000

    c. $100 000

    d. $1 000 000

CHAPTER 3

What Is Money?

CHAPTER SYNOPSIS/COMPLETIONS

Money has always been important to the economy because it promotes economic efficiency. Here we develop a current definition of money by addressing the functions of money, and learning about the different forms of money through history.

Money is anything that is generally accepted in payment for goods or services or in the repayment of debts. The definition of money includes currency (notes and coins) and chequing account deposits. Money is not the same as (1) _____ or (2) _____. A person's wealth includes the person's money, but it also includes other assets such as bonds, stock, art, land, and houses. Income is a flow of earnings per unit of time while money is a stock, which is measured at a given point in time.

Money has three primary functions. Money serves as a

- (3) _____ _____ _____. Money is used to pay for goods and services. The use of a medium of exchange is efficient for two reasons: It reduces transactions costs (the time spent exchanging goods or services), and it allows for specialization and the division of labor. In a barter economy—an economy without money—goods and services are exchanged directly for other goods and services. Transaction costs are high because an exchange requires a "double coincidence of wants."

- *unit of account*. Money is used to measure value in the economy. As a result, all prices are in terms of money. The use of money as a unit of account is efficient because it reduces transactions costs. In a barter economy, where all goods must be valued in terms of all other goods, the exchange of just a small number of goods requires an enormous number of prices. When money is a unit of account, there is only one price per good and transaction costs are small.

- (4) _____ _____ _____. Money is used as a repository of purchasing power. This allows people to earn money today, and spend it at a later date. Other assets are a store of value, and they may provide a greater rate of return, but people still hold money because of its (5) _____. During inflation, when prices are rising rapidly, people are reluctant to hold money because its value is falling.

The (6) _____ _____ has evolved. Most economic systems first employed (7) _____ _____, usually a valuable commodity or precious metal such as gold or silver. Because metals are difficult to transport, societies developed paper (8) _____ that was fully convertible into precious metals. More recently, paper currency has evolved into (9) _____ _____, money decreed by governments as legal tender but not convertible into the precious metal. Since coins and paper currency are easily stolen and hard to transport, modern banking has invented *cheques*. Cheques instruct your bank to transfer money from your bank account to another person's account. Cheques are efficient because some payments cancel each other out so no currency need be physically moved; cheques can be easily written for large amounts; cheques reduce loss from theft; and cheques provide receipts for purchases. But cheques take time to move from place to place, so the money is not available immediately when deposited, and cheques are expensive to process. Computers now allow for *electronic payment* of bills over the Internet. (10)_____ is money that exists only in electronic form, in the form of debit cards, stored-value cards, and (11) _____. Each type of money is more efficient than its predecessor because it lowers transactions costs.

Since there is no single measure of money that is accurate for all times and for all purposes, the Bank of Canada defines different measures of the money supply, known as (12) _____ _____. For example,

- M2 = currency outside banks + personal deposits at chartered banks+ non-personal demand and notice deposits at chartered banks
- M3 = M2 + non-personal term deposits at chartered banks + foreign currency deposits of residents at chartered banks

These two measures of the money supply do not always move together, so the proper choice of a measure of money by policymakers does matter for the conduct of monetary policy.

It is difficult to measure money for two reasons: It is hard to decide which monetary aggregate is best, and the Bank of Canada substantially revises earlier estimates of the monetary aggregates. The Bank of Canada revises earlier estimates because small depository institutions only report their deposits infrequently, and seasonal variation is revised as new data comes in. Revisions in the growth rates of the monetary aggregates are great enough that we should not be too concerned with short-run movements in the money supply and should only be concerned with longer-run movements.

HELPFUL HINTS

1. One of the functions of money is to serve as a (13) _____ _____ _____. When serving in this capacity, money expresses the relative value between all goods. That is, when all prices are established in terms of money, money is the common denominator across all goods. If an apple costs 25 cents, while an orange costs 50 cents, we know that it takes two apples to get an orange. The relative value between the goods has been established.

2. The M2 monetary aggregate includes personal deposits and other demand and notice deposits at chartered banks. Note that it is not the cheque that is part of the money supply. It is the balance in the account that is money. A fresh cheque book with 25 cheques is of no value unless there is a positive balance in the account.

3. As we move from M1 to M2, we include slightly less liquid assets. M1 only includes perfectly liquid assets in that the items in M1 don't need to be converted into anything else in order to be exchanged for goods and services. The additional assets in M2 are highly liquid, but they require some small expense or effort to convert them into cash.

EXERCISES

Practice Problems

1. Which of the three functions of money (medium of exchange, unit of account, store of value) is illustrated by each of the following situations?
a.   Susan purchases a case of soda at the grocery store with a cheque.

_____

b.   Bryce puts $3000 in his chequing account and plans to spend it next month when he pays his college tuition.

c.   To avoid confusion, prisoners in a POW camp value all of their tradable items in terms of cigarettes.

d.   Joe goes shopping for meat. At the meat counter, he notices that fresh fish is priced at $10 per pound while frozen fish is priced at $5 per pound. He immediately recognizes that he could get twice as much frozen fish as fresh fish for the same expenditure.

e.   Lisa is willing to specialize as an economics professor and receive payment in dollars because she is confident that she can go to the market and spend those dollars for food, clothing, and shelter.

f.   A prisoner in a POW camp keeps 100 cigarettes in his locker even though he does not smoke, because he believes that he will be able to buy chocolates with them next week when packages from home arrive.

g.   For tax purposes Jennifer's Flower Shop values the store's inventory, which includes a variety of different types of flowers, at $40 000.

h.   Joe buys ten gallons of gasoline with a $20 bill.

2.   Suppose there are four goods produced in an economy—apples, oranges, pears, and bananas.
a.   If this is a barter economy, list the prices needed in order to exchange any good for any other good. How many are there?

b.   Suppose dollars are introduced into the economy and universally circulate as money. What are the prices needed in order to exchange any good for any other good? How many are there?

c.   Which system has lower transactions costs, the barter system or the one with money? Does the difference in transactions costs increase or decrease as the economy expands? Explain.

3.   What type of payment (commodity money, fiat money, cheques, electronic payment, e-money) is employed in each of the following situations?
a.   While in France, you use a 100 euro note to purchase a bottle of wine.

b.   On the island of Yap, stone wheels are used to purchase all goods and services.

c.   You have your mortgage and life insurance premiums automatically paid each month by your bank directly out of your chequing account.

d.   One hundred fifty years ago, your great-great-grandfather purchased a new suit with a $20 gold piece.

e.   You write a cheque each month on your account at your bank and mail it your auto insurance company to pay your premium.

f.   You buy a new lawnmower at Sears and pay directly out of your chequing account with your debit card.

_____

g.   You buy a soda with a ten dollar bill.

_____

h.   You purchase $20 worth of subway rides in Toronto. Instead of tickets, you receive a disposable paper card with a magnetic strip on the back (similar to the back of a credit card). You feed it into the turnstile each time you ride the train, and you continue to use it until the $20 has been used up.

_____

4. The price of one good in terms of another is referred to as the barter price or exchange rate. The benefits of using money are best appreciated by thinking of a barter economy. Between any two goods there is one barter price or exchange rate. But as the number of goods increases, the number of barter prices or exchange rates grows more rapidly. Complete the following table which dramatically illustrates the virtues of a unit of account.

Number of Prices in a Barter Versus a Money Economy

Number of Goods	Number of Prices in a Barter Economy	Number of Prices in a Money Economy
5	_____	5
25	_____	25
50	_____	_____
500	124,750	_____
5000	_____	_____

5. People accept fiat money because they expect that they will be able to trade the money for goods and services today and in the future. The government plays a large role in maintaining universal acceptance of a currency by promoting expectations that the currency will continue to be used in the future. Suppose that you learn that the government is issuing a new currency tomorrow and that, after today, no one will be legally required to accept dollars. Explain why your reaction will likely be to spend all of your dollars today. Now suppose that you learn that the new currency will be issued next week rather than tomorrow. Explain why your reaction continues to be to spend all of your dollars today, as long as you think that other people have the same expectations that you do regarding the new currency.

_____

_____

_____

Short-Answer Questions

1.   What is income? What is wealth? Does someone who has a high income or who is wealthy necessarily have a lot of money? Explain.

_____

_____

2.   What is a barter economy? What are transactions costs? What are two reasons why transactions costs are high in a barter system?

_____

_____

3.   What are the necessary characteristics of a commodity if it is to function effectively as money?

_____

4. Why do people hold money as a store of value when there are many other assets, such as houses and bonds, that earn a greater rate of return and are also a store of value?

_____

_____

5. What are some advantages of using cheques as a means of payment? What are some shortcomings?

_____

_____

6. What are the assets included in M1? What separates them from the assets in M2?

_____

_____

7. Which is the larger monetary aggregate, M1 or M2? Why?

_____

_____

8. Does it matter what definition of money policy makers use as the true measure of money when making monetary policy decisions? Why?

_____

_____

9. Why does the Bank of Canada revise its earlier estimates of the monetary aggregate?

_____

_____

10. Are short-run movements in the money supply important? Explain.

_____

_____

Critical-Thinking Questions

You are with your best friend at the bank when she cashes her paycheque for cash. She takes the $500 of currency and, with a frown on her face, she says, "Money is just becoming paper these days. I should go the Bank of Canada and demand that they give me gold in exchange for this paper. Then I'd have some real money."

1. Explain to your friend what type of money she received.

_____

_____

2. What are some of the advantages and disadvantages of this type of money?

_____

_____

3.   What type of money does your friend think she wants? Explain. Would the Bank of Canada redeem her currency in gold? Why or why not?

_____

_____

SELF-TEST

True-False Questions

Circle whether the following statements are true (T) or false (F).

T   F   1.   Since cheques are accepted as payment for purchases of goods and services, economists consider chequing account deposits as money.

T   F   2.   Of its three functions, it is as a unit of account that money is distinguished from other assets.

T   F   3.   Money is a unique store of value, since physical goods depreciate over time.

T   F   4.   Money can be traded for other goods quickly and easily compared to all other assets. Thus money is said to be liquid.

T   F   5.   Money proves to be a good store of value during inflationary episodes, since the value of money is positively related to the price level.

T   F   6.   Paper currency evolved because it is less costly to transport than is commodity money.

T   F   7.   Inflation may reduce economic efficiency if it induces people to resort to barter.

T   F   8.   The major impetus behind the move to expand electronic payment systems is the relatively high cost of transporting and processing cheques.

T   F   9.   In times past, when only currency functioned as money, measuring money would have been conceptually much easier.

T   F   10. The past behaviour of M1 and M2 indicates that using only one monetary aggregate to guide policy is sufficient, since they move together very closely.

T   F   11. For economists, money, income, and wealth have the same meaning.

T   F   12. Fiat money is a paper currency decreed by governments and is convertible into precious metals.

T   F   13. M2++ equals M2+ plus Canada Savings Bonds and non-money-market mutual funds.

T   F   14. Money has an advantage as a store of value over all other types of assets.

T   F   15. The M2 monetary aggregate includes currency plus non-personal demand and notice deposits at chartered banks.

Multiple-Choice Questions

Circle the appropriate answer.

1.   Money is measured as a _____ of dollars, while income is measured as a _____ of dollars.

   a. medium; stock

   b. flow; stock

   c. liquidity; flow

   d. stock; flow

2. When an economist talks about the impossibility of barter, she really means to imply that
   a. barter transactions are relatively costly.
   b. barter has no useful place in today's world.
   c. it is impossible for barter transactions to leave the parties to an exchange better off.
   d. each of the above is true.

3. The resources expended trying to find potential buyers or sellers and negotiating over price and terms are called
   a. barter costs.
   b. transaction costs.
   c. information costs.
   d. enforcement costs.

4. If cigarettes serve as a medium of exchange, a unit of account, and a store of wealth, cigarettes are said to function as
   a. bank deposits.
   b. reserves.
   c. money.
   d. loanable funds.

5. Because money reduces both the time it takes to make exchanges and the necessity of a double coincidence of wants, people will find that they can more easily pursue their individual comparative advantages. Thus money
   a. encourages nonproductive pursuits.
   b. encourages specialization.
   c. forces people to become too specialized.
   d. causes a waste of resources due to the duplication of many activities.

6. As the transaction costs of selling an asset rise, the asset is said to become
   a. more valuable.
   b. more liquid.
   c. less liquid.
   d. more money like.

7. The conversion of a barter economy to one that uses money
   a. increases efficiency by reducing the need to exchange goods.
   b. increases efficiency by reducing transaction costs.
   c. has no effect on economic efficiency since efficiency is a production concept, not an exchange concept.
   d. decreases efficiency by reducing the need to specialize.

8. Which of the following is an example of fiat money?
   a. Cigarettes traded in a prisoner-of-war camp.
   b. Canadian paper currency that is not redeemable in gold.
   c. Canadian paper currency that is redeemable in gold.
   d. Silver coins.

9. Which of the following is not a desirable characteristic of money?
   a. Money must be difficult to counterfeit.
   b. Money must be difficult to carry.
   c. Money must not deteriorate quickly.
   d. Money must be recognizable.

10. During the Depression, the government stopped redeeming paper currency for gold. When this happened,
    a. paper currency became fiat money.
    b. the money supply fell to zero.
    c. the dollar was no longer a unit of account.
    d. the dollar was no longer a store of value.

11. At many colleges students can use their identification card to pay for copies and meals, with the balance remaining on the card reduced after each purchase. These cards function as
    a. credit cards.
    b. commodity money.
    c. stored-value cards.
    d. M2.

12. Metal tokens can be used to play games at the video arcade but cannot be used for purchases at other stores. Why do tokens, unlike Canadian coins, not function as money everywhere?
    a. Tokens are too large to transport.
    b. Tokens are easily stolen.
    c. Tokens are not widely accepted by merchants.
    d. Tokens are not a good store of value.

13. During a period of hyperinflation,
    a. money is a poor store of value.
    b. the inflation rate is very high.
    c. money may stop being used as a medium of exchange.
    d. all of the above.

14. Which of the following are problems with a payments system based largely on cheques?
    a. Cheques are costly to process.
    b. Cheques are costly to transport.
    c. Cheques take time to move through the cheque-clearing system.
    d. All of the above.

15. Starting January 1, 1999,
    a. the exchange rates of countries entering the European Union were fixed permanently to the euro.
    b. the European Central Bank took over monetary policy from the individual national central banks.
    c. the governments of the member countries began issuing debt in euros.
    d. all of the above occurred.

16. Which of the following are true about the evolution of the payments system?
    a. The evolution of the payments system from barter to precious metals, then to fiat money, then to cheques can best be understood as a consequence of innovations that allowed traders to more easily escape oppressive taxes on exchange.
    b. Precious metals had the advantage of being widely accepted, being divisible into relatively small units, and being durable, but had the disadvantage of being difficult to carry and transport from one place to another.
    c. Paper money has the advantage of being easy to transport, but has the disadvantage of being less accepted than cheques.
    d. Only (a) and (b) of the above are true.

17. In Europe, individual currencies, such as the German mark, were recently replaced by a common currency called the euro. The anticipated effect was to
    a. reduce the need for money.
    b. change the unit of account.
    c. increase transaction costs.
    d. promote barter.

18. Generally, the problem of defining money becomes _____ troublesome as the pace of financial innovation _____.
    a. less; quickens
    b. more; quickens
    c. more; slows
    d. more; stops

19. The narrowest measure of money, called M1+, consists of
    a. currency and chequing account deposits.
    b. currency, chequing account deposits, and money market mutual funds.
    c. currency, chequing account deposits, and money market deposit account funds.
    d. currency, chequing account deposits, and traveller's cheques.

20. Which of the following is not included in the money aggregate M2?
    a. Currency.
    b. Personal savings deposits at chartered banks.
    c. Overnight repurchase agreements.
    d. Current accounts.

21. Economists do not define money as the sum of all currency because
    a. it is impossible to adequately measure currency.
    b. currency is sometimes stolen.
    c. other items besides currency function as money.
    d. currency is fiat money.
    e. e-cash is stored on computers.

22. Which of the following statements regarding monetary aggregates is true?
    a. M1+ is always greater than M2.
    b. The growth rate of M2 is always greater than the growth rate of M1+.
    c. The Bank of Canada rarely revises estimates of M1+ and M2.
    d. The Bank of Canada is concerned mainly with longer-run, rather than short-run, movements in money aggregates.
    e. None of the above.

23. Generally speaking, the initial data on the monetary aggregates reported by the Bank of Canada are
    a. not a reliable guide to the short-run behaviour of the money supply.
    b. a reliable guide to the long-run behaviour of the money supply.
    c. a reliable guide to the short-run behaviour of the money supply.
    d. both (a) and (b) of the above.
    e. both (b) and (c) of the above.

24. When prices are rising rapidly
    a. money is not a good store of value.
    b. money fails as a good unit of account.
    c. money fails as a good medium of exchange.
    d. money fails as a good standard of value.

25. Money is a medium of exchange because it
    a. eliminates the need for a double coincidence of wants.
    b. encourages specialization.
    c. lowers transaction costs.
    d. does all of the above.
    e. does only (a) and (b) of the above.

26. Hyperinflation refers to inflation rates higher than _____ per _____.
    a. 100%; month
    b. 50%; month
    c. 50%; year
    d. 100%; year

27. Which of the following is not part of M2+:
    a. Deposits at trust and mortgage loan companies.
    b. Non-money-market mutual funds.
    c. Life insurance company individual annuities.
    d. Money market mutual funds.

28. What is hyperinflation?
    a. A rapid increase in the price level, money loses value rapidly, individuals are reluctant to hold money.
    b. A rapid decrease in the price level, money gains value rapidly, individuals want to hold as much money as possible.
    c. An inflation where the inflation rate exceeds 50% per month.
    d. An inflation where the inflation rate exceeds 100% per month.
    e. An inflation where the inflation rate exceeds 50-100% per year.

29. The primary objective of what invention was to reduce the problem of transporting paper currency and coins?
    a. E-money.
    b. Electronic payment.
    c. Cheques.
    d. E-Cash.

30. Which of the following assets is most appropriately associated with the potential use as a medium of exchange?
    a. A Group of Seven painting.
    b. A notice deposit account with a trust company.
    c. A 90-day Canadian Treasury Bill.
    d. One share of RIM stock.
    e. All of the above.

CHAPTER **4**

Understanding Interest Rates

CHAPTER SYNOPSIS/COMPLETIONS

This chapter establishes what interest rates are and addresses the ways in which they are measured. The most accurate measure of *interest rates* is (1) _____ _____ _____. The concept of yield to maturity reveals that bond prices and interest rates are negatively related, and the longer the maturity of the bond, the greater the change in the price of the bond from a given change in the interest rate. Interest rates are important because they affect how much people and firms wish to save or borrow. The terms defined in this chapter will be employed throughout the book.

(2) _____ _____ (or present discounted value) is today's value of a future cash payment given an interest rate of i. The basic present value formula is:

$$PV(1+i)^n = CF \text{ or } PV = CF/(1+i)^n$$

where PV = present value, CF = future cash flow, and n = number of years to maturity.

For example, a (3) _____ _____ of $100 (the present value) at 6% for one year (n = 1) generates a future cash flow payment of $100(1.06) = $106 one year from today. Alternatively, the present value of a future cash payment of $106 to be received one year from today is $106/1.06 = $100 today.

There are four basic types of credit market instruments: a simple loan, a fixed-payment loan (also known as a fully amortized loan), a (4) _____ _____, and a (5) _____ _____ (also known as a zero-coupon bond). A simple loan and a discount bond require the borrower to make one payment at the end of the loan, which includes both the principal and interest. Fixed-payment loans (installment loans such as auto loans and mortgages) and coupon bonds require the borrower to make periodic payments to the lender until a maturity date. The payments on a fixed-payment loan are all the same size and each payment includes a combination of interest and principal. The periodic payments on a coupon bond are interest payments alone, and the final payment at maturity includes the face-value or principal of the bond.

The most important and accurate way to calculate the interest rate is *yield to maturity*, which is the interest rate that equates the present value of cash flow payments received from a debt instrument with its price or value today. The price or value today of any instrument is equal to the sum of the present value of all of its future cash flow payments. Since a simple loan and a discount bond generate only one future cash flow payment, yield to maturity on each of those instruments can be calculated with the present value formula provided above. If the value today and the future cash flow values are known, one can use the formula above to solve for i, which is the yield to maturity. For the simple one year case, $i = (CF - PV)/PV$, which is also our formula for simple interest.

We follow the same general process for finding the yield to maturity for fixed-payment loans and coupon bonds, but since they generate periodic future cash flow payments, we must sum the present value of each future cash flow payment and equate it to the value or price of the instrument today. The general formula for an instrument generating annual payments until some future maturity date is:

$$\text{Value today (price)} = CF/(1 + i) + CF/(1 + i)^2 + CF/(1 + i)^3 + \ldots + CF/(1 + i)^n$$

If the price of the instrument and the future cash flow payments are known, we can solve for i and get the yield to maturity. Because this calculation is not easy, many pocket calculators have been programmed to solve this problem.

When the formula above is applied to a coupon bond, the following facts emerge:

- If the yield to maturity equals the (6) _____ _____ (coupon/face value), the price of the bond equals its (7) _____ _____.
- If the yield to maturity is above the coupon rate, the price of the bond is below its face value, and vice versa.
- The price of the bond and its yield to maturity are negatively related. This is also true for a discount bond.

A (8) _____ or (9) _____ is a coupon bond with no maturity. For a perpetuity, $P = C/i$, or $i = C/P$, where P is the price of the perpetuity, C = annual coupon, and i = yield to maturity. This formula is also an approximation of yield to maturity for any long-term coupon bond, and it is known as (10) _____ _____ when used in this manner. The greater the maturity of the bond, the better current yield approximates yield to maturity.

The actual (11) _____ _____ _____ earned by the holder of a coupon bond includes the capital gains or losses on the bond from fluctuations in the price of the bond. The formula for the *return* on a bond held from time t to $t + 1$ is:

$$Return = (C + P_{t+1} - P_t)/P_t$$

where C = coupon payment, P_t = price of the bond at t, and P_{t+1} = price of the bond at $t + 1$. General findings from this concept include:

- The return on a bond equals the yield to maturity if the holding period is equal to maturity (the bond is held to maturity).
- An increase in interest rates causes the price of a bond to fall, resulting in a capital loss on bonds with maturity greater than the holding period.
- The longer to maturity, the greater is the change in price (and capital gain or loss) from a change in interest rates, and the greater is the impact on the return on the bond.
- Thus, a bond with a high yield to maturity can have negative returns if interest rates rise and the bond is sold before maturity (has a short holding period).

Prices (and therefore returns) are more volatile on long-term bonds than short-term bonds. This volatility in returns that results from changes in the interest rate is known as (12) _____ _____ _____.

The (13) _____ _____ _____ has not been corrected for the effects of inflation. The *real interest rate* has been adjusted for inflation so that it more accurately reflects the true cost to borrowers and true return to lenders. The Fisher equation shows the necessary adjustment,

$$i_r = i - \pi^e$$

where i = nominal interest rate, i_r = real interest rate, and π^e = expected inflation. Borrowers and lenders respond to real interest rates. When real rates are low, there are greater incentives to borrow and fewer incentives to lend.

HELPFUL HINTS

1.   We can use the present value formulas in this chapter to solve for the yield to maturity (interest rate) on an instrument if we know the price (value today) of the instrument and its future cash flow payments. Alternatively, and equally important, we can use the present value formulas in this chapter to solve for the price of an instrument given the interest rate and its future cash flow payments. Using the formulas in this alternative way, one can clearly see the main points developed in this chapter. When interest rates rise, the present value of future (14) _____ _____ decrease and the price of existing instruments fall. Longer-term instruments have more terms to be discounted at higher powers, so the longer to maturity, the greater is the change in the price of an instrument from the same size change in the interest rate. Thus, long-term bonds can generate greater capital gains and losses when held for short holding periods, demonstrating that long-term bonds are not considered to generate a sure return when held for short periods.

2.   *Yield to maturity* is the return the owner of an instrument would realize if the owner held the instrument to maturity. If the holding period is less than maturity, the return to the holder may differ from the yield to maturity. If the yield to maturity on comparable instruments rises (the interest rate rises), then the price of the bond will fall and the returns to the holder of the bond will fall below the bond's original yield to maturity if the holder of the bond sells it before maturity.

EXERCISES

Practice Problems

1. Calculate the present value of each of the following.
a. $1000, to be received one year from today, and the interest rate is 4%.

_____

b. $1000, to be received one year from today, and the interest rate is 8%.

_____

c. $1000, to be received two years from today, and the interest rate is 4%.

_____

d. Compare your answers to *a* and *b* above. What happens to the present value of a future cash flow if the interest rate rises? Why?

_____

e. Compare your answers to *a* and *c* above. What happens to the present value of a future cash flow as the future cash flow is received farther into the future? Why?

_____

_____

2. The following questions are based on a $1000 face value coupon bond with a coupon rate of 10%.
a. Suppose the bond has one year to maturity and you buy it for $1018.52. What is the yield to maturity on the bond? Is the yield to maturity above or below the coupon rate of 10%? Why?

_____

b. Since the equation is often considered too difficult to solve, simply write down the equation that one would have to solve to find the yield to maturity if the bond has two years to maturity, and you paid $965 for the bond. If this equation were solved, would the resulting yield to maturity be above or below the coupon rate of 10%? Why?

_____

c. What price would the bond sell for if it had two years to maturity and the interest rate (and therefore the yield to maturity) on the bond is 7%?

_____

d. What price would the bond sell for if it had two years to maturity and the interest rate (and therefore the yield to maturity) on the bond is 8%?

_____

e. Compare *c* and *d* above. What happens to the price of a bond if the interest rate rises? Make a general statement with regard to the price of any coupon bond and the interest rate.

_____

_____

f. What price would the bond sell for if it has one year to maturity and the interest rate is 7%? What is the price of the bond if the interest rate is 8%? Using your results from *c* and *d* above, how much did the price change on the two-year bond when the interest rate rose to 8% from 7%? How much did the price change for the one-year bond when the interest rate rose to 8% from 7%? Make a general statement with regard to the sensitivity of bond prices to changes in interest rates.

_____

_____

_____

3.   What is the value of the real interest rate in each of the following situations?
a.   The nominal interest rate is 15%, and the expected inflation rate is 13%.

b.   The nominal interest rate is 12%, and the expected inflation rate is 9%.

c.   The nominal interest rate is 10%, and the expected inflation rate is 9%.

d.   The nominal interest rate is 5%, and the expected inflation rate is 1%.

e.   In which of the above situations would you prefer to be the lender? Why?

f.   In which of the above situations would you prefer to be the borrower? Why?

4.   The formula $PV = FV/(1+i)^n$ (or $FV = PV * (1+i)^n$) allows one to determine equivalent values in different time periods. Obviously, fifty dollars received in the year 2011 has a value of fifty dollars in the year 2011. However, in the year 2011 the value (PV) of fifty dollars received in the year 2012 is $50 / (1+i)$. Likewise, in the year 2011 the value (FV) of fifty dollars received in the year 2010 is $50 * (1+i)$. This simply illustrates the principle that dollars received in the future are worth less today while dollars received in the past are worth more today. Complete the following table by calculating the value in the Year Payment Valued of receiving fifty dollars in the Year Payment Received.

Year	Year Payment Received		
Payment Valued	2010	2011	2012
2010	$50	(a) _____	(b) _____
2011	$50 * (1 + i)$	$50	$50/(1 + i)$
2012	(c) _____	(d) _____	$50

5.   For discount bonds with a face value of $1000, fill in the yield to maturity (annual rate) and the yield on a discount basis in the following table.

Price of the Discount Bond	Maturity	Yield on a Discount Basis	Yield to Maturity
$900	1 year (365 days)		
$950	6 months (182 days)		
$975	3 months (91 days)		

Note: For bonds with a maturity of 6 months, the yield to maturity at an annual rate equals $[(1 + i_6)^2 - 1]$, where i_6 is the return over 6 months; for bonds with a maturity of 3 months, the yield to maturity at an annual rate equals $[(1 + i_3)^4 - 1]$, where i_3 is the return over 3 months.

Short-Answer Questions

1.   If a lender makes a simple loan of $500 for one year and charges 6%, how much will the lender receive at maturity? If a lender makes a simple loan of $500 for one year and charges $40 interest, what is the simple interest rate on that loan?

2. What is the alternative name for a fixed-payment loan? How is it similar to a coupon bond? How is it different?

_____

_____

3. What is a bond's coupon rate? Does it change over the life of the bond? If a bond's yield to maturity exceeds its coupon rate, what is its price compared to par (or face value)? Why?

_____

_____

4. What is a consol or perpetuity? What is the price of a perpetuity if it pays an annual coupon of $70, and its yield to maturity is 7%? What is its price if the yield to maturity rises to 14%?

_____

_____

5. What is the yield to maturity on a consol that pays an annual coupon of $70, and it sells for $700? What is the *current yield* of the consol? Explain the relationship between yield to maturity and current yield on a consol.

_____

_____

Critical-Thinking Questions

Your friend just won a state lottery that claims to pay the winner $30 000. The lottery actually pays the holder of the winning ticket $10 000 per year for the next three years. The first $10 000 payment arrives immediately. The second arrives one year from today. And the third arrives two years from today. Your friend excitedly says to you, "I need all the money right now because I want to make a down payment on a house. Since you have saved some money, why don't you just give me the $30 000 and I'll give you the ticket. Then you can collect the $30 000 and we'll be even."

1. Should you give your friend $30 000 for the winning lottery ticket? Why or why not?

_____

_____

2. Suppose the interest rate is 5%. What price would you pay for the winning lottery ticket?

_____

_____

3. Suppose the interest rate is 8%. What price would you pay for the winning lottery ticket?

_____

_____

4. Which interest rate implies a greater present value for the lottery ticket? Why?

_____

_____

SELF-TEST

True-False Questions
Circle whether the following statements are true (T) or false (F).

T F 1. Most people would prefer to receive $100 one year from today than receive $100 today because the present discounted value of a future cash flow is greater than the future cash flow.

T F 2. A fixed-payment loan requires the borrower to make a single payment to the lender when the loan matures, and that single payment includes both the principal and interest.

T F 3. The coupon rate on a bond is the coupon divided by the face value (par) of the bond.

T F 4. Yield to maturity is what economists mean when they use the term "interest rate."

T F 5. If a $1000 face value bond pays annual coupons of $50, has two years to maturity, and has a yield to maturity of 7%, it will sell for $963.84.

T F 6. If the yield to maturity on a bond exceeds its coupon rate, the price of the bond will be above its face value.

T F 7. The price of a bond and its yield to maturity are negatively related.

T F 8. The yield to maturity on a treasury bill that sells for $9500 today, has a face value of $10 000, and matures in one year, is 5%.

T F 9. If the nominal interest rate is 7% and expected inflation is 2%, then the real interest rate is 9%.

T F 10. Current yield is a better estimate of yield to maturity for short-term bonds than for long-term bonds.

T F 11. Current yield and yield to maturity on a perpetuity are the same.

T F 12. If a bondholder pays $1000 for a 20-year bond that pays $40 annual coupons, holds the bond for one year, and than sells the bond for $1050, the rate of return for that year for the bondholder is 9%.

T F 13. A security that pays the holder $500 five years from today is preferred to a security that pays the holder $100 per year for the next five years.

T F 14. If the interest rate falls the same amount for both short-term and long-term bonds, bondholders would prefer to be holding short-term bonds.

T F 15. Borrowers have a greater desire to borrow when the nominal interest rate is 15% and the expected inflation rate is 13% than when the nominal interest rate is 6% and the expected inflation rate is 2%.

Multiple-Choice Questions

Circle the appropriate answer.

1. With an interest rate of 5%, the present value of a security that pays $52.50 next year and $110.25 two years from now is
    a. $162.50.
    b. $50.
    c. $100.
    d. $150.

2. The present value of a security that pays you $55 next year and $133 three years from now is $150 if the interest rate is
   a. 10%.
   b. 5%.
   c. 15%.
   d. 20%.

3. Which of the following payment terms should a professional athlete prefer in his "ten million dollar" contract if he wants to obtain the greatest present value of income?
   a. Receive $2 million in each of the next five years.
   b. Receive $6 million next year and then receive $1million in each of the subsequent four years.
   c. Receive $1 million in each of the next four years and then receive $6 million in the subsequent year.
   d. All of the above have the same present value of income.

4. The present value of A plus B is
   a. the present value of A multiplied by B.
   b. the present value of A plus B divided by the future value.
   c. the present value of A plus the present value of B.
   d. the present value of A multiplied by the present value of B.

5. A $5000 coupon bond with a coupon rate of 5% has a coupon payment every year of
   a. $50.
   b. $500.
   c. $250.
   d. $100.
   e. none of the above.

6. If a security pays you $105 next year and $110.25 the year after that, what is its yield to maturity if it sells for $200?
   a. 4%.
   b. 5%.
   c. 6%.
   d. 7%.

7. The yield to maturity on a $20 000 face value discount bond that matures in one year's time and currently sells for $15 000 is
   a. 20%.
   b. 25%.
   c. 33 1/3 %.
   d. 66 2/3 %.

8. Which of the following $1000 face value securities has the lowest yield to maturity?
   a. 5% coupon bond selling for $1000.
   b. 5% coupon bond selling for $1200.
   c. 5% coupon bond selling for $900.
   d. 10% coupon bond selling for $1000.
   e. 10% coupon bond selling for $900.

9. Which of the following $1000 face value securities has the highest yield to maturity?
    a. 5% coupon bond selling for $1000.
    b. 5% coupon bond selling for $900.
    c. 10% coupon bond selling for $1000.
    d. 10% coupon bond selling for $900.

10. If a $5000 face value discount bond maturing in 1 year is selling for $4000, its yield to maturity is
    a. 5%.
    b. 10%.
    c. 25%.
    d. 50%.

11. People who own a bond do not like to read that the interest rate increased because
    a. their coupon payments will fall.
    b. their return will rise.
    c. the yield to maturity on their bond will fall.
    d. the price of their bonds has fallen.

12. A bond that makes a fixed coupon payment forever is known as a
    a. Real Return Bond.
    b. discount bond.
    c. nominal bond.
    d. consol.

13. A discount bond
    a. pays the bondholder the same amount every period until the maturity date.
    b. at the maturity date pays the bondholder the face value of the bond plus an interest payment.
    c. pays the bondholder a fixed interest payment every period and repays the face value at the maturity date.
    d. pays the bondholder the face value at the maturity date.

14. The current yield on a $5000 10% coupon bond selling for $4000 is
    a. 5%.
    b. 10%.
    c. 12.5%.
    d. 15%.

15. The yield on a discount basis
    a. always moves in the same direction as the yield to maturity.
    b. is a somewhat misleading measure of the interest rate.
    c. understates the interest rate as measured by the yield to maturity.
    d. all of the above.

16. The current yield is a
    a. more accurate approximation of the yield to maturity, the nearer the bond's price is to the par value and the shorter the maturity of the bond.
    b. less accurate approximation of the yield to maturity, the nearer the bond's price is to the par value and the longer the maturity of the bond.
    c. more accurate approximation of the yield to maturity, the nearer the bond's price is to the par value and the longer the maturity of the bond.
    d. more accurate approximation of the yield to maturity, the farther the bond's price is to the par value and the shorter the maturity of the bond.

17. The yield on a discount basis of a 180-day $1000 treasury bill selling for $975 is
    a. 5.2%.
    b. 10.5%.
    c. 20.5%.
    d. 50%.

18. Today, Canadian government treasury bill dealers report the yield on a discount basis because
    a. dealers historically reported the discount yield.
    b. the discount yield is the interest rate that is most preferred by economists.
    c. the discount yield is difficult to calculate.
    d. the yield to maturity cannot be calculated for treasury bills.

19. If it is reported that the interest rate rose by six basis points, then the interest rate rose by
    a. .06%.
    b. 6%.
    c. 6 cents.
    d. $6.00
    e. none of the above.

20. If you buy a discount bond for $980 with 90 days until maturity and a face value of $1000, then the yield on a discount basis is
    a. 9.5%.
    b. 8.3%.
    c. 7.5%.
    d. 6.3%.
    e. 5.5%.

21. What is the return on a 15% coupon bond that initially sells for $1000 and sells for $700 next year?
    a. 15%.
    b. 10%.
    c. −5%.
    d. −15%.

22. If a discount bond, which matures in one year, is purchased and held until it matures, then the yield to maturity and _____ are identical.
    a. the coupon rate
    b. the discount yield
    c. the capital gain
    d. the return
    e. current yield

23. Which of the following cannot be calculated at the time that a bond is purchased?
    a. The current yield.
    b. The return.
    c. The yield to maturity.
    d. only (a) and (b) of the above.
    e. only (b) and (c) of the above.

24. If Edmund pays $900 for a bond with a $1000 face value and a coupon payment of $70, and if he sells the bond next year for $936, then Edmund's rate of capital gain is

    a. 2%.

    b. 3%.

    c. 4%.

    d. 5%.

    e. 6%.

25. In which of the following situations would you rather be borrowing?

    a. The interest rate is 20% and expected inflation rate is 15%.

    b. The interest rate is 4% and expected inflation rate is 1%.

    c. The interest rate is 13% and expected inflation rate is 15%.

    d. The interest rate is 10% and expected inflation rate is 15%.

26. If a bond has a coupon rate of 4% and a face value of $20 000, then the yearly coupon payment is

    a. $40.

    b. $80

    c. $400.

    d. $800.

27. Which of the following says that the nominal interest rate equals the real interest rate plus the expected rate of inflation?

    a. The Fisher equation.

    b. The Keynesian equation.

    c. The Marshall equation.

    d. The multiplier equation.

28. The price of a consol is $5000 which pays $150 annually. What is the yield to maturity on this consol?

    a. 5%.

    b. 3%.

    c. 4%.

    d. 2%.

29. What is the discount yield of a 30-day treasury bill that is selling for $490 and has a face value of $500?

    a. 2.04%.

    b. 10%.

    c. 24.48%.

    d. 24.83%.

30. What is the internal rate of return for a machine that costs $7000 and has $2000 revenue per year for 5 years?

    a. 15%.

    b. 10%.

    c. 13.2%.

    d. 42.8%.

CHAPTER 5

The Behaviour of Interest Rates

CHAPTER SYNOPSIS/COMPLETIONS

Interest rates fluctuate. In this chapter we employ both the bond market and the liquidity preference framework to see how a variety of shocks affects interest rates. We address how a change in the money supply affects the interest rate, both in the near term while other determinants of the interest rate are held constant, and in the long run when other determinants are allowed to adjust to the change in the money supply.

Before we address the demand for bonds, we first address the demand for assets in general, such as money, bonds, stock, and art. Holding everything else unchanged, the quantity demanded of any asset is:

1. Positively related to the wealth of the buyer.
2. Positively related to the (1) _____ _____ on the asset relative to that on an alternative asset.
3. Negatively related to the (2) _____ of the asset relative to that of alternative assets.
4. Positively related to the liquidity of the asset relative to that of alternative assets.

The bond (3) _____ _____ shows the relationship between the quantity demanded of bonds and the price of bonds, holding everything else constant. Recall that a high price of a bond corresponds to a low interest rate. Since the demander of bonds is a lender, at a high price of bonds (a low interest rate), the quantity demanded of bonds is low. Alternatively, at a low price of bonds (a high interest rate), the quantity demanded of bonds is relatively high. As a result, the bond demand curve has the usual downward slope when graphed in price/quantity space.

The bond (4) _____ _____ shows the relationship between the quantity supplied of bonds and the price of bonds, holding everything else constant. Since the supplier of bonds is the borrower, at a high price of bonds (a low interest rate), the quantity supplied of bonds is high, and the bond supply curve has the usual positive slope when graphed in price/quantity space.

The intersection of bond supply and bond demand determines the (5) _____ price and quantity of bonds. The equilibrium price generates a corresponding equilibrium interest rate.

Equilibrium interest rates change when there is a shift in the demand or supply of bonds.

The demand for bonds shifts right if there is an increase in (6) _____ (often from a business cycle expansion), a decrease in the riskiness of bonds relative to other assets, an increase in the (7) _____ of bonds relative to other assets, or an increase in the expected return on bonds relative to other assets. The expected return on bonds could rise due to a reduction in expected inflation (which raises real returns to lenders at each price of bonds) or a decrease in the expected interest rate (which would cause an increase in the price of bonds in the future and increase real returns).

The supply of bonds shifts right if there is an increase in the expected profitability of investment opportunities (from a business cycle expansion), an increase in expected inflation (which reduces real costs of borrowing at each price of bonds), or an increase in government deficits.

A rightward shift in the demand for bonds increases the price of bonds and reduces the interest rate. A rightward shift in the supply of bonds decreases the price of bonds and increases the interest rate. An increase in expected inflation causes bond supply to shift right, bond demand to shift left, the price of bonds to fall, and interest rates to rise. This effect is known as the (8) _____ _____.

The (9) _____ _____ _____ suggests that the interest rate is determined by the supply and demand for money. While the bond market best shows how expected inflation affects interest rates, the liquidity preference framework best shows how changes in income, the price level, and the money supply affect interest rates.

Because money earns little or no interest, the interest rate on bonds is the (10) _____ _____ of holding money. Therefore, at high interest rates, the opportunity cost of holding money is high, and the quantity demanded of money is low. Using similar logic, at low interest rates, the quantity demanded of money is high. As a result, the demand for money has the usual negative slope when graphed in interest rate/quantity of money space. Since we assume that the central bank controls the supply of money at some fixed quantity, the supply of money is a vertical line at the fixed quantity of money supplied. The intersection of money supply and money demand determines the equilibrium interest rate.

Changes in the supply or demand for money cause changes in the equilibrium interest rate. The (11) _____ _____ for money shifts right if there is an increase in income or if there is an increase in the price level. An increase in the money supply will shift the money supply curve to the right. Thus, other things held constant, an increase in income during a business cycle expansion will cause interest rates to rise, an increase in the price level will cause interest rates to rise, and an increase in the money supply will cause interest rates to fall. This last result is known as the liquidity effect.

An increase in the money supply, however, might not leave "other things equal." An increase in the money supply is expansionary, so it tends to raise national income, raise the price level, and increase expected inflation. Therefore, an increase in the growth rate of the money supply generates opposing effects on the interest rate: The liquidity effect suggests that interest rates should immediately fall, while the income, price-level, and expected-inflation effects suggest that the interest rate should rise. There are three possible outcomes. If the liquidity effect is larger than the other effects, an increase in the rate of money growth will cause interest rates to first fall, and then rise, but not to the level of the original interest rate. If the liquidity effect is smaller than the other effects, the interest rate will first fall, and then rise above the original interest rate. And if the liquidity effect is smaller than the other effects and we adjust quickly to expected inflation, then an increase in the rate of money growth only causes interest rates to rise. Empirical evidence suggests that an increase in money growth first causes the interest rate to fall, and then rise above the original interest rate.

HELPFUL HINTS

1. When dealing with the bond market, it is always helpful to remember that the bond suppliers are borrowers, and that the bond demanders are lenders. This distinction is particularly useful when dealing with disequilibrium. For example, if the price of bonds is above equilibrium, there is an (12) _____ of bonds. If there is an excess supply of bonds, then *desired borrowing exceeds desired lending*. Interest rates rise and the price of bonds falls until we reach equilibrium.

2. Supply and demand models can address both positive and negative shocks to variables that affect supply and demand. In the text and study guide, we often just explain the results of one direction of shock just to save space. For example, we show how an increase in inflation expectations in the bond market affects bond demand, bond supply, the price of bonds, and the interest rate. It is helpful (and good practice) if you address the opposite shock from that demonstrated in the text and see if you can generate the opposite result. In the case described above, since the text demonstrated the case of an increase in expected inflation, you should see if you are able to demonstrate the case of a decrease in expected inflation in the bond market.

3. The phrase "liquidity preference" is an alternative term for "money demand." That is, our desire to hold money is our preference to be liquid, or liquidity preference. Therefore, a model that employs the supply and demand for money is termed the "liquidity preference framework."

4. The (13) _____ _____ approach (the bond market) and the liquidity preference framework are generally compatible. That is, they generally provide the same answer to the question of how interest rates should respond to a particular shock. We only employ both markets because each market provides a particularly

clear answer for how interest rates respond to a few important shocks. Specifically, the bond market provides a clear answer to how interest rates respond to changes in expected inflation, while the liquidity preference framework (market for money) provides a clear answer to how interest rates respond to changes in income, the price level, and the money supply.

EXERCISES

Practice Problems

1. Employ the theory of asset demand to determine whether you would increase or decrease your quantity demanded of bonds in response to the following events. Explain.
a. Your grandmother dies and leaves you a bequest of $100 000.

_____

_____

b. Your brokerage firm lowers its commissions on stock transactions but keeps its commissions the same on bond transactions.

_____

_____

c. You are risk averse. You anticipate more volatility in future stock returns.

_____

_____

d. You become more pessimistic about future returns in the stock market.

_____

_____

e. You wreck your uninsured automobile.

_____

_____

_____

2. a. Information is provided below for the demand and supply of $1000 face value, one-year discount bonds that pay no coupon, and are held to maturity (for the full year). Complete the table and plot demand and supply in the graph provided below. Record the corresponding interest rates on the graph in the box beside the related price. Quantities are in billions of dollars.

Price	Quantity demanded	Quantity supplied	Corresponding interest rate
$975	100	300	_____
$950	150	250	_____
$925	200	200	_____
$900	250	150	_____

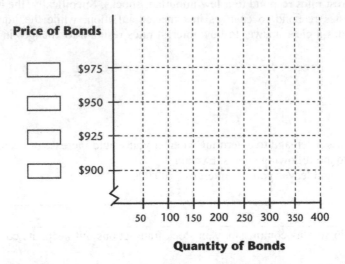

Quantity of Bonds

b.   What is the equilibrium price, interest rate, and quantity demanded of bonds?

_____

_____

c.   Suppose that the price of bonds is above the equilibrium price at, say, $950. Explain why this price is not the market-clearing price, and explain how and why the price of bonds and interest rates adjust to equilibrium.

_____

_____

d.   Suppose that wealth in the economy increases, causing the demand for bonds to increase by $100 billion at each price. Show this shift on the accompanying graph. What is the new equilibrium price, interest rate, and quantity of bonds?

_____

_____

3.   For each of the following events, describe the shift in the supply and/or demand for bonds, and describe the impact on the price of bonds and the interest rate. Use the graph provided to help you determine the answer.

a.   There is an increase in peoples' wealth.

_____

_____

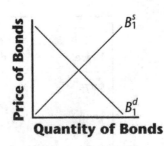

b.   An OSC ruling allows brokerage firms to reduce their commissions on bond transactions but not on stock transactions.

_____

_____

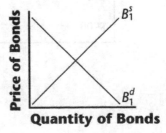

c.   The volatility of stock returns decreases.

_____

_____

d.   People expect higher interest rates in the future.

_____

_____

e.   There is an increase in the expected rate of inflation.

_____

_____

4.   For each of the following events, use the liquidity preference framework and shift money demand or money supply to determine the change in the equilibrium interest rate.

a.   There is a higher level of income due to a business cycle expansion.

_____

_____

b.   There is a higher price level.

_____

_____

c.   The Bank of Canada increases the money supply.

_____

_____

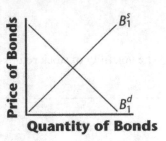

Short-Answer Questions

1.   In the theory of asset demand, what are the four factors that affect the decision about whether to buy one asset rather than another?

_____

_____

2.   Suppose you buy a one-year discount bond that pays no coupons, has a face value of $1000, and you hold it for the entire year. If you pay $963 for it, what is the corresponding interest rate?

_____

_____

3.   If there is an excess demand for bonds, is the price of bonds above or below the equilibrium price? Explain the price adjustment to equilibrium.

_____

_____

4.   Suppose people expect lower interest rates in the future. Use the bond market to explain the impact of this event on interest rates.

_____

_____

5.   What three events would shift the supply of bonds to the right?

_____

_____

6.   Suppose there is a decrease in expected inflation. Use the bond market to explain the impact of this event on interest rates.

_____

_____

7.   In question 6 above, the change in interest rates that results from a change in expected inflation is known as what?

_____

_____

8.   According to the liquidity preference framework, in what direction do interest rates move in response to an increase in the money supply, other things unchanging? What is the name of this effect?

_____

_____

Critical-Thinking Questions

You are watching the national news with your parents. The news anchor says that interest rates are higher than the historical average. Your parents know that you will begin looking to buy a house in a just few years. Your father says, "I hope that someone is appointed soon to run the Fed that will expand the money supply faster. If more money is available, borrowing rates will go down, and it will be much cheaper for you to buy a home."

1. If the liquidity effect is smaller than the income, price-level, and expected-inflation effects, is it true that increasing the growth rate in the money supply will decrease interest rates? Explain for both the near term and longer run.

_____

_____

_____

_____

2. If it is going to be a significant amount of time before you buy a home, is a faster or slower growth rate in the money supply likely to create lower interest rates for you? Explain.

_____

_____

_____

_____

SELF-TEST

True-False Questions

Circle whether the following statements are true (T) or false (F).

T   F   1.   According to the theory of asset demand, an increase in expected returns in the stock market decreases the quantity demanded of bonds.

T   F   2.   According to the theory of asset demand, an increase in the volatility of returns in the stock market decreases the quantity demanded of bonds.

T   F   3.   A one-year discount bond for which the owner pays $937, holds it for the entire one year, and receives $1000 at maturity, generates an interest rate of 6.7%.

T   F   4.   The price of a bond and the interest rate are always negatively related for any type of bond, whether a discount or coupon bond.

T   F   5.   If the price of bonds is below the equilibrium price, there will be an excess supply of bonds, and interest rates will rise.

T   F   6.   An increase the government's budget deficit shifts the supply of bonds to the right, decreases the price of bonds, and increases the interest rate.

T   F   7.   The asset market approach emphasizes flows rather than stocks of assets to determine asset prices.

T   F   8.   An increase in expected inflation decreases real returns at each price of bonds, causing bond demand to shift left, bond supply to shift right, the price of bonds to fall, and interest rates to rise.

T   F   9.   When expected inflation rises causing interest rates to rise, we have seen a demonstration of the Fisher effect.

T   F   10. An increase in the riskiness of bonds causes bond demand to increase, the price of bonds to rise, and interest rates to fall.

T   F   11. The liquidity preference framework suggests that the interest rate is determined by the supply and demand for bonds.

T   F   12. In the liquidity preference framework, an increase in incomes, *ceteris paribus*, causes money demand to shift left and interest rates to fall.

T   F   13. An increase in the money supply, other things held constant, causes interest rates to fall.

T   F   14. If there is an increase in the growth rate of the money supply and the resulting liquidity effect is smaller than the combined income, price-level, and expected-inflation effects, then the interest rate will eventually rise above the initial interest rate.

T   F   15. If there is an increase in the growth rate of the money supply, the resulting liquidity effect is smaller than the combined income, price-level, and expected-inflation effects, and inflationary expectations adjust quickly, then the interest rate will immediately rise and rise further over time.

Multiple-Choice Questions

Circle the appropriate answer.

1.   Which of the following assets is the least liquid?
   a. Currency.
   b. Automobile.
   c. Canada savings bond.
   d. Savings account.

2.   When the interest rate is below the equilibrium interest rate, there is an excess _____ for (of) bonds and the interest rate will _____.
   a. supply; fall
   b. supply; rise
   c. demand; rise
   d. demand; fall

3.   When brokerage commissions in the housing market are raised from 6 to 7% of the sales price, the _____ curve for bonds shifts to the _____.
   a. demand; right
   b. demand; left
   c. supply; left
   d. supply; right

4.   When rare coin prices become less volatile, the _____ curve for bonds shifts to the _____.
   a. demand; right
   b. demand; left
   c. supply; left
   d. supply; right

5. When the expected inflation rate decreases, the demand for bonds shifts to the _____, the supply of bonds shifts to the _____, and the interest rate _____.
   a. right; right; rises
   b. right; left; falls
   c. left; left; falls
   d. left; right; rises

6. When people revise downward their expectations of next year's short-term interest rate, the demand for long-term bonds shifts to the _____ and their interest rates _____.
   a. right; rise
   b. right; fall
   c. left; fall
   d. left; rise

7. In a recession, normally the demand for bonds shifts to the _____, the supply of bonds shifts to the _____ and the interest rate _____.
   a. right; right; rises
   b. right; left; falls
   c. left; left; falls
   d. left; right; rises

8. When the interest rate on a bond is _____ the equilibrium interest rate, in the bond market there is excess _____ and the price of bonds will _____.
   a. below; demand; rise
   b. above; demand; fall
   c. below; supply; fall
   d. above; supply; rise

9. If the government decides to exclude the interest earned on bonds from income taxation, then bond _____ will likely _____, and the interest rate will _____.
   a. demand; rise; fall
   b. supply; rise; fall
   c. demand; fall; rise
   d. supply; fall; rise

10. Since it has become easier in recent years to buy and sell stocks on the Internet, one expects that bond _____ has fallen since bonds are _____ liquid relative to stocks.
    a. demand; more
    b. supply; less
    c. demand; less
    d. supply; more

11. When equilibrium in the bond market changes, then
    a. the quantity of bonds bought and sold always increases.
    b. the equilibrium price and interest rate always move in opposite directions.
    c. either bond demand or bond supply or both curves have shifted.
    d. only (a) and (b) of the above.
    e. only (b) and (c) of the above.

12. The bond demand curve is downward sloping because
    a. the quantity demanded of bonds rises when the expected return on bonds rises.
    b. the expected return on bonds rises when the price of bonds rises.
    c. the expected return on bonds rises when the interest rate falls.
    d. only (a) and (b) of the above.
    e. only (a) and (c) of the above.

13. Which of the following will lead to an interest rate increase in the bond market?
    a. The riskiness of stocks rises.
    b. The expected inflation rate rises.
    c. The government deficit falls.
    d. The expected interest rate falls.
    e. None of the above.

14. As the interest rate on bonds _____, the opportunity cost of holding money _____, and the quantity of money demanded _____.
    a. rises; rises; rises
    b. rises; falls; falls
    c. falls; rises; falls
    d. falls; falls; rises
    e. falls; falls; falls

15. If interest rates are predicted to rise in the future, then bond _____ will _____.
    a. demand; fall
    b. supply; fall
    c. demand; rise
    d. supply; rise

16. The bond supply curve is upward sloping because
    a. the quantity supplied of bonds rises when the cost to borrow by issuing bonds falls.
    b. the cost to borrow by issuing bonds falls when the price of bonds rises.
    c. the cost to borrow by issuing bonds falls when the interest rate rises.
    d. only (a) and (b) of the above.
    e. only (a) and (c) of the above.

17. In the money market, when the interest rate is below the equilibrium interest rate, there is an excess _____ for (of) money, people will try to sell bonds, and the interest rate will _____.
    a. demand; rise
    b. demand; fall
    c. supply; fall
    d. supply; rise

18. If the price level falls, the demand curve for money will shift to the _____ and the interest rate will _____.
    a. right; rise
    b. right; fall
    c. left; rise
    d. left; fall

19. In the Keynesian liquidity preference framework, when income is _____ during a business cycle contraction, interest rates will _____.
    a. rising; rise
    b. rising; fall
    c. falling; rise
    d. falling; fall

20. In the liquidity preference framework, the price-level effect of a one-time increase in the money supply will have its maximum impact on interest rates
    a. at the moment the price level hits its peak (stops rising) because both the price-level and expected-inflation effects are at work.
    b. immediately after the price level begins to rise, because both the price-level and expected-inflation effects are at work.
    c. at the moment the expected inflation rate hits its peak.
    d. at the moment the inflation rate hits its peak.

21. The demanded quantity of an asset _____ as the risk of its return falls, and it _____ as the asset gets more liquid.
    a. decreases; decreases
    b. increases; decreases
    c. decreases; increases
    d. increases; increases

22. If the Bank of Canada wants to permanently lower interest rates, then it should raise the rate of money growth if
    a. there is a fast adjustment of expected inflation.
    b. there is slow adjustment of expected inflation.
    c. the liquidity effect is smaller than the expected-inflation effect.
    d. the liquidity effect is larger than the other effects.

23. When the growth rate of the money supply is increased, interest rates will rise immediately if the liquidity effect is _____ than the other money supply effects and there is _____ adjustment of expected inflation.
    a. larger; fast
    b. larger; slow
    c. smaller; slow
    d. smaller; fast

24. In the liquidity preference framework, the difference between the price-level and expected-inflation effects of a one-time increase in the money supply can be stated as follows:
    a. The increase in the interest rate caused by the rise in the price level remains once the price level has stopped rising, but the increase in the interest rate caused by expected inflation will be reversed once the price level stops rising.
    b. The increase in the interest rate caused by the rise in the expected inflation rate remains once the price level has stopped rising, but the increase in the interest rate caused by the rise in the price level will be reversed once the price level stops rising.
    c. Once the price level stops rising, the interest rate declines, but the expected-inflation effect remains.
    d. There is no difference, as both effects cause the interest rate to rise.

25. The most plausible explanation for why interest rates rose in the 1970s is
    a. the contractionary monetary policy pursued by the Bank of Canada.
    b. the decline in the money supply caused by the many failures of commercial banks.
    c. the rapidly rising level of income.
    d. the continual increase in expected inflation.

26. If prices in the market for fine art become less uncertain, then
    a. the demand curve for bonds shifts to the left and the interest rate rises.
    b. the demand curve for bonds shifts to the left and the interest rate falls.
    c. the demand curve for bonds shifts to the right and the interest rate falls.
    d. the supply curve for bonds shifts to the right and the interest rate falls.

27. If the expected inflation rate increases, then the _____ for (of) bonds increases while the _____ curve shifts to the left.
    a. demand; demand
    b. demand; supply
    c. supply; demand
    d. supply; supply

28. When the bond market becomes less volatile, the _____ for (of) bonds shifts to the right, and when the expected inflation increases, the _____ curve shifts to the _____.
    a. supply; demand; right
    b. supply; demand; left
    c. demand; supply; right
    d. demand; supply; left

29. In the late 1990s, Japan experienced a recession and deflation. Deflation caused the demand for bonds to _____ and the supply of bonds to _____. The outcome was a _____ in bond price and a _____ in the interest rate.
    a. fall, rise; fall; rise
    b. rise; fall; rise; fall
    c. fall; fall; rise; rise
    d. rise; rise; fall; fall

30. The income effect and the expected-inflation effect of a decrease in the money supply are a _____ and a _____ in the interest rate, respectively.
    a. rise; rise
    b. fall; fall
    c. rise; fall
    d. fall rise

CHAPTER 6

The Risk and Term Structure of Interest Rates

CHAPTER SYNOPSIS/COMPLETIONS

There are many different interest rates. Due to differences in risk, liquidity, and tax treatment, bonds with the same term to maturity may have different interest rates. The relationship between these interest rates is known as the (1) _____ *of interest rates*. Bonds with different terms to maturity (but that are otherwise the same) also have different interest rates. The relationship between these interest rates is known as the (2) _____ *of interest rates*.

Bonds with the same term to maturity may have different interest rates because they have differences in
- Risk of default.
- Liquidity.
- Income tax treatment.

Default occurs when the issuer of a bond is unable to make interest payments or pay off the face value when the bond matures. Treasury bonds are considered to be (3) _____ _____ _____ because they have no risk of default. The (4) _____ is the spread between the interest rate on bonds with default risk and the interest rate on default-free bonds, both of the same maturity. It shows how much bondholders must be compensated to hold a bond with default risk. The risk premium can be demonstrated by analyzing the separate markets for default-free Treasury bonds and corporate bonds of the same maturity. Suppose the price in each market is originally the same, and therefore the interest rate is the same. Since corporations have some possibility of default, the expected return on corporate bonds is lower. The corporate bond's return is also more uncertain. Since the relative expected return is lower and the risk is higher, the theory of asset demand tells us that the demand for corporate bonds will decrease, or shift left. At the same time, the relative return on default-free government bonds is higher and their risk is lower, so the demand for Treasury bonds increases, or shifts right. The price of corporate bonds falls, and their interest rate rises. The price of Treasury bonds rises, and their interest rate falls. The difference between the two interest rates is the risk premium. An increase in default risk on corporate or municipal bonds will increase the risk premium on those bonds. (5) _____ _____ rate the quality of corporate and municipal bonds in terms of the probability of default. Similar risk premiums can be calculated between bonds with different bond ratings.

According to the theory of asset demand, (6) _____ is a desirable attribute. Treasury bonds are more widely traded, and thus are easier to sell quickly and at lower cost than comparable corporate bonds. Similar to the analysis of default risk described above, the difference in liquidity between Treasury securities and corporate bonds causes a further decrease in the demand for corporate bonds and a further increase in the demand for Treasury bonds. Thus, differences in liquidity across bonds increase the "risk and liquidity premium," which is simply called the (7) _____ _____ by convention.

Interest payments received from holding municipal bonds are exempt from federal income tax. Other things being the same, if a bondholder were in the 35% tax bracket, a 10% return on taxable Treasury bonds would net the holder 6.5% after tax. The bondholder might prefer a similar municipal security even though it pays less than 10% as long as it pays more than 6.5%. Alternatively, applying the analysis from above, the tax exempt status of municipal bonds increases the demand for municipal bonds, which increases their price and decreases their interest rate. The taxable status of Treasury bonds decreases their demand and increases their interest rate. Thus, municipal bonds usually pay lower rates than Treasury bonds.

Bonds that are otherwise the same may have different interest rates if the time to maturity is different. A (8) _____ _____ is a plot of interest rates for a particular type of bond with different terms to maturity. That is, a yield curve shows the term structure of interest rates. A theory of the term structure must explain the following three empirical facts:

- Interest rates on bonds of different maturities move together over time.
- When short-term rates are low, yield curves tend to be upward sloping; when short-term rates are high, yield curves tend to be downward sloping, or (9) _____ .
- Yield curves almost always slope upward.

There are three theories of the term structure of interest rates. The (10) _____ *theory* argues that, if bonds of different maturities are perfect substitutes, then the interest rate on a long-term bond is the average of short-term interest rates that people expect to prevail over the life of the bond. For example, if the one-year interest rate is 6%, and next year's expected one-year rate is 7%, the current two-year rate must be (6% + 7%)/2 = 6.5%. As a result, a bondholder would be indifferent between holding sequential one-year bonds earning first 6% and then 7%, and holding a two-year bond earning 6.5%. This theory can explain the first two empirical facts listed above. However, since short-term rates are as likely to rise as fall, the expectations theory suggests that yield curves should generally be flat.

The (11) _____ _____ *theory* of the term structure argues that, if bonds of different maturities are not substitutes at all, then interest rates for different maturity bonds are completely separate, and the interest rate for each maturity is determined by the supply and demand for bonds of that maturity. Since the demand for short-term bonds is greater than for long-term bonds, the prices of short-term bonds will be higher and their interest rates lower than long-term bonds. This theory can explain the third empirical fact listed above.

The (12) _____ *theory* of the term structure combines components of the previous two theories. This theory suggests that bonds of different maturities are substitutes, but not perfect substitutes. As a result, the liquidity premium theory argues that the interest rate on long-term bonds is an average of short-term interest rates expected to occur over the life of the long-term bond (from the expectations theory) plus a positive term that represents the liquidity premium (from the segmented markets theory). Since people prefer short-term to long-term bonds, the liquidity premium is larger on long-term bonds. The (13) _____ _____ *theory* is the same as the liquidity premium theory if bondholders prefer short-term bonds. While the expectations theory and the segmented markets theory can each explain some of the three empirical facts about the term structure of interest rates, the liquidity premium theory and preferred habitat theory can explain all three. In addition, the liquidity premium/preferred habitat theories allow us to infer future movements in short-term interest rates from the yield curve as follows:

- A steeply upward-sloping yield curve indicates that short-term rates are expected to rise.
- A mildly upward-sloping yield curve suggests that short-term rates are expected to stay the same.
- A flat curve indicates that short-term rates are expected to decline slightly.
- An inverted curve (downward sloping) indicates that short-term rates are expected to decline substantially.

HELPFUL HINTS

1.   The segmented markets theory of the term structure is based on the argument that bonds of different maturities are not substitutes. This will be true if people won't accept any interest rate risk. If people won't accept any interest rate risk, they will only buy bonds of a maturity that perfectly matches their expected holding period. If you are saving for next year's vacation, you will only buy bonds in the market for one-year bonds. If you are saving for your retirement, you will only buy bonds in the market for 30-year bonds, and so on. As such, the interest rate for any particular maturity bond is unrelated to the interest rate for any other maturity bond.

2.   The preferred habitat theory is a more general theory of the term structure than the liquidity premium theory. The preferred habitat theory leaves open what length to maturity bondholders might prefer. If we argue that, other things

the same, bondholders would always prefer short-term bonds, then long-term bonds require an interest rate premium in order to get people to buy them, and the preferred habitat theory and the liquidity premium theory become the same.

EXERCISES

Practice Problems

1. Suppose that the health of the economy improves so that the probability of corporations defaulting on their bonds decreases.
a. Describe the shifts in the supply and demand curves for corporate bonds and Treasury bonds from the event described above.

_____

_____

b. What happens to the price and interest rate on corporate bonds?

_____

c. What happens to the price and interest rate on Treasury bonds?

_____

d. What happens to the risk premium? Explain.

_____

_____

2. Describe the shifts in supply and demand in the financial markets that would result from each of the following events, and then describe the impact on the relevant spread or risk premium.
a. A major AAA-rated corporation defaults on its bonds. What happens in the markets for corporate bonds and Treasury bonds, and the spread?

_____

_____

b. The volume of transactions in the corporate bond market increases so that corporate bondholders are more confident that they can find a buyer easily should they decide to sell their corporate bonds. What happens in the markets for corporate bonds and Treasury bonds, and the spread?

_____

c. A major BBB-rated corporation defaults on its bonds. What happens in the markets for bonds rated BBB and corporate bonds rated AAA and the spread between BBB and AAA bonds?

_____

_____

3. The following questions address the term structure of interest rates.
a. Suppose people expect the interest rate on one-year bonds for each of the next four years to be 4%, 5%, 6%, and 7%. Calculate the implied interest rate on bonds with a maturity of one year, two years, three years, and four years if the expectations theory of the term structure of interest rates is correct.

_____

_____

b. Plot the yield curve generated by this data if the expectations theory of the term structure of interest rates is correct.

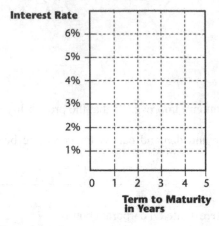

c. Can the yield curve you derived in *b* above be used to explain why yield curves almost always slope upward? Explain.

_____

_____

d. Since short-term interest rates are just as likely to rise as fall, in the long run people on average expect short-term interest rates to be steady. Suppose that people expect the one-year bond rate to remain at 4% for each of the next four years. If the liquidity premium theory of the term structure is correct, what are the liquidity premiums implied by a yield curve that looks like the one you plotted in *b* above?

_____

_____

4. What is the market predicting about the movement of future short-term interest rates (assuming there is a mild preference for shorter maturity bonds) if the yield curve looks like the one in Figure 6A? Figure 6B?

_____

_____

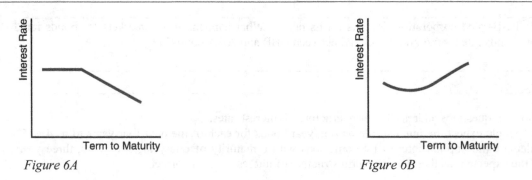

Figure 6A   *Figure 6B*

Short-Answer Questions

1. What three characteristics of a bond are collectively embedded in the risk structure of interest rates? How does a change in each affect the spread or risk premium?

_____

_____

2. What are the two main credit-rating agencies? What are these firms advising investors about? What name do we attach to bonds rated BAA (or BBB) or higher? What name to we attach to bonds rated below BAA (or BBB)?

    _____

    _____

3. How does the expectations theory of the term structure of interest rates explain the fact that interest rates on bonds of different maturities move together over time?

    _____

    _____

4. How does the segmented markets theory of the term structure of interest rates explain the fact that yield curves almost always slope upward?

    _____

    _____

Critical-Thinking Questions

You are presented with two alternatives: You can buy a three-year bond with a yield to maturity of 7%, or you can buy a one-year bond with a yield to maturity of 6%, then purchase another one-year bond with a yield to maturity of 7%, and when the second bond matures, purchase another one-year bond with a yield to maturity of 8%.

1. What is your expected annual rate of return for the first strategy?

    _____

2. What is your expected annual rate return for the second strategy?

    _____

3. What can you say about the two expected returns?

    _____

4. If the liquidity premium theory of the term structure of interest rates is correct, which one of these choices would you pick? Why?

    _____

    _____

SELF-TEST

True-False Questions

Circle whether the following statements are true (T) or false (F).

T   F   1.   The term structure of interest rates is the relationship among interest rates of bonds with the same maturity.

T   F   2.   The greater a bond's default risk, the higher is its interest rate.

T   F   3.   The expected returns on perfect substitute bonds are equal.

T   F   4.   The risk premium on a bond only reflects the amount of risk this bond has relative to a default-free bond.

T   F   5.   A plot of the interest rates on default-free government bonds with different terms to maturity is called a term structure curve.

T   F   6. The difference between the expectations theory of the term structure and the liquidity premium theory is that the liquidity premium theory allows for a risk premium while the expectations theory does not.

T   F   7. The expectations theory of the term structure assumes that bonds of different maturities are perfect substitutes.

T   F   8. The segmented markets theory of the term structure is unable to explain why yield curves usually slope upward.

T   F   9. The liquidity premium theory combines elements of both the segmented markets theory and the expectations theory.

T   F   10. The liquidity premium theory assumes that bonds of different maturities are not substitutes.

T   F   11. The relationship among interest rates on bonds with different terms to maturity is called the term structure of interest rates.

T   F   12. The bond price is positively related to the interest rates and when the price rises, the interest rates rise too.

T   F   13. The higher the default risk is, the larger the risk premium will be.

T   F   14. The interest rate on bonds of different maturities differ, because the short-term interest rates are expected to have different values at future dates.

T   F   15. An inverted yield curve means that short-term interest rates are expected to fall moderately.

Multiple-Choice Questions

Circle the appropriate answer.

1. Which of the following long-term bonds tend to have the highest interest rate?
   a. Corporate BBB bonds.
   b. Canada bonds.
   c. Corporate CCC bonds.
   d. Municipal bonds.

2. When the default risk on corporate bonds increases, other things being equal, the demand curve for corporate bonds shifts to the _____ and the demand curve for Canada bonds shifts to the _____.
   a. right; right
   b. right; left
   c. left; right
   d. left; left

3. When the corporate bond market becomes less liquid, other things being equal, the demand curve for corporate bonds shifts to the _____ and the demand curve for Canada bonds shifts to the _____.
   a. right; right
   b. right; left
   c. left; left
   d. left; right

4. The risk premium on corporate bonds falls when
   a. brokerage commissions fall in the corporate bond market.
   b. a flurry of major corporate bankruptcies occurs.
   c. the Canada bond market becomes more liquid.
   d. both (b) and (c) of the above occur.

5. The interest rate on tax-exempt municipal bonds in the United States rises relative to the interest rate on U.S. corporate bonds when
   a. there is a major default in the municipal bond market in the United States.
   b. income tax rates are raised.
   c. U.S. Treasury securities become more widely traded.
   d. U.S. corporate bonds become riskier.

6. Because municipal bonds in the United States bear substantial default risk, their interest rates
   a. tend to be higher than interest rates on default-free U.S. Treasury bonds indicating that the default premium exceeds the tax advantages of municipal bonds.
   b. tend to be higher than interest rates on default-free U.S. Treasury bonds indicating that the default premium falls short of the tax advantages of municipal bonds.
   c. tend to be lower than interest rates on default-free U.S. Treasury bonds indicating that the default premium exceeds the tax advantages of municipal bonds.
   d. tend to be lower than interest rates on default-free U.S. Treasury bonds indicating that the default premium falls short of the tax advantages of municipal bonds.

7. When income tax rates are _____ , the interest rates on taxable bonds _____ relative to the interest rate on tax-exempt bonds.
   a. lowered; fall
   b. lowered; rise
   c. raised; fall
   d. raised; do not change

8. The risk structure of interest rates is explained by three factors:
   a. risk of default, liquidity, and the income tax treatment of the security.
   b. risk of default, maturity, and the income tax treatment of the security.
   c. liquidity, maturity, and the income tax treatment of the security.
   d. risk of default, maturity, and the liquidity of the security.

9. Why does the interest rate on junk bonds rise relative to the interest rate on Canadian treasury bills after a big drop in the stock market?
   a. Income tax rates rise.
   b. The risk of default for Canadian treasury bills rises.
   c. The risk of default for junk bonds rises.
   d. The term premium for Canadian treasury bills falls.

10. Bonds with a low risk of default are labelled _____ while bonds with a high risk of default are labelled _____ .
    a. corporate; Canada
    b. junk; corporate
    c. investment-grade; high-yield
    d. risky; safe

11. If the interest rates of corporate bonds and government bonds are the same in a country, then it is likely that
    a. there is no term premium.
    b. government bonds are not default-free bonds.
    c. the liquidity premium has disappeared.
    d. bonds of different maturities are perfect substitutes.

12. Which of the following theories of the term structure is able to explain the fact that when short-term interest rates are low, yield curves are more likely to slope upward?
    a. Expectations theory.
    b. Segmented markets theory.
    c. Liquidity premium theory.
    d. Both (b) and (c) of the above.
    e. Both (a) and (c) of the above.

13. If the expected path of one-year interest rates over the next three years is 4%, 1%, and 1% then the expectations theory predicts that today's interest rate on the three-year bond is
    a. 1%.
    b. 2%.
    c. 3%.
    d. none of the above.

14. If the expected path of one-year interest rates over the next five years is 2%, 2%, 4%, 3%, and 1%, the expectations theory predicts that the bond with the highest interest rate today is the one with a maturity of
    a. one year.
    b. two years.
    c. three years.
    d. four years.

15. According to the liquidity premium theory,
    a. a steeply rising yield curve indicates that short-term interest rates are expected to rise in the future.
    b. a moderately rising yield curve indicates that short-term interest rates are expected to decline in the future.
    c. interest rates on bonds of different maturities need not move together over time.
    d. only (a) and (b) of the above.

16. The _____ of the term structure states the following: the interest rate on a long-term bond will equal an average of short-term interest rates expected to occur over the life of the long-term bond but investors do not prefer short-term over long-term bonds.
    a. segmented markets theory
    b. expectations theory
    c. liquidity premium theory
    d. liquidity preference theory.

17. Why, according to the expectations theory, does the interest rate on a long-term bond equal the average of expected short-term interest rates over the life of the long-term bond?
    a. Because only then will the public hold both long- and short-term bonds.
    b. Because long- and short-term bonds are not perfect substitutes.
    c. Because people prefer short-term bonds.
    d. None of the above.

18. The segmented markets theory assumes that
    a. long-term bonds are preferred to short-term bonds.
    b. people are not rational.
    c. bonds of different maturities are not substitutes.
    d. the risk of default does not influence bond demand.

19. Which of the following is an empirical fact regarding the term structure of interest rates?
    a. Interest rates on bonds of different maturities move together.
    b. When short-term interest rates are low, yield curves are likely to slope upward.
    c. Yield curves usually slope upward.
    d. All of the above.

20. People prefer shorter-term bonds to longer-term bonds because
    a. the maturity length is longer for shorter-term bonds.
    b. the risk of default is greater for shorter-term bonds.
    c. the interest rate risk is greater for longer-term bonds.
    d. only (a) and (b) of the above.

21. According to the expectations theory of the term structure, if people expect that the short-term interest rate will be 6% on average over the coming three years, then the interest rate on a bond with three years to maturity will be
    a. less than 6%.
    b. greater than 6%.
    c. exactly 6%.
    d. exactly 2%.

22. According to the liquidity premium and preferred habitat theories, a flat yield curve indicates that
    a. future short-term interest rates are expected to rise.
    b. future short-term interest rates are expected to remain constant.
    c. the liquidity premium has disappeared.
    d. future short-term interest rates are expected to fall.

23. If the yield curve slopes upward mildly for short maturities and then slopes sharply upward for longer maturities, the liquidity premium theory (assuming a mild preference for short-term bonds) indicates that the market is predicting
    a. a rise in short-term interest rates in the near future and a decline further out in the future.
    b. constant short-term interest rates in the near future and a rise further out in the future.
    c. a decline in short-term interest rates in the near future and a rise further out in the future.
    d. a decline in short-term interest rates in the near future which levels off further out in the future.

24. An inverted yield curve signals that the market expects interest rates to
    a. fall in the future.
    b. rise in the future.
    c. remain constant in the future.
    d. be random in the future.

25. During the Great Depression, the difference between interest rates on low-quality corporate bonds and Canada bonds
    a. increased significantly.
    b. decreased significantly.
    c. decreased moderately.
    d. did not change.

26. In reality, short-term interest rates are just as likely to fall as to rise; this is the major shortcoming of the
    a. segmented markets theory.
    b. expectations theory.
    c. liquidity premium theory.
    d. separable markets theory.

27. When yield curves slope upward, the long-term interest rates are _____ the short-term interest rates; when yield curves are _____, short- and long-term interest rates are the same.
    a. above; flat
    b. above; downward-sloping
    c. below; downward-sloping
    d. below; flat

28. If the expected path of one-year interest rates over the next four years is 4%, 3%, 2%, and 1%, the expectations theory predicts that interest rates on three-year and four-year bonds are _____ and _____ and the yield curve is _____.
    a. 2%; 1%; flat
    b. 2%; 2.5%; upward sloping
    c. 3%; 2.5%; downward sloping
    d. 3%; 2.5%; upward sloping

29. In the expectations theory and in the segmented markets theory, bonds with different maturities are _____ and _____, respectively.
    a. perfect substitutes; not substitutes at all
    b. perfect substitutes; substitutes
    c. substitutes; perfect substitutes
    d. not substitutes at all; perfect substitutes

30. Suppose that the one-year interest rates over the next six years are expected to be 2%, 4%, 5%, 6%, 7%, and 9%. In addition, the liquidity premiums for holding short-term bonds for one-year to six-year bonds are 0%, 0.5%, 1%, 1.5%, 2%, and 2.5%, respectively. What is the interest rate on a three-year bond and a five-year bond?
    a. 6.8%; 4.67%
    b. 5%; 7%
    c. 6%; 9%
    d. 4.67%; 6.8%

The Stock Market, the Theory of Rational Expectations, and the Efficient Markets Hypothesis

CHAPTER SYNOPSIS/COMPLETIONS

There are a variety of fundamental theories that underlie the valuation of stocks and other securities. These theories require that we understand how expectations affect stock market behavior, because to value a stock, people must form expectations about a firm's future dividends and the rate to discount future values. The *theory of* (1) _____ _____, when applied to financial markets, implies the (2) _____ _____ _____.

(3) _____ have voting rights within the firm and are claimants on the firm's (4) _____ _____ _____. Stockholders also receive (5) _____ from the net earnings of the corporation. The value of any investment is the present discounted value of all expected cash flows the investment will generate over its life. A one-period model of stock price determination would suggest that P_0 = $[Div/1+k_e]+[P_1/(1+k_e)]$, where P_0 = the current price of the stock, Div = the dividend paid at the end of the year, k_e = the required return on investments on equities, and P_1 = the price of the stock at the end of the period. The (6) _____ _____ _____ extends the single period model by discounting all future expected cash flows. Since the sale price is so far in the future, it is discounted to such a degree that its value can be ignored. Thus, the generalized dividend model says that the current price of a stock is the sum of the present value of the future dividends. This is difficult to calculate because it requires that we estimate all future dividends. The (7) _____ _____ _____ is a simplified version of generalized dividend model that assumes a constant growth rate of dividends. Thus, $P_0 = Div_0(1 + g)/(k_e - g) = Div_1/(k_e - g)$, where Div_0 = the most recent past dividend, Div_1 = the next future dividend, and g = the expected constant growth rate of dividends.

On a day-to-day basis, stock prices are set by the interaction of traders in the stock market. As with an auction, the price of a stock is determined by the buyer who values the stock the greatest. Based on the Gordon growth model, the trader who values the stock the greatest either has less uncertainty regarding its future cash flows or estimates its cash flows to be greater than other traders do. New information that causes even small changes in expectations about dividend growth rates or required returns causes large changes in stock prices, so stock markets are often volatile.

Monetary policy affects stock prices by altering the required rate of return on equities (k_e) and by altering the performance of the economy, which alters the expected growth rate of dividends (g).

The evaluation of stock prices requires that people form expectations about firms' future cash flows and the discount rate. An older theory, called (8) _____ _____, suggests that expectations of a variable are based on an average of past values of that variable. A more modern theory, called (9) _____ _____, suggests that expectations are identical to (10) _____ _____ (the best guess of the future), which uses all available information. This does not mean that rational expectations are perfectly accurate. Expectations can still be rational even if an additional factor is important in the prediction but was not available to the forecaster. It would be irrational if additional information were available but the forecaster ignored it or was unaware of it.

It is logical that people form rational expectations because there is a cost to people whose expectations are not based on the optimal forecast. As a result:

- If there is a change in the way a variable moves, the way in which expectations of this variable are formed will change as well.
- The forecast errors of expectations will on average be zero, and they cannot be predicted ahead of time.

The application of the theory of rational expectations to financial markets is called the (11) _____ _____ _____. It suggests that prices of securities fully reflect all available information. The above statement is derived from the following: Since the expected return on a security equals the equilibrium return, and if rational expectations hold the expected return equals the optimal forecast of the return, then it follows that the optimal forecast of the return equals the equilibrium return. Therefore, current prices in a financial market are set so that the optimal forecast of a security's return equals the equilibrium return.

In an efficient market, since prices of securities fully reflect all available information, all (12) _____ _____ _____ will be eliminated by (13) _____. For example, if the optimal forecast of tomorrow's price of a stock is higher than today's price, buying today at the lower price would generate abnormally high returns. This would cause people to buy the stock, driving its price up and its returns down until the optimal forecast of the returns is reduced and equals the equilibrium return. This does not require that all market participants be well informed. "Smart money" will eliminate the profit opportunities.

The stronger version of the efficient market hypothesis suggests that not only are the prices of securities the result of optimal forecasts, they reflect the true fundamental value of the securities, or what is known as the (14) _____ _____ (the items that have a direct impact on future income streams of the securities). If this is true, one investment is as good as any other.

The efficient market hypothesis suggests that hot tips and investment advisor's published recommendations cannot help an investor outperform the market because this information is already fully incorporated into the price of securities. One would need to have the information before others have it in order to outperform the market. In addition, stock prices will respond to announcements only when the information being announced is unexpected. Most investors should engage in a "buy and hold" strategy, which will generate the average market return in the long run but with lower costs due to fewer brokerage commissions.

Some economists think that stock market crashes are evidence that the stronger version of efficient markets is not true. However, other economists use *rational bubbles* to explain crashes. A (15) _____ is when the price of an asset differs from its fundamental market value. It may not be irrational to hold an asset when its price exceeds its fundamental value if you think that the price will go even higher before it falls.

(16) _____ _____ applies concepts from other social sciences like psychology to understand securities prices. Loss aversion may stop smart money from engaging in (17) _____ _____ even when a stock is overvalued. In addition, investor overconfidence and social contagion can explain why trading volume is so high, why stocks get overvalued, and why speculative bubbles occur.

Helpful Hints

1. When most people hear the phrase "rational expectations," they think that it cannot be true because they know some very irrational people. However, the theory of rational expectations does not require that all or even most people are rational. It only requires that enough people are rational, what we call *smart money*, that their behavior removes all profit opportunities by moving securities prices to their equilibrium values. This also helps explains why studies employing survey data will find that many people engage in irrational behavior while stock market studies usually show that market outcomes support the theory of rational expectations.

2.   Rational bubbles are related to the "greater fool" theory. The "greater fool" theory suggests that an investor will buy an asset at a price that exceeds the fundamental value of the asset if the investor thinks that there will be an even greater fool who will pay even more for it in the future. Therefore, if an investor believes that the fundamental value of a stock is $50, he will be willing to buy it at $100 if he thinks he can sell it $150 before its value falls back to $50.

EXERCISES

Practice Problems

1.   Suppose that a stock is expected to pay a $1 dividend at the end of this year and that your required return on equity investments is 9%.

a.   Using a one-period model of stock price determination, what would you pay for the stock if you expect to sell it in one year for $17.50?

_____

_____

b.   Using the Gordon growth model, what would you pay for the stock if you expected the dividends to grow at 3% per year?

_____

_____

c.   Suppose that you meet the CEO of the firm and you are so impressed that you consider the company to be of lower risk that you previously thought, and so you reduce your required return on this equity investment to 7%. Using the Gordon growth model, what would you pay for this stock?

_____

_____

d.   Suppose the CEO provides you with inside information that the dividends are going to grow at 4% per year. Using the Gordon growth model, if your required return on this equity investment remains at 7%, what price would you pay for the stock?

_____

_____

e.   Compare your answers from *b*, *c*, and *d*. According to the Gordon growth model of stock price determination, for a given dividend payment, what are the only things that can increase the price of a stock?

_____

_____

2.   If the efficient market hypothesis is true, how will each of the following events affect the price of IBM stock? Explain your answer.

a.   IBM announces profits of $100 million. Stock analysts had predicted profits of $300 million.

_____

_____

b.   IBM announces profits of $300 million. Stock analysts had predicted profits of $300 million.

_____

_____

c.   IBM announces a merger with Dell Computer. The deal is so complex that only financial analysts and other financially sophisticated people can correctly assess that it will make both firms much more efficient and profitable. The average person is simply confused.

_____

_____

3. Recall from Chapter 5 that there are three different outcomes for long-term interest rates when the Bank of Canada slows the growth of the money supply. Describe the interest rate outcome for each of the following conditions listed below.

a. The Bank of Canada action was widely anticipated.

_____

_____

_____

b. The Bank of Canada action was unanticipated and people expect that the slower growth of money will be permanent.

_____

_____

_____

c. The Bank of Canada action was unanticipated and people do not expect that the inflation rate will be lower.

_____

_____

_____

d. What does the example here suggest about the difficulty of conducting monetary policy when expectations are rational?

_____

_____

_____

4.

a. Suppose that a share of Microsoft had a closing price yesterday of $115, but new information was announced after the market closed, causing a revision in the forecast of next year's price to go to $100. If the annual equilibrium return on Microsoft is 17%, what will the price be when the market opens today?

_____

_____

b. The annual equilibrium return on Microsoft is 17%. What would happen if the optimal forecast of the return is an annual rate of 45%?

_____

_____

c. Could this situation be maintained under the efficient markets condition?

_____

_____

Short-Answer Questions

1. John values ABC stock at $10 per share. Susan values it at $15 per share, and Bill values it at $20 per share. In a free-market auction, who will buy ABC stock? Why? What is the range for the price of ABC stock? Explain.

_____

_____

2. Suppose a person has better information about a firm than others and so has greater certainty regarding the future cash flows of the firm. Other things being the same, will that person be willing to pay more, the same, or less than others for stock in that firm? Explain.

    _____

    _____

3. Suppose there is a change in the way a variable moves. If adaptive expectations accurately represent how people form expectations, are forecast errors zero on average, and unpredictable? Explain.

    _____

    _____

4. Suppose there is a change in the way a variable moves. If rational expectations accurately represent how people form expectations, are forecast errors zero on average, and unpredictable? Explain.

    _____

    _____

5. Can a stock market bubble be rational? Explain.

    _____

    _____

6. If the efficient market hypothesis is correct, what investment strategy is best for most investors?

    _____

    _____

Critical-Thinking Questions

You are watching a broadcast of the Financial Market Report on CNN with a friend. The host reports that a tropical storm in the Gulf of Mexico named Katrina has just been upgraded to hurricane status. It is expected to hit the entire gulf coast of the United States and destroy most of the sugar beet farms. Your friend says, "We should purchase stock in C&H Sugar because they produce only pure cane sugar from outside the Gulf region, and its stock price will surely rise after the storm damages its competitors."

1. Is it likely that you can make abnormally high returns by using this information to buy stock in C&H Sugar? Why or why not?

    _____

    _____

2. Suppose that a friend of your works for the Weather Bureau. She calls you late at night, and in casual conversation tells you that weather satellites have detected cloud movements that suggest that an enormous storm is in the process of forming. The weather bureau has not yet reported this information. It is afraid of causing panic because there are no evacuation plans in place. Can you earn abnormally high returns using this information? Why or why not?

    _____

    _____

3. What will happen to the price and returns to stock in C&H Sugar as you (and later others) buy stock in C&H Sugar? Can abnormally high returns be maintained? Explain.

    _____

SELF-TEST

True-False Questions

Circle whether the following statements are true (T) or false (F).

T   F   1. Technical analysis is the only method that beats the market and creates higher returns on stocks.

T   F   2. Expectations that are formed solely on the basis of past information are known as rational expectations.

T   F   3. The theory of rational expectations argues that optimal forecasts need not be perfectly accurate.

T   F   4. An important implication of rational expectations theory is that when there is a change in the way a variable behaves, the way expectations of this variable are formed will change as well.

T   F   5. If the optimal forecast of a return on a financial asset exceeds its equilibrium return, the situation is called an unexploited profit opportunity.

T   F   6. In an efficient market, all unexploited profit opportunities will be eliminated.

T   F   7. Everyone in a financial market must be well informed about a security if the market is to be considered efficient.

T   F   8. The efficient markets theory suggests that published reports of financial analysts can guarantee that individuals who use this information will outperform the market.

T   F   9. The overwhelming majority of statistical studies indicate that financial analysts do indeed pick financial portfolios that outperform the market average.

T   F   10. According to the efficient markets hypothesis, picking stocks by throwing darts at the financial page is an inferior strategy compared to employing the advice of financial analysts.

T   F   11. The Black Monday crash of 1987 and the Tech crash of 2000 show that expectations in the financial markets are not rational.

T   F   12. As long as stock market crashes are unpredictable, the rational expectation theory holds.

T   F   13. The forecast errors of expectations will on average be greater than zero and can be predicted ahead of time.

T   F   14. In efficient markets, all unexploited profit opportunities will be eliminated.

T   F   15. The random-walk theory implies that the future changes in stock prices should, for all practical purposes, be predictable.

Multiple-Choice Questions

Circle the appropriate answer.

1. Suppose you read a story in the financial section of the local newspaper that announces the proposed merger of Dell Computer and Gateway. The announcement is expected to greatly increase the profitability of Gateway. If you should now decide to invest in Gateway stock, you can expect to earn

   a. above average returns since you will get to share in the higher profits.

   b. above average returns since your stock will definitely appreciate as the profits are earned.

   c. a normal return since stock prices adjust to reflect changed profit expectations almost immediately.

   d. none of the above.

2. Evidence of chaotic dynamics in stock prices

   a. implies that prediction is possible over short periods of time.

   b. implies that prediction is possible over both short and long periods of time.

   c. is questionable because of the reliability of the existing chaos tests.

   d. only (a) and (b) of the above.

3. In countries experiencing rapid rates of inflation, announcements of money supply increases are often followed by immediate increases in interest rates. Such behaviour is consistent with which of the following?

   a. Rational expectations.

   b. Expectations of higher inflation in the near future.

   c. A tight current monetary policy.

   d. Both (a) and (b) of the above.

4. The efficient markets hypothesis suggests that purchasing the published reports of financial analysts

   a. is likely to increase one's returns by an average of 10%.

   b. is likely to increase one's returns by an average of about 3% to 5%.

   c. is not likely to be an effective strategy for increasing financial returns.

   d. is likely to increase one's returns by an average of about 2% to 3%.

5. After the announcement of higher quarterly profits, the price of a stock falls. Such an occurrence is

   a. clearly inconsistent with the efficient markets hypothesis.

   b. possible if market participants expected lower profits.

   c. consistent with the efficient markets hypothesis.

   d. not possible.

6. Since a change in regulations permitting their existence in the mid-1970s and the explosive growth in the number of people who surf the Internet, discount brokers have grown rapidly. Efficient markets theory would seem to suggest that people who use discount brokers

   a. will likely earn lower returns than those who use full-service brokers.

   b. will likely earn about the same as those who use full-service brokers, but will net more after brokerage commissions.

   c. are going against evidence that suggests that the financial analysis provided by full-service brokers can help one outperform the overall market.

   d. are likely to be poor.

7. The efficient markets hypothesis suggests that stock prices tend to follow a "random walk." Thus the best strategy for investing is

   a. a "churning strategy" of buying and selling often to catch the market swings.

   b. turning over your stock portfolio each month, selecting stocks by throwing darts at the stock page.

   c. a "buy and hold strategy" of holding onto stocks to avoid brokerage commissions.

   d. to do none of the above.

8. Rational expectations theory suggests that forecast errors of expectations

   a. tend to be persistently high or low.

   b. are unpredictable.

   c. are more likely to be negative than positive.

   d. are more likely to be positive than negative.

9. Unexploited opportunities are quickly eliminated in financial markets through
    a. changes in asset prices.
    b. changes in dividend payments.
    c. accounting conventions.
    d. exchange-rate translations.

10. Stockbrokers have at times paid newspaper reporters for information about articles to be published in future editions. This suggests that
    a. your stockbroker's hot tips will help you outperform the overall market.
    b. financial analysts' reports contain information that will help you earn a return that exceeds the market average.
    c. insider information may help ensure returns that exceed the market average.
    d. each of the above is true.

11. If expectations are formed rationally, forecast errors of expectations will on average be _____ and therefore _____ be predicted ahead of time.
    a. positive; can
    b. positive; cannot
    c. zero; cannot
    d. zero; can

12. That stock prices do not always rise when favourable earnings reports are released suggests that
    a. the stock market is not efficient.
    b. people trading in stocks sometimes incorrectly estimate companies' earnings.
    c. stock prices tend to be biased measures of future corporate earnings.
    d. all of the above are true.

13. According to the theory of efficient capital markets, since all relevant, publicly available information is discounted in asset prices as soon as it becomes available,
    a. investors cannot construct systematically profitable trading rules based only on this information.
    b. investors have no incentive to buy stock based on favourable information, since the market will have already discounted it.
    c. investors have an incentive to buy stock based on favourable information, since the market takes time to discount it.
    d. both (a) and (b) of the above.

14. Mutual funds that outperform the market in one period are
    a. highly likely to consistently outperform the market in subsequent periods due to their superior investment strategies.
    b. likely to underperform the market in subsequent periods to average the funds' returns.
    c. not likely to consistently outperform the market in subsequent periods.
    d. not likely to outperform the market in any subsequent periods.

15. According to the theory of efficient capital markets,
    a. incorrectly valued assets are quickly discovered and bought or sold until their prices are brought into line with their correct underlying value.
    b. most investors will not earn excess returns from spending resources on technical market analysis.
    c. the best strategy for most investors is to buy and hold a well-diversified portfolio of securities.
    d. all of the above are true.

16. The stockholders are residual claimants to all _____ of the firm.
    a. cash flows
    b. expenses
    c. fundamentals
    d. liabilities

17. According to the one-period valuation model, which of the following is not important to the value of a stock?
    a. The stock dividend.
    b. The stock purchase price this period.
    c. The stock sales price next period.
    d. The required return on equity investments.

18. According to the generalized dividend valuation model, if the required return on equity investments rises, then the stock price
    a. rises.
    b. falls.
    c. remains constant.
    d. does not change in a predictable manner.

19. Even if company XYZ does not routinely pay dividends on its stock, the generalized dividend model predicts that company XYZ stock has value because
    a. company XYZ paid dividends in the past.
    b. the required return on equity investment is never zero.
    c. buyers expect company XYZ to pay dividends in the future.
    d. all companies must legally pay dividends.

20. According to the Gordon growth model, as the _____ rises, the value of a stock _____.
    a. required return on equity investments; rises
    b. expected growth rate of dividends; rises
    c. the most recent dividend paid; falls
    d. All of the above.

21. If the required return on equity investments is 8%, then according to the one-period dividend model, what is the value of a stock that will pay a dividend of $0.50 next year and that is expected to sell for $30 next year?
    a. $28.24.
    b. $27.18.
    c. $10.00.
    d. $3.81.

22. If the required return on equity investments is 11% and if the expected constant growth rate of dividends is 6%, then according to the Gordon growth model, what is the value of a stock that will pay a dividend of $0.61 next year?
    a. $57.55.
    b. $12.20.
    c. $3.59.
    d. $0.55.

23. New information may lead to an immediate change in the price of a stock because
    a. the required return on this equity investment may change.
    b. the expected constant growth rate in dividends may change.
    c. the forecast of the future sales price of the stock may change.
    d. all of the above.

24. If uncertainty about the future cash flow of a stock rises, then the price of the stock falls because
    a. the amount of future dividends falls.
    b. the amount of future dividends rises.
    c. the required return on the stock falls.
    d. the required return on the stock rises.

25. The value of a company's stock may fall when the economy enters a recession because
    a. the value of expected future dividends falls.
    b. the required return on equity investments falls.
    c. the expected growth rate of dividends falls.
    d. only (a) and (c) of the above.

26. The term "optimal forecast" in rational expectations theory is best defined as the
    a. correct forecast.
    b. correct guess.
    c. actual outcome.
    d. best guess.

27. If stock prices follow a "random walk," then stock prices
    a. will rise, then fall, then rise again.
    b. will rise and fall in a predictable manner.
    c. tend to follow trends.
    d. cannot be predicted based on past trends.

28. The average industry PE ratio for firm X is 41. What is the current price of firm X's stock if earnings per share is projected to be 1.22?
    a. $50
    b. $33.61
    c. $9
    d. $41

29. The optimal forecast of return and the equilibrium return for a given security are –10% and 5%, respectively. In such a case, based on the efficient markets hypothesis, the current price of this security will _____ and its R^{of} will _____.
    a. fall; fall
    b. rise; rise
    c. fall; rise
    d. rise; fall

30. The value of a firm's stock can be obtained by
    a. multiplying the firm's price earnings ratio by the expected earnings per share.
    b. dividing the average industry price earnings ratio by the expected earnings per share.
    c. multiplying the average industry price earnings ratio by the expected earnings per share.
    d. none of the above

CHAPTER 8

An Economic Analysis of Financial Structure

CHAPTER SYNOPSIS/COMPLETIONS

The financial structure is designed to promote economic efficiency. The efficiency of the financial system affects the performance of the macroeconomy.

There are eight basic facts about the financial structure that this chapter will explain.

- *Stocks are not the most important source of external financing for businesses.* In the United States, only 11% of external financing comes from stock. In other developed countries it is much less.
- *Issuing marketable debt and equity securities is not the primary way in which businesses finance their operations.* Stocks and bonds combined only add up to 43% of the external source of funds to U.S. businesses; it is even less in other countries.
- *Indirect finance, which involves the activities of financial intermediaries, is many times more important than direct finance, in which businesses raise funds directly from lenders in financial markets.* Since most of the newly issued securities of firms are sold to financial intermediaries, less than 10% of external funding is truly direct finance.
- *Financial intermediaries, particularly banks, are the most important source of external funds used to finance businesses.* While this is true for the United States, it is even more the case in developing nations.
- *The financial system is among the most heavily regulated sectors of the economy.* Regulations promote the provision of information and stability of the system.
- *Only large, well-established corporations have easy access to the securities market to finance their activities.* Small firms obtain their funding from banks.
- (1) _____ *is a prevalent feature of debt contracts for both households and businesses.* Collateralized debt, known as (2) _____ _____, requires the borrower to pledge an asset to the lender to guarantee payment of the debt.
- Debt contracts typically are extremely complicated legal documents that place substantial restrictions on the behaviour of the borrower. Loan contracts usually contain (3) _____ _____ that restrict the activities in which the borrower can engage.

Understanding transaction costs and information costs will help explain the eight facts above.

People with only a small amount to loan cannot lend through the financial markets because the brokerage fees are too large and the denominations of issues may be too large. To lower transaction costs, mutual funds take advantage of (4) _____ _____ _____ by combining many small savers' funds and buying a widely diversified portfolio. Financial intermediaries also gain *expertise* in carrying out customer transactions, which reduces transaction costs further. This cost reduction allows money market mutual funds to provide (5) _____ _____.

(6) _____ _____ is when each party to a transaction has unequal knowledge about the other party. This leads to two problems: (7) _____ _____ before the transaction and (8) _____ _____ after the transaction. Adverse selection occurs when bad credit risks are the ones who most desire to borrow. Moral hazard occurs when borrowers engage in activities that are undesirable from the lender's point of view. The analysis of how asymmetric information affects economic behaviour is known as (9) _____ _____.

If a buyer can't determine if a product for sale is a lemon, he will pay only a low value. Sellers of good products won't want to sell at the lower price. The market becomes small and inefficient at moving goods from sellers to buyers. In financial markets, the adverse selection problem suggests that risky firms benefit more from borrowing. If lenders can't distinguish between good and bad firms, they will pay only low prices for securities (that is, charge high interest rates). Good firms won't bother to sell securities at the low price, so the market is small and inefficient. This is a reason why stocks and bonds are not the primary source of financing for businesses.

There are tools to help reduce the asymmetric information problem that caused the lemons problem. These tools help lenders distinguish good firms from bad.

- *Private production and sale of information.* Standard and Poor's, Moody's, and Value Line gather information and sell it. However, the (10) _____ _____ _____ (those not paying for the information still benefit from it) reduces the production of private information.

- *Government regulation to increase information.* The Securities and Exchange Commission (SEC) requires firms to have independent (11) _____, use standard accounting principles, and disclose information about sales, assets, and earnings. Thus, the financial system is heavily regulated. This reduces the asymmetric information problem, but does not eliminate it.

- *Financial intermediation.* Since it is so hard for individuals to acquire enough information to make completely informed loans, most people lend to financial intermediaries, such as a bank, who then lend to the ultimate borrower. The bank becomes an expert in sorting good credit risks from bad. There is no free-rider problem because the bank makes private, non-traded loans rather than buying securities. The larger and more established the firm, the more likely it is that they will issue securities rather than borrow from an intermediary.

- *Collateral and net worth. Collateral* is property promised to the lender if the borrower defaults, which reduces the consequences to the lender of a default. (12) _____ _____, or equity capital, is the difference between a firm's assets and liabilities. Large net worth lowers the probability of default, and acts as collateral in the event of default.

The (13) _____ _____ _____ causes a particular type of moral hazard in equity contracts. Managers (agents) act in their own interests rather than the interests of the stockholders (principals). The following are tools that help solve the principal-agent problem.

- *Production of information: monitoring.* Stockholders can engage in (14)_____ _____ _____ , which is the monitoring of the firm through auditing and observing management. It is expensive and suffers from the free-rider problem.

- *Government regulation to increase information.* Governments impose standard accounting principles and punish fraud.

- *Financial intermediation.* (15)_____ _____ firms pool resources of their partners and help entrepreneurs start new businesses. In exchange they receive equity and membership on the board of directors, which provides lower-cost verification activities.

- *Debt contracts.* Since a lender receives a fixed amount of interest as opposed to a portion of the profits, the principal-agent problem is much smaller with debt finance when compared to equity finance. This explains why debt contracts are more prevalent than equity contracts.

    Although debt contracts suffer from moral hazard less than equity contracts, there is still an incentive for the borrower to behave in a more risky fashion than the lender wants. The following tools help solve the moral hazard problem in debt contracts by making the contracts (16) _____ _____.

- *Net worth and collateral.* When borrowers have more to lose, moral hazard is reduced.

- *Monitoring and enforcement of restrictive covenants.* Covenants can discourage undesirable behaviour (avoid risky behaviour), encourage desirable behaviour (require life insurance for the borrower), keep collateral valuable, and provide information (periodic accounting reports).

- *Financial intermediation.* Monitoring and restrictive covenants still suffer from the free-rider problem. Financial intermediaries make private loans that don't have this problem, which explains why financial intermediaries are predominate.

Financial institutions achieve (17) _____ _____ _____ by offering many services that utilize the same information resource. (18) _____ _____ _____ occur, however, when financial service providers serve multiple interests and misuse or conceal information needed for funds to be channelled to those with productive investment opportunities. Three major types of financial services suffer from conflicts of interest, causing firms to distort information and reduce efficiency.

- *Underwriting and research in investment banking:* An investment bank serves the firm for whom it is issuing the securities and the investors to whom it sells the securities. Issuers benefit from optimistic research while investors want unbiased research. If revenue from underwriting exceeds brokerage commissions, the information about the firm may be overly favourable. (19) _____ occurs when investment banks allocate profitable *initial public offerings* to executives of other companies to gain their investment banking business.
- *Auditing and consulting in accounting firms:* Accounting firms offer auditing services and *management advisory services*—advice on taxes, accounting or management information systems, and business strategies. Auditors feel pressure to make favourable reports to avoid losing management advisory services business, to avoid criticizing the management advice given to the client from the nonauditing portion of the accounting firm, and to retain the client's auditing business.
- *Credit assessment and consulting in credit-rating agencies:* Since firms pay to have their debt rated, credit-rating agencies have an incentive to provide a favourable rating while investors and regulators want an impartial rating. Also, there is pressure for credit-rating agencies to provide favourable ratings because they wish to secure consulting contracts to advise firms on the structure of debt issues.

Two major policy measures have been implemented to reduce conflicts of interest: the Sarbanes-Oxley Act of 2002 and the Global Legal Settlement of 2002 against the ten largest investment banks.

HELPFUL HINTS

1. Transaction costs and information costs explain the proportion of external finance done through stocks, bonds, and intermediation. High transaction costs suggest that only large borrowers and lenders use the direct financial markets, so most people and firms use intermediaries. Information costs due to adverse selection and moral hazard further explain why most external finance is through intermediaries. Information costs also explain why most of the remaining direct finance is done with debt rather than equity.
2. Markets are efficient when all mutually beneficial transactions take place. Therefore, markets become inefficient when there are impediments to trade that reduce the number of participants in the market. In the case of the financial markets, transaction costs and information costs reduce the amount of participants in the direct finance markets, reducing the efficiency of the direct finance markets and providing an opportunity for financial intermediaries to improve efficiency.

EXERCISES

Practice Problems
1. The following questions refer to the adverse selection problem generated by asymmetric information known as the "lemons problem."
a. In general, what is the "lemons problem?"

_____

_____

b. What tools have been developed to reduce the lemons problem in direct financial markets?

_____

_____

c. Have these tools completely solved the problem? Explain.

_____

_____

2. The following questions are based on the principal-agent problem.
a. What is the principal-agent problem?

_____

b. What tools have been developed to reduce the principal-agent problem in direct financial markets?

_____
_____

c. Have these tools completely solved the problem? Explain.

_____
_____

3. Which of the following, transaction costs, adverse selection, or moral hazard, help explain the eight facts about financial structure below? Explain.
a. Stocks are not the most important source of finance for businesses.

_____

b. Issuing marketable securities is not the primary way businesses finance their operations.

_____

c. Indirect finance is many times more important than direct finance.

_____

d. Financial intermediaries, particularly banks, are the most important source of external funds to business.

_____

e. The financial system is heavily regulated.

_____

f. Only large, well-established corporations have access to securities markets to finance their activities.

_____

g. Collateral is a prevalent feature of debt contracts.

_____

h. Debt contracts are complicated documents often placing restrictions on the behaviour of borrowers.

_____

4.
a. List the four factors in the economic environment that can lead to a substantial deterioration of firms' balance sheets that can worsen adverse selection and moral hazard problems in financial markets, eventually leading to a financial crisis.

1. _____

2. _____

3. _____

4. _____

b. Most financial crises in Canada have begun with the following four factors:

1. _____

2. _____

3. _____

4. _____

5. The performer David Bowie raised over $55 million by issuing personal bonds, which he agreed to pay off when they mature in ten years. As collateral, Bowie offered royalty sales from his past albums. Which asymmetric information problem would exist if Bowie offered royalty sales from future albums as collateral?

_____

_____

Short-Answer Questions

1. How are financial intermediaries able to lower transaction costs?

_____

2. How does the free-rider problem reduce efficiency in financial markets?

_____

3. Is adverse selection a problem before or after a loan transaction? Is moral hazard a problem before or after a loan transaction? Explain each.

_____

4. Which are more important sources of external funds to businesses, stocks and bonds or banks? Are banks becoming more or less important over time? Why?

_____

5. When lenders require a borrower to have a high net worth and collateral, are they trying to reduce adverse selection or moral hazard or both? Explain.

_____

_____

6. Why do debt contracts have fewer principal-agent problems than equity contracts?

_____

_____

Critical-Thinking Questions

Suppose that you have worked all summer and accumulated $5000. You would like to save it, but you might need it one year from this fall for tuition payments. Your friends all have ideas about where you should save it.

1. One friend says, "Lend it to my brother. He's starting a new restaurant that is sure to make big profits." Is this a good choice? Explain.

_____

2. Another friend says, "You should buy stocks and bonds. The market has been doing very well lately. Use my broker. Here's his card." Is this a good choice? Explain.

_____

3. Yet another friend says, "Given your small amount of funds and your need to be liquid, you should buy either a money market mutual fund or simply deposit it in a bank." Is this a good choice? Explain.

_____

_____

SELF-TEST

True-False Questions

Circle whether the following statements are true (T) or false (F).

T F 1. Stocks are the most important source of external funds for businesses.

T F 2. Bonds are a more important source of external funds than stocks.

T F 3. Although banks are the most important source of external funds to businesses worldwide, their role is shrinking slightly over time.

T F 4. Over 90% of households own securities.

T F 5. Financial intermediaries, such as mutual funds, take advantage of economies of scale to reduce transaction costs by combining many small savers funds and buying a diversified portfolio.

T F 6. Banks reduce the free-rider problem in information production because they make private nontraded loans rather than purchasing securities that are traded in financial markets.

T F 7. Adverse selection occurs when borrowers use borrowed funds in a manner that lenders find objectionable.

T F 8. Bonds create a greater moral hazard problem than stocks.

T F 9. The adverse selection problem in financial markets is eliminated by the private production and sale of information about borrowers by companies such as Standard and Poor's, Moody's, and Value Line.

T F 10. When lenders cannot sort good borrowers from bad ones, they lend less and the financial markets become inefficient.

T F 11. The principal-agent problem occurs when managers act in their own interests rather than the interests of stockholders.

T F 12. Firms with relatively low net worth and little collateral are more likely to default on their loans.

T F 13. To make a debt contract more incentive compatible, lenders may include restrictive covenants requiring the borrower to keep the collateral valuable.

T F 14. The Sarbanes-Oxley Act of 2002 reduced conflicts of interest in investment banking by fining the ten largest investment banks $1.4 billion for past exploitation of their conflicts of interest.

T F 15. When financial institutions attempt to achieve economies of scope, their operations tend to become subject to conflicts of interest.

Multiple-Choice Questions

Circle the appropriate answer.

1. The recovery process from an economic downturn can be short-circuited by a substantial decline in the price level that reduces firms' net worth, a process called

    a. adverse selection.

    b. moral hazard.

    c. debt deflation.

    d. insolvency.

2. Which of the following statements concerning external sources of financing for nonfinancial businesses in Canada are true?

    a. Issuing marketable securities is not the primary way businesses finance their operations.

    b. Direct finance is many times more important than indirect finance as a source of external funds.

    c. Banks are not the most important source of external funds used to finance businesses.

    d. All of the above.

3. Poor people have difficulty getting loans because
   a. they typically have little collateral.
   b. they are less likely to benefit from access to financial markets.
   c. of both (a) and (b) of the above.
   d. of neither (a) nor (b) of the above.

4. Financial intermediaries provide their customers with
   a. reduced transaction costs.
   b. increased diversification.
   c. reduced risk.
   d. all of the above.
   e. only (b) and (c) of the above.

5. Because of the adverse selection problem,
   a. lenders are reluctant to make loans that are not secured by collateral.
   b. lenders may choose to lend only to those who "do not need the money."
   c. lenders may refuse loans to individuals with high net worth.
   d. only (a) and (b) of the above.

6. That most used cars are sold by intermediaries (i.e., used car dealers) provides evidence that these intermediaries
   a. help solve the adverse selection problem in this market.
   b. profit by becoming experts in determining whether an automobile is of good quality or a lemon.
   c. are unable to prevent purchasers from free-riding off the information they provide.
   d. do only (a) and (b) of the above.

7. Mishkin's analysis of adverse selection indicates that financial intermediaries in general, and banks in particular, because they hold a large fraction of non-traded loans _____.
   a. play a greater role in moving funds to corporations than do securities markets as a result of their ability to overcome the free-rider problem.
   b. provide better-known and larger corporations a higher percentage of their external funds than they do to newer and smaller corporations, which tend to rely on the new issues market for funds.
   c. both (a) and (b) of the above.
   d. neither (a) nor (b) of the above.

8. The principal-agent problem arises because
   a. principals find it difficult and costly to monitor agents' activities.
   b. agents' incentives are not always compatible with those of the principals.
   c. principals have incentives to free-ride off the monitoring expenditures of other principals.
   d. of all of the above.

9. Equity contracts
   a. are agreements by the borrowers to pay the lenders fixed dollar amounts at periodic intervals.
   b. have the advantage over debt contracts of a lower-cost state verification.
   c. are used much more frequently to raise capital than are debt contracts.
   d. are none of the above.

10. Factors that lead to worsening conditions in financial markets include
    a. declining interest rates.
    b. declining stock prices.
    c. unanticipated increases in the price level.
    d. only (a) and (c) of the above.
    e. only (b) and (c) of the above.

11. The "lemons problem" is a term used to describe the
    a. moral hazard problem.
    b. adverse selection problem.
    c. free-rider problem.
    d. principal-agent problem.

12. The _____ problem helps to explain why _____ cannot be eliminated solely by the private production and sale of information.
    a. free-rider; adverse selection
    b. free-rider; moral hazard
    c. principal-agent; adverse selection
    d. principal-agent; moral hazard

13. Equity contracts are subject to a particular example of _____ called the _____ problem.
    a. adverse selection; principal-agent
    b. moral hazard; principal-agent
    c. adverse selection; free-rider
    d. moral hazard; free-rider

14. Debt-deflation occurs when the price level _____, reducing the value of business firms' _____.
    a. rises; net worth
    b. rises; collateral
    c. falls; net worth
    d. falls; collateral

15. Important factors leading up to the financial crises in both Mexico and East Asia in the mid- to late 1990s include
    a. weak supervision of banks by regulators.
    b. lack of expertise in screening and monitoring borrowers at banking institutions.
    c. an increase in indebtedness due to depreciation of their currencies.
    d. all of the above.
    e. only (a) and (b) of the above.

16. The largest source of external funds for businesses is _____ while the smallest source is _____.
    a. stock; bonds
    b. bank loans; stock
    c. bonds; stock
    d. bank loans; nonbank loans
    e. bonds; bank loans

17. Small investors cannot easily purchase financial instruments because
    a. transaction costs are too small.
    b. the minimum purchase price is often too small.
    c. brokerage fees may be a small part of the purchase price.
    e. none of the above.

18. Compared to large companies, small companies are less likely to borrow funds through issuing
    a. debt.
    b. equity.
    c. collateral.
    d. only (a) and (b) of the above.

19. Adverse selection problems in financial markets can often be reduced by
    a. providing collateral.
    b. monitoring borrower behaviour.
    c. enforcement of restrictive covenants.
    d. all of the above.

20. Accurate accounting information
    a. reduces problems from adverse selection and moral hazard.
    b. is generally required of publicly traded firms by the Ontario Securities Commission.
    c. is subject to the free-rider problem.
    d. all of the above.

21. Government fiscal imbalances in emerging market countries may lead to a contraction in economic activity because
    a. the government may default on its debt, which lowers bank assets.
    b. the government is issuing too little debt.
    c. the value of the currency may rise.
    d. bank lending may rise.

22. The financial crisis in Argentina in 2001 was accompanied by
    a. large government surpluses.
    b. a banking panic.
    c. a rise in the value of Argentina's currency.
    d. only (a) and (b) of the above.
    e. only (b) and (c) of the above.

23. A venture capital firm avoids the free-rider problem in the face of moral hazard by
    a. acquiring equity in the start-up firm.
    b. placing its own people on the board of directors of the start-up firm.
    c. requiring collateral for loans.
    d. not allowing others to purchase start-up firm equity shares.

24. Types of restrictive covenants that reduce moral hazard in debt contracts include
    a. covenants to keep collateral valuable.
    b. covenants to discourage desirable behaviour.
    c. covenants to provide information.
    d. both (a) and (c) of the above.

25. The pecking order hypothesis
    a. claims that small firms can more easily issue securities.
    b. claims that lesser known firms can more easily issue securities.
    c. claims that information about the quality of a firm does not influence whether or not it can issue securities.
    d. none of the above.

26. High net worth solves the moral hazard problem because it
    a. makes the debt contract incentive compatible.
    b. collateralizes the debt contract.
    c. state verifies the debt contract.
    d. does none of the above.

27. Which of the following events would be least likely to cause a financial crisis?
    a. Increase in interest rates.
    b. Bank panic.
    c. Increase in uncertainty.
    d. Stock market decline.

28. _____ keeps security markets such as the stock markets and bond markets from being effective in channelling funds from savers to borrowers.
    a. Transaction cost
    b. Economies of scale
    c. Lemons problem
    d. Lack of expertise

29. Four categories of factors can trigger financial crises:
    a. decrease in interest rates, increase in uncertainty, adverse selection, conflict of interests.
    b. decrease in interest rates, increase in uncertainty, moral hazard, conflict of interests.
    c. decrease in interest rates, decrease in uncertainty, moral hazard, conflict of interests.
    d. increase in interest rates, increase in uncertainty, asset market effects on balance sheets, and problems in the banking sector.

30. A sharp _____ in the stock market is one factor that can cause a serious deterioration in a firm's balance sheet, which in turn _____ adverse selection and moral hazard problems and can provoke financial crises.
    a. decline; decreases
    b. decline; increases
    c. increase; decreases
    d. increase; increases

CHAPTER 9

Financial Crises and the Subprime Meltdown

CHAPTER SYNOPSIS/COMPLETIONS

Financial crises are major disruptions in financial markets characterized by a decline in asset prices and the failure of many firms. This chapter explains why the most recent financial crisis occurred, why these crises are so prevalent, and why these crises tend to be followed by severe economic contractions.

A financial crisis occurs when a disruption in the financial system causes an increase in asymmetric information, which increases adverse selection and moral hazard problems. As a result, financial markets fail to channel funds efficiently from savers to productive investment opportunities, causing a reduction in lending and a severe contraction in economic activity. Six categories of factors cause financial crises.

- Asset market effects on balance sheets: Events that reduce the net worth of borrowing firms effectively reduce borrowing firms' collateral, increasing moral hazard and adverse selection because borrowing firms have less to lose. Things that reduce the net worth of the borrowing firm include (1) a decline in the stock market that reduces the firm's value; (2) an unanticipated decline in the price level that raises the real burden of the firm's debt payments when debt payments are fixed in nominal terms; (3) an unanticipated decline in the value of the domestic currency that raises the real burden of the firm's debt payments when debt payments are denominated in a foreign currency; and (4) asset write-downs that reduce the value of assets on the borrowing firm's balance sheet.

- Deterioration in financial institutions' balance sheets: A deterioration of a financial institution's balance sheet reduces its capital and reduces its ability to lend.

- Banking crisis: A severe deterioration in a financial institution's balance sheet will cause it to fail. Due to asymmetric information problems, depositors may remove their deposits from both risky and sound banks, causing even some sound banks to fail. A (1) _____ _____ occurs when many banks fail simultaneously, which reduces lending and raises interest rates.

- Increases in uncertainty: An increase in uncertainty makes it more difficult for lenders to screen good credit risks from bad ones, which reduces lending.

- Increases in interest rates: At higher interest rates, good credit risks no longer wish to borrow, while bad credit risks are still willing to borrow, increasing the adverse selection problem and reducing lending. In addition, an increase in interest rates raises interest payments and reduces a firm's cash flow, causing it to use more borrowed funds rather than internal funds for expansion. But due to information asymmetry, lenders will not lend as much as the firm would have had internally at a lower interest rate.

- Government fiscal imbalances: If private investors fear that the government will default on its debt, private investors won't purchase government bonds and private banks may be forced to buy them. If the value of these bonds decreases, it will reduce bank capital, and bank lending will decrease. Fear of a government default may also cause a reduction in the domestic currency's value, leading to an increase in adverse selection and moral hazard problems described above.

Past financial crises in the United States have progressed in two or three stages.

Stage one: Initiation of financial crisis. A financial crisis can begin in several ways.

- A financial crisis often begins with (2) _____ _____, the elimination of restrictions on financial markets and institutions, or when there are financial innovations that avoid regulation. Often a (3) _____ _____ results and financial firms take on excessive risk. To avoid a bank panic, governments often provide a safety net for depositors. The safety net, unfortunately, increases moral hazard, causing banks to take on even more risk. Government regulators usually lack the resources and expertise to control the risk-taking. Loan losses reduce bank capital, causing a reduction in bank lending, known as (4) _____. Depositors withdraw their funds, further reducing bank lending, and economic activity contracts.

- An (5) _____ _____ _____ , caused by a credit boom, causes asset prices to rise above their fundamental values. When the bubble bursts, the net worth of borrowers is reduced, increasing asymmetric information and reducing lending. The deterioration of balance sheets of financial institutions also reduces lending. This happened in the 1990s and again with the recent housing price bubble.

- In the 19th century, spikes in interest rates caused an increase in adverse selection and moral hazard, reducing the number of creditworthy borrowers willing to borrow at the high rates.

- An increase in uncertainty, due to the failure of a major financial firm or a stock market crash, reduces lending because the reduction in information increases adverse selection and moral hazard.

Stage two: Banking crisis. Due to the uncertainty about their banks' health, depositors begin to withdraw funds from banks, causing a bank panic. This increases adverse selection and moral hazard, reducing bank lending. Bank panics are a feature of all U.S. financial crises in the last 200 years.

Stage three: Debt deflation. If the resulting economic downturn leads to a sharp reduction in prices, debt deflation can result. This occurs when a substantial unanticipated decline in the price level increases firms' burden of indebtedness. This can reduce economic activity for a long time. The most significant case of debt deflation in U.S. history was the Great Depression.

Mismanagement of financial innovation in the subprime residential mortgage market and a bursting of a housing price bubble initiated the financial crisis of 2007–2008.

- In recent times, borrowers with less-than-perfect credit have been able to get mortgages, called subprime mortgages. Other borrowers with higher-than-average default rates could get (6) _____ _____. Through the process of (7) _____, these mortgages were bundled into standardized securities, called (8) _____ _____ _____. Further (9) _____ _____ generated sophisticated financial products called (10) _____ _____ _____, which are instruments based on the cash flows of underlying assets such as mortgages. Most noteworthy is a (11) _____ _____ _____ (CDO), which paid out the cash flows from different risk subgroups within a subprime mortgage-backed security, with the highest-rated group paying first, etc.

- A housing price bubble developed, aided by foreign cash flows and the expansion of subprime mortgage-backed securities. The resulting higher housing prices increased mortgage lending even more because lenders felt secure that borrowers were unlikely to default when their homes had appreciated.

- Agency problems arose because the subprime mortgage market was based on the originate-to-distribute business model. The mortgage originator had little incentive to lend to good credit risks, and risky borrowers had incentives to buy houses in a rising market. Lax regulations didn't require lenders to disclose information about the borrower's ability to repay the loan. Rating agencies were subject to conflicts of interest because they were earning fees from the clients whose mortgage-backed securities they were rating.

- Information problems surfaced because financial engineering had created structured products that were so complicated that they were hard to value correctly.

- The housing price bubble burst. Since lending standards had been weak, and borrowers had made very small down payments and now owed more than the value of the houses, defaults rose sharply.

- Although the crisis originated in the United States, the crisis spread globally when European banks suffered losses on U.S. mortgage-backed securities, causing the interbank lending market to freeze up in Europe and the United States.

- Banks' balance sheets deteriorated because, as U.S. housing prices decreased, the value of mortgage-backed securities decreased. Banks had to deleverage (reduce lending). With no one else able to step in to collect information and make loans, the increase in adverse selection and moral hazard reduced loans and economic activity.
- High-profile financial firms failed, including Bear Stearns, Fannie Mae, Freddie Mac, and Lehman Brothers.
- A controversial bailout package for Wall Street was enacted, but the stock market crash accelerated, and unemployment continued to rise.

Emerging market economies are economies in an earlier stage of market development that have recently opened up their markets for goods, services, and capital to the rest of the world. Financial crises in these economies develop along two paths: Mismanagement of financial liberalization/globalization or severe fiscal imbalances.

- Mismanagement of financial liberalization/globalization: Due to weaker financial supervision in emerging market economies, financial liberalization creates an even bigger lending boom in emerging market economies. High risk loans fail, causing a lending crash. The deterioration in banks' balance sheets is even more harmful here because the securities markets are less developed.
- Governments in emerging market economies with a fiscal imbalance often force their banks to buy the government's debt. When the value of the debt decreases, it causes the deterioration of the banks' balance sheets. The instability of the government also adds to uncertainty.

In response to the deterioration in the banks' balance sheets, participants in the foreign exchange markets engage in a (12) _____ _____ on the currency, selling the currency and driving its value down. The speculative attack on the domestic currency could also come from a severe fiscal imbalance where investors fear that the government cannot repay its debts.

The decline in the value of the domestic currency causes a sharp rise in the debt burden of firms, which leads to a decline in firms' net worth, causing an increase in adverse selection and moral hazard. In addition, the depreciation of the currency leads to an increase in import prices and an increase in inflation and interest rates, reducing firm's net worth even more. The inability of firms to repay their debts to the banks and the increase in the value of the banks' foreign-currency denominated deposits causes a banking crisis, even greater adverse selection and moral hazard problems, a reduction in lending, and a severe contraction in economic activity.

The previous discussion helps explain the recent financial crises in Mexico, East Asia, and Argentina.

HELPFUL HINTS

1. Financial crises are associated with financial liberalization or innovation, combined with a government safety net. The unregulated financial liberalization causes a lending boom, and the government safety net exaggerates the problem by making the loans appear to be less risky.

2. At some point in a financial crisis, the lending boom turns into a lending crash. Regardless of the source, in the end, an increase in adverse selection and moral hazard in the credit markets reduces lending to a point that it substantially reduces investment and economic activity and increases unemployment.

EXERCISES

Practice Problems

1. Explain how each of the following events affects the state of a borrowing firm's balance sheet, and thus how it affects the severity of asymmetric information problems in the financial system.
a. A decline in the stock market

_____

_____

b. An unanticipated decline in the price level

_____

_____

c.   An unanticipated decline in the value of the domestic currency

_____

_____

d.   A write-down in the value of assets

_____

_____

2.   The following questions address debt deflation.
a.   What is debt deflation?

_____

b.   How does debt deflation affect economic activity? Explain.

_____

c.   What event in U.S. history is the greatest example of debt deflation?

_____

d.   How much did prices fall during this period? What was the rate of unemployment during this period?

_____

3.   The following questions address the subprime mortgage crisis.
a.   What is a subprime mortgage?

_____

b.   What is a mortgage-backed security?

_____

c.   Explain the agency problem in the originate-to-distribute business model.

_____

_____

d.   How did the factors described in *a*, *b*, and *c* combine to create a housing price bubble?

_____

_____

e.   What happens when an asset bubble pops?

_____

_____

4.   Describe the two stages of a typical financial crisis.
a.   Stage One:

_____

b.   Stage Two:

_____

_____

c.   Describe the additional set of events that occur if the crisis develops into a debt deflation.

_____

_____

5.

a. List the factors that contributed to worsening conditions in the Canadian ABCP market in 2007.

_____

_____

b. How did regulators respond?

_____

_____

c. Explain the Montreal Accord.

_____

_____

Short-Answer Questions

1. Why does an increase in adverse selection and moral hazard reduce aggregate economic activity?

_____

2. Why do financial crises in emerging market economies tend to be more severe compared to those in developed economies?

_____

3. How can a government's fiscal imbalance cause a financial crisis?

_____

4. How can a spike in interest rates cause a financial crisis?

_____

5. What type of crisis is common to all financial crises? Why?

_____

6. Why does a financial crisis often begin with financial liberalization or innovation?

_____

7. Does a government safety net increase or decrease adverse selection and moral hazard? Explain.

_____

8. What was the source of the recent subprime financial crisis?

_____

_____

Critical-Thinking Questions

You are watching a financial news show on CNN with your roommate. The commentator is discussing the recent subprime financial crisis. Your roommate says, "I don't know why we are having difficulty figuring out the causes and cures for our financial crisis. There was a financial crisis in Russia in 1998 and in Argentina 2001-2002. Why don't we just study their crises and copy their solutions. All of these financial crises are the same."

1.   What is an "emerging market economy?"

_____

_____

2.   What was the main source of the financial crises in Russia and Argentina in the late 1990s and early 2000s?

_____

_____

3.   What was the main source of the most recent subprime financial crisis in the United States?

_____

_____

4.   Are the sources of financial crises (and therefore the solutions to financial crises) the same in countries at different levels of development? Explain.

_____

_____

_____

_____

SELF-TEST

True-False Questions

Circle whether the following statements are true (T) or false (F).

T   F   1.   An increase in adverse selection and moral hazard in the credit markets tends to increase bank lending.
T   F   2.   An increase in interest rates tends to drive high-risk borrowers from the loan market, reducing adverse selection and moral hazard.
T   F   3.   Financial crises often begin with financial liberalization or innovation.
T   F   4.   An unanticipated decline in the price level raises the real burden of a firm's debt payments when these debt payments are fixed in nominal terms.
T   F   5.   An increase in adverse selection and moral hazard increases the lender's screening and monitoring costs, thereby reducing the amount of loans extended.
T   F   6.   A government safety net in the credit markets that guarantees a borrower's repayment causes banks to be more conservative in their lending practices, and thus reduces their risk exposure.
T   F   7.   Sooner or later, an asset-price bubble must burst because the price of an asset cannot stay above its fundamental value forever.
T   F   8.   The originate-to-distribute business model reduces agency problems in the mortgage market.
T   F   9.   The securitization of mortgages reduces the risk that the securitized mortgages will default.
T   F   10. A subprime loan is a loan for which the interest rate is below the prime rate.
T   F   11. Financial crises in emerging market economies are often more severe than those in more developed economies.
T   F   12. In an emerging market economy, the concurrent crises of a financial crisis and a currency crisis are often referred to as the "twin crises."
T   F   13. Events that reduce the net worth of a borrowing firm reduce the firm's capital, effectively reducing the borrowing firm's collateral and increasing adverse selection and moral hazard.
T   F   14. A reduction in the value of a country's currency improves the condition of domestic firms' balance sheets and reduces the risk of default on loans.
T   F   15. Bank panics are a feature of all financial crises in emerging market economies, but bank panics have never been associated with a financial crisis in the United States.

Multiple-Choice Questions

Circle the appropriate answer.

1. Borrowers with risky investment projects have the greatest desire to borrow, creating a problem known as
    a. uncertainty.
    b. interest rate risk.
    c. adverse selection.
    d. moral hazard.

2. After a borrower receives a loan, the borrower has an incentive to use the loan in a riskier fashion than specified in the loan contract, creating a problem known as
    a. financial engineering.
    b. deleveraging.
    c. adverse selection.
    d. moral hazard.

3. Which of the following does not cause a reduction in the net worth of the borrowing firm in a loan market?
    a. A decline in the stock market that reduces the value of the firm.
    b. An unanticipated increase in the price level that reduces the value of the firm's liabilities.
    c. An unanticipated decline in the value of the domestic currency when the firm's debt is denominated in terms of a foreign currency.
    d. Asset write-downs on the firm's balance sheet.

4. Financial crises
    a. are prevalent in all industrial economies.
    b. only occur in emerging market economies.
    c. rarely have an impact on aggregate economic output.
    d. tend to be more severe in financially advanced countries.

5. Which of the following is an example of debt deflation?
    a. A credit boom deflates into a credit crunch.
    b. An unanticipated decrease in the price level increases the burden of indebtedness.
    c. There is a write-down in the value of assets.
    d. An asset-price bubble bursts and deflates.

6. A subprime mortgage is
    a. a loan with a lower-than-prime interest rate.
    b. a securitized loan.
    c. denominated in a foreign currency.
    d. a loan to someone with less-than-excellent credit.

7. The recent subprime financial crisis began with
    a. mismanagement of financial innovations in the subprime residential mortgage market.
    b. a spike in interest rates for subprime borrowers.
    c. an excessive government fiscal imbalance where the government forced banks to buy its subprime bonds.
    d. the bailout of subprime Wall Street firms.

8. Financial crises in emerging market economies tend to be more severe than in financially advanced economies because
    a. there is weaker financial supervision in emerging market economies.
    b. bankers in emerging market economies are less experienced with screening and monitoring for adverse selection and moral hazard.
    c. bank panics are more crippling to an emerging market economy because the financial markets are less developed.
    d. all of the above.

9. Securitization is a process by which
    a. deposits are insured by the CDIC against default.
    b. loans are insured against default.
    c. loans are bundled into standardized securities.
    d. securities are rated as investment grade or less-than-investment grade.

10. The main problem with the originate-to-distribute business model for mortgage lending is that
    a. the interest rate is driven so high that borrowers default.
    b. it reduces funds flowing into the mortgage market.
    c. it is subject to a significant principle-agent problem.
    d. it only works efficiently when packaging subprime mortgages.

11. What economic process is believed to have caused the Great Depression to last so long?
    a. Debt deflation.
    b. Securitization.
    c. The stock market crash.
    d. The bursting of the asset-price bubble.

12. Regardless of the original source of the financial crisis, all credit booms end in a credit crash because of
    a. corruption in the mortgage industry.
    b. an increase in adverse selection and moral hazard in the loan market.
    c. massive government deficits.
    d. collateralized debt obligations.

13. Why does a financial crisis ultimately cause a substantial reduction in economic activity?
    a. The government responds to the crisis with excessive regulation.
    b. Only corrupt bankers survive the crisis.
    c. The financial crisis causes a fiscal deficit.
    d. The resulting credit crash severely reduces investment for productive activities.

14. Which of the following is unlikely to cause a reduction in lending?
    a. A decline in the stock market.
    b. A bank panic.
    c. A decrease in interest rates.
    d. An unanticipated decline in the price level.

15. In an emerging market economy, what two types of financial crises are often referred to as the "twin crises?"
    a. A banking crisis and a currency crisis.
    b. A fiscal crisis and a monetary crisis.
    c. An asset crisis and a liability crisis.
    d. A lending crisis and a borrowing crisis.

16. Which of the following is one of the main sources of a financial crisis in an emerging market economy?
    a. Excessive government regulation.
    b. A restriction on the extension of credit.
    c. Severe government fiscal imbalances.
    d. All of the above.

17. Which of the following has not been a source of past financial crises in the United States?
    a. Severe government fiscal imbalances.
    b. Mismanagement of financial liberalization or innovation.
    c. A spike in interest rates.
    d. The bursting of an asset-price bubble.

18. Deleveraging occurs when banks
    a. increase their lending.
    b. contract their lending.
    c. increase their capital.
    d. reduce the interest rates they charge on loans.

19. Which of the following statements is true when there is an increase in adverse selection and moral hazard in the loan market?
    a. Banks tend to lend more, which generates an asset-price bubble.
    b. Banks tend to reduce interest rates.
    c. Banks tend to reduce lending because fewer firms want to borrow.
    d. Banks tend to reduce lending because they cannot separate good credit risks from bad ones as efficiently.

20. Severe government fiscal imbalances may cause a financial crisis because the fiscal imbalance may cause the government to
    a. increase taxes.
    b. decrease spending.
    c. sell high-risk government securities to domestic banks.
    d. restrict financial innovations.

21. Banking crises in emerging-market economies indicate that
    a. government fiscal imbalances are also to blame.
    b. a government safety net for depositors increases moral hazard.
    c. expertise in screening borrowers cannot prevent loan losses.
    d. deregulation combined with poor regulatory supervision raises moral hazard incentives.

22. Banking crises in emerging-market economies started with
    a. corrupt bankers.
    b. financial liberalization or innovation.
    c. excessive regulation.
    d. a crisis in the United States.

23. In response to the subprime meltdown, the Canadian government
    a. increased deposit insurance.
    b. decreased deposit insurance.
    c. banned subprime mortgages.
    d. allowed subprime mortgages.

24. With regard to the subprime financial crisis, countries around the world are now considering
    a. expanding their subprime mortgage markets.
    b. lower capital requirements for their financial institutions.
    c. establishing government-sponsored enterprises like Fannie Mae and Freddie Mac.
    d. implementing Canadian-style reforms of their financial markets.

25. Capital requirements of Canadian banks
    a. are illegal.
    b. are higher than global peers.
    c. increase the bank's risk.
    d. are unregulated.

26. Which of the following statements regarding banking crises in emerging market economies is true?
    a. The causes of banking crises are unique to each country.
    b. Emerging-market economies have strong supervision by bank regulators.
    c. These countries are experts in the screening and monitoring of borrowers.
    d. The dynamics are similar to those found in Canada and the United States.

27. High bank capital helps to prevent bank failures because it
    a. provides a cushion against potential losses.
    b. means that the bank has a higher income.
    c. allows loans to be more easily sold.
    d. makes it easier to call in loans.

28. During the recent Canadian banking crisis
    a. shares of Canadian banks fell by about 50%.
    b. the Canadian government had to bail out many banks.
    c. Canadian banks fared worse than many U.S. banks.
    d. all of the above.

29. Important factors leading up to emerging-market financial crises in include
    a. worsening of adverse selection and moral hazard problems.
    b. the development of a foreign exchange crisis.
    c. the decline of economic activity.
    d. all of the above.

30. Which of the following events would be least likely to cause a financial crisis?
    a. Increase in interest rates.
    b. Bank panic.
    c. Increase in uncertainty.
    d. Stock market decline.

CHAPTER 10

Economic Analysis of Financial Regulation

CHAPTER SYNOPSIS/COMPLETIONS

In this chapter, we use economic analysis to show why financial institutions and banks are so heavily regulated. Financial regulation, however, is not always successful. Banking and financial crises cause regulators to reform existing regulations.

Much of banking regulation is based on the presence of asymmetric information, which causes adverse selection and moral hazard problems in banking. Banking regulations can be grouped into the following categories:

- *The government safety net.* Depositors lack information about the quality of a bank's private loans. Thus, before deposit insurance, depositors were reluctant to put funds in a bank, and even small negative shocks to the banking system could cause bank panics and the contagion effect. In response, the CDIC was established in 1967. Bank failures are handled through either the (1) _____ method or the (2) _____ _____method, which guarantees all deposits.

  In addition to deposit insurance, central banks can act as the "lender of last resort" to troubled institutions. A government safety net fixes one set of problems but causes a moral hazard problem (financial institutions take on excessive risk), and an adverse selection problem (risk-loving entrepreneurs may choose to enter the financial industry). Since the failure of a very big financial institution may cause a financial disruption, some institutions have been considered "too big to fail" so their insolvencies were handled by the purchase and assumption method, which further increases the moral hazard problem. The consolidation of the financial industry causes more financial institutions to be "too big to fail," and conglomerate financial firms may receive a safety net for nonbanking activities.

- *Restrictions on asset holdings.* Because depositors and creditors of financial institutions cannot easily monitor the institution's assets, regulations restrict banks from holding risky assets such as common stock and regulations require banks to diversify.

- *Capital requirements.* Banks have capital requirements that establish a minimum (3) _____ _____ (capital asset ratio) of 5%. The (4) _____ _____ increases the capital-asset ratio for risky banks by establishing risk-based capital requirements for banks in over 100 countries.

- (5) _____ _____: *chartering and examination.* Chartering financial institutions limits adverse selection by preventing undesirable people from controlling them. On-site examinations and the application of the CAMELS rating to a bank's activities reduce moral hazard. Banks also file quarterly call reports.

- *Assessment of risk management.* Since banks can take on more risk than is apparent from their balance sheets, regulators are interested in a bank's management processes for controlling risk of fraud, risky trading activities, and interest rate risk.
- *Disclosure requirements.* Due to the free-rider problem, depositors and creditors don't create enough information about the bank's condition. Regulators respond by requiring financial institutions to adhere to standard accounting principles and to disclose substantial information. Financial firms are required to employ mark-to-market accounting ((6) _____ _____ _____) where assets are valued at what they would sell for. During a financial crisis, however, prices of financial instruments may fall below their true value, reducing a lender's capital, and causing lenders to reduce their lending, making the crisis worse.
- *Consumer protection.* As a result of asymmetric information, "truth in lending" laws require lenders to be clear about financing charges. Other legislation also requires creditors, especially credit card issuers, to provide information on the method of assessing finance charges and requires that billing complaints be handled quickly.
- *Restrictions on competition.* Competition may increase moral hazard by causing financial institutions to assume greater risk to maintain profits. Governments in many countries have instituted regulations to protect financial institutions from competition.

It is difficult to successfully regulate financial institutions because financial institutions have incentives to avoid the regulations, the regulations may have unintended consequences, and regulators are subject to political pressure to regulate more easily.

Because the same types of asymmetric information problems exist in banking everywhere, financial regulation in foreign countries is similar to that in Canada—financial institutions are chartered, supervised, regulated, and insured. International financial institutions are particularly difficult to regulate because they can shift their business from one country to another.

Few banks failed from 1923 to 1985. In the mid-1980s, however, the situation in Canada changed with the failure of two chartered banks and the financial difficulties of a large number of other financial institutions. This happened for the following reasons. Financial innovation decreased the profitability of banks by increasing competition for both their source of funds and their use of funds, causing banks to make riskier loans to maintain profits. Deposit insurance increased moral hazard. In addition, the sharp rise in interest rates produced rising costs of funds for the banks that were not matched by higher earnings on bank assets like long-term residential mortgages. Regulators responded by adopting a stance of (7) _____ _____: they refrained from exercising their regulatory right to put the insolvent banks out of business. The loss of public confidence in the Canadian banking system led to the financial reforms of 1987–1992 and the consolidating of financial institution supervision under the Office of the Superintendent of Financial Institutions.

Extensive parallels exist between the banking crises in Canada and those in other countries, indicating that similar forces are at work. All banking crises start with financial liberalization or innovation combined with a weak bank regulatory system and a government safety net. The cost associated with the banking crisis of the 1980s varies when taken as a percent of GDP – only 3% for the United States but over 50% for Argentina and Indonesia.

The recent subprime financial crises will likely lead to additional financial regulations. Future regulations to reduce the agency problems associated with the originate-to-distribute model of credit may include:

- Increased regulation of mortgage brokers to prevent them from encouraging borrowers to take on more debt than they can afford.
- Fewer subprime mortgage products will be available because these products may be too complicated for unsophisticated borrowers.
- Regulation of compensation for those involved in the distribution of mortgage-related securities.
- Higher capital requirements for financial firms to compensate for their increased risk.
- Additional regulation of privately owned, government-sponsored enterprises (such as Fannie Mae) to reduce their risk exposure.
- Heightened regulation to limit financial institutions' risk taking.
- Increased regulation of credit-rating agencies to increase the accuracy of the information provided to investors.
- Additional regulation of derivatives, particularly credit-default swaps.

There is a danger that overregulation will stifle future financial innovation.

HELPFUL HINTS

1. Depositors face the same problems of adverse selection and moral hazard when depositing money in banks as banks face when lending depositors money. To avoid these asymmetric information problems in private financial markets, banks screen borrowers, employ restrictive covenants preventing borrowers from investing in risky activities, employ restrictive covenants requiring that their borrowers maintain a minimum net worth, and monitor borrowers. Similarly, on behalf of depositors, regulators require banks to have a charter, restrict risky asset holdings of banks, impose capital requirements on banks, and examine banks.

2. The moral hazard problem in banking increases when a bank nears insolvency. When a bank is technically insolvent, the bank is lending the depositors' money with no contribution from the owners because the bank no longer has a positive net worth. That is, the owners have nothing to lose. Thus, the incentive is for the bank to seek out the highest risk loans possible. If the loans fail to perform, the depositors or CDIC may lose, but the owners lose nothing. If the loans perform, the owners gain. It is as if the bank is allowed to gamble with someone else's money. If the gamble loses, the bank doesn't care because it's someone else's money. But if the gamble pays off, the bank gets to keep the winnings.

EXERCISES

Practice Problems

1. Depositors and regulators face an adverse selection and moral hazard problem that is similar to what banks and private lenders face in their loan markets. (See Helpful Hint 1.)
a. What are the main four ways that financial regulators reduce the adverse selection and moral hazard problems in banking? What problem does each regulation reduce—adverse selection or moral hazard?

_____

b. Match the answers you provided in *a* above to the solutions banks and private lenders have used to reduce the same problems in their loan markets.

_____

_____

2. Some banks have been considered by regulators to be "too big to fail."
a. What two ways can the CDIC handle an insolvent bank? If a regulator decides that a bank is "too big to fail," how does the regulator handle an insolvent bank, and what does it mean to the depositors and creditors of the bank?

_____

b. What is the purpose of a policy that designates some banks as "too big to fail?"

_____

c. What problem is exaggerated by this policy? Explain.

_____

d. How does financial consolidation affect the "too big to fail" policy? Explain.

_____

e. There are two methods the CDIC can use to handle an insolvent bank. Which method generates the least moral hazard? Why?

_____

_____

3. Ironically, the existence of deposit insurance increases the likelihood that depositors will require deposit protection, because the threat of withdrawals no longer constrains the managers of banks from taking on too much risk. List some of the problems that deposit insurance creates or makes worse.

a. _____

b. _____

c. _____

4. John Smith has the following deposits with XYZ Bank, a CDIC member bank (all funds CAD except where noted):

Chequing Account:	$5 000
Savings Account:	$25 000
USD Term Deposit:	$15 000
3-Year GIC:	$50 000
7-Year GIC:	$20 000

a. In the event of a bank failure, how much of John Smith's deposits is insured by the CDIC?

_____

_____

b. If the CDIC decides XYZ Bank is too big to fail, what will happen? What method will they use to handle the bank?

_____

_____

c. Why might the CDIC declare XYZ Bank too big to fail?

_____

_____

Short-Answer Questions

1. What two problems are solved by deposit insurance? Explain.

_____

_____

2. What two problems are created by deposit insurance? Explain.

_____

_____

3. Why do regulators require that banks maintain a minimum capital-to-asset ratio?

_____

_____

4. What does a CAMELS rating measure?

_____

_____

5. What problem is caused by too much competition in banking? What problems did these regulations to restrict competition cause?

_____

_____

Critical-Thinking Questions

Suppose you are watching television. An advertisement for Risky Bank suggests that it is a bank that seeks risky speculative loans and junk bonds, and it is willing to pay 10% on its certificates of deposit. Immediately following that advertisement is a commercial for Safe Bank. Safe Bank screens and monitors its borrowers so that the loans are sure to be repaid. However, it only pays 5% on its certificates of deposit.

1. If the CDIC insures all deposits, where would you choose to place your deposit? Why?

_____

_____

2. If there were no deposit insurance, where would you likely choose to place your deposit? Why?

_____

_____

3. Explain how this example shows why countries charter and supervise their banks. What problems are reduced by requiring bank charters and by supervising banks?

_____

_____

SELF-TEST

True-False Questions

Circle whether the following statements are true (T) or false (F).

T F 1. The presence of deposit insurance from the CDIC reduces moral hazard and adverse selection problems in the banking industry.

T F 2. It is usually cheaper for the taxpayer if the CDIC resolves an insolvent institution by the "purchase and assumption method."

T F 3. A policy of "too big to fail" provides a competitive advantage to very large banks because the policy effectively guarantees repayment to all depositors and creditors of a large bank in the event of a bank failure rather than just the insured depositors and creditors.

T F 4. Requiring banks to be chartered reduces adverse selection in banking because it reduces the chances that undesirable or risk-loving people can gain control of a bank.

T F 5. The Basel Accord requires all signing countries to provide deposit insurance to their depository institutions.

T F 6. A bank's balance sheet alone provides an accurate picture of the degree of risk to which the bank is exposed.

T F 7. The requirement that banks employ mark-to-market accounting may cause lenders to contract lending during a financial crisis.

T F 8. Capital requirements are intended to reduce moral hazard in banking by making a bank failure more costly to the owners of the bank.

T   F   9.   The leverage ratio is defined as the amount of equity capital divided by the bank's liabilities.

T   F   10.   A sharp decrease in interest rates at the beginning of the 1980s caused losses for banks and a few failures.

T   F   11.   Banking crises in different countries almost always begin with embezzlement by corrupt bankers.

T   F   12.   Future financial regulations will likely allow for the expansion of subprime mortgage lending.

T   F   13.   One problem with the too-big-to-fail policy is that it increases the moral hazard incentive for large banks.

T   F   14.   The Schedule II and Schedule III banks are permitted to opt out of CDIC membership.

T   F   15.   The cost of the banking crisis in the United States measured as a percent of GDP far exceeds comparable crises in other countries around the world.

Multiple-Choice Questions

Circle the appropriate answer.

1.   Which of the following is <u>not</u> true of a banking system with deposit insurance?
    a.   Depositors are more likely to deposit their money in a bank.
    b.   Depositors are less likely to withdraw their money in the event of a crisis.
    c.   Depositors are less likely to collect information about the quality of the bank's loans.
    d.   The moral hazard problem in banking is reduced.

2.   If a bank becomes insolvent and the CDIC reorganizes the bank by finding a willing merger partner, the CDIC resolved this insolvency problem through the
    a.   payoff method.
    b.   safety net method.
    c.   purchase and assumption method.
    d.   CAMELS method.

3.   The presence of deposit insurance increases the *adverse selection* problem in banking by
    a.   attracting risk-loving people into bank ownership.
    b.   increasing risky loans in banking.
    c.   reducing bank capital.
    d.   reducing the amount of deposits in the bank.

4.   If the CDIC considers an insolvent bank to be "too big to fail," it will resolve the insolvency through the
    a.   payoff method, which guarantees all deposits.
    b.   payoff method, which guarantees only deposits that do not exceed $100 000.
    c.   purchase and assumption method, which guarantees all deposits.
    d.   purchase and assumption method, which guarantees only deposits that do not exceed $100 000.

5.   The "too big to fail" policy of the CDIC
    a.   decreases the moral hazard incentives for large banks.
    b.   increases the moral hazard incentives for large banks.
    c.   decreases the moral hazard incentives for small banks.
    d.   increases the moral hazard incentives for small banks.

6.   Which of the following banking regulations is most focused on reducing adverse selection in banking?
    a.   Consumer protection laws.
    b.   Disclosure requirements requiring banks to use standard accounting principles.
    c.   Periodic on-site examinations.
    d.   Bank charter requirements.

7. A bank's capital-to-asset ratio is also known as its
    a. leverage ratio.
    b. profit ratio.
    c. equity ratio.
    d. liability ratio.

8. Regulators impose capital requirements on banks because a low capital-to-asset ratio dramatically
    a. increases a bank's adverse selection.
    b. increases a bank's moral hazard.
    c. increases a bank's CAMELS rating.
    d. decreases a bank's rate of return on equity.
    e. All of the above are true.

9. When a bank is well-capitalized, the bank has _____ to lose if it fails and is thus _____ likely to pursue risky activities.
    a. more; more
    b. more; less
    c. less; more
    d. less; less

10. The primary objective of the Basel Accord was to standardize
    a. deposit insurance across international boundaries.
    b. bank examinations across international boundaries.
    c. bank capital requirements across international boundaries.
    d. branching restrictions across international boundaries.

11. One problem with the too-big-to-fail policy is that it _____ the incentives for _____ by big banks.
    a. increases; moral hazard
    b. decreases; moral hazard
    c. increases; adverse selection
    d. decreases; adverse selection

12. The premium rates for CDIC member institutions in Canada depend on which of the following criteria?
    a. Capital adequacy.
    b. Profitability.
    c. Asset concentration.
    d. All of the above.

13. Banking crises in other countries indicate that
    a. deposit insurance is to blame in each country.
    b. a government safety net for depositors need not increase moral hazard.
    c. expertise in screening borrowers cannot prevent loan losses.
    d. deregulation combined with poor regulatory supervision raises moral hazard incentives.

14. Most banking crises around the world started with
    a. corrupt bankers.
    b. financial liberalization or innovation.
    c. excessive regulation.
    d. a crisis in the United States.

15. Banking crises episodes differ in that
    a. deposit insurance is to blame in many of the countries.
    b. deposit insurance has played an important role in many of the countries.
    c. deposit insurance has not played an important role in many of the countries.
    d. deposit insurance is not to blame in many of the countries.

16. With regard to the subprime financial crisis, future financial regulations will likely
    a. expand the subprime mortgage market.
    b. lower capital requirements for financial institutions.
    c. increase the size and scope of government-sponsored enterprises such as Fannie Mae and Freddie Mac.
    d. provide greater incentives for credit-rating agencies to provide reliable ratings.

17. Eliminating deposit insurance has the disadvantage of
    a. reducing the stability of the banking system due to an increase in the likelihood of bank runs.
    b. not being a politically feasible strategy.
    c. encouraging banks to engage in excessive risk taking.
    d. all of the above.
    e. only (a) and (b) of the above.

18. Off-balance-sheet activities of a bank
    a. are illegal.
    b. reduce bank profits.
    c. increase the bank's risk.
    d. are unregulated.

19. Mark-to-market accounting
    a. helps banks lend more during a financial crisis.
    b. requires financial firms to value assets at what they would sell for.
    c. increases a bank's capital in a financial crisis.
    d. none of the above.

20. Which of the following statements regarding banking crises throughout the world is true?
    a. The causes of banking crises are so unique across countries that any solution must be tailored specifically to the needs of that country.
    b. The 1980s savings and loan and banking crisis in the United States was more costly as a percent of GDP than any modern banking crisis in the rest of the world.
    c. Japan is the only industrialized country to avoid banking crises altogether in the post-WWII period.
    d. None of the above is true.

21. The Differential Premiums By-law that came into effect on March 31, 1999,
    a. reduces the moral hazard incentives of banks to take on higher risk.
    b. encourages banks to hold more capital.
    c. increases the incentives of uninsured depositors to monitor the risk-taking activities of banks.
    d. only (a) and (b) of the above.

22. The Insurance Companies Act of 1992
    a. replaced the Canadian and British Insurance Companies Act and the Foreign Insurance Companies Act.
    b. set rules for life insurers and P&C insurers.
    c. allowed insurance companies to own Schedule II chartered banks.
    d. followed the same format as the Bank Act.
    e. all of the above.

23. The Trust and Loan Companies Act of 1992
    a. replaced the Trust Companies Act and the Loan Companies Act, both passed in 1914.
    b. set rules for TMLs reporting to the OSFI.
    c. required large, formerly closely held TMLs to become 35% widely held.
    d. all of the above.
24. The Argentine banking crisis of 2001
    a. included a banking panic in which customers rushed to withdraw their deposits.
    b. was fuelled by the rise in the value of the Argentine peso.
    c. will not cost much relative to GDP.
    d. began despite low levels of Argentine government debt.
25. A large amount of bank capital helps to prevent bank failures because it
    a. is useful in absorbing deposit outflow losses.
    b. means that the bank has a higher income.
    c. allows loans to be more easily sold.
    d. makes it easier to call in loans.
26. Financial consolidation poses two challenges to banking regulation. First, it increases the _____ problem and second, it _____.
    a. moral hazard, creates adverse selection
    b. too-big-to-fail, increases the government's safety net
    c. moral hazard, increases the possibility of bank panics
    d. adverse selection, increases the government's safety net
27. Which of the following can be used by regulators to make banks avoid too much risk?
    a. Restricting banks from holding common stocks.
    b. Promoting diversification in assets and loans.
    c. Forcing the banks to hold large amounts of equity capital.
    d. All of the above.
28. _____ and _____ of the banking system have triggered banking crises in most countries.
    a. Adverse selection, privatization
    b. Real estate booms, privatization
    c. Adverse selection, deregulation
    d. Collapse of real estate, deregulation
29. The 1980s' Canadian banking crisis was the result of
    a. the sharp increases in interest rates from 1979 to 1981.
    b. the severe recession in 1981–1982.
    c. the collapse in the price of energy and agriculture products.
    d. all of the above.
30. In Canada, a chartered bank obtains a charter through either an Act of Parliament or through
    a. an application to the Governor of the Bank of Canada.
    b. an application to the Minister of Finance.
    c. an application to the President of the Treasury Board.
    d. all of the above.

CHAPTER 11

Banking Industry: Structure and Competition

CHAPTER SYNOPSIS/COMPLETIONS

Banks are financial intermediaries in business to earn profits. Compared to the United States, Canada has six large commercial banks that typically dominate the industry. In this chapter we examine the structure of the Canadian banking industry, and we address the competitiveness, efficiency, and soundness of the banking system.

The history of banking in Canada has left us with a small number of banks chartered by the federal government. Multiple agencies regulate chartered banks: the Office of the Superintendent of Financial Institutions (OSFI), the Bank of Canada, and the Canada Deposit Insurance Corporation (CDIC). The Big Six (the Royal Bank of Canada, Canadian Imperial Bank of Commerce, Bank of Montreal, Scotiabank, TD Canada Trust, and the National Bank of Canada) together with the *Desjardins Institutions* dominate the deposit-taking industry in Canada.

In the United States there is a (1) _____ _____ system, with commercial banks chartered by the states and the federal government. Restrictive (2) _____ _____ regulations that prohibited branching across state lines led to a large number of small commercial banks in the United States. The large number of commercial banks in the United States reflects the past *lack* of competition, not the presence of vigorous competition.

A change in the financial environment will stimulate a search by financial institutions for innovations that are likely to be profitable. The research and development of new financial products and services is known as (3) _____ _____ Financial innovation has come from three basic sources that often interact with each other:

- *Responses to changes in demand conditions*. The increasing volatility of interest rates since the 1970s has increased interest-rate risk resulting in an increase in the demand for adjustable-rate mortgages and (4) _____ _____ such as *futures contracts* to *hedge* interest-rate risk.

- *Responses to changes in supply conditions*. Improvements in *information technology* have lowered the cost of processing financial transactions so financial institutions can supply new products and services, and improved information acquisition making it easier for firms to issue securities. As a result, there has been an increase in the use of bank credit and debit cards and electronic banking such as the (5) _____, ABM, and virtual bank. Lesser-known firms are now able to issue junk bonds and commercial paper. *Securitization* has allowed illiquid loans to be bundled into standardized amounts and sold to a third party. This innovation was at the center of the subprime mortgage crisis of the mid 2000s.

- *The desire to avoid costly regulations*. Two particularly burdensome regulations that have caused loophole mining and innovation are reserve requirements, which acted as a tax on deposits, and (6) _____ _____ _____ known as (7) _____

_____, which caused deposit withdrawal known as (8) _____. In response, we find growth in money market mutual funds and (9) _____ _____.

Financial innovation has reduced banks' cost advantages in acquiring funds and their income advantages on their assets. Banks' cost advantage in acquiring funds was reduced when competitive pressures caused the elimination of Regulation Q. Banks' income advantages on assets have been reduced due to competition from junk bonds, securitization, and commercial paper. As a result, banks' traditional lines of business (making loans funded by deposits) have become less profitable, leading to a decline in traditional banking and an expansion in the shadow banking system. Banks have responded by making riskier loans for real estate and for corporate takeovers and leveraged buyouts, and by pursuing off-balance-sheet activities.

In Canada, as of January 2009, there were 73 chartered banks with over 8000 (10) _____. Until 1981, foreign banks were not allowed to operate in Canada. Today, we have 49 foreign bank subsidiaries and branches, operating as (11) _____ _____ _____. They have the same powers as the domestic banks but differ in the ownership structure permitted. That is, all Schedule I banks must be widely held, whereas Schedule II and III banks can be closely held if small.

Another important feature of the structure of the banking industry in Canada until recently was the separation of the banking and other financial services industries—such as securities, insurance, and real estate. Regulations enforced the separation of institutions according to their core financial service, and only four distinct types of financial services were identified: banking, brokerage, trusts, and insurance. This approach to regulation by institution (versus regulation by function) has been known as the (12) _____ _____ _____. The separation of the four pillars prohibited chartered banks from engaging in insurance and real estate activities. In turn, it prevented investment banks and insurance companies from engaging in commercial banking activities and thus protected banks from competition.

The regulation and structure of the near banks (trust and mortgage loan companies, and credit unions and *caisses populaires*) parallel closely the regulation and structure of the chartered banks. Federally incorporated near banks are regulated and supervised by the OSFI. They must also register in all the provinces in which they do business and must conform to the regulations of those provinces.

With the rapid growth of world trade since 1960, international banking has grown dramatically. Canadian banks engage in international banking activities by opening branches abroad and owning controlling interests in foreign banks. Foreign banks operate in Canada by owning a subsidiary Canadian bank or by operating branches or agency offices in Canada. International banking has undergone rapid growth due to three factors. First, the rapid growth of international trade and multinational corporations has caused firms to need banking services in foreign countries. Second, Canadian banks have become involved in global investment banking. Third, Canadian banks have become involved in the Eurocurrencies market.

The 2001 (13) _____ _____ _____ introduced a bank holding company structure, new ownership rules, expanded access to the payments and clearance system, and new opportunities for strategic alliances and joint ventures. These changes are reshaping the financial services marketplace in Canada by making it easier to introduce new financial products and services and increasing the competitive environment in the industry.

HELPFUL HINTS

1. Under the new legislation of the Bank Act Reform, bank financial groups have the option of expanding via (14) _____ _____ _____ (BHCs). A holding company is a corporation that exists to hold stock in other companies. A BHC holds stock in banks and bank-related companies. A lead bank that wishes to expand but cannot open branch offices creates a holding company and sells its stock to the holding company. The original stockholders of the lead bank now own stock in the BHC rather than the bank itself. While the bank could not buy other banks, the BHC can purchase other banks. The banks that are owned by the holding company are considered "affiliates" of the BHC but not branches. That is, the affiliates are still technically separate corporations and the flow of funds between those affiliates is restricted. When banks are allowed to branch, funds can flow freely between branches because each branch is simply a separate office of the same bank, and deposits from one branch can be loaned out from another branch. BHCs are considered inefficient substitutes for branching, and given the option banks will expand through branching rather than through BHCs.

EXERCISES

Practice Problems

1. The following questions address financial innovation in banking.
a. List the three main sources for financial innovation and provide examples of the banking industry's responses to each.

_____

_____

_____

b. Assume there is no interest on bank reserves. For every $1000 in deposits, how much would banks lose in forgone interest (opportunity cost) because of reserve requirements if banks charged 8% on loans and the required reserve ratio was 10%?

_____

_____

c. For every $1000 in deposits, how much would banks lose in forgone interest (opportunity cost) because of reserve requirements if banks charged 12% on loans and the require reserve ratio was 20%?

_____

_____

d. Use your answers to *b* and *c* above to make a general statement regarding how interest rates and reserve requirements affect the cost to banks of holding required reserves.

_____

_____

2. The following questions address trends in banks traditional lines of business.
a. Has there been an increase or a decrease in banks' traditional lines of business of making loans funded by deposits? Why?

_____

_____

b. What factor reduced banks' cost advantage in acquiring funds? Explain.

_____

_____

c. What three factors reduced banks' income advantages on its assets?

_____

_____

_____

d. How have banks responded to these events?

_____

_____

3. Explain why the rise of the junk bond market reduced the demand for bank loans.

_____

_____

4. List the two financial innovations that U.S. banks have used to get around the restrictions to branch banking.

a. _____

b. _____

Short-Answer Questions

1. Has Canada always had a central bank? What is the name of the Canadian central bank?

    _____

    _____

2. What is a dual banking system? How did the United States arrive at such a system?

    _____

    _____

3. What did Regulation Q do? When it was repealed, what two effects did it have on the banking system?

    _____

    _____

4. Why has the growth in junk bonds and commercial paper market reduced the demand for bank loans?

    _____

    _____

5. What three factors have caused the rapid growth in international banking?

    _____

    _____

6. What are the three main ways Canadian banks engage in international banking?

    _____

    _____

Critical-Thinking Questions

Your roommate is reading an article in *The Globe and Mail* about trends in banking. It states that, due to mergers and acquisitions, the number of banks is expected to drop in the future. Your roommate says, "The drop in the number of banks is clearly reducing competition. Borrowers are sure to be forced to pay higher interest rates in the future. This drop in the number of banks has to be bad for consumers."

1. How many banks does Canada have compared to other countries? Why the great disparity?

    _____

    _____

2. Which banking system would be more competitive: A banking system where 1000 banks serve 1000 towns and each town is served by one bank, or a banking system where ten banks, each with 1000 offices, serve 1000 towns so each town has ten banks from which to choose? Why?

    _____

    _____

3. Which are generally more efficient and have lower risk, large banks or small banks? Why?

    _____

    _____

4. Is a reduction in the number of banks evidence of lack of competition? Explain.

    _____

    _____

5. Is your roommate's statement correct? That is, is it true that having fewer banks is likely to be bad for the consumer? Explain.

    _____

    _____

SELF-TEST

True-False Questions

Circle whether the following statements are true (T) or false (F).

T   F   1. Economic analysis suggests that banks will devise ways around regulations which restrict certain banking activities.

T   F   2. Noting the lack of strong regulation, many economists argue that bank failures in the first half of the nineteenth century resulted from fraudulent practices.

T   F   3. The Canada Deposit Insurance Corporation (CDIC) has been granted the sole responsibility for supervising bank holding companies in Canada.

T   F   4. Regulations that restrict competition in the banking industry are often justified by the desire to prevent bank failures.

T   F   5. Periodic examinations of banks help regulators identify problems at banks before they have a detrimental effect on the financial soundness of the economy.

T   F   6. It has been argued that the small number of commercial banks in Canada can be seen as an indication of the absence of competition rather than the presence of competition.

T   F   7. One impetus in the early 1980s leading to an increase in the number of foreign banks in Canada was the absence of competition in the Canadian financial services industry.

T   F   8. Information technology has lowered the costs of processing financial transactions.

T   F   9. The rise of the junk bond market has contributed to the decline in banking.

T   F   10. The same technological forces that have hurt the competitiveness of banks in Canada also seem to be at work abroad, helping to explain the decline of banking in other nations.

T   F   11. Two sets of regulations that restricted the ability of the U.S. banks to make profits are reserve requirements and restrictions on interest paid on deposits.

T   F   12. The simultaneous rise of cost and income advantages has resulted in reduced profitability of the traditional banking system.

T   F   13. A change in the financial environment will stimulate a search by financial institutions for innovations that are likely to be less profitable.

T   F   14. High volatility of interest rates leads to a higher level of interest-rate risk.

T   F   15. During the 1970s and early 1980s, a large proportion of the bank's foreign lending was in sovereign loans.

Multiple-Choice Questions

Circle the appropriate answer.

1. Which of the following is a bank regulatory agency?
   a. Office of the Superintendent of Financial Institutions Canada.
   b. Bank of Canada.
   c. Canada Deposit Insurance Corporation.
   d. All of the above.

2. The bundling of a portfolio of mortgage or auto loans into a marketable capital market instrument is known as
   a. "fastbacking."
   b. arbitrage.
   c. computerization.
   d. securitization.

3. Near banks (TMLs and CUCPs) are regulated by
   a. the Bank of Canada.
   b. the CDIC.
   c. the Office of the Superintendent of Financial Institutions Canada.
   d. all of the above.
   e. only (b) and (c) of the above.

4. Which of the following factors explain the rapid growth in international banking in the past 25 years?
   a. Rapid growth of world trade in this period.
   b. Decline in world trade since 1960.
   c. Creation of the League of Nations.
   d. None of the above.

5. When economists argue that banking regulations have been a mixed blessing, they are referring to the fact that
   a. bank regulations foster competition at the expense of banking system safety.
   b. bank regulations foster banking system safety at the expense of competition.
   c. branch banking, while desired by consumers, leads to less competition.
   d. bank regulations foster competition by limiting branching.

6. The U.S. banking system has been labelled a dual system because
   a. banks offer both chequing and savings accounts.
   b. it actually includes both banks and thrift institutions.
   c. it is regulated by both federal and state governments.
   d. it was established during the Civil War, thus making it necessary to create separate regulatory bodies for the North and South.

7. A *caisse populaire* is usually
   a. regulated by the provincial government.
   b. an investor in mortgage loans.
   c. linked to the Canadian Payments System through a *Centrale*.
   d. all of the above.

8. A *caisse populaire* is usually

   a. more profitable than a Schedule I bank.

   b. regulated by the OSFI.

   c. regulated by a *Centrale*.

   d. an investor in mortgage loans.

9. Credit unions are usually

   a. regulated by the provincial government.

   b. regulated by the Bank of Canada.

   c. investors in mortgage loans.

   d. both (a) and (c) of the above.

10. Credit unions and *caisses populaires*

    a. are funded almost entirely by deposits.

    b. are regulated and supervised by the OSFI.

    c. are investors in commercial loans.

    d. none of the above.

11. Trust and mortgage loan companies outside Quebec

    a. are funded almost entirely by deposits, guaranteed investment certificates, and debentures.

    b. are directly covered by the CDIC.

    c. are bigger than TMLs in Quebec.

    d. both (a) and (b) of the above.

12. Financial innovation has caused banks' cost advantages to _____, and their income advantages to _____.

    a. increase; increase

    b. increase; decrease

    c. decrease; increase

    d. decrease; decrease

13. The most important developments that have reduced banks' cost advantages in the past thirty years include:

    a. the elimination of Regulation Q ceilings in the United States.

    b. the competition from money market mutual funds.

    c. the competition from junk bonds.

    d. all of the above.

    e. only (a) and (b) of the above.

14. The most important developments that have reduced banks' income advantages in the past thirty years include:

    a. the growth of the junk bond market.

    b. the competition from money market mutual funds.

    c. the growth of securitization.

    d. only (a) and (b) of the above.

    e. only (a) and (c) of the above.

15. Schedule II banks are

    a. regulated by the OSFI.

    b. more profitable than Schedule I banks.

    c. small, universal, and domestic.

    d. all of the above.

16. An improvement in technology stimulates financial innovations by
    a. lowering the cost of providing new services.
    b. raising the demand of providing new services.
    c. reducing the competition from those providing financial services.
    d. doing all of the above.

17. Adjustable-rate mortgages are offered by banks because these mortgages
    a. lower interest rate risk for banks.
    b. guarantee the maximum monthly payment from borrowers.
    c. are the only mortgages that households desire.
    d. have a payment that remains fixed over the life of the loan.

18. A large number of banks started providing credit card services
    a. before World War II.
    b. after computer technology reduced transaction costs of these services.
    c. in order to earn profit from loan defaults.
    d. despite the fact that these services are generally not profitable.

19. Financial derivatives were created by the Chicago Board of Trade in the 1970s and they
    a. are essentially a futures contract in financial instruments.
    b. protect institutions from interest-rate risk.
    c. have a payoff that is linked to previously issued financial securities.
    d. all of the above.
    e. only (a) and (b) of the above.

20. A bank bundling together a collection of student loans and selling claims to principal and interest payments to a third party is known as
    a. collateralization.
    b. selling junk bonds.
    c. securitization.
    d. selling commercial paper.
    e. modernization.

21. The Four Pillars refers to
    a. banks, life insurance companies, P&C insurance companies, and pension funds.
    b. the Bank of Canada, the Big Six, the OSFI, and the CDIC.
    c. banks, insurance companies, finance companies, and merchant banks.
    d. banks, insurance companies, trust companies, and mutual funds.

22. Sweep accounts, which transform corporate chequing accounts into overnight securities, have which advantage for banks?
    a. Sweep accounts reduce costs since they require few transactions.
    b. Sweep accounts are not subject to corporate income taxation.
    c. Sweep accounts reduce costs since they are not subject to reserve requirements.
    d. None of the above.

23. The possible benefits of larger banking institutions and nation-wide banking include
    a. raising the efficiency of the banking sector through more competition.
    b. an increase in lending to small businesses.
    c. decreased diversification of banks' loan portfolios.
    d. only (a) and (b) of the above.

24. As compared to banks, credit unions
    a. have customers that share a common bond.
    b. tend to be larger.
    c. are only provincially chartered.
    d. have no deposit insurance.

25. Economies of scope refers to the idea that
    a. larger banks are more efficient than smaller banks.
    b. taxes are reduced for banks that consolidate.
    c. one resource can be used to provide many products and services.
    d. international banking is generally more profitable than domestic banking.

26. Which of the following are true statements?
    a. Schedule I and Schedule II banks have identical powers.
    b. Widely held foreign banks can own 100% of a Canadian bank subsidiary.
    c. A Schedule II bank may have a significant shareholder (more than 10%) for up to 10 years after chartering.
    d. All of the above.

27. Bank holding companies
    a. own almost all large banks.
    b. are largely not restricted in branch banking.
    c. have grown tremendously in the past decade.
    d. All of the above are true.
    e. Only (a) and (c) are true.

28. A foreign bank can enter the Canadian banking industry as either a Schedule _____ or as a Schedule _____ bank. In the former case, it will be a Canadian subsidiary of a foreign bank, whereas in the latter case, it is allowed to branch directly into Canada.
    a. I; II   b. I; III   c. II; III   d. III; II

29. The near-banks in Canada are
    a. trust and mortgage loan companies.
    b. Ontario saving office and credit unions.
    c. credit unions and *caisses populaires*.
    d. both (a) and (c).

30. According to the three-tiered ownership regime, small, medium-size, and large banks have _____, _____, and _____ billion dollars of equity capital, respectively.
    a. under 5; between 5 and 20; more than 20
    b. under 5; between 5 and 10; more than 10
    c. under 1; between 1 and 5; more than 5
    d. under 1; between 1 and 10; more than 10

CHAPTER 12

Nonbank Financial Institutions

CHAPTER SYNOPSIS/COMPLETIONS

In our economy, nonbank finance also plays an important role in channelling funds from lender-savers to borrower-spenders. Furthermore, the process of financial innovation has increased the importance of nonbank finance and is blurring the distinction between different financial institutions. This chapter examines in more detail how institutions engaged in nonbank finance operate, how they are regulated, and recent trends in nonbank finance.

Insurance providers, which are regulated by the OSFI and the provinces, acquire funds by selling policies that pay out benefits if catastrophic events occur. Property and casualty insurance companies hold more liquid assets than life insurance companies because of greater uncertainty regarding the benefits they will have to pay out. All insurers face moral hazard and adverse selection problems that explain the use of insurance management tools, such as information collection and screening of potential policyholders, risk-based premiums, restrictive provisions, prevention of fraud, cancellation of insurance, deductibles, coinsurance, and limits on the amount of insurance. (1) _____ is the conversion to a stock company. (2) _____ _____ _____ is sold one policy at a time, whereas (3) _____ _____ _____ is sold to a group of people under a single policy. There are two principal forms of individual life insurance policies: (4) _____ _____ _____ and (5) _____ _____ _____ (such as term insurance). Permanent life insurance policies have a constant premium throughout the life of the policy. Permanent insurance is also called endowment insurance. Insurance companies have also begun to sell investment vehicles for retirement such as annuities, arrangements whereby the customer pays an annual premium in exchange for a future stream of annual payments. Reinsurance allocates a portion of the risk to another company in exchange for a portion of the premium and is particularly important for small insurance companies.

Pension plans provide income payments to people when they retire after contributing to the plans for many years. If the benefits are determined by the contributions into the plan and their earnings, the pension is a (6) _____ _____ _____; if future income payments (benefits) are set in advance (usually based on the highest average salary and the number of years of pensionable service), the pension is a (7) _____ _____ _____. Pension funds have experienced very rapid growth as a result of encouragement by federal tax policy and now play an important role in the stock market. A defined-benefit plan is (8) _____ _____ if the contributions into the plan and their earnings over the years are sufficient to pay out the defined benefits when they come due. Many pension plans are (9) _____, which means that in future years they will have to pay out higher benefits than the value of their contributions and earnings. Registered pension plans (RPPs) are voluntary, employer-sponsored plans, with the contributions usually shared between employer and employee. Government-administered pension plans are the Old Age Security (OAS) program, Canada Pension Plan (CPP), and in Quebec, the Quebec Pension Plan (QPP). An alternative to both public pension plans and private pension plans is (10) _____ _____ _____.

Finance companies raise funds by issuing commercial paper and stocks and bonds and use the proceeds to make loans that are particularly suited to consumer and business needs. Virtually unregulated in comparison to chartered banks and near banks, finance companies have been able to tailor their loans to customer needs very quickly and have grown rapidly. There are three types of finance companies: sales, consumer, and business.

When a corporation decides which kind of financial instrument it will issue, it offers them to (11) _____—investment bankers that guarantee the corporation a price on the securities and then sell them to the public. Investment bankers assist in the initial sale of securities in primary markets, whereas securities brokers and dealers assist in the trading of securities in the secondary markets, some of which are organized into exchanges. Organized stock exchanges function as a hybrid of an auction market (in which buyers and sellers trade with each other in a central location) and a dealer market (in which dealers make the market by buying and selling securities at given prices). Securities are traded on the floor of the exchange with the help of a special kind of dealer-broker called a (12) _____. The provinces and the federal government regulate the financial institutions in the securities markets and ensure that adequate information reaches prospective investors.

Mutual funds sell shares and use the proceeds to buy securities. Open-end funds issue shares that can be redeemed at any time at a price tied to the asset value of the firm. Closed-end funds issue nonredeemable shares, which are traded like common stock. They are less popular than open-end funds because their shares are not as liquid. Money market mutual funds hold only short-term, high-quality securities, allowing shares to be redeemed at a fixed value. (13) _____ _____ _____ are state-owned investment funds that invest in foreign assets. The growing importance of mutual funds and pension funds, known as (14) _____ _____, has resulted in their controlling a large share of total financial sector assets. (15) _____ _____ are a special type of investment fund, with estimated assets of more than $1 trillion. Private equity funds make long-term investments in companies that are not traded publicly and are of two types: (16) _____ _____, which make investments in start ups and (17) _____ _____, which make investments in established companies, often taking publicly traded firms private.

To provide credit to residential housing and agriculture, the U.S. government has created a number of government agencies. Particularly important are government-sponsored enterprises (GSEs), which are federally sponsored agencies that function as private corporations with close ties to the government. Because the government provides an implicit guarantee for GSE debt, market discipline to limit excessive risk-taking by GSEs is weak. The resulting moral hazard problem has led to major taxpayer bailouts, especially the recent bailout of Fannie Mae and Freddie Mac, which involved US$200 billion of government funds.

HELPFUL HINTS

1.   The financial intermediation business of transforming one type of asset into another for the public is not limited to banks. For example, insurance companies use the premiums paid on policies to invest in assets such as bonds, stocks, mortgages, and other loans; the earnings from these assets are then used to pay out claims on the policies. The economic concepts of adverse selection and moral hazard discussed also apply to other financial intermediaries.

EXERCISES

Practice Problems

1. Explain the difference between the following:

a.   life insurance companies and property and casualty companies.

_____

b.   defined-contribution plans and defined-benefit plans

_____

c.   fully funded and underfunded plans

_____

    d.   private pension plans and public pension plans

    e.   investment banks and securities dealers

    f.   venture capital funds and capital buyout funds

Short-Answer Questions

1. Why do people buy insurance policies?

2. How does reinsurance benefit insurance companies?

3. Insurance companies supply credit insurance. Explain the two ways they do this.

4. Explain the impact of tax policies on the asset growth of pension plans.

5. Why do you think pension plans are also considered financial intermediaries?

Critical-Thinking Questions

It has been reported that Fannie Mae and Freddie Mac have cost the U.S. taxpayer billions of dollars in bailout money.

1. Why did government regulation and supervision fail to make sure that these institutions did not take on excessive risk?

2. How did Fannie and Freddie carry out their mission to promote affordable housing?

3. Explain the conflict of interest problem faced by those institutions.

SELF-TEST

True-False Questions

Circle whether the following statements are true (T) or false (F).

T   F   1.   Demutualization is the conversion of mutuals to stock companies.

T   F   2.   Group life insurance is sold to a group of people under a single policy.

T   F   3.   An annuity is the same as endowment insurance.

T   F   4.   Only defined-benefit plans can be underfunded.

T   F   5.   Vesting refers to the length of time a person has to be retired before receiving benefits.

T   F   6.   Private pension plans are different from the Canada Pension Plan.

T   F   7.   Benefits in government pension plans are tied closely to a participant's past contributions.

T   F   8.   Finance companies do not deal with consumers.

T   F   9.   Securities brokers and investment dealers can be thought of as 'financial facilitators.'

T   F   10. Brokerage firms can act as brokers, dealers, and investment bankers.

T   F   11. Organized stock exchanges function as a hybrid of an auction market and a dealer market.

T   F   12. Mutual funds pool the resources of institutional investors.

T   F   13. Hedge funds are specialized because they use strategies to avoid risk.

T   F   14. The Canadian government is involved in financial intermediation.

T   F   15. GSEs are federally sponsored agencies that function as private corporations.

Multiple-Choice Questions

Circle the appropriate answer.

1.   Demutualization refers to

   a. the conversion of insurance companies from being owned by policyholders to stockholders.

   b. the conversion of mutual fund companies from being owned by policyholders to stockholders.

   c. the conversion of insurance companies from being owned by stockholders to policyholders.

   d. the conversion of mutual fund companies from being owned by stockholders to policyholders.

2.   Individual life insurance

   a. is regulated by the Bank of Canada.

   b. is sold one policy at a time.

   c. has been extremely volatile over time.

   d. is sold to a group of people at a time.

3.   Which of the following is an example of term insurance?

   a. The policyholder can borrow against the cash value.

   b. It provides an annuity until death.

   c. The premium is constant through the life of the policy.

   d. The premium is matched every year to the amount needed to match against death.

4.   Which of the following is likely to occur if lawsuits involving Property and Casualty insurance and amounts awarded rise dramatically?

   a. Insurance companies leave premiums unchanged.

   b. Insurance companies raise premiums.

   c. Insurance companies hold less liquid assets to earn more income.

   d. Insurance companies keep insurance rates low.

5.   Reinsurance

   a. allows the insured to reduce the premium by accepting a portion of the risk that would otherwise be allocated to the insurance company.

   b. allows insurance companies to reduce their risks of exposure by allocating a portion of the risk to another company in exchange for a portion of the premium.

   c. allows insurance companies to reduce their risks of exposure by allocating a portion of the risk to the insured in exchange for a rebate on the premium.

   d. none of the above.

6. An example of permanent insurance is _____ insurance, and an example of temporary insurance is _____ insurance.

    a. term; variable life

    b. term; whole life

    c. whole life; variable life

    d. whole life; term

7. A defined-contribution plan

    a. has borrowed from the public.

    b. has purchased foreign currency.

    c. sets future income payments in advance.

    d. has agreed to make periodic payments for a specific period of time.

8. Which of the following is an example of financial intermediation?

    a. A pension fund providing income payments on retirement.

    b. Issuing a bond that is sold to a retired person.

    c. Issuing common stock that is sold to a college student.

    d. All of the above are examples of financial intermediation.

9. Which of the following is an example of a fully funded plan?

    a. Contributions are sufficient to pay out the benefits but earnings are not.

    b. Contributions and earnings are not sufficient to pay out the benefits.

    c. Contributions and earnings are sufficient to pay out the benefits.

    d. Earnings are sufficient to pay out the benefits but contributions are not.

10. In a defined-contribution plan, future benefits

    a. are set in advance.

    b. are determined by the contributions into the plan and their earnings.

    c. are government administered.

    d. are registered with the federal regulatory authority.

11. The Canada Pension Plan

    a. is a government-administered pension plan.

    b. is a 'pay-as-you-go' system.

    c. is underfunded.

    d. is all of the above.

12. Personal pension plans

    a. are different from RRSPs.

    b. cannot be converted to annuity or a RRIF on retirement.

    c. provide tax-sheltered, self-financed retirement funds.

    d. are government-administered.

13. The term "bank" generally includes all of the following institutions except

    a. chartered banks.

    b. credit unions.

    c. trust and mortgage loan companies.

    d. finance companies.

14. The three types of finance companies are

    a. sales, investment, and business.

    b. sales, consumer, and business.

    c. credit, consumer, and business.

    d. credit, consumer, and bank.

15. Non-deposit-taking financial institutions that acquire funds by issuing commercial paper or stock and bonds or borrowing from banks, and that use the proceeds to make loans, are known as

    a. theft companies.

    b. redistribution companies.

    c. barter companies.

    d. finance companies.

16. In financial markets, when a firm issuing new securities has previously issued securities, these securities are called

    a. investment-grade issues.
    b. seasoned issues.
    c. an initial public offering.
    d. secondary issues.

17. A/an _____ _____ is an example of a security which is currently selling on the market.

    a. seasoned issue

    b. new issue

    c. IPO issue

    d. IB issue

18. Which of the following transactions would involve an investment bank?

    a. New shares of stock are issued by a corporation.

    b. One corporation buys a bond issued by another corporation.

    c. A pension fund manager buys a bond in the secondary market.

    d. Both (b) and (c) of the above.

19. Which of the following is true?

    a. Insider information is public information.

    b. Brokerage firms act as brokers, dealers, and investment bankers.

    c. Dealers are pure intermediaries who act as agents.

    d. Brokers make their living by selling securities at a higher price than what they paid for them.

20. Mutual funds were created

    a. in order to provide insurance to all households.

    b. in order to limit interest rates that are paid on deposits.

    c. to pool the savings of small investors and use the proceeds to invest on their behalf.

    d. only (a) and (b) of the above.

21. Which of the following are the primary assets of mutual fund companies?

    a. Stocks and bonds.

    b. Premiums from policies.

    c. Chequing accounts.

    d. All of the above.

22. Shares in open-end funds are_____ while shares in closed-end funds are _____.

    a. redeemable; not redeemable

    b. not redeemable; redeemable

    c. front load; no-load

    d. no-load; front load

23. Institutional funds can be a concern because they
    a. include individuals between 50 and 70.
    b. lead to lower interest rates.
    c. control a large share of total financial assets.
    d. have no clout with corporate boards.

24. Sovereign Wealth Funds can be a concern because they
    a. could cause market instability.
    b. raise national security issues.
    c. are secretive.
    d. all of the above.

25. Money-market mutual funds invest in
    a. stocks.
    b. bonds.
    c. short-term debt.
    d. short-term and long-term debt.

26. Which of the following is true about hedge funds?
    a. Hedge funds are the same as mutual funds.
    b. Hedge funds require that investors commit their funds short-term.
    c. Hedge funds use strategies that avoid risk.
    d. Hedge funds have a minimum investment requirement between $100 000 and $20 million.

27. Which of the following funds make investments in new startup businesses?
    a. Capital buyout funds.
    b. Venture capital funds.
    c. Mutual funds.
    d. LBO funds.

28. Examples of Crown finance companies are
    a. the Bank of Canada and the Office of the Superintendent of Financial Institutions Canada.
    b. the Bank of Canada and Canada Deposit Insurance Corporation.
    c. the Canada Mortgage and Housing Corporation, Farm Credit Canada, and Export Development Canada.
    d. both (a) and (b) of the above.

29. To promote and assist in the establishment of business enterprises in Canada, the government created the
    a. stock market
    b. bond market
    c. Business Development Bank.
    d. Bank of Canada.

30. Fannie Mae and Freddie Mac
    a. are U.S. government agencies that provide funds to the mortgage market.
    b. are the names of U.S. central banks.
    c. demonstrated great stability during the subprime crisis.
    d. are pivot points in the business cycle.

CHAPTER 13

Banking and the Management of Financial Institutions

CHAPTER SYNOPSIS/COMPLETIONS

This chapter focuses on how commercial banks are managed in order to maximize profits. We concentrate on commercial banks because they are the most important financial intermediaries.

A bank's (1) _____ _____ lists its sources of funds (liabilities, such as deposits) and uses of funds (assets, such as loans). It has the characteristic that total assets = total liabilities + capital. A bank's liabilities include demand and notice deposits, fixed-term deposits, and borrowings. Bank capital is on the liability side and is the bank's net worth.

The bank's assets are its uses of funds, which include cash reserves, cash items in process of collection, deposits at other banks, securities, loans, and other assets (mostly physical capital). The (2) _____ _____ _____ or (3) _____ _____ sets the percentage of chequable deposits that must be held as *required reserves*. The bank may choose to hold *excess reserves*.

Banks make profits from asset transformation. They borrow short (accept relatively short-term deposits) and lend long (make loans that are relatively longer). When a bank receives additional deposits, it gains an equal amount of reserves. When it loses deposits, it loses an equal amount of reserves. In the simplest case, banks make profits by lending the excess reserves generated from a deposit and charging a higher interest rate on the loan than they pay on the deposit.

Banks engage in (4) _____ _____ to be prepared for *deposit outflows*. For this reason, banks hold excess reserves and secondary reserves even though they earn less interest than less liquid assets such as loans. First, when a bank faces deposit outflow, it need not change other parts of its balance sheet if it has ample excess reserves. Second, the bank could sell some of its securities with relatively low transaction costs. Third, it could get an advance from the Bank of Canada, but it would have to pay the (5) _____ _____ , the interest rate charged by the Bank of Canada. Finally, it could call in loans or sell loans to another bank, but this is the costliest way to acquire funds and is to be avoided.

Banks engage in (6) _____ _____ to seek the highest returns possible, reduce risk, and provide liquidity. They do this by seeking borrowers who will pay high rates but are a low risk of default, buying securities with high returns and low risk, buying a variety of assets to lower risk through diversification, and maintaining just enough liquid assets to insure against deposit outflows. (7) _____ _____ used to be a staid affair because 60% of their liabilities were chequable deposits for which they could not compete by paying interest, and there was no well-developed federal funds market. Post-1960, large (8) _____ _____ _____ began selling negotiable CDs and borrowing from other banks. Thus, banks began to actively seek funds if they found productive loan prospects.

Banks must manage the amount of capital they hold in order to lessen the chance of a bank failure (assets < liabilities) and to meet capital requirements set by regulatory authorities, which is known as (9) _____ _____ _____. Bank capital is the cushion for the reduction in the value of assets that results from bad loans. Other things the same, the greater the capital account, the more bad loans the bank can sustain and remain solvent (have positive net worth). However, the lower the bank capital, the higher the return on equity for the owners of the bank, causing a trade-off between safety and return to equity holders. This relationship is demonstrated by the definition of *return on equity* (ROE). ROE = net profit after taxes/equity capital. Reducing capital increases ROE. Due to the cost of holding capital, regulatory authorities enforce minimum bank capital requirements. To increase the amount of capital relative to assets, a bank can issue more common stock, reduce the bank's dividends to increase retained earnings, or reduce the bank's assets by selling off loans or securities. In a financial crisis, it is difficult for banks to raise capital, so banks usually reduce loans, causing a credit crunch.

Credit risk is the risk associated with the probability of default on a loan. To avoid the asymmetric information problems of adverse selection and moral hazard, banks engage in five activities. First, banks (10) _____ _____ _____ borrowers by collecting information on borrowers prior to the loan, specializing in lending to particular industries to gain expertise in screening, and monitoring and enforcing restrictive covenants to ensure that the borrower uses the loan for the prescribed activities. Second, banks develop *long-term customer relationships* to more efficiently gather information on the borrower and to provide the borrower with an incentive to reduce moral hazard for future borrowing. Third, banks issue (11) _____ _____, which promotes long-term customer relationships. Fourth, banks require (12) _____ _____ _____ *balances* from the borrower. Compensating balances act as collateral and help the bank monitor the spending of the loan. Finally, the bank can engage in (13) _____ _____, refusing to make a loan even at a high interest rate or making a loan for a smaller amount that was originally requested.

Interest-rate risk is the riskiness of earnings associated with changes in interest rates. If a bank has more rate-sensitive (short-term) liabilities than assets, a rise in interest rates will reduce bank profits. This is because the increase in interest a bank pays on its liabilities will exceed the increase in interest it receives on its assets. Alternatively, a decline in interest rates will raise bank profits. Basic (14) _____ _____ can measure the sensitivity of bank profits to changes in interest rates. Gap = rate-sensitive assets – rate-sensitive liabilities. Gap × change in interest rate = change in bank profits. (15) _____ _____ measures the interest rate sensitivity of the market value of the bank's assets and liabilities, and thus shows the change in net worth of the bank from a change in interest rates. Percent change in market value of security = – percentage-point change in interest rate × duration in years. Both measures indicate that banks with more rate-sensitive liabilities tend to suffer when interest rates rise and gain when they fall. Managing interest-rate risk can be costly if it requires changing the average duration of a bank's assets or liabilities.

(16) _____ _____ _____ *activities* involve trading financial instruments and generating income from fees and loan sales, which affect bank profits but don't appear on the balance sheet. A (17) _____ _____, or secondary loan participation, is when a bank sells all or part of a loan's cash stream. Fee income is earned from foreign exchange trades for a customer, servicing mortgage-backed securities, guaranteeing debt such as banker's acceptances, providing backup lines of credit, and creating structured investment vehicles (SIVs). Trading activities can be profitable but risky, requiring the bank to put risk assessment procedures in place and restrict employees from taking on too much risk.

HELPFUL HINTS

1. Prior to 1960, more than 60% of a bank's liabilities were chequable deposits. Since banks could not actively compete for those deposits by paying interest on them, a bank's size was largely determined by its local source of funds. Post-1960, banks with exceptionally profitable loan opportunities can actively seek funds by borrowing in ways that didn't exist prior to the 1960s. Thus, a bank now has more influence over its size and growth rate than prior to 1960.
2. Capital protects a bank from bankruptcy or insolvency. Insolvency is when the value of a bank's assets falls below the value of its liabilities. Thus, a bank can sustain a reduction in the value of its assets by the amount of its capital. If a bank has $1 billion in capital, the value of its assets could fall by up to $1 billion and the bank would still be technically solvent.

EXERCISES

Practice Problems

1.

a.   Fill in the T-account of the First Bank if Shirley Student deposits $2000 in cash into her chequing account at this bank.

First Bank

Assets	Liabilities

b.   Fill in the T-accounts of the First Bank and the Second Bank when Shirley writes a $1000 cheque written on her account at the First Bank to pay her tuition at the University of Toronto, which in turn deposits the cheque in its accounts at the Second Bank.

First Bank

Asset	Liabilities

Second Bank

Assets	Liabilities

c.   What is the net effect of the transactions in A and B on the reserve position at the two banks?

_____

2.   Suppose that the First Bank has the following balance-sheet position and that the desired reserve ratio on deposits is 20% (in millions of dollars).

Assets		Liabilities	
Reserves	$25	Deposits	$100
Loans	75	Bank capital	10
Securities	10		

a.   If the bank suffers a deposit outflow of $6 million, what will its balance sheet now look like? Show this by filling in the amounts in the following balance sheet.

Assets		Liabilities	
Reserves		Deposits	
Loans		Bank capital	
Securities			

Must the bank make any adjustment in its balance sheet? _____

Why? _____

b.   Suppose the bank is hit by another $4 million deposit outflow. What will its balance-sheet position look like now? Show this by filling in the amounts in the following balance sheet.

Assets		Liabilities	
Reserves		Deposits	
Loans		Bank capital	
Securities			

Must the bank make any adjustment in its balance sheet? _____

Why? _____

c. If the bank satisfies its reserve requirements by selling off securities, how much will it have to sell?

_____

Why? _____

d. After selling off the securities to meet its reserve requirements, what will its balance sheet look like? Show this by filling in the amounts in the following balance sheet:

Assets		Liabilities	
Reserves		Deposits	
Loans		Bank capital	
Securities			

e. If, after selling off the securities, the bank is hit by another $10 million of withdrawals of deposits and it sells off all its securities to obtain reserves, what will its balance sheet look like? Again show this by filling in the amounts in the following balance sheet:

Assets		Liabilities	
Reserves		Deposits	
Loans		Bank capital	
Securities			

If the bank is now unable to call in or sell any of its loans and no one is willing to lend funds to this bank, then what will happen to the bank and why?

_____

_____

3. On July 1, 1935, S.D.K deposited $200 dollars into the Bank of Cambridge. The bank requires that its deposits have a reserve ratio of 25%. At this point the bank's balance sheet is:

Assets		Liabilities	
Reserves	$50	Deposits	$180
Loans	130	Bank capital	20
Securities	20		

a. On July 2, 1935, the government withdraws $50 from the Bank of Cambridge to finance its expenditure. What changes occur in the bank's balance sheet?

Assets		Liabilities	
Reserves		Deposits	
Loans		Bank capital	
Securities			

b.   What does the new bank balance sheet say about the initial level of reserves that the bank holds?

_____

c.   What four actions could be taken to restore the reserve ratio?

_____

d.   Why is it important for banks to hold excess reserves? What is the downfall of holding a very large amount of excess reserves?

_____

4.   Below you will find balance sheets for High Capital Bank and Low Capital Bank. Numbers are in millions.

High Capital Bank

Assets		Liabilities	
Reserves	90	Deposits	540
Loans	510	Bank capital	60
Securities	0		

Low Capital Bank

Assets		Liabilities	
Reserves	90	Deposits	560
Loans	510	Bank capital	40
Securities	0		

a.   How many dollars of bad loans can each bank sustain before it becomes insolvent? As a result, which bank has the lower probability of becoming insolvent?

_____

b.   Suppose net profit after taxes is $6 million for each bank. What is each bank's return on assets (ROA)? What is each bank's return on equity (ROE)? Which bank is more profitable to its owners?

_____

c.   What does this example say about the relationship between safety and returns to equity holders? What is regulatory response to this situation?

_____

_____

5. Suppose that Rate-Sensitive Bank has the following balance sheet. All values are in millions of dollars.

Rate-Sensitive Bank

Assets		Liabilities	
Variable-rate loans	$5	Variable-rate CDs	$30
Short-term loans	10	Money market	
Short-term securities	15	deposit accounts	20
Reserves	10	Chequable deposits	10
Long-term loans	30	Savings deposits	10
Long-term securities	30	Long-term CDs	20
		Equity capital	10

a. Employ basic gap analysis to determine this bank's "gap."

b. If interest rates suddenly increase by two percentage points, by how much do the bank's profits change?

c. If, instead, interest rates decrease by three percentage points, by how much do the bank's profits change?

d. If a bank has more rate-sensitive liabilities than assets, how do bank profits move with respect to the interest rate?

e. Suppose the average duration of the assets of this bank is four years while the average duration of the liabilities is two years. Use duration analysis to determine the change in the net worth of the bank if interest rates rise by three percentage points.

Short-Answer Questions

1. What are secondary reserves? What purpose do they serve? What advantage do they have over excess reserves?

2. What category of assets generates the greatest profits for commercial banks? Why would banks receive more profit from this type of asset?

3. If a bank has $1000 in deposits and the required reserve ratio is 10%, how much are the bank's required reserves? In what form must the bank hold them?

4. When banks engage in asset management, they seek high-return, low-risk, liquid assets. Why is this difficult?

5. If a depositor withdraws $100 from his deposit at a bank, what happens to the bank's reserves?

Critical-Thinking Questions

You are watching the news with a friend. The news anchor says that the Fed has just increased the interest rate for the eighth meeting in a row. Your friend says, "I bet banks just love these increases in the interest rate. Banks must be making enormous profits charging those high interest rates. Bank stock prices must just be going through the roof."

1. Use a description of gap analysis to explain to your friend how a rising interest rate tends to affect a bank's profits.

    _____

    _____

2. Use a description of duration analysis to explain to your friend how a rising interest rate tends to affect a bank's net worth.

    _____

    _____

SELF-TEST

True-False Questions

Circle whether the following statements are true (T) or false (F).

T	F	1.	A bank's assets are its sources of funds.
T	F	2.	Bank capital equals the total assets of the bank minus the total liabilities.
T	F	3.	Savings accounts are the most common type of chequable deposit.
T	F	4.	Chequable deposits are usually the lowest-cost source of bank funds.
T	F	5.	Chequable deposits are the primary source of bank funds.
T	F	6.	Interest paid on deposits makes up over half of total bank operating expenses.
T	F	7.	Banks are only able to borrow reserves from the Bank of Canada.
T	F	8.	Loans provide banks with most of their revenue.
T	F	9.	Providing backup lines of credit is an off-balance-sheet activity.
T	F	10.	Off-balance-sheet activities have declined in importance for banks over the past two decades.
T	F	11.	The currency that is physically held by banks is called vault cash.
T	F	12.	Canadian banks are required to hold cash reserves.
T	F	13.	Opening a savings account leads to an increase in the bank's reserves equal to the increase in savings deposits.
T	F	14.	A bank will maximize its profits by issuing loans to a limited number of specific sectors in the economy.
T	F	15.	If the average duration of a bank's assets exceeds the average duration of a bank's liabilities, an increase in interest rates will increase a bank's net worth.

Multiple-Choice Questions

Circle the appropriate answer.

1. Which of the following bank assets is the most liquid?
    a. Consumer loans.
    b. Provincial and local government securities.
    c. Physical capital.
    d. Canadian government securities.

2. Reserves
    a. equal the deposits banks hold at the Bank of Canada.
    b. include bank holdings of Canadian government securities.
    c. can be divided up into desired reserves plus excess reserves.
    d. equal both (a) and (c) of the above.

3. When a $1000 cheque written on the Bank of Montreal is deposited in an account at the Royal Bank, then
    a. the liabilities of the Bank of Montreal increase by $1000.
    b. the reserves of the Bank of Montreal increase by $1000.
    c. the liabilities of the Royal Bank fall by $1000.
    d. the reserves of the Royal Bank increase by $1000.

4. When you deposit a $100 cheque in your bank account at the First Bank of Calgary and you withdraw $50 in cash, then
    a. the liabilities of First Bank rise by $100.
    b. the reserves of First Bank rise by $100.
    c. the assets of the First Bank rise by $100.
    d. the liabilities of the First Bank rise by $50.
    e. none of the above occur.

5. If a bank has $1 million of deposits and a desired reserve ratio of 5%, and it holds $100 000 in reserves, then it must rearrange its balance sheet if there is a deposit outflow of
    a. $51 000.
    b. $20 000.
    c. $30 000.
    d. none of the above.

6. A bank will want to hold less excess reserves (everything else equal) when
    a. it expects to have deposit inflows in the near future.
    b. brokerage commissions on selling bonds rise.
    c. both (a) and (b) of the above occur.
    d. neither (a) nor (b) of the above occurs.

7. When a bank faces a reserve deficiency because of a deposit outflow, it will try to do which of the following first?
    a. Call in loans.
    b. Borrow from the Bank of Canada.
    c. Sell securities.
    d. Borrow from other banks.

8. A bank failure is more likely to occur when
    a. a bank holds more Canadian government securities.
    b. a bank suffers large deposit outflows.
    c. a bank holds more excess reserves.
    d. a bank has more bank capital.

9. When interest rates are expected to fall in the future, a banker is likely to
    a. make short-term rather than long-term loans.
    b. buy short-term rather than long-term bonds.
    c. buy long-term rather than short-term bonds.
    d. do both (a) and (b) of the above.

10. Banks want to hold _____ as an insurance against the costs associated with deposit outflows.
    a. interbank deposits
    b. excess reserves
    c. securities
    d. both (a) and (b)

11. Items listed on the liability side of banks' balance sheets include
    a. bank capital.
    b. loans.
    c. reserves.
    d. all of the above.

12. Collectively, reserves, cash items in process of collection, and deposits at other banks are referred to as _____ in a bank balance sheet.
    a. secondary reserves
    b. total cash reserves
    c. liquid items
    d. compensating balances

13. In less uncertain times, bank managers might want to hold _____ capital, have a _____ equity multiplier, and thereby _____ the return on equity.

    a. less; high; increase
    b. more; high; decrease
    c. less; low; increase
    d. more; high; increase

14. For a given return on _____, the _____ is bank capital, the _____ is the return for the owners of the bank.
    a. liabilities; lower; lower
    b. assets; lower; higher
    c. assets; higher; higher
    d. liabilities; lower; higher

15. Chequable deposits
    a. include time deposits.
    b. are the most expensive way for banks to acquire funds.
    c. are an asset for the bank.
    d. none of the above.

16. Which of the following financial instruments are commercial banks legally not allowed to hold?

    a. Bonds issued by a local government.

    b. Stock issued by a foreign company.

    c. Stock issued by a domestic company.

    d. Only (a) and (b) of the above.

    e. Only (b) and (c) of the above.

17. Banks generally earn the highest rate of return on which of their assets?

    a. Reserves.

    b. Certificates of deposit.

    c. Canadian government securities.

    d. Loans.

    e. Deposits at other banks.

18. If Steve writes a cheque for $200 to Beth that she deposits into her account, and if Steve and Beth use the same bank, then

    a. the bank eventually loses reserves equal to $200.

    b. total liabilities of the bank rise by $200.

    c. total assets of the bank fall by $200.

    d. excess reserves increase by $200.

    e. none of the above.

19. In order to reduce excess reserves after a deposit inflow, a bank can

    a. purchase loans from another bank.

    b. borrow from the Bank of Canada.

    c. call in loans.

    d. sell securities.

20. For a given return on assets, a bank with more capital has a _____ risk of insolvency and a _____ return on equity.

    a. lower; higher

    b. lower; lower

    c. higher; lower

    d. higher; higher

21. A bank has $100 in chequable deposits, reserves of $15, and the reserves requirement is 10%. Suppose the bank suffers a $10 deposit outflow. If the bank chooses to borrow from the Bank of Canada to meet its reserve requirement, how much does it need to borrow?

    a. $0.

    b. $1.50.

    c. $4.

    d. $5.

    e. $10.

22. Which of the following is not true regarding how banks manage their assets? Banks seek assets that

    a. are liquid.

    b. provide diversification.

    c. have no default risk.

    d. generate high returns.

23. Suppose that a bank's balance sheet consists of the following: On the liability side it has $93 of deposits and $7 of capital, while on the asset side it has $10 of reserves and $90 of loans. How many dollars of bad loans can this bank sustain before it become insolvent?

    a. $0.

    b. $7.

    c. $9.30.

    d. $10.

24. Other things being the same, a bank with a greater amount of capital

    a. has a lower risk of failure.

    b. has a higher rate of return on equity to the owners.

    c. is more liquid.

    d. All of the above are true.

25. Which of the following is not a method by which banks reduce their credit risk?

    a. Collect information on prospective borrowers to screen out high-risk borrowers.

    b. Use gap analysis to help balance a bank's rate-sensitive assets and liabilities.

    c. Develop long-term relationships with borrowers.

    d. Enforce restrictive covenants in the loan contract.

26. Banks often specialize in providing loans to firms in a particular industry because this activity

    a. reduces the cost of acquiring and analyzing information about the borrower.

    b. reduces the bank's exposure to interest-rate risk.

    c. allows the bank to increase the diversification of its loan portfolio.

    d. is required by law.

27. Suppose a bank has a "gap" of –$50 million dollars. What will happen to its profits if interest rates rise by 2%?

    a. Profits rise by $100 million.

    b. Profits fall by $100 million.

    c. Profits rise by $1million.

    d. Profits fall by $1 million.

28. Which of the following statements about interest-rate risk is true?

    a. A commercial bank usually has a larger "gap" than an equivalent-size savings and loan.

    b. An increase in interest rates always increases commercial bank profits.

    c. If a bank has more rate-sensitive liabilities than assets, an increase in interest rates reduces bank profits.

    d. Banks tend to have more rate-sensitive assets than liabilities.

29. Which of the following does not describe an off-balance-sheet activity?

    a. A bank guarantees a firm's debt by signing a banker's acceptance.

    b. A bank writes a mortgage and sells it to a life insurance company.

    c. A bank makes a loan to a large corporate customer.

    d. A bank exchanges dollars for euros for a large corporate customer.

30. Using duration analysis, if a bank's assets have an average duration of 4 years, and if the interest rate rises by 2%, what will happen to the value of the bank's assets?

    a. The value of the assets will rise by 8%.

    b. The value of the assets will fall by 8%.

    c. The value of the assets will rise by 2%.

    d. The value of the assets will fall by 2%.

CHAPTER 14

Risk Management with Financial Derivatives

CHAPTER SYNOPSIS/COMPLETIONS

Beginning in the 1970s and continuing into the 1980s and 1990s, interest rates and foreign exchange rates became more volatile, increasing the risk to financial institutions. To combat this, managers of financial institutions have demanded financial instruments to better manage risk. These instruments, called *financial derivatives*, have become an important source of profits for financial institutions, particularly larger banks. In this chapter, we investigate the use of forward contracts, financial futures, options, and swaps to reduce risk.

When financial institutions (1)_____, they write a financial contract that reduces or eliminates risk. A long contract means that the holder agrees to buy the asset in the future while the (2)_____ contract holder agrees to sell the asset. The principle of hedging risk involves offsetting a long position by taking an additional short position, or offsetting a short position by taking an additional long position.

A forward contract is an agreement for the exchange of assets in the future. An *interest-rate forward contract* exchanges debt instruments such as bonds. The price and date of the exchange are agreed upon up front. Forward contracts have the advantage of being as flexible as the parties want them to be, but they have the disadvantages of lacking liquidity (finding a counterparty may be difficult) and being subject to default (3)_____, if one or the other party chooses not to complete their end of the bargain.

An *interest-rate futures contract* reduces risk because when the price of the underlying asset moves one way, the price of the futures contract will move by the same amount in the (4)_____ direction, effectively cancelling any gains or losses due to unanticipated movements in interest rates. An interest-rate futures contract is similar to an interest-rate forward contract, but differs in ways that overcome liquidity and default problems of forward contracts. For example, the quantities delivered and the delivery dates of interest-rate futures are (5)_____ so that it is easier to find a counterparty. Moreover, interest-rate futures contracts can be traded again at any time until the delivery date, and, in the case of a Canada bond futures contract, any Canada bond that neither matures nor is callable for 15 years can be deliverable on the delivery date. These three features increase the liquidity of interest-rate futures.

A micro hedge occurs when a futures contract is purchased or sold to hedge one particular security. Macro hedges occur when futures contracts are purchased or sold to offset an entire portfolio. A clearinghouse for the exchange requires that both buyers and sellers must make a *margin requirement* into a margin account at their brokerage firm. This feature of financial futures contracts (6)_____ the risk of default. Additionally, to protect the exchange from loss, they are *marked to market* every day. This means that at the end of every trading day, the change in the value of the futures contract is added or subtracted from a margin account. If the margin account falls too low, the investor must replenish it.

A final advantage that futures have over forward contracts is that most futures contracts do not result in delivery of the underlying asset on the expiration date, (7)_____ transaction costs compared to forward contracts that do require delivery. A trader who sells short a futures contract can avoid making delivery on the expiration date by making an offsetting purchase of a long futures contract.

Alternatives to using forward and futures contracts to hedge risk are options and swaps. Options are contracts that give the purchaser the option, or (8)_____, to buy or sell the underlying financial instrument at the (9)_____ (exercise) price. Although the seller of an option is obligated to buy or sell, the owner (buyer) need not exercise the option. Because the right to buy a financial instrument at a specified price has value, one must pay a *premium* to buy an option. American options can be exercised at any time up to the expiration date; (10)_____ options can be exercised only on the expiration date.

Options on individual stocks are called stock options. Options on financial futures, commonly called futures options, were developed in 1982 and have become the most widely traded option contracts. A call option is a contract that gives the owner the right to buy a financial instrument at the exercise price. A put option gives the owner the right to (11)_____ a financial instrument at the strike price.

Interest-rate swaps are an important tool for controlling interest-rate risk. In a simple swap, called the *plain vanilla swap*, one firm agrees to pay a fixed rate of interest on a stated sum and another firm agrees to pay a floating interest rate on the same sum. The advantage of this arrangement is that it effectively converts fixed-rate assets into floating rate assets and vice versa. A bank that finds that it has more interest rate-sensitive liabilities than assets can protect itself (hedge) from an increase in interest rates by agreeing to pay a fixed rate on a swap in exchange for receiving floating rate payments. What this does is convert fixed rate assets into floating-rate assets.

The use of swaps to eliminate interest-rate risk can be cheaper than rearranging a bank's balance sheet. Swaps have an advantage over futures because swaps can be written for (12)_____ periods of time. The disadvantage of swaps is that they suffer from the liquidity and default risk that plague the forward market. Intermediaries have set up markets in swaps that help alleviate these problems. For example, Citicorp will match firms together and each firm will deal exclusively with the bank.

Credit derivatives are a new type of derivative that offer payoffs on previously issued securities that have credit risk. These derivatives—credit options, swaps, and credit linked notes—can be used to hedge credit risk.

HELPFUL HINTS

1. There are three concerns about the dangers of derivatives: They allow financial institutions to more easily increase their leverage and take big bets (by effectively enabling them to hold a larger amount of the underlying assets than the amount of money put down), and they expose financial institutions to large credit risks because the huge notional amounts of derivative contracts greatly exceed the capital of these institutions. The second danger seems to be overplayed, but the danger from increased leverage using derivatives is very real, as events in the subprime financial crisis revealed.

EXERCISES

Practice Problems

1. List four features that distinguish futures contracts from forward contracts.

   a. _____

   b. _____

   c. _____

   d. _____

2. *Fill in the blanks.*

   a. A firm with a portfolio of Canada bonds may hedge by _____ futures contracts.

   b. A _____ contract is where the investor agrees to sell an asset at some time in the future at an agreed-upon price.

   c. Forward contracts are subject to _____ risk since the counterparty could go bankrupt.

d.   The elimination of riskless profit opportunities in the futures markets is referred to as _____, and it guarantees that the price of the futures contract at expiration equals the price of the underlying asset to be delivered.

e.   Because futures contracts are _____, it is easier for an investor to find a counterparty.

f.   Each day futures contracts are marked to market, helping to _____ the chance of losses to the exchange.

3.   *Fill in the blanks.*

a.   A contract that gives the purchaser the right to buy or sell an asset is a(n)_____.

b.   A _____ option gives the holder the right to buy an underlying asset.

c.   A _____ option gives the holder the right to sell an underlying asset.

d.   The price that the holder of a call option can demand from exercising the option is the _____ price.

e.   An option that cannot be exercised until maturity is called a _____ option.

f.   An option that can be exercised any time up until maturity is called an _____ option.

g.   A _____ can be used to reduce interest-rate risk without requiring the firm to restructure its balance sheet.

Short-Answer Questions

1.   The most common type of interest-rate swap is called the _____ _____, which specifies:

   1. _____

   2. _____

   3. _____

   4. _____

2.   List two advantages of interest-rate swaps:

   1. _____

   2. _____

3.   List three disadvantages of interest-rate swaps:

   1. _____

   2. _____

   3. _____

Critical-Thinking Questions

Suppose that in January you purchase $100 000 face value Canada bonds for a price of $95 000. Assume that the bonds mature in fifteen years and that you plan to sell the bonds at the end of March.

1. In Table 13.A, calculate the gain or loss (indicate loss with a negative) of the March sale that you incur for each potential bond selling price.

Table 13.A Gain or Loss

	Price of Asset				
	$85 000	$90 000	$95 000	$100 000	$105 000
Selling Canada bonds					
Selling futures contract					
Purchasing put option					

2. Suppose that you want to hedge your long position by selling a futures contract for Canada bonds for $95 000 (95 points). Thus, at the end of March, the buyer of the futures contract agrees to buy from you Canada bonds for $95 000. In Table 13.A, calculate the gain or loss (indicate loss with a negative) that you incur from selling the futures contract for each potential bond selling price.

3. Suppose instead that you want to hedge your long position by purchasing a put option on a Canada bond futures contract with a strike price of $95 000 (95 points) and a premium of $2000. Thus, at the end of March, you have the option of selling a futures contract for $95 000. In Table 13.A, calculate the gain or loss (indicate loss with a negative) that you incur from exercising (if profitable to do so) the put option for each potential futures contract price. Be sure to include the option premium in your gain or loss. If it is not profitable to exercise the put option, show the loss incurred from the premium.

SELF-TEST

True-False Questions

Circle whether the following statements are true (T) or false (F).

T   F   1. Interest-rate futures can be used to reduce the risk of selling goods overseas.

T   F   2. Forward contracts are more flexible than futures contracts because they are not standardized.

T   F   3. To hedge against interest rate increases, a bank with a portfolio of Canada securities could sell futures contracts.

T   F   4. A serious problem for the market in financial futures contracts is that it may be difficult to make the financial transaction or that it will have to be made at a disadvantageous price; in the parlance of financial economists, this market suffers from a lack of liquidity.

T   F   5. To corner a market means that someone has purchased the bulk of a particular asset so that high prices can be charged when contracts are settled.

T   F   6. Open interest refers to the number of futures contracts that have not been settled.

T   F   7. Option premiums are generally higher the greater the exercise price.

T   F   8. Option premiums are higher the greater the volatility of the underlying asset.

T   F   9. A call option gives the holder the right to buy the underlying asset.

T   F   10. A swap is a financial contract that obligates one party to exchange a set of payments it owns for another set of payments owned by another party.

T   F   11. An interest-rate future contract and an interest-rate forward contract have the same meaning.

T   F   12. A call with asset price equal to the exercise price is said to be in the money.

T   F   13. At the expiration date of a futures contract, the price of the contract is higher than the price of the underlying asset to be delivered.

T   F   14. A put option is a contract that gives the owner the right to buy a stock at the exercise price within a specific period of time.

T   F   15. The greater the term to expiration, the higher the premiums for both call and put options.

Multiple-Choice Questions

Circle the appropriate answer.

1. An investor who chooses to hedge in the futures market
   a. gives up the opportunity for gains.
   b. reduces the opportunity for losses.
   c. increases her earnings potential.
   d. does both (a) and (b) of the above.

2. A portfolio manager with $100 million in Canada securities could reduce interest-rate risk by
    a. selling financial futures.
    b. going long on financial futures.
    c. buying financial futures.
    d. both (b) and (c) are true.

3. A bank sold a futures contract that perfectly hedges its portfolio of Canada securities; if interest rates fall,
    a. the bank suffers a loss.
    b. the bank has a gain.
    c. the bank's income is unchanged.
    d. none of the above.

4. When an investor agrees to buy an asset at some time in the future he is said to have gone
    a. long.
    b. short.
    c. ahead.
    d. back.

5. The main advantage of a forward contract is that it
    a. is standardized, thereby reducing the cost of finding a counterparty.
    b. is default risk free since the contract is between the exchange and the investor.
    c. is flexible because it can be written any way the parties desire.
    d. both (a) and (b) are true.

6. At the expiration date of a futures contract, the price of the contract is
    a. equal to the price of the underlying asset to be delivered.
    b. equal to the price of the counterparty.
    c. equal to the hedge position.
    d. equal to the value of the hedged asset.

7. Futures markets have been successful and have grown rapidly because
    a. of standardization of the futures contract.
    b. of the ability to buy or sell the contract up to the maturity.
    c. of the reduced risk of default in the futures market.
    d. of all of the above.

8. When compared to forward contracts, financial futures have the advantage that
    a. they are standardized, making it more likely that different parties can be matched, thereby increasing liquidity in the market.
    b. they specify that more than one bond is eligible for delivery, to reduce the possibility that someone might corner the market and "squeeze" traders who have sold contracts.
    c. they cannot be traded at any time before the delivery date, thereby increasing liquidity in the market.
    d. all of the above are true.
    e. only (a) and (b) of the above are true.

9. Option premiums are increased when
    a. time to maturity increases.
    b. volatility is lower on the underlying asset.
    c. strike price is lower.
    d. both (b) and (c) are true.

10. An option that lets the holder buy an asset in the future is a
    a. put option.
    b. call option.
    c. swap.
    d. premium.

11. An option that lets the holder sell an asset in the future is a
    a. put option.
    b. call option.
    c. swap.
    d. premium.

12. The holder of an option
    a. limits his gains.
    b. limits his losses.
    c. limits both his gains and his losses.
    d. has no limits on his gains and losses.

13. An important tool for managing interest-rate risk that requires the exchange of payment streams on assets is a
    a. futures contract.
    b. forward contract.
    c. swap.
    d. micro hedge.

14. Which of the following is a disadvantage of the swap as a method for controlling interest-rate risk?
    a. Swaps, unlike forward contracts, are not subject to default risk.
    b. Swaps are more expensive than simply restructuring the balance sheet.
    c. Swaps, like forward contracts, lack liquidity.
    d. All of the above are disadvantages of swaps.
    e. Only (a) and (b) of the above are disadvantages of swaps.

15. Which of the following is an advantage of interest-rate swaps?
    a. Swaps lower interest-rate risk more cheaply than simply restructuring the balance sheet.
    b. Swaps, unlike forward contracts, are quite liquid.
    c. Swaps, unlike forward contracts, are not subject to default risk.
    d. All of the above are advantages of swaps.
    e. Only (a) and (b) of the above are advantages of swaps.

16. The principle of hedging risk involves offsetting a _____ position by taking an additional _____ position.
    a. risky; risk-free
    b. long; future
    c. short; long
    d. put; call
    e. risky; short

17. Arbitrage is best defined as
    a. the pricing of options.
    b. the pricing of futures.
    c. the elimination of riskless profit opportunities.
    d. the right to buy or sell a security.

18. At the expiration date of a futures contract, the price of the contract is _____ the price of the underlying asset to be delivered.

    a. the same as

    b. less than

    c. greater than

    d. unrelated to

19. A _____ hedges the interest-rate risk for a specific asset that a financial institution is holding.

    a. put

    b. stock

    c. micro hedge

    d. none of the above

20. If you want to hedge $4 million worth of Canada bonds, and if the contract size is $50,000, then how many bond futures contracts must you sell?

    a. 4000.

    b. 540.

    c. 400.

    d. 100.

    e. 80.

21. The likelihood that someone will corner a bond market, and therefore discourage futures contract trading, is reduced because

    a. the size of futures contracts is standardized.

    b. more than one bond is eligible for delivery in a futures contract.

    c. futures contracts can be traded before the delivery date.

    d. clearinghouses usually have margin requirements.

22. Financial futures options

    a. are more common than options on bonds.

    b. are not very common.

    c. are the same as stock options.

    d. only (a) and (c) of the above.

    e. none of the above.

23. A call option on a futures contract will be exercised if

    a. the strike price is below the premium.

    b. the option is "out of the money."

    c. the current futures contract price is below the strike price.

    d. it is profitable to exercise a put option on the same futures contract.

    e. none of the above.

24. Which of the following is an example of a long position?

    a. A bank purchases $10 million in mortgage-backed securities.

    b. A financial institution purchases financial futures put options.

    c. An investment bank sells 10 euros in the forward currency market.

    d. only (a) and (b) of the above.

    e. only (b) and (c) of the above.

25. As compared to financial futures contracts, options on financial futures contracts
    a. usually require delivery of the underlying financial asset.
    b. are usually subject to greater potential loss.
    c. can provide greater potential gains.
    d. only (a) and (c) of the above.
    e. none of the above.

26. If interest rates _____ in the future then you will profit if you sold a short futures contract.
    a. rise
    b. fall
    c. remain the same
    d. fluctuate

27. Which type of option gives the owner the right to sell a financial instrument at the exercise price within a specified period of time?
    a. A call option.
    b. A put option.
    c. A specified option.
    d. A European option.
    e. A class option.

28. At the expiration date of a futures contract, the price of the contract is _____ the price of the underlying assets to be delivered.
    a. the same as
    b. lower than
    c. higher than
    d. larger than or equal to

29. A call is said to be in the money when _____, and the net profit of exercising this call is _____.
    a. $C<X$; $C-\alpha$
    b. $C<X$; C
    c. $C>X$; $C-\alpha$
    d. $C>X$; C

30. Which of the following financial instruments is not considered a derivative financial instrument?
    a. Bonds.
    b. Interest-rate future contracts..
    c. Stock index options
    d. Swaps.

CHAPTER 15

Central Banks and the Bank of Canada

CHAPTER SYNOPSIS/COMPLETIONS

This chapter describes the goals and institutional structure of the Bank of Canada, the Federal Reserve, the European Central Bank, and other foreign central banks. Knowing the institutional structure of a central bank will help you to understand who controls the central bank, what motivates its behavior, and who holds the reigns of power within the central bank. A key feature of the institutional structure of a central bank is the degree to which it is independent of political pressures from government officials outside of the central bank. This chapter examines the advantages and disadvantages of central bank independence.

The overall responsibility for the operation of the Bank of Canada rests with a (1)_____ _____ _____ . The Board consists of fifteen members: the governor, the senior deputy governor, the deputy minister of finance, and twelve outside directors. The Board appoints the governor and senior deputy governor with the government's approval, for a renewable term of seven years. The outside directors are appointed by the minister of finance, with cabinet approval, for a three-year term and they are required to come from all regions of Canada representing a variety of occupations with the exception of banking.

The governor of the Bank is the chief executive officer and chairman of the Board of Directors. In 1994 the Board of Directors made some changes in the internal organization of the Bank. It established a new senior decision-making authority within the Bank, called the (2)_____ _____ . The Council is chaired by the governor and is composed of the senior deputy governor and the four deputy governors. Since this change, the Governing Council assumes responsibility for the Bank's policy. This system of 'collective responsibility' ensures that the governor of the Bank of Canada is not personally identified with the Bank's policy.

The European Central Bank (ECB) was created on January 1, 1999 and is based in Frankfurt, Germany. It is the central bank of the euro area, currently consisting of 12 countries. The Eurosystem is the term used to refer to the ECB and the 12 national banks of the countries that have adopted the euro. The European System of Central Banks is the term used to refer to the ECB, the 12 national banks of the countries that have adopted the euro, and the national central banks of the 3 European Union countries (Denmark, Sweden, and the United Kingdom) that have not yet adopted the euro.

Of all the central banks in the world, the Federal Reserve System in the United States has the most unusual structure, reflecting Americans' distrust of the concentration of power in banking. Although responsibility is formally shared across separate, cooperating entities, the Federal Reserve is fundamentally a hierarchical organization. At the top is the (3)_____ _____ _____—a group of seven members appointed to lengthy terms by the president of the United States and confirmed by the Senate. One member is chosen as chairman who serves a four-year term and may be reappointed. The chairman of the Board of Governors wields great power in Washington, D.C.

In the United States, monetary policy decisions are determined by a majority vote of the twelve-member Federal Open Market Committee or FOMC. The voting members of the committee consist of the seven members of the Board of Governors, the president of the Federal Reserve Bank of (4)_____ _____, and four presidents from other Federal Reserve banks.

While the Bank of Canada retains a relatively high degree of independence, it is not free from political pressure. Politicians need favourable economic conditions to help them win reelection, while lenders and the housing industry want low (5)_____ rates, and still other groups (such as those who have retired on fixed incomes) want low inflation. Given these pressures, the theory of (6)_____ behaviour suggests that the Bank of Canada will do best for itself by avoiding conflict with these groups.

A short survey of the structure and independence of the central banks in Canada, the United States, England, Japan, and the new European Central Bank indicates that we have been seeing a remarkable trend toward greater (7)_____. Both theory and evidence suggest that more independent central banks produce better monetary policy, thus providing an impetus for this trend. Good arguments have been made both for retaining the Bank of Canada's independence and for restricting it. The strongest argument to be made for an independent Bank of Canada rests on the belief that subjecting the Bank to more political pressure would impart an (8)_____ bias to monetary policy. However, critics of an independent central bank contend that it is (9)_____ to have monetary policy controlled by a group that is not directly responsive to the electorate. The jury is still out on how best to improve monetary policy (see Chapter 21 on recent research), but recognition that the Bank of Canada is subject to political and bureaucratic forces helps one to better understand current and past monetary policy and helps one to predict how the Bank of Canada will respond to future events.

HELPFUL HINTS

1.   Price stability is the most important goal of monetary policy. Central banks have successfully achieved price stability using monetary targeting, inflation targeting, dual mandates, and hierarchical mandates.

2.   The key point to understand about the institutional structure of the Bank of Canada and other central banks is how institutional structure relates to independence. Independent central banks are less likely to create excessive inflation and a *political business cycle*. On the other hand, an independent central bank is potentially less accountable for its policies. Worldwide there has been a greater movement toward central bank independence in recent years. As predicted by theory, greater central bank independence has been associated with lower inflation.

Exercises

Practice Problems

1.   The Bank of Canada (founded in 1934) is the federal government's fiscal agent and is responsible for monetary policy in the country. Match the Bank of Canada entity to its responsibilities and duties given on the left by placing the appropriate letter in the space provided.

Responsibilities and Duties	Bank of Canada Entity
_____ 1. *Monetary Policy Report*	a. Board of Directors
_____ 2. Overall operation of the Bank of Canada	
_____ 3. *Monetary Policy Report Update*	
_____ 4. Appointed by the Board of Directors of the Bank of Canada	
_____ 5. Serves a renewable 7-year term	b. Governor of the Bank of Canada
_____ 6. Chairman of the Board of Directors	
_____ 7. Appoints the Senior Deputy Governor	
_____ 8. Monetary policy	
_____ 9. Sets the operating band of the overnight rate	c. Governing Council

2.

a. List three arguments made by those who support a Bank of Canada that is independent of direct control from either the executive or legislative branches of government.

1. _____

2. _____

3. _____

b. List three arguments that favour a Bank of Canada that is brought under the control of the government.

1. _____

2. _____

3. _____

Short-Answer Questions

1.

a. What are the four functions of the Bank of Canada that are mentioned on the Bank's web page?

1. _____

2. _____

3. _____

4. _____

b. List the entities of the Federal Reserve System of the United States.

1. _____

2. _____

3. _____

4. _____

5. _____

2. What does it mean for a commercial bank to be a member of the Federal Reserve System?

    _____

    _____

3. In what ways can the President and Congress influence the Federal Reserve?

    _____

    _____

4. How did the Bank of Japan Law, which took effect in 1998, affect the independence of the Bank of Japan?

    _____

    _____

5. Do countries with greater central bank independence have higher unemployment or greater output fluctuations?

    _____

    _____

Critical-Thinking Questions

Suppose a Senator introduces a bill to Congress that would require the Federal Reserve to establish a single goal of low inflation.

1. How would passage of this bill affect the Fed's goal and instrument independence?

    _____

    _____

2. Would passage of this bill make the Fed more or less like the European Central Bank? Explain your answer.

    _____

    _____

3. Would passage of this bill make it more or less likely that the Fed would pursue policies that would lead to a political business cycle? Explain your answer.

    _____

    _____

SELF-TEST

True-False Questions

Circle whether the following statements are true (T) or false (F).

T   F   1.   The Bank of Canada was created by the Bank of Canada Act in 1934.

T   F   2.   The Bank of Canada is not responsible for monetary policy.

T   F   3.   Base money consists of currency in circulation and bank deposits.

T F 4. It would be accurate to say that the European Central Bank was modeled after the U.S. Federal Reserve System.

T F 5. In the United States, district Federal Reserve Banks essentially have no input regarding monetary policy decisions, since the Board of Governors has sole responsibility for monetary policy.

T F 6. Open-market operations, believe it or not, were not envisioned as a monetary policy tool when the Bank of Canada was created.

T F 7. The theory of bureaucratic behaviour may help explain why the Bank of Canada seems to be so preoccupied with the level of short-term interest rates.

T F 8. Although all 12 Federal Reserve Bank presidents attend the FOMC meetings, only those five presidents who have a vote actively participate in the deliberations.

T F 9. Placing the Bank of Canada under the control of the government may lead to a monetary policy that is more responsive to political pressures.

T F 10. Supporters of placing the Bank of Canada under control of the government believe that the electorate should have more control over monetary policy.

T F 11. A change in the monetary base has no impact on the money supply.

T F 12. Central banks' actions affect interest rates and the money supply, but have no effect on the aggregate output and inflation.

T F 13. The central bank goal of low inflation is directly linked to the objective of stable economic growth.

T F 14. An independent central bank is less likely to produce a political business cycle.

T F 15. A disadvantage of central bank independence is that it tends to result in higher inflation.

Multiple-Choice Questions

Circle the appropriate answer.

1. The main motivation for the formation of the Bank of Canada in 1934 was
   a. political.
   b. the need for Canada to reflect its growing political independence from Britain.
   c. the need for Canada to coordinate its international economic policy.
   d. all of the above.

2. The theory of bureaucratic behaviour indicates that
   a. government agencies attempt to increase their power and prestige.
   b. government agencies attempt to avoid conflicts with the legislative and executive branches of government.
   c. both (a) and (b) of the above are true.
   d. neither (a) nor (b) of the above are true.

3. Which of the following are entities of the Bank of Canada?
   a. The Board of Directors.
   b. The Governing Council.
   c. The Canada Deposit Insurance Corporation (CDIC).
   d. Both (a) and (b) of the above.

4. While the regional Federal Reserve Banks in the United States "establish" the discount rate, in truth, the discount rate is determined by

    a. Congress.

    b. the President of the United States.

    c. the Board of Governors.

    d. the Federal Reserve Advisory Council.

5. A majority of the Federal Open Market Committee is comprised of

    a. the 12 Federal Reserve Bank presidents.

    b. the five voting Federal Reserve Bank presidents.

    c. the seven members of the Board of Governors.

    d. none of the above.

6. Which of the following is an element of the Bank of Canada?

    a. The Office of the Superintendent of Financial Institutions Canada (OSFI).

    b. The Governing Council.

    c. The Federal Open Market Committee.

    d. The Federal Reserve Advisory Council.

7. Power within the U.S. Federal Reserve is essentially located in

    a. New York.

    b. Washington, D.C.

    c. Boston.

    d. San Francisco.

8. While the Fed enjoys a relatively high degree of independence for a government agency, it feels political pressure from the President and Congress because

    a. Fed members desire reappointment every 3 years.

    b. the Fed must go to Congress each year for operating revenues.

    c. Congress could limit Fed power through legislation.

    d. of all of the above.

    e. of only (b) and (c) of the above.

9. Which of the following functions are not performed by the Bank of Canada?

    a. Cheque clearing.

    b. Conducting economic research.

    c. Setting interest rates payable on time deposits.

    d. Issuing new currency.

10. Supporters of keeping the Bank of Canada independent from both the executive and legislative branches of government believe that a less independent Bank of Canada would

    a. pursue overly expansionary monetary policies.

    b. be more likely to pursue policies consistent with the political business cycle.

    c. ignore short-run problems in favour of longer-run concerns.

    d. do only (a) and (b) of the above.

11. In its role as the federal government's fiscal agent, the Bank of Canada provides debt management services for the federal government such as

    a. advising on federal government borrowings.

    b. managing new debt offerings by the federal government.

    c. servicing the federal government's outstanding debt.

    d. all of the above.

12. Although the Bank of Japan has new powers and greater autonomy under 1998 legislation, critics

    a. contend that the central bank's independence is limited because the Ministry of Finance has veto power over a portion of the bank's budget.

    b. contend that the central bank's independence is too great because the central bank need not pursue a policy of price stability even if that is the popular will of the people.

    c. contend that the central bank's independence is too great because the central bank can now ignore concerns of the Ministry of Finance since it no longer has veto power over the bank's budget.

    d. contend that the central bank's independence is limited because the Ministry of Finance retained the power to dismiss senior bank officials.

13. In its role as provider of banking services, the Bank of Canada

    a. serves as a lender of last resort if a deposit-taking institution faces a liquidity crisis.

    b. plays a central role in Canada's national payments system.

    c. is responsible for the government's operating accounts and for managing the government's foreign exchange reserves.

    d. all of the above.

14. Under the current "joint responsibility system,"

    a. the Bank of Canada and the minister of finance consult regularly.

    b. in the event of a serious policy conflict the minister of finance can issue a directive that the Bank of Canada must follow.

    c. the government accepts full responsibility for monetary policy.

    d. the Bank of Canada has considerable autonomy in the conduct of day-to-day monetary policy.

    e. all of the above.

15. The ability of a central bank to set reserve requirements is an example of

    a. goal independence.

    b. the theory of bureaucratic behaviour.

    c. independent review.

    d. instrument independence.

    e. the public interest view.

16. Which of the following statements concerning the 14-year term for members of the Board of Governors is *false*?

    a. The 14-year term is nonrenewable.

    b. The 14-year term allows great independence from political considerations.

    c. Most governors serve out the entire 14-year term.

    d. The President of the United States appoints governors to a 14-year term.

17. Which of the following are entities of the Eurosystem?
    a. The European Central Bank.
    b. The Executive Board of the European Central Bank.
    c. The Governing Council of the European Central Bank.
    d. All of the above.

18. Which of the following is an example of the U.S. Fed becoming more transparent?
    a. Since 1994, the results of the FOMC meetings are immediately released.
    b. The Board of Governors does not release its "blue" and "green" books.
    c. The Chairman of the Board of Governors is appointed to a 4-year term.
    d. All of the above.
    e. None of the above.

19. A political business cycle is _____ likely to be caused by a more independent central bank as compared to a less independent central bank.
    a. less
    b. more
    c. just as
    d. none of the above

20. The principal-agent problem is _____ for an independent Bank of Canada than for politicians, because it has _____ incentives to act against the interests of the public.
    a. greater; more
    b. less; more
    c. greater; fewer
    d. less; fewer

21. Worldwide data show that a more independent central bank leads to
    a. a higher inflation rate.
    b. a higher unemployment rate.
    c. greater output fluctuations.
    d. none of the above.

22. Central banks' actions are capable of affecting _____.
    a. money supply
    b. interest rates
    c. the amount of credit
    d. all of the above

23. During the Great Depression, from 1929 to 1933, Canadian real GDP fell by almost _____ and the unemployment rate increased _____.
    a. 5%; twofold
    b. 30%; twofold
    c. 5%; sevenfold
    d. 30%; sevenfold

24. The president of the Federal Reserve Bank of _____ is the only permanent member of the FOMC among the Federal Reserve bank presidents.
    a. Chicago
    b. San Francisco
    c. New York
    d. Atlanta

25. The Bank of England has _____ goal independence as the Bank of Canada, but _____ goal independence than the Fed.
    a. the same; less
    b. the same; more
    c. less; less
    d. more; more

26. Political business cycle means that just before an election, _____ policies are pursued to _____ the unemployment rate and interest rates.
    a. expansionary; raise
    b. contractionary; lower
    c. expansionary; lower
    d. monetary; control

27. _____ determines monetary policy, and the responsibility for policy rests with _____.
    a. The Bank of Canada; the government
    b. The Bank of Canada; the Bank of Canada
    c. The government; the Bank of Canada
    d. The government; the government

28. The ultimate goal of the Bank of Canada is to
    a. keep the unemployment rate low.
    b. control the money supply.
    c. keep inflation low.
    d. both (a) and (c) of the above.

29. Recent research shows that inflation performance is the best for countries with the _____ independent central banks, and these countries are _____ likely to have high unemployment.
    a. least; less
    b. least; no more
    c. most; less
    d. most; no more

30. The overall responsibility for the operation of the Bank of Canada rests with the_____, which consists of _____ members.
    a. Board of Directors; 15
    b. Board of Directors; 17
    c. Governing Council; 15
    d. Governing Council; 17

CHAPTER 16

The Money Supply Process

CHAPTER SYNOPSIS/COMPLETIONS

This chapter describes the money supply process. Bank deposits are by far the largest component of the money supply. This chapter begins by showing how banks create deposits and how deposit creation affects the money supply. It then derives the *money multiplier*. After deriving a more realistic money multiplier, this chapter describes the sources of movement in the monetary base, the money multiplier, and the money supply.

The money supply process involves three players: the central bank (the Bank of Canada), banks (depository institutions), and depositors. Of these three players, the central bank—the Bank of Canada—is the most important.

The simplified Bank of Canada balance sheet is as follows:

Bank of Canada

Assets	Liabilities
Government securities	Notes in circulation
Advances to banks	Reserves

The sum of the Bank of Canada's liabilities, currency in circulation (*C*) plus (1) _____ (*R*) is called the (2) _____ _____ (*MB*). Reserves equal *desired reserves* plus *excess reserves*. The ratio of desired reserves to deposits is called the *desired reserve ratio* (*r*). The desired reserve ratio is established by the commercial banks and plays an important role in the deposit creation process.

The Bank of Canada exercises control over the monetary base through its buying and selling of securities on the open market, called (3) _____ _____ _____ through its extension of advances to banks. The Bank of Canada has more (but not complete) control over the total of the monetary base than the components of the monetary base (currency and reserves). Actions by the nonbank public can change the mix of currency and reserves in the monetary base, but those actions leave the total monetary base unchanged. When the Bank of Canada conducts an *open market purchase* of a $100 bond from a bank, reserves, and therefore the monetary base, increase by $100. When the Bank of Canada conducts an open market purchase of a $100 bond from the nonbank public, the monetary base again increases by $100. But the increases could take the form of an increase in reserves if the nonbank public deposits the proceeds of the sale into a chequing account, or it could take the form of an increase in currency in circulation if the nonbank public decides to hold the proceeds of the sale in currency. Obviously some intermediate case is possible as well; the nonbank public can hold some currency and some deposits.

The main point is that the Bank of Canada is able to precisely increase the monetary base by $100, but actions by the nonbank public, not the Bank of Canada, determine the mix of reserves and currency in circulation. When the Bank of Canada makes a $100 advance to a bank, the monetary base increases by $100. When a bank pays off a $100 advance from the Bank of Canada, the monetary base decreases by $100. The interest rate that the Bank of Canada charges on advances is called the (4) _____ _____ .

Two sources of change in the monetary base that are outside of the Bank of Canada's control are Government of Canada deposits at the Bank of Canada and *float*. Float occurs when the Bank of Canada clears cheques. The Bank of Canada often credits the account of the bank presenting the cheque for payment before it debits the account of the bank that the cheque is drawn on. For that brief period of time before the debit occurs, reserves in the banking system rise. Government of Canada deposits and float complicate but do not prevent the Bank of Canada from accurately controlling the monetary base.

The Bank of Canada does not have complete control over the monetary base because banks decide when they want to borrow from the Bank of Canada at the Bank rate. Bank borrowing from the Bank of Canada is called (5) _____ _____ (*BR*). If we subtract borrowed reserves (*BR*) from the monetary base we get the (6) _____ _____ _____ (*MB_n*). The nonborrowed monetary base is directly under the control of the Bank of Canada and is affected only by open market operations.

In order to derive the *simple deposit multiplier*, we assume that banks hold no excess reserves (they loan them out as soon as they get them) and the nonbank public holds no currency (only deposits). To illustrate how the deposit multiplier works, suppose the Bank of Canada makes an open market purchase of $100 bond from First National Bank. First National Bank will loan out that extra $100 in reserves by creating a $100 chequing account deposit for the borrower. By creating that chequing account balance, First National Bank has created $100 of new money and the money supply, which includes chequing account balances, has increased by $100. This "creation" of money by the bank is key to understanding the *multiple deposit creation* process. But the creation of money does not stop with First National Bank's creation of a deposit. Presumably, the borrower of the $100 will spend that money and, by doing so, that money will work its way into some other bank account (the bank account of the store owner where the purchase was made). Assuming that the store owner banks at Bank A, Bank A will now find itself with $100 in new deposits, and assuming the required reserve ratio is 10%, Bank A will keep $10 of that $100 deposit in reserves and loan out the remaining $90 to a new borrower. As was the case with the First National Bank, Bank A will make the loan by creating a chequing account deposit for the borrower. Thus, at this stage of the process, Bank A has created an additional $90 of money. That $90 gets spent and the process continues. At the next stage, Bank B will receive a $90 deposit and it will keep 10% or $9 in required reserves and loan out the remaining $81. Thus, Bank B creates $81 of new money. This process continues with Banks C, D, and E creating money each time they lend the excess reserves. Once this process is complete, the total amount of deposits (and therefore money) that will have been created by the banking system will be $1000. In general, the relationship between the initial change in reserves and the total change in deposits in this simple example is given by the simple deposit multiplier $\Delta D = (1/r) \times \Delta R$, where ΔR is the initial change in reserves, r is the required reserve–deposit ratio and ΔD is the total change in deposits by the banking system. Although this formula is helpful for understanding the multiple deposit creation process, the actual creation of deposits is much less mechanical than the simple model indicates. If some of the proceeds from loans are held as currency, or if banks choose to hold all or some of their excess reserves, the money supply will not increase by as much as the simple model of multiple deposit creation tells us.

The money supply is positively related to the *nonborrowed monetary base* (*MB_n*) as well as the level of *borrowed reserves* (*BR*) from the Bank of Canada. The money supply is negatively related to the required reserve ratio *r*. The money supply is negatively related to currency holdings as well as the amount of excess reserves.

Three players—the Bank of Canada, depositors, and banks—directly influence the money supply. The Bank of Canada influences the money supply by controlling *borrowed reserves*, the *nonborrowed monetary base,* and the required reserve ratio, *r*. Depositors influence the money supply through their decisions about currency holdings, and banks influence the money supply with their decisions about excess reserves. Depositors' behaviour also influences bankers' decisions to hold excess reserves.

The relationship between the monetary base and the money supply is $M = m \times MB$, where *m* denotes the money multiplier. The monetary base is also called (7) _____ _____ _____ because a $1 change in the monetary base leads to a more than $1 change in the money supply. The size of the money multiplier, *m*, is negatively related to the *desired reserve ratio*, *r*. The money multiplier is also negatively related to the *currency ratio*, *c*, which equals the ratio of the publics' holdings of currency to deposits (*C/D*) and the *excess reserves ratio*, *e*, which equals ratio of excess reserves held by banks to deposits (*ER/D*). The formula for the money multiplier is $m = (1 + c)/(r + e + c)$. An important difference between the money multiplier and the deposit multiplier is that the money multiplier is smaller because it is multiplying the monetary base, not just deposits. Although there is multiple expansion of deposits, there is no such expansion for currency. When *e* is small, as is typically the case, changes in *e* have a small impact on the money supply and the multiplier. However, during both the subprime financial crisis and the Great Depression, *e* was much larger and its movements had a substantial effect on the money supply and the money multiplier.

HELPFUL HINTS

1. The monetary base is the sum of the two Bank of Canada liabilities: reserves and currency in circulation. The two primary ways that the Bank of Canada causes changes in the monetary base are through open-market operations and Bank lending. The Bank of Canada has more precise control over the monetary base than the mix of reserves and currency. The mix of currency and reserves is determined by the nonbank public. The key to understanding the deposit multiplier is to understand that when a bank makes a loan, it creates a deposit, which is part of the money supply. The money multiplier tells us what multiple of the monetary base is transformed into the money supply. Anything that reduces the amount of loans that banks make reduces the size of the multiplier and therefore the money supply. Increases in *r*, *e*, or *c* reduce the quantity of funds that banks have available to lend, which reduces the size of the multiplier and the money supply.

EXERCISES

Practice Problems

1.

a. Fill in the entries in the following T-accounts when the Bank of Canada sells $100 000 of T-bills to First Bank.

First Bank		**The Bank of Canada**	
Assets	**Liabilities**	**Assets**	**Liabilities**

What has happened to reserves in the banking system? _____

b. If, instead, First Bank pays off a $100 000 Bank of Canada advance, what will be the entries in the T-accounts below?

First Bank		**The Bank of Canada**	
Assets	**Liabilities**	**Assets**	**Liabilities**

What has happened to reserves in the banking system? _____

2.

a. Assume that the desired reserve ratio is 0.20 and that the Bank of Canada purchases $1000 in government bonds from the First Bank of Toronto, which, in turn, lends the $1000 of reserves it has just acquired to a customer for the purchase of a used car. If the used car dealer deposits the proceeds from the sale in Bank A, how much in additional loans can Bank A make?

_____

_____

b. Suppose that this loan is used to purchase a computer, and that the computer store deposits the proceeds into Bank B. What has been the total change in chequable deposits at Bank A?

_____

_____

c. Assume a similar process occurs for Bank B, Bank C, and Bank D. Complete the following table for these banks (see Table 16-1 in the text for an example) and the totals for all banks.

Bank	Change in Deposits	Change in Loans	Change in Reserves
First Bank of Toronto	+$0.00	+$1000.00	+$0.00
A	+1000.00	+800.00	+200.00
B	+800.00	+640.00	+160.00
C	_____	_____	_____
D	_____	_____	_____
•	•	•	•
•	•	•	•
•	•	•	•
Total All Banks	_____	_____	_____

3.

a. Write down the formula for the simple deposit multiplier.

_____

b. Assuming that the desired reserve ratio is 0.20, what is the change in reserves when the Bank of Canada sells $10 billion of government bonds and extends advances of $5 billion to commercial banks?

_____

c. Using the simple deposit multiplier formula, calculate the resulting change in chequable deposits.

_____

4. The Bank of Canada can cause changes in the monetary base through open market operations. Suppose the Bank of Canada purchases $5000 of bonds from a bank and there is no change in currency circulation.

a. What happens to the T-account for the banking system?

_____

_____

b. What happens to the T-account for the Bank of Canada?

_____

_____

c.   What is the net result of the open market purchase?

_____

_____

5. a.   Write the formula for the money multiplier.

_____

    b.   Calculate the currency ratio and the money multiplier for the following numbers:

        $r = 0.10$ $C = \$280$ billion

        $D = \$800$ billion $ER = \$40$ billion

        $c =$ _____

        $m =$ _____

    c.   Calculate desired reserves (DR), total reserves (R), and the monetary base (MB).

        $DR = \$$_____

        $R\ \ = \$$_____

        $MB = \$$_____

    d.   Calculate the new money multiplier and money supply assuming that banks lower the desired required reserve ratio on chequable deposits to 0.08. Assume that c remains unchanged.

        $m =$ _____

        $M = \$$_____

    e.   Calculate the new level of deposits (D) and currency in circulation (C).

        $D = \$$_____

        $C = \$$_____

    f.   Calculate the new level of desired reserves (DR) and excess reserves (ER).

        $DR = \$$_____

        $ER = \$$_____

6.

a. Given the following values, calculate the money multiplier and the money supply:

        $r = 0.10$ $c = 0.40$

        $ER = 0$ $MB_n = \$400$ billion

        $m =$ _____

        $M = \$$_____

b. Calculate the level of currency (C), the level of deposits (D), the level of desired reserves (DR), and the level of total reserves (R) in the banking system.

$C = \$$_____ $DR = \$$_____

$D = \$$_____ $R = \$$_____

c. Suppose that bankers suddenly increase the desired reserve ratio to 0.16. Calculate the new money multiplier, the new money supply, the level of deposits, currency in circulation, and the amount of desired reserves that banks will now hold.

$m =$ _____

$M = \$$_____

$D = \$$_____

$C = \$$_____

$DR = \$$_____

Short-Answer Questions

1. List the three players in the money supply process. Which of these players is most important?

_____

_____

2. Use the simple deposit multiplier to show what would happen to total deposits in the banking system as a result of a $100 open market purchase by the Federal Reserve. Assume that the banking system holds no excess reserves, the nonbank public holds no currency, and the required reserve deposit ratio is 10%.

_____

_____

3. How does an increase in the monetary base that arises from an increase in currency affect the overall money supply compared to an increase in the monetary base that arises from an increase in reserves?

_____

_____

4. How does an increase in currency holdings affect the money multiplier and the money supply?

_____

_____

5. Why is it important to distinguish between the nonborrowed monetary base and borrowed reserves?

_____

_____

Critical-Thinking Questions

Back in the 1950s, economist Milton Friedman proposed setting the required reserve ratio equal to 100%.

1. What would the value of the multiplier be under Friedman's proposal?

_____

2. Describe the roles of banks, depositors, and the Fed in controlling the money supply under Friedman's proposal.

_____

3. Compare the Bank of Canada's ability to control the money supply under Friedman's proposal to the current situation in which reserve requirements are much lower.

_____

4. How would Friedman's proposal change the nature of banking?

_____

SELF-TEST

True-False Questions

Circle whether the following statements are true (T) or false (F).

T   F   1. Currency held by depository institutions (banks) is added to currency circulating in the hands of the public to get total currency in circulation.

T   F   2.. If the First Security Bank of Calgary has $50 in excess reserves, it will be able to lend more than an additional $50 as long as the desired reserve ratio is below 100%.

T   F   3. Assuming that the desired reserve ratio is 20%, an open market sale of $100 in government bonds by the Bank of Canada will cause chequable deposits to fall by $500 in the simple deposit expansion model.

T   F   4. When a bank chooses to purchase securities instead of making loans, deposit expansion is diminished.

T   F   5. In the simple model, deposits in the banking system contract by a multiple of the loss in reserves caused by a Bank of Canada sale of government bonds.

T   F   6. Whether a bank chooses to use its excess reserves to make loans or to purchase securities, the effect on deposit expansion is the same.

T   F   7. The effect of open market operations on the monetary base is much more certain than its effect on reserves.

T   F   8. The ratio that relates the change in the money supply to a given change in the monetary base is called the money multiplier.

T   F   9. Another name for the nonborrowed base is high-powered money.

T   F   10. The banking system's desired reserve ratio is negatively related to the market interest rate.

T   F   11. The desired reserve ratio is negatively related to expected deposit outflows.

T   F   12. When individuals reduce their holdings of currency by depositing these funds in their bank accounts, the money multiplier increases.

T   F   13. As the currency ratio falls, fewer reserves are available to support chequable deposits causing a decrease in the money supply.

T   F   14. The money multiplier from the money supply model that includes depositor and bank behaviour is larger than the simple deposit multiplier.

T   F   15. The money multiplier and the money supply are positively related to the currency ratio.

Multiple-Choice Questions

Circle the appropriate answer.

1. The monetary base is comprised of
    a. currency in circulation and Bank of Canada notes.
    b. currency in circulation and government securities.
    c. currency in circulation and reserves.
    d. reserves and government securities.

2. When the Bank of Canada simultaneously purchases government bonds and extends advances to banks,
    a. chequable deposits unambiguously fall.
    b. chequable deposits unambiguously rise.
    c. the net effect on chequable deposits cannot be determined because the two Bank of Canada actions counteract each other.
    d. the Bank of Canada action has no effect on chequable deposits.

3. When the Bank of Canada wants to reduce reserves in the banking system, it will
    a. purchase government bonds.
    b. extend advances to banks.
    c. print more currency.
    d. sell government bonds.

4. The First Bank of London has $150 in excess reserves. If the desired reserve ratio is 10%, how much extra can the First Bank lend?
    a. $1500.
    b. $750.
    c. $150.
    d. $0.

5. A sale of government bonds by the Bank of Canada
    a. is called an open market sale.
    b. reduces the monetary base, all else the same.
    c. increases currency in circulation, all else the same.
    d. does all of the above.
    e. does only (a) and (b) of the above.

6. Which of the following are found on the asset side of the Bank of Canada's balance sheet?
    a. Government securities.
    b. Government deposits.
    c. Advances to banks.
    d. Only (a) and (c) of the above.

7. When float increases,
    a. currency in circulation falls.
    b. the monetary base falls.
    c. the monetary base rises.
    d. the monetary supply falls.

8. Commercial banks create money whenever they
   a. issue loans.
   b. buy government securities.
   c. create chequable deposits.
   d. only (a) and (b) of the above.
   e. only (a) and (c) of the above.

9. If banks hold excess reserves, then the simple deposit multiplier _____ the impact of an increase in reserves on the increase in chequable deposits.
   a. overstates
   b. understates
   c. is unrelated to
   d. perfectly describes

10. When the Bank of Canada issues advances to banks, Bank assets _____ and the monetary base _____.
    a. rise; rises
    b. fall; rises
    c. rise; falls
    d. fall; falls

11. All else the same, the monetary base, also known as high-powered money, will fall when the Bank of Canada
    a. increases bank reserves.
    b. decreases currency in circulation.
    c. increases the amount of government securities that it holds.
    d. decreases the desired reserve ratio.
    e. only (b) and (d) of the above.

12. Suppose that Mary deposits $60 in cash into her chequing account at Redwood Bank and that the desired reserve ratio is 5%. If no excess reserves are held by the banking sector or cash withdrawn by the public, then which of the following statements is *false*?
    a. Vault cash at Redwood Bank rises by $60.
    b. Redwood Bank will be able to increase loans by $54.
    c. The value of the simple deposit multiplier is 20.
    d. The change in total chequable deposits in the banking system will be $1200.

13. If Ernie writes Beth a cheque for $30, and if Beth deposits the cheque and immediately withdraws $20 in cash, then which of the following statements is true if the desired reserve ratio is 10%?
    a. The total increase in chequable deposits in the banking sector will be $300.
    b. The total increase in chequable deposits in the banking sector will be $100.
    c. The total decrease in chequable deposits in the banking sector will be $300.
    d. The total decrease in chequable deposits in the banking sector will be $200.

14. If the simple deposit multiplier is equal to one, then the desired reserve ratio is equal to
    a. 1%.
    b. 10%.
    c. 50%.
    d. 100%.

15. A bank can only lend as much as its excess reserves because
    a. the Bank of Canada will refuse to release these reserves to other banks.
    b. the bank will lose reserves when deposits find their way to other banks.
    c. both (a) and (b) of the above.
    d. neither (a) nor (b) of the above.

16. Canadian banks are required to hold _____ of their deposits as reserves.
    a. 4%
    b. 6%
    c. 10%
    d. none of the above.

17. Which of the following statements is true?
    a. When the Bank of Canada purchases or sells foreign currency deposits, the monetary base will change.
    b. An open market operation has a more certain effect on the monetary base than on reserves.
    c. When the desired reserve ratio is less than 100%, even a single bank can create a multiplier expansion of deposits.
    d. Both (a) and (b) of the above.

18. The effect of an open market purchase on the monetary base
    a. depends on whether the seller of the bonds keeps the proceeds from the sale in currency or in deposits.
    b. depends on whether the seller of the bonds keeps the proceeds from the sale in currency.
    c. depends on whether the seller of the bonds keeps the proceeds from the sale in deposits.
    d. is always the same whether the seller of the bonds keeps the proceeds from the sale in currency or in deposits.

19. For the banking system as a whole, deposits creation will stop only when
    a. the total amount of desired reserves is greater than the reserve ratio.
    b. the total amount of desired reserves equals the Bank's liabilities.
    c. the total amount of desired reserves equals the total amount of reserves.
    d. the total amount of desired reserves is greater than the Bank's liabilities.

20. The money multiplier increases in value as the
    a. currency ratio increases.
    b. desired reserve ratio increases.
    c. desired reserve ratio decreases.
    d. monetary base increases.

21. The Bank of Canada lacks complete control over the monetary base because
    a. it cannot set the desired reserve ratio on chequable deposits.
    b. it cannot perfectly predict the amount of borrowing by banks.
    c. it cannot perfectly predict shifts from deposits to currency.
    d. of each of the above.
    e. of only (a) and (b) of the above.

22. The money multiplier is negatively related to
    a. the desired reserve ratio on chequable deposits.
    b. the currency ratio.
    c. the currency ratio and the desired reserve ratio.
    d. all of the above.
    e. only (a) and (b) of the above.

23. For a given level of the monetary base, a drop in the desired reserve ratio means
    a. an increase in the money supply.
    b. an increase in the monetary base.
    c. an increase in the nonborrowed base.
    d. all of the above.

24. For a given level of the monetary base, a drop in the currency ratio means
    a. an increase in the nonborrowed base, but a decrease in the borrowed base of equal magnitude.
    b. an increase in the borrowed base, but a decrease in the nonborrowed base of equal magnitude.
    c. an increase in the money supply.
    d. a decrease in the money supply.

25. If banks reduce their holdings of reserves,
    a. the monetary base will increase.
    b. the money supply will increase.
    c. both (a) and (b) of the above will occur.
    d. neither (a) nor (b) of the above will occur.

26. The monetary base less advances to banks is called
    a. reserves.
    b. high-powered money.
    c. the nonborrowed monetary base.
    d. the borrowed monetary base.

27. If the desired reserve ratio is one-fourth, currency in circulation is $400 billion, excess reserves are not held, and chequable deposits are $1200 billion, then the money multiplier is approximately
    a. 2.3.
    b. 2.8.
    c. 2.0.
    d. 1.8.

28. All else the same, which of the following will lead to a decrease in bank reserves?
    a. An increase in the desired reserve ratio.
    b. An increase in the money supply.
    c. An increase in the currency ratio.
    d. An increase in the monetary base.

29. If the desired reserve ratio is 0.03, currency in circulation is $600 billion, chequable deposits is $700 billion, and excess reserves is $1 billion, then the money multiplier is equal to
    a. 3.09.
    b. 3.29.
    c. 2.29.
    d. 2.09.

30. If the desired reserve ratio is 0.10, currency in circulation is $1000 billion, chequable deposits is $500 billion, and total reserves is $80 billion, then the excess reserves ratio is
    a. 0.10.
    b. 0.09.
    c. 0.06.
    d. 0.04.

CHAPTER 17

Tools of Monetary Policy

CHAPTER SYNOPSIS/COMPLETIONS

The Bank of Canada uses three tools to manipulate the money supply and interest rates: open market operations, government (1)_____ _____, and (2)_____ to banks. This chapter looks at how the Bank of Canada uses these tools to influence the market for reserves and the overnight interest rate. The (3) _____ _____ is the interest rate that banks charge each other for overnight loans. The chapter ends with a discussion of the tools of monetary policy used by central banks other than the Bank of Canada.

Currently, the Bank of Canada implements monetary policy by changing the overnight interest rate. In fact, the Bank's operational objective is to keep the overnight rate within a band of 50 basis points. The upper limit of the operating band for the overnight interest rate defines the bank rate and the lower limit is the rate that the Bank pays LVTS participants with positive settlement balances at the end of the day.

Since December 2000, the Bank has operated under a system of eight "fixed" dates throughout the year for announcing any changes to the operating band for the overnight rate, keeping the option of acting between the fixed dates in "extraordinary circumstances."

By far the most important monetary policy tool at the Bank of Canada's disposal is its ability to buy and sell government (4)_____. Open market operations is the Bank's most important monetary policy tool, because it is the primary determinant of changes in reserves. There are two types of open market operations. Open market operations designed to change the level of settlement balances in an effort to influence economic activity are called (5)_____ open market operations. Defensive open market operations are intended to offset movements in other factors that affect the monetary base, such as changes in government deposits and float.

Most of the time, the Bank of Canada engages in repurchase agreements (repos) or reverse repurchase agreements (reverse repos). A repo is actually a temporary open market (6)_____ that will be reversed within a few days, and it is often argued to be an especially effective way of conducting defensive open market operations. Matched sale-purchase transactions or (7)_____ _____ are used when the Bank of Canada wants to temporarily drain reserves from the banking system.

Open market operations have several advantages over the other tools of the Bank of Canada that make them particularly desirable:

1. Open market operations occur at the initiative of the Bank. The Bank has complete control over the volume of open market operations, giving it control over the overnight funds interest rate.

2. Open market operations can be varied in any degree. Thus, open market operations are said to be (8)_____.

3. Open market operations are easily reversed.

4. Open market operations can be implemented quickly.

HELPFUL HINTS

The overnight rate is determined by the demand and supply for reserves. The key to understanding how the Bank of Canada's monetary policy tools affect the overnight rate is to understand how those tools affect the demand and supply for reserves. The Bank of Canada mostly uses open market operations to manipulate nonborrowed reserves in order to target the federal funds rate. The discount rate serves as an upper limit on the federal funds rate and allows the Bank of Canada to serve its role as lender of last resort. The interest rate the Bank of Canada pays on reserves serves as a lower bound on the bank rate.

EXERCISES

Practice Problems

1.
a. Why are open market operations the most important monetary policy tool?

_____

_____

b. What are the two types of open market operations?

   1. _____

   2. _____

c. List the advantages of open market operations.

   1. _____

   2. _____

   3. _____

   4. _____

2.
a. List the two types of Bank of Canada loans.

   1. _____

   2. _____

b. Why might it be important to have a lender of last resort even with the existence of deposit insurance?

_____

_____

3. One noticeable change in monetary policy is that many central banks have recently reduced or eliminated reserve requirements. This reduces the "tax" that banks implicitly pay because reserves do not pay interest. The reduction of reserve requirements makes banks more competitive with other financial institutions when trying to attract funds. List two reasons why changes in reserve requirements are rarely used as a policy tool to conduct monetary policy in those countries that still require banks to hold reserves against their deposit liabilities.

a. _____

b. _____

Short-Answer Questions

1. What monetary policy tool does the Bank of Canada use to control the amount of nonborrowed reserves?

    _____

    _____

2. What are the advantages of open market operations?

    _____

    _____

3.. What are the advantages and disadvantages of the Bank of Canada's lending policy?

    _____

    _____

4. What is the Eurosystem's equivalent of the Bank of Canada's discount rate?

    _____

    _____

Critical-Thinking Questions

Use the demand and supply diagram for reserves to illustrate and explain how the Bank of Canada limits the fluctuations in the overnight rate using its current policy with regard to the bank rate and the rate it pays on reserves.

_____

_____

_____

_____

SELF-TEST

True-False Questions

Circle whether the following statements are true (T) or false (F).

T   F   1. Open market operations are the most important monetary policy tool because they are the most important determinant of changes in the money multiplier, which is the main source of fluctuations in the money supply.

T   F   2. Open market buyback operations by the Bank of Canada are intended to change the level of reserves and the monetary base in an effort to influence economic activity.

T   F   3. When the Bank of Canada purchases or sells a security in the open market, it is most likely trading in Canada bonds.

T   F   4. The Bank of Canada has less than complete control over the volume of open market operations because banks can refuse to buy Canada securities.

T   F   5. Because banks in agricultural areas experience greater demands for funds in the spring, the Bank of Canada issues adjustment credit to these banks when they have deficient reserves.

T   F   6. Central banks in many countries have recently reduced or eliminated reserve requirements.

T   F   7. The Bank of Canada's role of lender of last resort may still be useful even though deposit insurance has reduced the probability of bank panics.

T   F   8. Banks view Bank of Canada lending as a substitute for borrowing overnight funds.

T   F   9. Open market operations are usually carried out once a month.

T   F   10. When the overnight interest rate rises, the quantity of excess reserves demanded falls.

T   F   11. If the quantity of reserves demanded is larger than the quantity supplied by the Bank of Canada, the equilibrium overnight interest rate will be higher than the bank rate.

T   F   12. SPRAs and SRAs are introduced to reduce the undesired downward and upward pressures, respectively, on the overnight rate.

T   F   13. The open market purchases expand both the bank reserves and the monetary base, thereby lowering short-term interest rates and raising the money supply.

T   F   14. If the overnight rate increases towards the upper limit of the operating band, then the Bank will lend at the bank rate to put a ceiling on the overnight rate.

T   F   15. The European Central Bank has no reserve requirements.

Multiple-Choice Questions

Circle the appropriate answer.

1. Open market operations are of two types:
    a. defensive and offensive.
    b. dynamic and reactionary.
    c. actionary and passive.
    d. dynamic and defensive.

2. If the Bank of Canada wants to inject reserves into the banking system, it will usually
    a. purchase government securities.
    b. raise the bank rate.
    c. sell government securities.
    d. lower reserve requirements.
    e. do either (a) or (b) of the above.

3. To temporarily raise reserves in the banking system, the Bank of Canada engages in
    a. a repurchase agreement.
    b. a reverse repo.
    c. a matched sale-purchase transaction.
    d. none of the above.

4. When float increases, causing a temporary increase in reserves in the banking system, the Bank of Canada can offset the effects of float by engaging in
    a. a repurchase agreement.
    b. an interest rate swap.
    c. a matched sale-purchase transaction.
    d. none of the above.

5. The bank rate is the rate at which
    a. the Bank of Canada lends funds to financial institutions.
    b. banks lend funds to their best customers.
    c. banks borrow overnight funds in the interbank market.
    d. none of the above.

6. The interest rate at which the Bank of Canada lends to participating financial institutions is called
    a. prime rate.
    b. overnight rate.
    c. bank rate.
    d. deposit rate.

7. A reduction in desired reserves causes the money supply to rise, since the change causes
    a. the money multiplier to fall.
    b. the money multiplier to rise.
    c. reserves to fall.
    d. reserves to rise.

8. The lower limit of the operating band for the overnight interest rate defines
    a. the bank rate.
    b. the prime rate.
    c. the rate the Bank of Canada pays LVTS participants with positive settlement balances at the end of the banking day.
    d. the rate the Bank of Canada charges LVTS participants with negative settlement balances at the end of the banking day.

9. When the Bank of Canada engages in a sale and repurchase agreement, it _____ securities that the other party agrees to _____ back within a few days.
    a. buys; buy
    b. buys; sell
    c. sells; buy
    d. sells; sell

10. When the Bank of Canada wants to conduct a _____ open market _____, it engages in a _____.
    a. permanent; purchase; reverse repo
    b. permanent; purchase; repurchase agreement
    c. temporary; sale; reverse repo
    d. temporary; sale; repurchase agreement
    e. temporary; purchase; reverse repo

11. If the operating band for the overnight interest rate is from 3.5 to 4.0 percent, then
    a. the bank rate is 4.0 percent.
    b. the bank rate is the upper limit of the operating band.
    c. the bank rate is the rate the Bank of Canada charges LVTS participants with negative settlement balances at the end of the banking day.
    d. all of the above.

12. If either government deposits or foreign deposits at the Bank of Canada are predicted to _____, a _____ open market _____ would be needed to offset the expected decrease in the monetary base.
    a. rise; dynamic; purchase
    b. fall; dynamic; sale
    c. rise; defensive; purchase
    d. fall; defensive; purchase

13. The operating band for the overnight interest rate

    a. is 50 basis points wide.

    b. defines the rate of interest the Bank of Canada charges LVTS participants with negative settlement balances at the end of the banking day.

    c. defines the rate of interest the Bank of Canada pays LVTS participants with positive settlement balances at the end of the banking day.

    d. all of the above.

    e. only (a) and (b) of the above.

14. When the Bank of Canada lowers the operating band for the overnight interest rate, it

    a. lowers the bank rate by the same amount.

    b. encourages LVTS participants to borrow reserves either from each other or from the Bank of Canada.

    c. reduces the monetary base and ultimately the money supply.

    d. all of the above.

    e. only (a) and (b) of the above.

15. The overnight interest rate

    a. is the shortest-term rate available.

    b. forms the base of any term structure of interest rates relation.

    c. is the rate of interest the Bank of Canada charges LVTS participants with negative settlement balances at the end of the banking day.

    d. only (a) and (b) of the above.

16. The overnight market in Canada is

    a. the key market for finance and monetary policy.

    b. the market where the bank rate is determined.

    c. the market where banks borrow overnight funds from each other.

    d. only (a) and (c) of the above.

17. If the Bank of Canada wanted to lower the overnight funds rate, then it would

    a. lower the required reserve ratio.

    b. increase the bank rate.

    c. conduct an open market sale of securities.

    d. lower the operating band.

18. The trading desk at the Federal Reserve Bank of New York contacts primary dealers

    a. in order to learn how dealers view the securities markets.

    b. when the Fed wants to sell government securities.

    c. to ask whether the Fed should buy or sell securities.

    d. all of the above.

    e. only (a) and (b) of the above.

19. A rise in the operating band for the overnight rate of interest is a signal that

    a. the Bank of Canada would like higher short-term interest rates.

    b. the Bank of Canada would like lower short-term interest rates.

    c. the Bank of Canada would like an increase in the monetary base.

    d. none of the above.

20. A fall in the operating band for the overnight rate of interest is a signal that
    a. the Bank of Canada would like higher short-term interest rates.
    b. the Bank of Canada would like lower short-term interest rates.
    c. the Bank of Canada would like a decrease in the monetary base and the money supply.
    d. none of the above.

21. The Channel/Corridor system for setting interest rates
    a. has been adopted by Canada, Australia, and New Zealand.
    b. allows central banks to target interest rates even if there are zero reserve requirements.
    c. strictly limits the amount that banks may borrow from the central bank.
    d. all of the above.
    e. only (a) and (b) of the above.

22. What is the main reason why reserve requirements have been declining around the world?
    a. Central banks are taxing banks in order to raise revenue.
    b. Central banks are trying to make banks more competitive with other financial intermediaries.
    c. The spread between the bank and the market interest rate is growing.
    d. Reserve requirements are a blunt tool for monetary policy.

23. To lower interest rates, the Bank of Canada could
    a. buy government securities.
    b. sell government securities.
    c. raise the operating band.
    d. raise the bank rate.

24. If the Bank of Canada wants to _____ reserves _____ in the banking system, it will execute a repurchase agreement.
    a. increase; temporarily
    b. increase; permanently
    c. decrease; temporarily
    d. decrease; permanently

25. The goal of the Bank of Canada is to keep the inflation rate within a target range of _____ to _____.
    a. 2%; 4%
    b. 1%; 3%
    c. 1%; 4%
    d. 0%; 2%

26. "Core CPI" excludes _____ from "headline CPI".
    a. volatile components
    b. health care costs
    c. housing costs
    d. both (b) and (c) of the above

27. When the Bank of Canada increases the overnight lending rate, the value of the Canadian dollar _____, and the inflation rate _____.
    a. goes up, falls
    b. goes up, rises
    c. remains unchanged, rises
    d. remains unchanged, falls

28. Which of the following is true?
    a. The Bank of Canada has complete control over volumes of SPRAs and SRAs.
    b. Changes in interest rate due to SPRAs and SRAs are not accurate.
    c. SPRA and SRA transactions can be implemented quickly.
    d. both (a) and (c) of the above.

29. The European Central Bank imposes a _____ reserve requirement on all deposit-taking institutions.
    a. 0%
    b. 2%
    c. 3%
    d. 5%

30. The federal funds rate _____ when the Fed makes an open market _____ or lowers reserve requirements.
    a. falls; sale
    b. falls; purchase
    c. rises; sale
    d. rises; purchase

CHAPTER 18

The Conduct of Monetary Policy: Strategy and Tactics

CHAPTER SYNOPSIS/COMPLETIONS

The last chapter described how the tools of monetary policy affect the market for reserves and the interest rate. This chapter looks at the strategies and tactics central banks use to conduct monetary policy and evaluates the Bank of Canada's conduct of monetary policy in the past.

A central feature of monetary policy strategies in these countries is also the use of a (1) _____ _____, a nominal variable such as the inflation rate or the money supply that policymakers use to tie down the price level. The role of the nominal anchor is to guide a nation's monetary authority to conduct monetary policy to keep the nominal anchor variable— the inflation rate or the money supply—within a narrow range.

Adherence to the nominal anchor can limit the (2)_____ _____ _____ for monetary policymakers. The time-inconsistency problem arises because the effect that monetary policy has on the economy depends on people's expectations. If workers and firms expect the central bank to pursue a tight monetary policy to keep inflation low—because that is the announced policy of the central bank—then the central bank has an incentive to renege on this promise and adopt an (3)_____ policy to boost output and lower unemployment. Knowing that policymakers may on occasion renege on policy announcements—that is, be inconsistent over time—workers and firms will (4)_____ central bank announcements. Thus, to make its announcements credible, the central bank will want to commit to a nominal anchor that limits its discretion.

Monetary targeting was adopted by a number of industrialized countries in the 1970s to bring down inflation. Of these countries, both Germany and Switzerland were the most persistent in sticking to this strategy. It is because of their success in keeping inflation under control that monetary targeting still has strong advocates. Germany and Switzerland have shown that monetary targeting can restrain inflation in the long run even when monetary targets are missed by wide margins. Despite frequent misses of announced targets, both countries have openly communicated to the public their intention of keeping inflation under control.

The chapter presents six basic goals most often mentioned by personnel at the Bank of Canada and other central banks as objectives of monetary policy:

(5)_____

(6)_____

(7)_____

(8)_____

(9)_____

(10)_____

By high employment, economists mean a level of unemployment consistent with labour market equilibrium. This level of unemployment is the (11)_____ _____ of unemployment.

Because exchange rate fluctuations have a greater relative impact on the domestic economy now that international financial and goods markets have become more integrated, the Bank of Canada no longer treats Canada as a closed economy. Now, when deciding the course of monetary policy, the Bank of Canada pays careful attention to the expected change in the value of the dollar.

Hierarchical mandates put the goal of price stability first, and state that other goals can only be pursued if this goal is achieved. The Bank of Canada and the Bank of England are among the central banks that are following this type of mandate. A (12)_____ _____ has two objectives; these two goals must be achieved at the same time.

The main advantage of monetary targeting is the flexibility it provides to the central bank for dealing with (13)_____ considerations. The principal problem with monetary targeting occurs when the relationship between the monetary target and the goal variable proves to be too weak to guarantee that the goal can be achieved.

It is because of this breakdown between monetary aggregates and goal variables that many countries have recently adopted (14)_____ _____ as their monetary policy regime. New Zealand, Canada, and the United Kingdom were the first to adopt explicit inflation-targeting regimes in the early 1990s. Inflation targeting requires a commitment to emphasizing stability as the primary, long-run goal of monetary policy; public announcement of numerical inflation targets, including the plans and objectives of monetary policymakers; and increased accountability of the central bank to attain its inflation objectives. Consider this last requirement. The governor of the Reserve Bank in (15)_____ _____ can be dismissed if the publicly announced goals are not satisfied. All three countries have succeeded in bringing inflation down, albeit at the initial cost of higher unemployment.

Inflation targeting is readily understood by the public and is thus highly (16)_____; it permits monetary policymakers to respond to shocks to the domestic economy, and does not depend on a stable relationship between money and inflation. Because an explicit numerical inflation target increases the (17)_____ of the central bank, inflation targeting reduces the likelihood that the monetary authority will fall into the time-consistency trap. Indeed, the success of the Bank of England's inflation-targeting regime proved to be instrumental in the government's decision to grant the Bank its operational independence. An inflation-targeting regime makes it more palatable to have an independent central bank that focuses on long-run objectives, but is consistent with a democratic society because it is accountable.

Critics of inflation targeting contend that long lags in the effects of monetary policy make it too difficult for markets to determine the stance of monetary policy. Also, they claim that inflation targeting limits the discretion of central bankers to respond to domestic shocks, creates the potential for increased fluctuation in aggregate (18)_____, and lowers the economic growth of output and employment. Although the available empirical evidence does not lend much support to these criticisms, some economists claim that targeting nominal GDP would guard against a slow-down in economic activity. A variant of inflation targeting, a nominal GDP targeting regime would suffer the problem of announcing a long-term target for GDP growth, which would be difficult to forecast and politically risky. Moreover, since GDP is not a statistic that is reported monthly, it would make targeting GDP difficult in practice. Inflation targeting has almost all the benefits of nominal GDP targeting, but without its problems.

In recent years, the U.S. Fed has pursued a policy of targeting an (19)_____ nominal anchor in the form of an overriding concern to control inflation in the long run. The Fed's "just do it" approach has many of the advantages of an explicit inflation-targeting regime, but has a disadvantage in that the Fed's policy is much less transparent. In addition, some question whether the Fed's approach is consistent with democratic principles, given the lack of transparency to the Fed's implicit anchor. Perhaps the most serious problem with the "just do it" approach is the strong dependence on the preferences, skills, and trustworthiness of the individuals in charge of the central bank. For these reasons, the "just do it" approach may give way to an explicit inflation-targeting regime.

A controversial theory suggesting how the Bank of Canada should set the overnight funds interest rate has been proposed by Stanford economist John Taylor. The Taylor-rule setting for the overnight funds rate is equal to the inflation rate plus the weighted average of two gaps: (1) an inflation gap: current inflation minus a target rate, and (2) an output gap: the percentage deviation of real GDP from an estimate of its full employment potential.

HELPFUL HINTS

Monetary policy strategies and tactics vary across countries and over time. It is important to keep in mind that each strategy has advantages and disadvantages. Moreover, as illustrated in the discussion of the Fed's past policies, sometimes the disadvantages are discovered only after the policy has resulted in a recession or excessive inflation.

EXERCISES

Practice Problems

1. a. List the advantages of monetary targeting.

    _____

    _____

    b. List the one disadvantage of monetary targeting.

    _____

    _____

2. a. List the advantages of inflation targeting.

    1. _____

    2. _____

    3. _____

    4. _____

    5. _____

    b. List the disadvantages of inflation targeting.

    1. _____

    2. _____

    3. _____

    4. _____

3. a. List the advantages of the U.S. Fed's "just do it" monetary policy strategy.

    1. _____

    2. _____

    3. _____

    b. List the disadvantages of the U.S. Fed's "just do it" monetary policy strategy.

    1. _____

    2. _____

    3. _____

4. a. Show graphically the effect of a central bank's targeting on:

    1. Reserve aggregates.

2. The interest rate.

b. What does your graphical analysis imply about the simultaneous use of the two policy instruments?

_____

_____

c. What criteria should be used to determine the desirability of using either of the two policy instruments?

_____

_____

d. Is one preferable to another?

_____

_____

5. a. Briefly explain the Taylor rule.

_____

_____

b. What is the equation for the Taylor rule?

_____

_____

c. Suppose the equilibrium real overnight interest rate is 3%, the target for inflation is also 3%, the inflation rate is 5%, and the real GDP is 2% above its potential. What should the overnight interest rate be?

_____

_____

Short-Answer Questions

1. Explain why the Bundesbank's monetary targeting regime was deemed a success despite the fact that they frequently missed their monetary aggregate growth targets.

_____

_____

2. What are the three criteria that a central bank uses to choose a policy instrument?

_____

_____

3. Explain why a central bank must choose either a reserve aggregate or an interest rate as its policy instrument, but it cannot choose both at once.

_____

_____

4. What is the difference between an operating instrument and an intermediate target?

_____

_____

5. Which type of bubble are policymakers more likely to identify while it is happening?

_____

_____

Critical-Thinking Questions

Suppose the central bank's goal for inflation is 2%, and the equilibrium overnight rate is 2%.

1. Assume that GDP is currently at potential and inflation is 2%. Use the Taylor rule to calculate the target overnight rate and the value of the *real* federal funds rate that is implied by that target rate. Is monetary policy expansionary, contractionary, or neutral? How will GDP growth and inflation be affected by this monetary policy?

_____

_____

2. Now assume that GDP is 1% below potential and inflation is 1%. Use the Taylor rule to calculate the target overnight rate and the value of the *real* overnight rate that is implied by that target rate. Is monetary policy expansionary, contractionary, or neutral? How will GDP growth and inflation be affected by this monetary policy?

_____

_____

3. Now assume that GDP is 1% above potential and inflation is 3%. Use the Taylor rule to calculate the target overnight rate and the value of the *real* overnight rate that is implied by that target rate. Is monetary policy expansionary, contractionary, or neutral? How will GDP growth and inflation be affected by this monetary policy?

_____

_____

SELF-TEST

True-False Questions

Circle whether the following statements are true (T) or false (F).

T   F   1.   A key fact about monetary targeting regimes in Germany and Switzerland is that the targeting regimes were not like a Friedman-type monetary targeting rule, in which a monetary aggregate is kept on a constant-growth-rate path and is the primary focus of monetary policy.

T   F   2.   The European Central Bank has adopted a hybrid monetary policy strategy that has much in common with the monetary targeting strategy previously used by the Bundesbank but also has some elements of inflation targeting.

T   F   3. A key reason why monetary targeting has been reasonably successful in both Germany and Switzerland, despite frequent target misses, is that the objectives of monetary policy are clearly stated and both central banks actively engaged in communicating the strategy of monetary policy to the public, thereby enhancing the transparency of monetary policy and the accountability of the central banks.

T   F   4. The Bank of Canada desires interest rate stability because it reduces the uncertainty of future planning.

T   F   5. The Bank of Canada attempts to get the unemployment rate to zero, since any unemployment is wasteful and inefficient.

T   F   6. According to hierarchical mandates, price stability and maximum employment are the most important goals of central banks.

T   F   7. A disadvantage of inflation targeting is that it relies on a stable relationship between money and the price level.

T   F   8. Two problems with the U.S. Fed's "just do it" approach to monetary policy are the lack of transparency and the low degree of accountability, since the Fed does not announce its long-run goals for policy.

T   F   9. Governments of countries that have their own currencies have an incentive to over-expand the money supply to gain the revenue called seignorage. This explains why dollarization may be an effective monetary strategy to convince the public that the monetary authority is serious about reducing inflation.

T   F   10. Achieving price stability in the long run and the natural rate of unemployment are not consistent with each other as goals of the central bank.

T   F   11. Price stability is desirable because a rising price level creates uncertainty in the economy, and that uncertainty might hamper economic growth.

T   F   12. A central bank will have better inflation performance in the long run if it does not conduct unexpected expansionary policies.

T   F   13. In the long run, there is inconsistency between the price stability goal and other goals of monetary policy.

T   F   14. It is better for an economy to operate under a hierarchical mandate than a dual mandate.

T   F   15. When the economy is at full employment, the supply of labour equals the demand for labour, implying that the unemployment rate is zero.

Multiple-Choice Questions

Circle the appropriate answer.

1. Using Taylor's rule, the Bank of Canada should raise the overnight funds interest rate when inflation _____ the Bank's inflation target or when real GDP _____ the Bank's output target.

   a. rises above; drops below

   b. drops below; drops below

   c. rises above; rises above

   d. drops below; rises above

2. Bank of Canada watchers are hired by financial institutions in order to
    a. collect data that the Bank of Canada does not share with the public.
    b. explain past Bank of Canada policy.
    c. sell or purchase securities from the Bank of Canada.
    d. predict future monetary policy.
    e. all of the above.

3. The Bank of Canada should not set zero unemployment as a policy goal since
    a. frictional unemployment may be helpful to the economy.
    b. monetary policy cannot eliminate structural unemployment.
    c. it cannot affect the unemployment rate.
    d. all of the above.
    e. only (a) and (b) of the above.

4. A breakdown in the relationship between money growth and inflation is
    a. a disadvantage for countries that use a monetary-targeting regime.
    b. not a disadvantage for countries that use a monetary-targeting regime.
    c. a disadvantage for countries that use an inflation-targeting regime.
    d. both (b) and (c) of the above.

5. Critics of inflation targeting complain that
    a. the signal between monetary policy actions and evidence of success is too long delayed.
    b. it imposes a rule on monetary policymakers that is too rigid, taking away their ability to respond to shocks to the economy.
    c. it has the potential for making output fluctuations more pronounced.
    d. it does all of the above.
    e. it does only (a) and (b) of the above.

6. Some economists question the desirability of the U.S. Fed's implicit targeting strategy by pointing out that
    a. the lack of transparency in the Fed's policy creates uncertainty that leads to unnecessary volatility in financial markets.
    b. the opacity of its policymaking makes it hard to hold the Fed accountable to Congress and the public.
    c. the policy has not been very successful, as inflation and unemployment were too high in the 1990s.
    d. all of the above.
    e. only (a) and (b) of the above.

7. The 1985 Plaza Agreement between central banks from the largest economies
    a. is an example of international policy coordination.
    b. sought to lower the value of the U.S. dollar versus other currencies.
    c. sought to lower inflation in the United States.
    d. only (a) and (b) of the above.
    e. only (a) and (c) of the above.

8. (I) If the relationship between the monetary aggregate and the goal variable is weak, monetary aggregate targeting will not work. (II) Canada was the first country to formally adopt inflation targeting in 1990.
    a. Both are true.
    b. Both are false.
    c. I is true, II is false.
    d. I is false, II is true.

9. Disadvantages of nominal GDP targeting include:
    a. the lack of timely information on nominal GDP since it is reported quarterly, not monthly.
    b. the potential confusion that might arise with the public between nominal and real GDP.
    c. the difficulty that policymakers would encounter in trying to calculate long-run potential GDP growth.
    d. all of the above.
    e. only (a) and (b) of the above.

10. A _____ is used by every central bank to control the price level.
    a. seignorage
    b. nominal anchor
    c. currency board
    d. real GDP target
    e. none of the above

11. The time-inconsistency problem in monetary policy exists because people's behaviour depends on
    a. what the central bank did in the past.
    b. current central bank behaviour.
    c. what the central bank will do in the future.
    d. what people believe the central bank will do in the future.

12. One solution to the time-inconsistency problem is for the central bank to
    a. have discretion over monetary policy.
    b. try to surprise people with unexpected policy.
    c. announce and commit to a policy strategy rule.
    d. only (a) and (c) of the above.
    e. only (b) and (c) of the above.

13. Which of the following statements regarding speculative attacks on currencies is *false*?
    a. Speculative attacks do not strike industrialized countries.
    b. Speculative attacks can be more damaging to emerging market economies than to industrialized economies.
    c. Speculators attack a currency when they believe that the central bank is not willing to increase interest rates high enough to defend the currency.
    d. A speculative attack on one currency may happen if that currency is pegged to another currency.
    e. All of the above.

14. The example of the German and Swiss monetary targeting policy strategies teaches us that
    a. inflation can be restrained even if the monetary target is often missed.
    b. transparency and accountability can be increased by effective communication from the central bank.
    c. a strict policy rule is important to keeping inflation low.
    d. only (a) and (b) of the above.
    e. only (b) and (c) of the above.

15. One advantage of an inflation targeting policy strategy is that
    a. an inflation targeting policy is very transparent.
    b. the likelihood of the time-inconsistency problem in monetary policy is reduced.
    c. the inflation rate is easily controlled by the central bank.
    d. all of the above.
    e. only (a) and (b) of the above.

16. Which of the following is a feature of Federal Reserve monetary policy?

    a. The Federal Reserve uses "pre-emptive strikes" against the threat of inflation.

    b. The Federal Reserve sets an explicit inflation target.

    c. The Federal Reserve uses policy rules rather than exercising discretion.

    d. Federal Reserve policy is highly transparent.

17. A nominal anchor is

    a. necessary for a successful monetary policy.

    b. used to keep a central bank from letting the price level grow too quickly or fall too fast.

    c. a nominal variable that policymakers use as an intermediate target to achieve their goals.

    d. all of the above.

    e. only (a) and (c).

18. An inflation rate target _____ zero makes periods of deflation _____ likely.

    a. above; more

    b. above; less

    c. below; more

    d. below; less

19. _____ and _____ are two types of policy instruments at the disposal of the Bank of Canada.

    a. Nonborrowed reserves; the monetary base

    b. The monetary base; interest rates

    c. Reserve aggregates; interest rates

    d. Total reserves,;the monetary base

20. Which of the following is false?

    a. Inflation targeting is easily understood by the public.

    b. Inflation targeting gives an immediate signal about the achievement of a target.

    c. Inflation targeting relies on a stable money-inflation relationship.

    d. Both (b) and (c) of the above.

21. Which of the following is a criterion in choosing a policy instrument?

    a. The instrument must be easily observable.

    b. The instrument must be controllable.

    c. The instrument must be measurable.

    d. All of the above.

22. Assume that the equilibrium overnight rate is 4%, the target for inflation is 3%, the inflation rate is 5%, and real GDP is 2% below its potential. What will be the overnight rate, according to Taylor's rule?

    a. 10%.

    b. 9%.

    c. 11%.

    d. 12%.

23. Inflation targeting involves

    a. public announcement of medium-term numerical targets for inflation.

    b. an institutional commitment to price stability as the primary long-run goal of the monetary policy.

    c. increased transparency of the monetary policy strategy.

    d. all of the above.

24. The rate of inflation tends to remain constant when
    a. the unemployment rate falls faster than the NAIRU falls.
    b. the unemployment rate increases faster than the NAIRU increases.
    c. the unemployment rate equals the NAIRU.
    d. the unemployment rate is above the NAIRU.

25. Interest rates are difficult to measure because
    a. they fluctuate too often.
    b. they cannot be controlled by the Bank of Canada.
    c. real interest rates depend on the expected inflation rate and the expected inflation rate is hard to determine.
    d. all of the above.

26. Full employment indicates that
    a. the unemployment rate is zero.
    b. the unemployment rate is not zero because of frictional unemployment.
    c. the unemployment rate is not zero because of structural unemployment.
    d. both (b) and (c) of the above.

27. Which of the following is false?
    a. Low and stable inflation rates promote economic growth.
    b. Price stability should be the primary short-run goal of monetary policy.
    c. Attempts to keep inflation at the same level in the long run would likely lead to excessive output fluctuations.
    d. Both (b) and (c) of the above.

28. The rate of unemployment at which there is no tendency for inflation to change is called the
    a. full unemployment rate.
    b. frictional unemployment rate.
    c. structural unemployment rate.
    d. nonaccelerating inflation rate of unemployment.

29. The type of monetary policy that is used in New Zealand, Canada, and the United Kingdom is
    a. inflation targeting.
    b. monetary targeting.
    c. interest-rate targeting.
    d. both (a) and (c) of the above.

30. Using Taylor's rule, when the positive output gap is 4 percent, the equilibrium overnight rate is 3 percent, the target inflation rate is 2 percent, and the actual inflation rate is 4 percent, the overnight rate should be
    a. 5%.
    b. 10%.
    c. 8%.
    d. 6%.

CHAPTER 19

The Foreign Exchange Market

CHAPTER SYNOPSIS/COMPLETIONS

This is the first chapter in a two-chapter sequence on international finance and monetary policy. This chapter looks at the foreign exchange market. The next chapter looks at the international financial system.

The exchange rate is the price of one country's (1) _____ in terms of another's. Trades in the foreign exchange market typically involve the exchange of bank (2) _____ denominated in different currencies. Spot exchange rates involve the immediate exchange of bank deposits, while (3) _____ exchange rates involve the exchange of deposits at some specified future date. When a currency increases in value, it has (4) _____; when a currency falls in value and is worth fewer Canadian dollars, it has depreciated. Exchange rates are important because when a country's currency appreciates, its exports become (5) _____ expensive and foreign imports become less expensive. Conversely, when a country's currency depreciates, its goods become less expensive for foreigners, but foreign goods become more expensive (implying that net exports decline, all else constant).

The starting point for undertaking an investigation of how exchange rates are determined in the long run is the law of one price, which states the following: If two countries produce an identical good, the price of the good should be the same throughout the world no matter which country produces it. Applying the law of one price to countries' price levels produces the theory of (6) _____ _____ _____, which suggests that if one country's price level rises relative to another's, its currency should (7)_____.

The theory of purchasing power parity cannot fully explain exchange rate changes because goods produced in different countries are not identical and because many goods and services (whose prices are included in a measure of a country's price level) are not (8)_____ across borders. Other factors also affect the exchange rate in the long run, including trade barriers such as (9)_____ and quotas, the demand for imports and exports, and relative productivity.

The key to understanding the short-run behaviour of exchange rates is to recognize that an exchange rate is the price of domestic bank deposits in terms of foreign bank deposits. Because the exchange rate is the price of one asset in terms of another, the natural way to investigate the short-run determination of exchange rates is through an asset-market approach using the theory of asset demand.

The theory of asset demand indicates that the most important factor affecting the demand for both domestic (dollar) and foreign deposits is the (10) _____ _____ on these assets relative to one another. According to the interest parity condition, however, the expected return on both domestic and foreign deposits is identical in a world in which there is (11) _____ _____. Because the interest parity condition is an equilibrium condition, it provides a framework for understanding short-run movements in exchange rates as a result of factors that cause the expected return on either domestic or foreign deposits to change.

Therefore, changes in foreign interest rates, the domestic (12) _____ _____, or a change in the expected future exchange rate will cause the exchange rate to change in the short run. Because long-run determinants of the exchange rate influence the expected future exchange rate, the determinants of long-run exchange rates affect short-run exchange rates. For example, any factor that raises the expected return on domestic deposits relative to foreign deposits causes the domestic currency to appreciate. These factors include a (13)_____ in the domestic interest rate, a decline in the foreign interest rate, or any long-run factor that causes the expected future exchange rate to (14)_____.

A rise in domestic interest rates relative to foreign interest rates can result in either an appreciation or a depreciation of the domestic currency. If the rise in the domestic interest rate is due to a rise in expected inflation, then the domestic currency depreciates. If the rise in the domestic interest rate, however, is due to a rise in the real interest rate, then the domestic currency (15) _____. Higher domestic money growth leads the domestic currency to (16) _____.

Exchange rates have been very volatile in recent years. The theory of asset demand explains this volatility as a consequence of changing expectations that are also volatile, plays an important role in determining the demand for domestic assets and, thereby, affects the value of the exchange rate.

HELPFUL HINTS

In the long run, movements in exchange rates are mainly driven by relative inflation rates between countries. In the short run, movements in exchange rates are mainly driven by relative rates of returns on assets between countries.

EXERCISES

Practice Problems

1. Suppose the dollar/euro exchange rate is 1.20.
a. What is the euro/dollar exchange rate?

_____

b. What would the new euro/dollar exchange rate be if the euro appreciated by 5% relative to the dollar?

_____

c. Starting from the original exchange rate you calculated in *a*, what would the new euro/dollar exchange rate be if the euro depreciated by 5% against the dollar?

_____

2.
a. Suppose the law of one price holds for wheat and the price of wheat is $4.50 per bushel in Canada, and the peso/dollar exchange rate is 10. Calculate the price of wheat in terms of pesos.

_____

b. Now suppose that purchasing power parity holds between the Canada and Mexico. Calculate the new peso/dollar exchange rate if the price level in Mexico rises 10% relative to the price level in Canada.

_____

c. Now suppose a basket of goods in Canada costs $100, while the cost of the same basket of goods in Mexico costs 950 pesos. Calculate the real exchange rate assuming the peso/dollar exchange rate is 15.

_____

3. In the second column of the following table, indicate with an arrow whether the exchange rate will rise or fall as a result of the change in the factor. (Recall that a rise in the exchange rate is viewed as an appreciation of the domestic currency).

Change in Factor	Response of the Exchange Rate
Domestic interest rate $\downarrow$	_____
Foreign interest rate $\downarrow$	_____
Domestic price level $\downarrow$	_____
Tariffs and quotas $\downarrow$	_____
Import demand $\downarrow$	_____
Export demand $\downarrow$	_____
Domestic productivity $\downarrow$	_____

4. Use the demand–and–supply diagram for domestic assets to demonstrate the following.
a. Show what happens to the exchange rate E_t when the domestic interest rate i^D decreases.

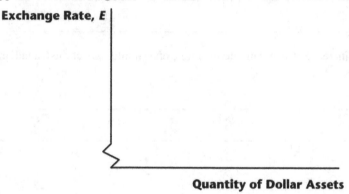

b. Show what happens to the exchange rate E_t when the foreign interest rate i^F increases.

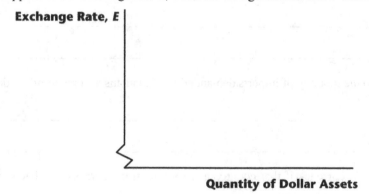

c.   Show what happens to the exchange rate E_t when the expected future exchange rate E_{t+1} increases.

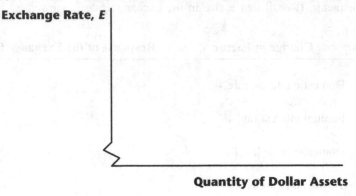

Quantity of Dollar Assets

5.   a.   The Economist Big Mac Index deals with the purchasing power parity of the currency of a number of currencies around the world. The Big Mac Index measures the price of Big Macs around the world, measured in converted US dollars. The purchasing power parity theory states that, in theory, in the long run, the price of Big Macs in adjusted US dollars should:

_____

_____

b.   If the Bank of Canada increases Canadian interest rates, one should expect the Canadian dollar to do what and why?

_____

_____

Short-Answer Questions

1.   What happens to the price of foreign imports into the Canada when the dollar depreciates?

_____

_____

2.   What is likely to happen to the quantity of imports demanded by Canadians as a result of the dollar depreciating?

_____

_____

3.   What happens to a country's currency if that country increases its trade barriers and becomes more productive relative to other countries?

_____

_____

4. What will happen to the exchange rate today if the expected future exchange rate declines?

_____

_____

5. What will happen to the value of the domestic currency when the domestic real interest rate rises?

_____

_____

6. What will happen to the value of the domestic currency when the domestic nominal interest rate rises and the increase is due to an increase in expected inflation?

_____

_____

7. What will happen to the value of the domestic currency when the money supply rises?

_____

_____

8. What is exchange rate overshooting and how does it happen?

_____

_____

_____

9. Why did the U.S. dollar appreciate during the subprime financial crisis?

_____

_____

Critical-Thinking Questions

Most of the analysis in this chapter looks at how a single factor, such as a change in domestic interest rates, affects the exchange rate, holding all other factors constant. But in the real world, many factors change at once and so sometimes it is not possible to predict the impact on exchange rates. For each of the following combinations of factors, state whether it is possible to predict the direction of the effect on the domestic exchange rate. For the cases where it is possible to predict the direction of effect, state what that direction is.

a.   The domestic interest rate rises, foreign interest rate falls, and expected import demand falls as well.

_____

_____

b.   The domestic price level rises, quotas are placed on imports, and productivity is expected to rise.

_____

_____

c.   Export demand is expected to rise, the domestic price level is expected to fall, and foreign interest rates are expected to fall as well.

_____

_____

SELF-TEST

True-False Questions

Circle whether the following statements are true (T) or false (F).

T   F   1.   Most trades in the foreign exchange market involve the buying and selling of bank deposits.

T   F   2.   When a country's currency appreciates, its goods abroad become less expensive and foreign goods in that country become more expensive, all else constant.

T   F   3.   Forward exchange rates involve the immediate exchange of bank deposits.

T   F   4.   The theory of purchasing power parity explains most of the movements in exchange rates in the short run.

T   F   5.   If purchasing power parity holds, the real exchange rate equals one.

T   F   6.   The quantity of domestic assets supplied increases as the exchange rate E_t rises.

T   F   7.   The quantity of domestic assets demanded increases as the exchange rate E_t falls.

T   F   8.   If the price level in Canada rises relative to the price levels in other countries, the dollar will appreciate.

T   F   9.   Increasing trade barriers causes a country's currency to appreciate in the long run.

T   F   10.   In the long run, as a country becomes more productive relative to other countries, its currency appreciates.

T   F   11.   When export demand rises, the domestic currency appreciates.

T   F   12.   When the domestic real interest rate rises, the domestic currency depreciates.

T   F   13.   When the domestic interest rate rises because of an expected increase in inflation, the domestic currency depreciates.

T   F   14.   Exchange rate overshooting occurs when an increase in the money supply causes the exchange rate to fall more in the long run than in the short run.

T   F   15.   The weakness of the U.S. dollar in the late 1970s and the strength of the U.S. dollar in the early 1980s can be explained by movements in nominal interest rates but not movements in real interest rates.

Multiple-Choice Questions

Circle the appropriate answer.

1. When the euro appreciates (holding everything else constant), then
   a. European chocolate sold in the Canada becomes more expensive.
   b. Canadian computers sold in Europe become more expensive.
   c. European watches sold in the Canada become less expensive.
   d. Canadian toothpaste sold in Europe becomes less expensive.
   e. a and c.
   f. a and d.

2. If the Mexican peso depreciates against the dollar, then
   a. it takes more dollars to buy a peso.
   b. it takes fewer pesos to buy a dollar.
   c. the dollar has appreciated against the peso.
   d. Canadian goods are less expensive in Mexico.

3. If transportation costs and trade barriers are low, and the exchange rate is .80 euros per dollar, then according to the law of one price, a computer that costs $1,00 in the Canada will cost
   a. 1000 euros in Europe.
   b. 1250 euros in Europe.
   c. 800 euros in Europe.
   d. 1800 euros in Europe.

4. According to the theory of purchasing power parity, if the price level in Canada rises by 5% while the price level in Mexico rises by 6%, then the dollar will
   a. appreciate 1% relative to the peso.
   b. depreciate 1% relative to the peso.
   c. appreciate 5% relative to the peso.
   d. depreciate 5% relative to the peso.

5. Reasons why the theory of purchasing power parity might not fully explain exchange rate movements include
   a. differing monetary policies in different countries.
   b. changes in the prices of goods and services not traded internationally.
   c. changes in the domestic price level that exceed changes in the foreign price level.
   d. changes in foreign price levels that exceed changes in the domestic price level.

6. If the cost of a market basket of goods in the Canada is $80, the cost of that same market basket in France is 90 euros, and the euro/dollar exchange rate is 0.77, the real exchange rate will be
   a. 0.68.
   b. 1.46.
   c. 1.
   d. 0.77.

7. If, in retaliation for "unfair" trade practices, government imposes a tariff on Chinese imports, but at the same time Chinese demand for Canadian goods increases, then in the long run
   a. the Chinese yuan will appreciate relative to the dollar.
   b. the Chinese yuan will depreciate relative to the dollar.
   c. the dollar will depreciate relative to the yuan.
   d. it is not clear whether the dollar will appreciate or depreciate relative to the yuan.

8. If Canadian products become popular in Europe and exports of Canadian products to Europe increase, then in the long run,

    a. the euro per dollar exchange rate will fall.

    b. European goods will become more expensive in the Canada.

    c. Canadian goods will become less expensive in Europe.

    d. the euro per dollar exchange rate will rise.

9. Holding everything else constant, an increase in the expected future exchange rate will cause the

    a. expected return on dollar assets in terms of foreign currency to rise.

    b. expected return on dollar assets in terms of foreign currency to fall.

    c. expected return on foreign assets in terms of dollars to rise.

    d. expected return on foreign assets in terms of dollars to fall.

    e. a and c.

    f. a and d.

10. All else held constant, an increase in the exchange rate E_t will lead to

    a. a rightward shift in the demand for domestic assets.

    b. a leftward shift in the demand for domestic assets.

    c. an increase in the quantity of domestic assets demanded.

    d. a decrease in the quantity of domestic assets demanded.

11. If the exchange rate is above the equilibrium exchange rate, then

    a. the quantity of domestic assets supplied is greater than the quantity of domestic assets demanded, and the domestic currency will appreciate.

    b. the quantity of domestic assets supplied is less than the quantity of domestic assets demanded, and the domestic currency will appreciate.

    c. the quantity of domestic assets supplied is greater than the quantity of domestic assets demanded, and the domestic currency will depreciate.

    d. the quantity of domestic assets supplied is less than the quantity of domestic assets demanded, and the domestic currency will depreciate.

12. A rise in the expected future exchange rate shifts the demand for domestic assets to the _____ and causes the domestic currency to_____.

    a. right; appreciate

    b. right; depreciate

    c. left; appreciate

    d. left; depreciate

13. A rise in the domestic interest rate shifts the demand for domestic assets to the _____ and causes the domestic currency to_____.

    a. right; appreciate

    b. right; depreciate

    c. left; appreciate

    d. left; depreciate

14. A rise in the foreign interest rate shifts the demand for domestic assets to the _____ and causes the domestic currency to_____.

    a. right; appreciate

    b. right; depreciate

    c. left; appreciate

    d. left; depreciate

15. If the domestic real interest rate rises, then
    a. the nominal interest rate will rise if there is no change in expected inflation.
    b. the return on domestic assets falls.
    c. the return on foreign deposits rises.
    d. the domestic currency depreciates.

16. Lowering the domestic money supply causes the domestic currency to
    a. depreciate more in the short run than in the long run.
    b. depreciate more in the long run than in the short run.
    c. appreciate more in the short run than in the long run.
    d. appreciate more in the long run than in the short run.

17. Exchange rates are volatile because
    a. central banks are constantly manipulating the value of foreign exchange.
    b. inflation rates are volatile.
    c. expectations about the variables that influence exchange rates change frequently.
    d. real interest rates are volatile.

18. According to the theory of monetary neutrality, a 10% increase in the money supply
    a. leads to a 10% increase in the price level in the long run.
    b. leads to less than a 10% increase in the price level in the long run.
    c. does not affect the price level in the long run.
    d. leads to a greater than 10% increase in the price level in the long run.

19. The rise in nominal interest rates in the United States in the 1970s caused the dollar to
    a. appreciate because the increase in nominal interest rates was due mainly to an increase in the real interest rate.
    b. appreciate because the increase in nominal interest rates was due mainly to an increase in expected inflation.
    c. depreciate because the increase in nominal interest rates was due mainly to an increase in the real interest rate.
    d. depreciate because the increase in nominal interest rates was due mainly to an increase in expected inflation.

20. Early models of exchange rate behaviour could not predict substantial fluctuations in exchange rates because
    a. they assumed purchasing power parity always holds.
    b. they did not emphasize changing expectations.
    c. they assumed the supply of domestic assets is fixed.
    d. they did not take into account monetary neutrality.

21. Reasons why the theory of purchasing power parity might not fully explain exchange rate movements include
    a. differing monetary policies in different countries.
    b. changes in the prices of goods and services not traded internationally.
    c. changes in the domestic price level that exceed changes in the foreign price level.
    d. changes in the foreign price level that exceed changes in the domestic price level.

22. An expected _____ in _____ productivity relative to _____ productivity (holding everything else constant) causes the domestic currency to _____.
    a. rise; foreign; domestic; depreciate
    b. rise; domestic; foreign; depreciate
    c. decline; foreign; domestic; depreciate
    d. rise; foreign; domestic; appreciate

23. When the domestic nominal interest rate falls because of a decrease in expected inflation, the expected appreciation of the dollar rises, R^F shifts _____ than R^D, and the exchange rate _____.

    a. less; falls

    b. less; rises

    c. more; falls

    d. more; rises

24. Lowering the domestic money supply causes the domestic currency to

    a. depreciate more in the short run than in the long run.

    b. depreciate more in the long run than in the short run.

    c. appreciate more in the short run than in the long run.

    d. appreciate more in the long run than in the short run.

25. According to the theory of purchasing power parity, the rupee will depreciate by 10% against the dollar if the Canadian price level increases by _____ and the Indian price level increases by _____.

    a. 10%; 10%

    b. 10%; 0%

    c. 10%; 20%

    d. 0%; 20%

26. Suppose that the current exchange rate is 1200 won per dollar. If inflation in South Korea is 8% while inflation in Canada is 5%, then PPP predicts that the exchange rate will become

    a. 1200 won per dollar.

    b. 1236 won per dollar.

    c. 1260 won per dollar.

    d. 1296 won per dollar.

27. Suppose that sunglasses cost 30 real in Brazil and 12 dollars in Canada. According to the law of one price, the exchange rate should be

    a. 24 dollars per real.

    b. 24 real per dollar.

    c. 0.4 real per dollar.

    d. 2.5 real per dollar.

28. Currencies are traded in markets

    a. that are organized into large centralized exchanges.

    b. with over $1 trillion in exchange volume per day.

    c. where banks trade deposits denominated in various currencies.

    d. only (b) and (c) of the above.

29. If the Mexican peso depreciates against the Canadian dollar, then which of the following is true?

    a. It takes more dollars to buy a peso.

    b. It takes fewer pesos to buy a dollar.

    c. Mexico has lost foreign exchange.

    d. The dollar has appreciated against the peso.

30. If Canada produces a new electric automobile that is very popular and Canada exports many to Europe, then over time

    a. the euro per dollar exchange rate will fall.

    b. European cars will become less expensive in Canada.

    c. Canadian wine will become less expensive in Europe.

    d. all of the above.

    e. none of the above.

CHAPTER **20**

The International Financial System

CHAPTER SYNOPSIS/COMPLETIONS

This is the second chapter in a two-chapter sequence on international finance and monetary policy. The last chapter looked at the foreign exchange market. This chapter looks at the structure of the international financial system and how that structure affects monetary policy. This chapter also looks at the evolution of the international financial system during the past half century.

The current international environment in which exchange rates fluctuate from day to day is called a managed-float or a (1)_____ float regime. In a managed-float regime, central banks allow rates to fluctuate but intervene in the foreign exchange market in order to influence exchange rates. Interventions are of two types. An unsterilized central bank intervention, in which the domestic currency is sold to purchase foreign assets, leads to a gain in international reserves, an (2)_____ in the money supply, and a depreciation of the domestic currency. Sterilized central bank interventions, which involve offsetting any increase in international reserves with equal open market sales of domestic securities, have little effect on the exchange rate.

The balance of payments is a bookkeeping system for recording all payments that have a direct bearing on the movement of funds between countries. The (3)_____ shows international transactions that involve currently produced goods and services. The difference between merchandise exports and imports is called the (4)_____ _____. The capital account shows the net receipts from capital transactions, such as sales of stocks and bonds to foreigners. The official reserves transaction balance is the sum of the current account balance plus the items in the capital account. It indicates the net amount of international reserves that must move between countries to finance international transactions.

Before World War I, the world economy operated under a gold standard, under which the currencies of most countries were convertible directly into gold, thereby fixing exchange rates between countries. After World War II, the Bretton Woods system was established in order to promote a (5)_____ exchange rate system in which the U.S. dollar was convertible into gold. The Bretton Woods agreement created the International Monetary Fund (IMF), which was given the task of promoting the growth of world trade by setting rules for the maintenance of fixed exchange rates and by making loans to countries that were experiencing balance of payments difficulties. The Bretton Woods agreement also set up the World Bank in order to provide long-term loans to assist developing countries to build dams, roads, and other physical capital.

A change in a country's holdings of international reserves leads to an equal change in its monetary base, which, in turn, affects the money supply. A currency like the U.S. dollar and the euro, which are used by other countries to denominate the assets they hold as international reserves, is called a (6)_____ _____. A reserve currency country (such as the United States) has the advantage over other countries that balance of payments deficits or surpluses do not lead to changes in holdings of international reserves and the monetary base.

The Bretton Woods system—because it did not allow for smooth and gradual adjustments in exchange rates when they became necessary—was often characterized by destabilizing balance-of-payments crises. Because countries resisted revaluing their currencies, they were often characterized by a "fundamental disequilibrium." The Bretton Woods system finally collapsed in 1971. The European Monetary System, because it is a (7)_____ exchange rate system like the Bretton Woods system, suffers the potential weakness of exchange rate crises characterized by "speculative attacks"—that is, a massive sale of a weak currency (or purchases of a strong currency) that would hasten the change in exchange rates.

Because capital flows were an important element in the currency crises in Mexico (1994), East Asia (1997), Brazil (1999), and Argentina (2001), politicians and some economists have advocated restricting capital mobility in emerging market countries. Controls on capital outflows could potentially prevent an emerging market country from being forced to (8)_____ its currency, which would otherwise exacerbate a financial crisis. Empirical evidence, however, indicates that controls are seldom effective during a crisis. Indeed, controls on capital outflows may be counterproductive because confidence in the government is weakened.

The case for controls on capital (9)_____ is stronger, as capital inflows can lead to a lending boom and excessive risk taking on the part of banks, which then helps trigger financial crisis. Although the case for controls on capital inflows seems plausible, this regulation can lead to corruption and a serious misallocation of resources in the emerging market country.

Three international considerations affect the conduct of monetary policy: direct effects of the foreign exchange market on the money supply, balance of payments considerations, and (10)_____ _____ considerations. If a central bank intervenes in the foreign exchange market to keep its strong currency from appreciating, as did the German central bank in the early 1970s, it (11)_____ international reserves, and the monetary base and the money supply (12)_____. In order to prevent balance of payments deficits, a country's central bank might pursue (13)_____ monetary policy.

Monetary policy is also affected by exchange rate considerations. Because an appreciation of the currency causes domestic businesses to suffer from increased foreign competition, a central bank might (14)_____ the rate of money growth in order to lower the exchange rate. Similarly, because a (15)_____ of the currency hurts consumers and stimulates inflation, a central bank might slow the rate of money growth in order to prop up the exchange rate. Because the United States has been a reserve-currency country in the post-World War II period, U.S. monetary policy has been less affected by developments in the foreign exchange market than is true for other countries.

HELPFUL HINTS

Unsterilized exchange rate interventions have exactly the same effect on the monetary base as open market operations. International reserves and government securities are both assets on the Bank of Canada's balance sheet. When the Bank of Canada conducts an open market purchase of securities, the monetary base increases. When the Bank of Canada purchases international reserves, the monetary base increases. When the Bank of Canada conducts an open market sale of government securities, the monetary base decreases. When the Bank of Canada sells international reserves, the monetary base decreases as well.

EXERCISES

Practice Problems

1. a. Show the T-account transactions for the case where the Bank of Canada buys $1 billion in foreign assets in exchange for $1 billion in currency.

Bank of Canada

Assets	Liabilities

b. What is the impact of this transaction on the monetary base?

_____

_____

c. Show the T-account transactions for the case where the Bank of Canada buys $1 billion in foreign assets in exchange for $1 billion in deposits.

Bank of Canada

Assets	Liabilities

d. What is the impact of this transaction on the monetary base?

_____

_____

e. Show the T-account transactions for the case where the Bank of Canada buys $1 billion in foreign assets in exchange for $1 billion in deposits. Assume that the Bank sterilizes this exchange rate intervention by selling $1 billion in government bonds.

Bank of Canada

Assets	Liabilities

f. What is the impact of these transactions on the monetary base?

_____

_____

2. a.   Draw the demand and supply curves for dollar assets and show what happens to the exchange rate in the short run and the long run when the Bank of Canada conducts an unsterilized sale of foreign assets.

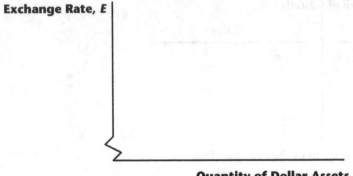

Exchange Rate, *E*

Quantity of Dollar Assets

b.   Explain why there is exchange rate overshooting in response to this exchange rate intervention.

_____

_____

_____

_____

c.   Draw the demand and supply curves for dollar assets and show what happens to the exchange rate in the short run and the long run when the Bank of Canada conducts a sterilized sale of foreign assets.

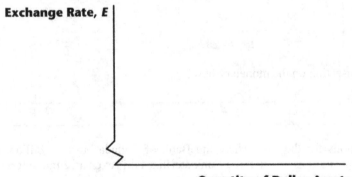

Exchange Rate, *E*

Quantity of Dollar Assets

3.

a.   Draw the demand and supply for dollar assets and show what happens to the exchange rate if the return on foreign assets increases, everything else held constant.

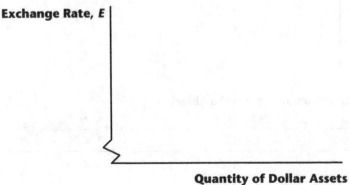

Exchange Rate, *E*

Quantity of Dollar Assets

b. Now assume that the central bank wishes to fix the exchange rate at its original level (the level it was at before the return on foreign assets increased). Describe the type of foreign exchange intervention that the central bank would undertake and use the diagram you constructed for part *a* to show the effect of this intervention on the exchange rate.

_____

_____

_____

_____

4. Consider an emerging market country with a fixed exchange rate that experiences a sudden decrease in the demand for its domestic assets. Despite the decrease in demand, the central bank continues to keep the exchange rate at its original value (its value before the decrease in demand for its assets).

a. Is this country's currency overvalued or undervalued?

_____

b. Describe the exchange rate intervention that this country would undertake in order to keep its exchange rate at par.

_____

c. What will happen to this country's international reserves as a result of this intervention?

_____

d. Under what circumstances would this country likely experience a speculative attack on its currency as a result of the decrease in demand for its domestic assets?

_____

e. How would a speculative attack affect this county's balance of payments? How would this country's central bank likely respond to such an attack?

_____

f. What possible action would the International Monetary Fund take to halt the speculative attack on this country's currency?

_____

g. Explain how that action by the IMF might create a moral hazard problem for emerging market economies.

_____

Short-Answer Questions

1. What is the difference between a sterilized exchange rate intervention and an unsterilized exchange rate intervention?

_____

_____

2. What is the difference between the current account and the trade balance?

_____

3.   Suppose the current account balance is –$725 billion and the capital account balance is $720 billion. Calculate the net change in government international reserves.

_____

_____

4.   What role does an anchor currency play in a fixed exchange rate regime?

_____

_____

5.   What is a dirty float exchange rate regime?

_____

_____

Critical-Thinking Questions

The U.S. current account deficit has approached nearly $1 trillion in recent years.

1.   What does a current account deficit of nearly $1 trillion imply about foreign claims on U.S. wealth?

_____

_____

2.   Is the U.S. increasing or decreasing its claims on foreign wealth?

_____

_____

3.   How will the U.S. current account deficit affect the wealth of future Americans? Why?

_____

_____

SELF-TEST

True-False Questions

Circle whether the following statements are true (T) or false (F).

T   F   1.   The capital account balance indicates whether the country is increasing or decreasing its claims on foreign wealth.

T   F   2.   The current account balance equals the difference between exports and imports.

T   F   3.   When the domestic currency is undervalued in a fixed exchange rate regime, the country's central bank must intervene in the foreign exchange market to purchase the domestic currency by selling foreign assets.

T   F   4.   The gold standard of the late nineteenth century always prevented inflation from developing.

T   F   5.   A particular problem with a fixed exchange rate system (or regime) is that it is periodically subject to speculative attacks on currencies.

T   F   6.   Special drawing rights (SDRs) are IMF loans to member countries.

T   F   7.   The World Bank makes loans to countries suffering balance of payments difficulties.

T F   8. The current international financial system is perhaps best described as a hybrid of fixed and flexible exchange rate systems.

T F   9. The IMF has, since the 1980s, been acting as an international lender of last resort.

T F   10. Monetary policy in a reserve currency country is less influenced by balance of payments deficits because they will be financed by other countries' interventions in the foreign exchange market.

T F   11. When the domestic currency is overvalued, the central bank must purchase domestic currency to keep the exchange rate fixed, but as a result it loses international reserves.

T F   12. A central bank's sale of domestic currency to purchase foreign assets in the foreign exchange market results in an equal rise in its international reserves and the monetary base.

T F   13. Under the Bretton Woods system, the U.S. dollar was overvalued if the equilibrium exchange rate was below the par value.

T F   14. A sterilized intervention in the foreign exchange market by a central bank will have no effect on the exchange rate because the central bank does not purchase or sell international reserves.

T F   15. An advantage of dollarization over a currency board is that it completely eliminates the possibility of a speculative attack on a country's currency.

Multiple-Choice Questions

Circle the appropriate answer.

1. Which of the following appear as payments in the Canadian balance of payments?
    a. French purchases of Canadian jeans.
    b. Purchases by Japanese tourists in Canada.
    c. Interest payments to Germans who hold Canadian bonds.
    d. Income earned by Nortel from its business abroad.

2. Which of the following appears in the current account part of the balance of payments?
    a. An Italian's purchase of Nortel stock.
    b. Income earned by Barclay's Bank of London, England, from subsidiaries in Canada.
    c. A loan by a Swiss bank to a Canadian corporation.
    d. A purchase by the Bank of Canada of an English Treasury bond.
    e. None of the above.

3. If Canadians are buying $1 billion more English goods and assets than the English are willing to buy from Canada, and so the Bank of England therefore sells $1 billion worth of pounds in the foreign exchange market, then
    a. England gains $1 billion of international reserves and its monetary base rises by $1 billion.
    b. England loses $1 billion of international reserves and its monetary base falls by $1 billion.
    c. England gains $1 billion of international reserves and its monetary base falls by $1 billion.
    d. England loses $1 billion of international reserves and its monetary base rises by $1 billion.
    e. England's level of international reserves and monetary base remains unchanged.

4. An important advantage for a reserve currency country is that
    a. its balance of payments deficits are financed by other countries' interventions in the foreign exchange market.
    b. it has more control over its monetary policy than non-reserve currency countries.
    c. it has more control over its exchange rate than non-reserve currency countries.
    d. both (a) and (b) of the above are true.

5. Under a gold standard in which one dollar could be turned into the U.S. Treasury and exchanged for 1/20th of an ounce of gold and one Swiss franc could be exchanged for 1/60th of an ounce of gold,

    a. at an exchange rate of 4 francs per dollar, gold would flow from the United States to Switzerland and the Swiss monetary base would fall.

    b. at an exchange rate of 4 francs per dollar, gold would flow from Switzerland to the United States and the Swiss monetary base would rise.

    c. at an exchange rate of 2 francs per dollar, gold would flow from the United States to Switzerland and the U.S. monetary base would fall.

    d. at an exchange rate of 2 francs per dollar, gold would flow from Switzerland to the United States and the U.S. monetary base would rise.

6. In a speculative attack against a weak currency under a fixed exchange rate system, the central bank for this country must shift the expected return schedule for domestic deposits further to the _____ through the _____ of international reserves.

    a. left; purchase

    b. right; sale

    c. left; sale

    d. right; purchase

7. Countries with deficits in their balance of payments often do not want to see their currencies depreciate because

    a. this would hurt consumers in their country by making foreign goods more expensive.

    b. this would stimulate inflation.

    c. this would hurt domestic businesses by making foreign goods cheaper in their country.

    d. this would hurt domestic businesses by making their goods more expensive abroad.

    e. of both (a) and (b) of the above.

8. The International Monetary Fund is an international organization that

    a. promotes the growth of trade by setting rules for how tariffs and quotas are set by countries.

    b. makes loans to countries to finance projects such as dams and roads.

    c. since the 1980s, has been acting as an international lender of last resort.

    d. does each of the above.

9. When a central bank buys its currency in the foreign exchange market,

    a. they acquire international reserves.

    b. they lose international reserves.

    c. the money supply will increase.

    d. both (a) and (b) of the above occur.

10. A central bank's international reserves rise when

    a. it sells domestic currency to purchase foreign assets in the foreign exchange market.

    b. it sells foreign currency to purchase domestic assets in the foreign exchange market.

    c. it buys domestic currency with the sale of foreign assets in the foreign exchange market.

    d. it buys gold with the sale of foreign assets in the foreign exchange market.

11. Under the Bretton Woods system, the U.S. dollar was _____ if the _____ exchange rate (expressed as units of foreign currency per dollar) was _____ the _____ value of the exchange rate.

    a. overvalued; equilibrium; below; par

    b. overvalued; equilibrium; above; par

    c. undervalued; par; above; equilibrium

    d. undervalued; equilibrium; below; par

12. A central bank that wants to _____ its currency is likely to adopt a _____ monetary policy.
    a. strengthen; less contractionary
    b. strengthen; more contractionary
    c. weaken; less expansionary
    d. weaken; more contractionary

13. A central bank _____ of domestic currency and corresponding _____ of foreign assets in the forcign exchange market leads to an equal decline in its international _____ and the monetary base.
    a. sale; purchase; reserves
    b. sale; sale; liabilities
    c. purchase; sale; reserves
    d. purchase; purchase; liabilities

14. A higher domestic money supply leads to a higher domestic price level in the long run, resulting in an expected _____ of the domestic currency that shifts the _____ schedule to the _____.
    a. depreciation; R^F; right
    b. appreciation; R^F; right
    c. depreciation; R^D; left
    d. appreciation; R^D; left

15. If the central bank decreases the money supply, domestic interest rates rise causing R^D to shift _____, while causing R^F to shift _____ because of the expected appreciation of the dollar.
    a. right; left
    b. right; right
    c. left; left
    d. left; right

16. A case can be made for controls on capital inflows because capital inflows
    a. can lead to a lending boom and encourage excessive risk taking.
    b. never go to financing productive investments.
    c. never finance productive investments and can lead to a lending boom and encourage excessive risk taking.
    d. are more effective in preventing financial crises than are policies that regulate banking activities.

17. A sterilized intervention in the foreign exchange market by a central bank will have no effect on the exchange rate because
    a. the central bank does not purchase or sell international reserves.
    b. the amount of international reserves held by the central bank is unchanged.
    c. the monetary base of the central bank is unchanged.
    d. the central bank simultaneously sells and buys foreign exchange.

18. When a central bank performs an unsterilized intervention in the foreign exchange market, the money supply _____ changes.
    a. always
    b. usually
    c. sometimes
    d. never

19. Which of the following will make the exchange rate rise from 3.5 Brazilian real per Canadian dollar to 3.7 real per dollar?

    a. The Brazilian central bank sells Brazilian government bonds.

    b. The Brazilian central bank sells Canadian dollars.

    c. The Bank of Canada sells Canadian dollars.

    d. The Bank of Canada sells Canada bonds.

    e. None of the above.

20. The current account balance may indicate future changes in the exchange rate because

    a. the current account shows what is happening to the demand for imports and exports.

    b. the current account indicates what will happen to claims on foreign wealth in the future.

    c. any change to the current account must be paid for by a change in net government international reserves.

    d. only (a) and (b) of the above.

    e. only (a) and (c) of the above.

21. If Singapore's current account is $300 billion, and its capital account is –$250 billion, then the central bank of Singapore _____ net holdings of international reserves by _____ .

    a. increased; $550 billion

    b. decreased; $550 billion

    c. increased; $50 billion

    d. decreased; $50 billion

22. If a newspaper reports that Nigeria's balance of payments has a deficit of $50 billion, then which of the following is true?

    a. The capital account is –$50 billion.

    b. The current account minus the capital account is $50 billion.

    c. The official reserve transactions balance is –$50 billion.

    d. The Nigerian central bank acquired $50 billion worth of international reserves.

23. One benefit of the gold standard is that

    a. a country has greater control of its money supply.

    b. inflation and deflation are less severe.

    c. exchange rates tend to return to their par value.

    d. gold is not traded between countries.

24. Countries experiencing a foreign exchange crisis, such as Mexico and Brazil did in the 1990s,

    a. are also experiencing a balance-of-payments crisis.

    b. may turn to the World Bank for help.

    c. are gaining international reserves.

    d. can revalue their currencies to end the crisis.

    e. only (a) and (c) of the above.

25. If the exchange rate between the Thai baht and the U.S. dollar is fixed, and if the Thai baht is overvalued, then Thailand will need to _____ international reserves or _____ the baht.

    a. sell; devalue

    b. purchase; revalue

    c. sell; revalue

    d. purchase; devalue

26. A disadvantage of capital controls in emerging market economies is that
    a. there are ways for capital to avoid the controls.
    b. they divert attention away from other important causes of financial instability.
    c. they may lead to corruption and bribery of governmental officials.
    d. all of the above.
    e. only (b) and (c) of the above.

27. If a central bank engages in a sterilized intervention, then there is no
    a. impact on the monetary base.
    b. effect on the exchange rate.
    c. impact on the money supply.
    d. all of the above.
    e. only (a) and (b) of the above.

28. The "rules of the game" under a gold standard mean that a country
    a. experiences deflation when world gold production increases.
    b. experiences inflation when world gold production slows.
    c. loses control over monetary policy.
    d. all of the above.
    e. only (a) and (c).

29. In the case of an unsterilized intervention, if the Bank of Canada decides to sell foreign assets, the Canadian price level will _____ in the long run and the expected future exchange rate will _____.
    a. fall; fall
    b. rise; rise
    c. rise; fall
    d. fall; rise

30. Exchange-rate targeting _____ the probability of speculative attacks, and provides _____ control on inflation.
    a. increases; more
    b. decreases; more
    c. increases; less
    d. decreases; less

CHAPTER 21

The Demand for Money

CHAPTER SYNOPSIS/COMPLETIONS

Earlier chapters looked at how the Bank of Canada, the public, and commercial banks all influence the money supply. This chapter looks at what determines money demand. Later in the text you will put money supply and demand together in order to study *monetary theory,* which is the study of how money affects the economy. The central question in monetary theory is whether or to what extent money demand is affected by interest rates.

The earliest treatment of the demand for money was offered by the classical economists. The classical economists—most notably Irving Fisher—argued that the demand for money was a function of nominal aggregate income. This followed from their assumptions regarding (1)_____ (the average number of times per year that a dollar is spent on final goods and services produced in the economy) and the equation of exchange.

The classical economists argued that the speed with which money is spent is a function of the institutional features of the economy. Although these features certainly change over time (due to improvements in technology, for example), velocity could be regarded as (2)_____ in the short run.

Nothing more than an identity, the equation of (3)_____ states that the quantity of money times velocity must equal nominal income. But when combined with Irving Fisher's assumption of a constant velocity, the equation of exchange is transformed into the quantity theory of (4)_____. Given the assumption of constant velocity, the quantity theory of money implies that changes in nominal income are determined solely by changes in the quantity of money. The classical economists also assumed that prices and wages were completely (5)_____, meaning that the economy would always remain at full employment. This last assumption meant that changes in the money supply had no effect on aggregate output and could therefore affect only the (6)_____.

Dividing both sides of the equation of exchange by the constant velocity makes clear that the quantity of money people hold is a constant fraction of nominal income. Thus, the classical economists regarded the demand for money as a demand for a medium of exchange.

John Maynard Keynes believed that a decline in velocity helped to explain the Great Depression, and his efforts to explain this decline in velocity led to his theory of money demand, which he called the (7)_____ _____ theory. Keynes contended that there were three separate and distinct motives for holding money: the transactions motive, the precautionary motive, and the (8)_____ motive.

It was the speculative motive that distinguished Keynes's theory from the other theories. Keynes argued that interest rates played an important role in determining the amount of wealth people desire to hold in the form of money. Though bonds pay interest, a rise in interest rates causes bond values to (9)_____, subjecting their holders to capital losses and even negative returns if bond values fall significantly. Thus, at low rates of interest, people reduce their holdings of bonds and hold more money as they expect interest rates to rise, returning to their normal levels. Therefore, Keynes concluded that the demand for money was (10)_____ related to the level of interest rates.

Since Keynes's early attempt, economists have improved on his analysis providing a better rationale for the (11)_____ relationship between interest rates and velocity. The works of Baumol and Tobin indicate that the transaction component (and, by extension, the precautionary component) of the demand for money is negatively related to the level of interest rates.

Friedman—noting that the interest rate paid on chequing deposits tends to move with market rates so that the differential between market interest rates and the interest rate paid on money remains relatively constant—believes that changes in interest rates will have little effect on the demand for money. This result does not require the absence of deposit rate ceilings, as banks pay implicit interest on deposits by providing "free" services such as branch offices, more tellers, or "free" chequing. Additionally, Friedman differs from Keynes in believing that the money demand function is stable and therefore velocity is predictable. To Friedman, the money supply is the main determinant of nominal income.

Milton Friedman has offered an alternative explanation for the (12)_____ behaviour of velocity. Rather than rely on the procyclical behaviour of interest rates, Friedman argues that since changes in actual income exceed changes in permanent income, velocity will tend to move procyclically.

Research on the demand for money indicates that while the demand for money is sensitive to interest rates, there is little evidence that the liquidity trap has ever existed. Also, because of the rapid pace of financial innovation, since 1973 the demand for money has been quite unstable. It is because of this instability that setting rigid money supply targets in order to control aggregate spending in the economy may not be an effective way to conduct monetary policy.

HELPFUL HINTS

Does money demand depend on the interest rate? The early classical economists said no. Keynes said yes. Friedman said yes, but no. Why does it matter? The more sensitive the demand for money is to the interest rate, the less influence the Fed has over aggregate spending. What is the evidence? Interest rates do influence money demand, but the demand for money is not extremely (or infinitely) sensitive to interest rates, which means the Fed can influence, but not completely control, aggregate spending.

EXERCISES

Practice Problems

1.

a.   Suppose nominal GDP is $15 trillion and the quantity of money is $5 trillion. Calculate the velocity of money.

_____

_____

b.   Now suppose that velocity is 5 and nominal GDP is $25 trillion. Calculate the quantity of money.

_____

_____

c.   What assumption transforms the equation of exchange into the quantity theory of money?

_____

_____

d. According to the quantity theory of money, what will happen to the price level if the money supply increases from $1 trillion to $1.3 trillion?

_____

_____

e. According to the quantity theory of money, what will the demand for money be if nominal income is $20 trillion and velocity is 2?

_____

_____

2. Suppose that people have come to expect that interest rates are normally 2%, but interest rates are currently 4%.
a. What will people expect to happen to the price of bonds as the interest rate returns to normal?

_____

_____

b. What will happen to the return on bonds as the interest rate returns to normal?

_____

_____

c. According to Keynes, what will happen to the demand for money if interest rates are above normal? Why?

_____

_____

3. Suppose you earn $1800 at the beginning of each month from your part-time job. Initially you cash your entire paycheck and spend your money evenly throughout the month.
a. What are your average cash balances?

_____

_____

b. What is your velocity of money?

_____

_____

c. Now suppose the interest rate increases and you decide to cash half of your paycheck at the beginning of the month, putting the remainder in bonds. Half way through the month you convert the bonds to cash. What are your average cash balances in this case?

_____

_____

d. What is your velocity of money?

_____

_____

e. What are the costs and benefits of holding money? Why did you decide to reduce your average cash balances when the interest rate rose?

_____

_____

_____

_____

4.

a. What are the two major differences between Friedman's money demand function and the Keynesian money demand function?

_____

_____

b. Suppose the rate of return on bonds rises. According to Friedman, what will happen to the rate of return on money? Explain how the rate of return on money changes even when money does not pay an explicit interest rate.

_____

_____

c. Use Friedman's money demand function to explain why velocity is procyclical.

_____

_____

_____

_____

Short-Answer Questions

1. What reasoning did Irving Fisher use to argue that the velocity of money is constant?

_____

_____

2. Why do classical economists believe that the level of output in the economy in normal times is at full employment?

_____

_____

3. Is the velocity of money constant?

_____

_____

4. According to Keynes, what are the three motives for holding money? Which of these motives is related to the interest rate?

_____

_____

5. What is the difference between nominal money balances and real money balances and what was Keynes's argument for why people desire to hold a certain level of real money balances?

_____

_____

6. Why do people hold precautionary money balances and how are those money balances related to income?

_____

_____

7. What does Keynes's liquidity preference theory predict about the relationship between interest rates and the velocity of money?

_____

_____

8. Explain why Keynes's liquidity preference theory predicts that the velocity of money is procyclical.

_____

_____

9. Why is it still unclear whether a speculative demand for money even exists?

_____

_____

10. What is permanent income and how does it differ from current income?

_____

_____

Critical-Thinking Questions

Suppose you read in the paper that the Bank of Canada has just increased the money supply by 20%. You decide to figure out what this means for the economy but, having just learned about three possible money demand functions, you know that your answer will depend on how money demand responds to the interest rate.

1. Analyze how this increase in the supply of money will affect the economy if the demand for money is the
a. quantity theory of money demand.

_____

_____

b. Keynesian liquidity preference function when there is a liquidity trap.

_____

_____

c. Keynesian liquidity preference function but the interest sensitivity of money demand is somewhere between ultrasensitive and completely insensitive.

_____

_____

d. Friedman's money demand.

_____

_____

2. Which one of your descriptions of the effect of the increase in the money supply on the economy is closest to what would likely happen in the real world? Why?

_____

_____

_____

3. What does you answer to Question 2 imply about the Bank of Canada's ability to influence nominal income?

_____

_____

_____

_____

SELF-TEST

True-False Questions

Circle whether the following statements are true (T) or false (F).

T F 1. The equation of exchange states that the product of the quantity of money and the average number of times that a dollar is spent on final goods and services in a given period must equal nominal income.

T F 2. Irving Fisher argued that velocity would be relatively constant in the short run, since institutional features of the economy, such as the speed at which cheques were cleared, were likely to change only slowly over time.

T F 3. The classical economists' contention that velocity could be regarded as a constant transformed the equation of exchange (an identity) into the quantity theory of money.

T F 4. Friedman believes that the demand for money is affected by changes in current income.

T F 5. At relatively low interest rates, people might be reluctant to hold money due to a concern about capital losses should interest rates rise.

T F 6. Keynes's liquidity preference theory offered an explanation for why velocity had fallen during the Great Depression.

T F 7. The demand for money approach developed by Keynes is consistent with the procyclical movements in velocity observed in Canada.

T F 8. Studies by economists show that the liquidity trap was common before 1973.

T F 9. James Tobin suggested that people might prefer to hold money to bonds as a store of wealth in an effort to reduce risk.

T   F   10. The permanent income argument in Friedman's demand for money formulation suggests that velocity will fluctuate with business cycle movements.

T   F   11. The main difference between Keynes's formulation and the classical demand for money is that the former relates it to the interest rate.

T   F   12. The liquidity preference theory of Keynes states that the demand for precautionary money is determined by the interest rate.

T   F   13. The transaction component of the demand for money is negatively related to the level of the interest rate.

T   F   14. Unlike Keynes's theory, Friedman's theory suggests that changes in interest rates should have little effect on the demand for money.

T   F   15. With Keynes's liquidity preference theory, permanent income is the primary determinant of money demand, and changes in interest rates should have little effect on the demand for money.

Multiple-Choice Questions

Circle the appropriate answer.

1. The quantity theory of money suggests that cutting the money supply by one-third will lead to
    a. a sharp decline in output by one-third in the short run and a decline in the price level by one-third in the long run.
    b. a decline in output by one-third.
    c. a decline in output by one-sixth and a decline in the price level by one-sixth.
    d. a decline in the price level by one-third.
    e. none of the above.

2. The classical economists believed that velocity could be regarded as constant in the short run, since
    a. institutional factors, such as the speed with which cheques were cleared through the banking system, changed slowly over time.
    b. the opportunity cost of holding money was close to zero.
    c. financial innovation tended to offset changes in interest rates.
    d. none of the above are true.

3. Empirical evidence supports the contention that
    a. velocity tends to be procyclical; that is, velocity declines (increases) when economic activity contracts (expands).
    b. velocity tends to be countercyclical; that is, velocity declines (increases) when economic activity contracts (expands).
    c. velocity tends to be countercyclical; that is, velocity increases (declines) when economic activity contracts (expands).
    d. velocity is essentially a constant.

4. Keynes's liquidity preference theory explains why velocity can be expected to rise when
    a. income increases.
    b. wealth increases.
    c. brokerage commissions increase.
    d. interest rates increase.

5. Keynes argued that people were more likely to increase their money holdings if they believed that
   a. interest rates were about to fall.
   b. bond prices were about to rise.
   c. bond prices were about to fall.
   d. none of the above are true.

6. The Baumol-Tobin analysis suggests that
   a. velocity is relatively constant.
   b. the transactions component of money demand is negatively related to the level of interest rates.
   c. the speculative motive for money is nonexistent.
   d. both (a) and (c) of the above are true.
   e. both (b) and (c) of the above are true.

7. One possible implication of the elimination of deposit rate ceilings is that the implicit interest rate on money will more closely approach bond rates. This suggests that changes in interest rates will
   a. have a greater impact on money demand.
   b. have less effect on the demand for money.
   c. no longer affect the speculative demand for money.
   d. cause velocity to become more volatile.

8. Milton Friedman argues that the demand for money is relatively insensitive to interest rates because
   a. the demand for money is insensitive to changes in the opportunity cost of holding money.
   b. competition among banks keeps the opportunity cost of holding money relatively constant.
   c. people base their investment decisions on expected profits, not interest rates.
   d. transactions are not subject to scale economics as wealth increases.

9. Friedman's belief regarding the interest insensitivity of the demand for money implies that
   a. the quantity of money is the primary determinant of aggregate spending.
   b. velocity is countercyclical.
   c. both (a) and (b) of the above are correct.
   d. neither (a) nor (b) of the above are correct.

10. In Friedman's view, because income tends to decline relative to permanent income during business cycle contractions, the demand for money with respect to actual income will increase, causing velocity to
    a. rise.
    b. decline.
    c. remain unchanged, since velocity is only sensitive to changes in interest rates.
    d. decline, provided that interest rates increase when the economy contracts.

11. The velocity of money is best defined as
    a. the average real money balances that are held in one month.
    b. the average number of times per year that a dollar is spent in buying aggregate output.
    c. the average amount of money that a person spends over one year.
    d. the average number of months that a currency bill circulates.

12. The equation of exchange, $MV = PY$,
    a. is an equation that is always true.
    b. is an equation that is never true.
    c. is an equation that holds only if velocity is constant.
    d. was disproved by Keynes.
    e. was proved correct by Friedman.

13. Which of the following may lead to a change in velocity?

    a. A reduction in the interest rate.

    b. A change in monetary institutions.

    c. A change in the money demand function.

    d. All of the above.

    e. None of the above.

14. The quantity theory of money predicts that movements in the price level result solely from changes in the quantity of money because

    a. velocity and aggregate real output are assumed to be constant in the short run.

    b. velocity is assumed to be constant in the short run.

    c. the price level changes slowly.

    d. the money supply is constant in the long run.

    e. None of the above.

15. Keynes's _____ motive states that people hold real money balances as a cushion against unexpected need.

    a. quantity

    b. speculative

    c. transactions

    d. savings

    e. precautionary

16. Keynes' speculative demand for money predicts that people will hold either money or bonds, but not both money and bonds at the same time. This shortcoming was overcome by Tobin who reasoned that _____ , in addition to expected return, was important to the demand for money.

    a. capital gain

    b. longevity

    c. risk

    d. the interest rate

17. According to Keynes, the demand for real money balances _____ and velocity falls when the interest rate _____ .

    a. falls; falls

    b. rises; falls

    c. falls; rises

    d. rises; rises

18. Friedman applied the theory of _____ to the demand for money.

    a. liquidity preference

    b. permanent wealth

    c. asset demand

    d. speculation

19. Friedman's concept of permanent income is best defined as

    a. transitory income.

    b. the opportunity cost of holding money.

    c. expected average holdings of stocks and bonds.

    d. expected average long-run income.

    e. none of the above.

20. According to Friedman, velocity is predictable because
    a. the relationship between income and permanent income is predictable.
    b. interest rates do not change very much.
    c. the money demand function is stable.
    d. only (a) and (b) of the above.
    e. only (a) and (c) of the above.

21. According to Keynes, when the interest rate was below a "normal" value, people would expect the price of bonds to _____ and the quantity demanded of money would _____.
    a. increase; increase
    b. increase; decrease
    c. decrease; increase
    d. decrease; decrease

22. If money demand is _____ sensitive to interest rates, then velocity will be _____ predictable.
    a. more; more
    b. less; more
    c. more; less
    d. less; less

23. The demand for real money will increase if
    a. interest rates increase.
    b. interest rates decrease.
    c. income increases.
    d. income decreases.
    e. both (b) and (c) of the above.

24. The liquidity preference theory indicates that a rise in the interest rate _____ velocity.
    a. decreases
    b. increases
    c. has no effect on
    d. might change

25. According to the demand for money model of Baumol and Tobin, in which case does the demand for transactions money increase?
    a. A rise in brokerage fees.
    b. An increase in interest rate.
    c. An increase in income.
    d. All of the above.

26. Which one of the following money demand functions includes inflation?
    a. Money demand function of Keynes.
    b. Money demand function of Fisher.
    c. Money demand function of Baumol and Tobin.
    d. Money demand function of Friedman.

27. According to Friedman's modern quantity theory of money, if the expected inflation rate is 5% and the expected return of money is 2.5%, then the demand for money will

    a. increase.

    b. decrease.

    c. remain unchanged.

    d. double.

28. Speculative component of money demand is sensitive to

    a. interest rate.

    b. expectations about interest rate.

    c. income and interest rate.

    d. both (a) and (b) of above.

29. It is believed that the main source of unstable money demand after 1973 is the

    a. increase in velocity.

    b. rapid pace of financial innovation.

    c. business cycles.

    d. fluctuations in interest rate.

30. Fisher emphasized _____ and ruled out any possible effect of interest rates on the demand for money in the _____.

    a. technological factors; long run.

    b. technological factors; short run.

    c. individual choice; long run.

    d. individual choice; short run.

CHAPTER 22

The ISLM Model

CHAPTER SYNOPSIS/COMPLETIONS

This chapter develops the *ISLM* model. The *ISLM* model explains how interest rates and total output produced in the economy are determined given a fixed price level. It is sometimes called the Keynesian *ISLM* model because it is based on the work of John Maynard Keynesian during the 1930s. In the next chapter we use the *ISLM* model to evaluate the effects of monetary and fiscal policy.

The Keynesian model arose from John Maynard Keynes's concern with explaining the cause of the Great Depression. Keynes came to the conclusion that the dramatic decline in economic activity was the result of insufficient (1)_____ _____. Aggregate demand in an open economy is the sum of four components of spending: consumer expenditure, (2)_____ _____, government expenditure, and net exports. A decline in any one of these components causes output to decline, potentially leading to recession and rising unemployment.

The Keynesian model, though highly simplified, provides a framework that is very useful for understanding fluctuations in aggregate output. This is more easily accomplished by examining the individual spending components separately.

Keynes argued that consumer expenditure is primarily determined by the level of disposable (3)_____. As income increases, consumers will increase their expenditures. The change in consumer expenditures that results from an additional dollar of disposable income is referred to as the (4)_____ _____ to consume, or simply *mpc*. At low levels of income it is likely that individuals consume more than their disposable income. Thus some amount of consumer expenditure is (5)_____, that is, independent of disposable income. This description of consumption behaviour is summarized by the consumption function, where autonomous consumption is represented by a constant term, *a*, and the positive slope of the function is given by the *mpc*.

Investment spending includes fixed investment (spending by business on equipment and structures, and by households on residential houses) and planned inventory investment. (6)_____ _____ is the spending by business on additional holdings of raw materials, parts, and finished goods.

Keynes believed that managers' expectations of future conditions, as well as interest rates, explained the level of planned investment. If actual investment (the sum of fixed investment and unplanned inventory investment) differs from desired investment (fixed investment plus (7)_____ inventory investment), then the actions of business firms will move the economy toward a new equilibrium. Consider a situation where business firms' inventories have risen above desired levels. Because firms find inventories costly to hold, they will cut production in an attempt to reduce their excess inventories. Aggregate output will fall and the desired level of inventories will eventually be restored.

After this equilibrium is achieved, business firms may become more optimistic about the future health of the economy. As business firms spend more, inventory levels will fall below desired levels, inducing a further expansion in aggregate output. Hence, the initial increase in investment spending is likely to cause a multifold increase in aggregate output. The ratio of the change in aggregate output to the change in investment spending is called the expenditure (8)_____.

An increase in investment spending causes aggregate output to expand by an amount greater than the initial change because consumer expenditure also increases. As firms expand output, they hire more factor inputs such as labour, raising households' disposable incomes. Consumers respond by spending more, leading to a further expansion in output and creating a multifold increase. Since this multifold increase is dependent on additional consumer expenditure, it is not surprising that the value of the *mpc* is used to determine the value of the multiplier.

Once government spending and taxes are added to the simple Keynesian model, policy decisions can be evaluated. Although the tax multiplier is smaller than the government expenditure multiplier, changes in either taxes or government spending can be effective in returning the economy to a full (9)_____ equilibrium.

The *ISLM* model allows one to determine the influence monetary policy has on the economy in the Keynesian framework. The (10)_____ curve illustrates that at lower interest rates, the level of investment spending and aggregate output is greater. Because the *IS* curve represents goods market equilibrium, the economy must be on the *IS* curve to be in general equilibrium. Goods market equilibrium is not, however, sufficient to guarantee general equilibrium; the economy must also be on the *LM* curve.

The *LM* curve slopes up, indicating that as income rises, a (11)_____ interest rate is required to maintain money market equilibrium. The increase in money demand due to an increase in (12)_____ must be exactly offset by the decrease in money demand due to the increase in the interest rate.

The *ISLM* model determines both the level of aggregate output and interest rates when the price level is fixed. Therefore, the *ISLM* model can be used to illustrate the effect on aggregate output and interest rates of monetary or fiscal policy actions, a topic extensively discussed in the next chapter.

HELPFUL HINTS

Changes in autonomous spending have a multiplier effect on aggregate output. Movements along the *IS* curve happen because an increase in the interest rate causes planned investment spending and net exports to decline, which leads to lower aggregate output (*Y*). Movements along the *LM* curve happen because higher aggregate output (*Y*) causes the demand for money to increase, which leads to higher interest rates. The equilibrium point is the point where both the goods market (described by the *IS* curve) and the money market (described by the *LM* curve) are in equilibrium at the same time.

EXERCISES

Practice Problems

1. Suppose that autonomous consumer expenditures are $300 billion and the marginal propensity to consume is 0.80.
a. Fill in the missing values in the table below using the information about consumption given above.

Point in Figure 3	Disposable Income, Y_D	Consumer Expenditure, C	Change in Disposable Income, ΔY_D	Change in Consumer Expenditure, ΔC
E	0	_____	_____	_____
F	200	_____	_____	_____
G	400	_____	_____	_____
H	800	_____	_____	_____

b. Use the data from the table you completed in part *a* to construct a consumption function graph. Label the points on the graph with the letters in the far left column (E through H).

2. Assume that the marginal propensity to consume is 0.90, and autonomous consumer expenditures equal $100 billion. Further, assume that planned investment spending is $300 billion, and government spending and net exports are zero.

a. Calculate equilibrium output.

_____

_____

b. Plot the aggregate demand function along with the 45^0 line and mark the equilibrium point on your graph.

c. Now suppose that autonomous consumer expenditures drop by $50 billion to $50 billion. Calculate the new equilibrium output.

_____

_____

d. Calculate the expenditure multiplier for this economy.

_____

_____

e. Now consider an economy with government spending and taxes. Assume that the marginal propensity to consume is 0.90. Calculate the change in equilibrium output that would result from a $10 billion increase in government spending.

_____

_____

f. Consider the same economy as in part *e* above. Calculate change in equilibrium output that would result from a $10 billion decrease in government spending.

_____

_____

3. a. Match each interest rate with the corresponding level of investment spending, aggregate demand, and equilibrium output:

i	I	Y^{ad}	Y^*
3%	100	$700 + 0.75Y$	4000
8%	200	$800 + 0.75Y$	2800
2%	400	$1{,}000 + 0.75Y$	3200

b. Label the points in the figure below using the numbers from part *a*.

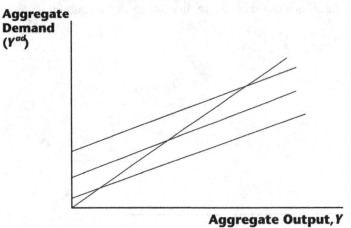

Aggregate Demand (Y^{ad})

Aggregate Output, Y

c.   Use the numbers from part *a* to construct an *IS* curve.

4.   Panel a in the figure below shows equilibriums in the money market corresponding to three different levels of aggregate income. Use the data from Panel a to construct an *LM* curve in Panel b.

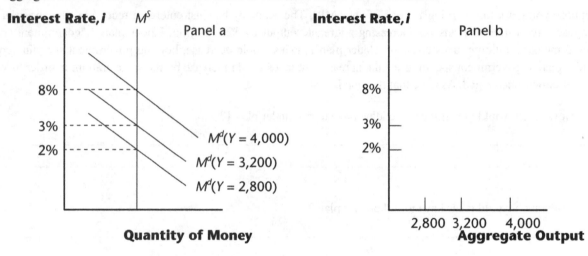

Short-Answer Questions

1.   What are the four types of spending that sum to total quantity demanded of the economy's output?

_____

_____

2.   Explain why, in the Keynesian model, an increase in nominal output is the same as an increase in real output.

_____

_____

3. Suppose that aggregate demand is $900 billion and aggregate output is $850 billion. What is the value of unplanned inventory investment in this economy, and what will happen to bring this economy back to equilibrium?

_____

_____

4. According to Keynes, what is the dominant source of instability in autonomous expenditures?

_____

_____

5. Suppose the *mpc* is 0.80 and net exports falls by $20 billion. Calculate the change in aggregate output.

_____

_____

Critical-Thinking Questions

Suppose you get a job working for one of your MPs. The economy has just entered a recession, and she asks you to propose three different plans for increasing aggregate output by $200 billion. Under plan 1, government spending would increase, holding taxes constant. Under plan 2, taxes would decrease, holding government spending constant. Under plan 3, government spending would increase, but taxes would increase by the same amount in order to keep the budget deficit unchanged. Assume that the *mpc* is 0.80.

1. How much would government spending have to rise under plan 1?

_____

_____

2. How much would taxes have to fall bunder plan 2?

_____

_____

3. How much would government spending and taxes both have to rise under plan 3?

_____

_____

SELF-TEST

True-False Questions

Circle whether the following statements are true (T) or false (F).

T   F   1. The investment spending component of aggregate demand does not include unplanned inventory investment.

T   F   2. Jean purchases 1000 shares of Exxon common stock through her broker. This transaction is included in the investment component of aggregate demand.

T   F   3. The 45-degree line in the Keynesian cross diagram represents all possible or potential equilibrium points.

T F 4. If the level of aggregate output exceeds aggregate demand, income will rise, causing the level of output to expand.

T F 5. Unplanned inventory investment occurs when the level of aggregate demand exceeds aggregate output.

T F 6. Business firms are likely to cut production in the face of unplanned rising inventory levels.

T F 7. The simple Keynesian model suggests that an increase in planned investment will actually lead to an expansion in aggregate output that exceeds the initial change in investment spending. This is known as the multiplier effect.

T F 8. Keynes believed that business cycle fluctuations were dominated by changes in autonomous consumer expenditure.

T F 9. The slope of the *IS* curve reflects the fact that investment is negatively related to the interest rate.

T F 10. At any point along an *IS* curve, the level of unplanned inventory investment is zero.

T F 11. The money demand curve is downward sloping, because a lower interest rate means that the opportunity cost of holding money is lower and therefore the quantity demanded of money is higher.

T F 12. Aggregate demand function y^{ad} is the horizontal sum of the consumption and planned investment spending.

T F 13. As long as output is below the equilibrium level, unplanned inventory investment will remain negative and firms will continue to raise production and output will continue to rise.

T F 14. The larger the marginal propensity to consume, the higher the expenditure multiplier.

T F 15. If the economy is located in the area to the right of the *LM* curve, there is an excess demand for money.

Multiple-Choice Questions

Circle the appropriate answer.

1. Which of the following describes the equilibrium condition in the simple Keynesian model?
   a. Aggregate output equals aggregate demand.
   b. Unplanned inventory investment is zero.
   c. Actual investment equals planned investment.
   d. All of the above.
   e. Only (a) and (b) of the above.

2. Keynes believed that the economy could achieve an equilibrium level of output
   a. only at the full-employment level of output.
   b. below the full-employment level of output.
   c. only if the government took a "hands-off" approach.
   d. by doing none of the above.

3. Inventory investment is distinguished from fixed investment in that
   a. fixed investment is never unplanned.
   b. inventory investment is never planned.
   c. unplanned inventory investment is always zero.
   d. there is no distinction.

4. If one knows the value of the multiplier and the change in the level of autonomous investment, one can determine
   a. the change in the interest rate.
   b. the change in the money supply.
   c. the change in the aggregate output.
   d. all of the above.

5. Keynes believed that fluctuations in aggregate output were largely the result of fluctuations in
   a. the money supply.
   b. autonomous investment spending.
   c. autonomous consumer expenditure.
   d. government spending.

6. If the MPC is 0.75, the multiplier is
   a. 3.00.
   b. 3.75.
   c. 0.25.
   d. 4.00.

7. Assume that an economy characterized by the simple Keynesian model is in equilibrium at full employment but the government budget is in deficit. If the government raises taxes to balance the budget, then
   a. the rate of unemployment will increase.
   b. the level of aggregate output will increase.
   c. the price level will increase.
   d. all of the above will occur.

8. An increase in the interest rate will cause
   a. investment spending to fall.
   b. investment spending to rise.
   c. tax rates to rise.
   d. no change in aggregate spending.

9. Points to the left of the *IS* curve represent interest rate and output combinations characterized by reductions in
   a. unplanned inventory accumulations.
   b. unplanned inventory reductions.
   c. an excess demand for money.
   d. an excess supply of money.

10. The money market is in equilibrium
   a. at any point on the *LM* curve.
   b. at only one point on the *IS* curve.
   c. at any point on the *IS* curve.
   d. at only one point on the *LM* curve.
   e. when only (a) and (b) of the above occur.

11. At points to the _____ of the *LM* curve there is an excess _____ of money which causes interest rates to fall.
   a. left; supply
   b. left; demand
   c. right; supply
   d. right; demand

12. If the economy is on the *IS* curve, but is to the _____ of the *LM* curve, then the _____ market is in equilibrium, but the interest rate is _____ the equilibrium level.

    a. left; goods; below

    b. left; goods; above

    c. right; money; below

    d. right; goods; above

13. The multiplier effect means that a given change in _____ expenditures will change equilibrium _____ by an amount _____ than the initial change in autonomous expenditures.

    a. autonomous; income; greater

    b. autonomous; income; less

    c. induced; income; greater

    d. induced; employment; greater

    e. autonomous; employment; less

14. If I^u is positive, firms will _____ production and output will _____.

    a. cut; rise

    b. cut; fall

    c. increase; rise

    d. increase; fall

15. In the Keynesian framework, as long as output is _____ the equilibrium level, unplanned inventory investment will remain negative and firms will continue to _____ production.

    a. below; lower

    b. above; lower

    c. below; raise

    d. above; raise

16. The price level in the Keynesian framework

    a. signals to firms whether they should increase or decrease production.

    b. is assumed to be constant.

    c. is the difference between real and nominal interest rates.

    d. changes in order for equilibrium to be reached.

    e. None of the above.

17. If Lisa finds $50 and purchases a sweater for $40 and saves the remaining $10, then her *mpc* is

    a. 0.10.

    b. 0.40.

    c. 0.80.

    d. $10.

    e. $40.

18. Aggregate demand includes _____ but it does not include _____.

    a. consumer expenditures; net exports

    b. planned investment spending; unplanned investment spending

    c. government spending; investment spending

    d. unplanned investment spending; planned investment spending

    e. unplanned investment spending; inventory investment

19. Which of the following is considered fixed investment?
    a. Government bonds.
    b. Raw materials.
    c. Inventory investment.
    d. A warehouse.
    e. All of the above.

20. If the MPC is 0.60, and if government spending rises by $500, then equilibrium output rises by
    a. $1250.
    b. $1000.
    c. $600.
    d. $500.
    e. $60.

21. Which of the following is a reason why the *IS* curve slopes downward?
    a. Investment rises as the interest rate rises.
    b. Net exports fall as the interest rate rises.
    c. Money demand rises as the interest rate rises.
    d. Only (a) and (b) of the above.
    e. Only (b) and (c) of the above.

22. If the consumption function is $C = 100 + 0.50Y_D$, then which of the following statements is true?
    a. Consumption is zero when disposable income is zero.
    b. Consumption is 100 when disposable income is zero.
    c. Consumption is 50 when disposable income is 100.
    d. Consumption is 100 when disposable income is 100.
    e. Consumption is 100 when disposable income is 50.

23. If the government raises taxes by $40 and simultaneously raises government spending by _____, then equilibrium output will _____.
    a. $40; fall
    b. $50; fall
    c. $0; rise
    d. $80; rise

24. The *ISLM* model differs from the Keynesian framework in that
    a. the price level is assumed to be constant.
    b. the interest rate is determined within the model.
    c. monetary policy can be studied within the model.
    d. only (a) and (b) of the above.
    e. only (b) and (c) of the above.

25. The LM curve slopes upward because as income rises, the _____ must _____ in order for the money market to remain in equilibrium.
    a. money supply; rise
    b. interest rate; fall
    c. money supply; fall
    d. interest rate; rise
    e. MPC; rise

26. If government purchases increase by $100 million and if autonomous taxes increase by $100 million, then in the simple Keynesian model
    a. aggregate output will increase by more than $100 million.
    b. aggregate output will increase by less than $100 million.
    c. aggregate output will increase by exactly $100 million.
    d. the effect on aggregate output cannot be determined.

27. In Keynes's model, if output is below equilibrium, then unplanned inventory investment will be negative, firms will _____ production, and output will _____.
    a. raise; rise
    b. raise; fall
    c. lower; rise
    d. lower; fall

28. Suppose that the consumption function is $C=100+0.8Y$ and that planned investment spending increases from $50 to $150. The equilibrium output will then rise by _____ dollars.
    a. 100
    b. zero
    c. 500
    d. 200

29. If autonomous spending decreases by $100 and planned investment spending increases by $100 at the same time, the equilibrium output
    a. increases by $100.
    b. decreases by $100.
    c. decreases by $200.
    d. remains unchanged.

30. When the interest rate is _____, few investments in physical capital will earn more than the cost of borrowed funds, so planned investment spending is _____.
    a. high; high
    b. high; low
    c. low; low
    d. low; high

CHAPTER 23

Monetary and Fiscal Policy in the ISLM Model

CHAPTER SYNOPSIS/COMPLETIONS

In this chapter we explore the mechanics of the *ISLM* model, discovering how monetary policy—the control of the money supply and interest rates—and (1)_____ policy—the control of government spending and taxes—affect the level of aggregate output and interest rates. Since policymakers have these two tools at their disposal they will be interested in knowing the effects each policy can be expected to have on the economy. The *ISLM* model provides a convenient but powerful framework for comparing the relative effects of proposed monetary and fiscal actions. By comparing these predicted effects, policymakers can better decide which policy is most appropriate.

The *ISLM* model also provides a framework that allows one to compare the desirability of interest rate targeting against money supply targeting. In addition, the aggregate demand curve is derived using the *ISLM* model. It is for these three important reasons that we study the *ISLM* model in the money and banking course.

As is true of any economic model, we can better comprehend the workings of the *ISLM* model by first examining the behaviour of the individual curves. Once this has been done, the effects that changes in fiscal and monetary variables will have on interest rates and aggregate output can be determined.

The (2)_____ curve shows the combinations of interest rates and aggregate output that ensure equilibrium in the goods market. Therefore, changes in autonomous consumer expenditures, autonomous (3)_____ spending, and government spending or taxes are all factors that shift the *IS* curve. For example, if the government enacts legislation to spend $100 billion over the next ten years to repair the decaying infrastructure (roads, bridges, canals) of the economy, the added government spending shifts the *IS* curve to the (4)_____. An example of a leftward shift in the *IS* curve is provided by the precipitous drop in autonomous investment spending during the Great Depression. It is important to distinguish between autonomous changes in investment and changes in investment due to changes in interest rates. A change in investment that results from a change in interest rates is shown as a movement along a given *IS* curve, not as a shift in the *IS* curve.

Interest rate and aggregate output combinations that represent equilibrium in the money market define an (5)_____ curve. Therefore, changes in either money supply or money demand can cause the *LM* curve to shift.

Consider the effect an increase in money supply has on the *LM* curve. At the initial interest rate, an increase in the money supply creates an (6)_____ supply of money. Holding output constant, equilibrium is regained in the money market by a fall in the interest rates. Alternatively, the interest rate held constant, equilibrium is regained in the money market when the increase in aggregate (7)_____ is sufficient to raise money demand to a level that eliminates the excess supply of money.

Changes in money demand also shift the *LM* curve. If more people come to expect a surge in the stock market, they will try to conserve their holdings of money, filling their portfolios with more stocks (recall the analysis of Chapter 5 on asset demand). The drop in money demand creates an excess supply of money at the initial interest rate. Therefore, interest rates will (8)_____, holding output constant, and the *LM* curve shifts to the (9)_____. Conversely, an increase in the demand for money shifts the *LM* curve left.

Putting the *IS* and *LM* curves together allows us to consider the effects of autonomous spending and policy changes on the equilibrium levels of the interest rate and aggregate output. For example, a tax cut aimed at reducing the budget surplus shifts the *IS* curve (10)_____ due to the increase in spending by consumers. The increase in output causes the demand for money to rise, which in turn creates an excess demand for money, putting upward pressure on interest rates. Although the rise in interest rates causes interest-sensitive investment to decrease, the decrease is not enough to offset the expansionary effects of the tax cut. No wonder tax cuts are so popular among incumbent politicians: a tax cut may cause rising employment and a net gain of votes on election day.

Some economists contend that there is a tendency for the money supply to expand prior to elections. Since the *ISLM* model indicates that an increase in the money supply causes aggregate output to (11)_____ and interest rates to fall, and since both are likely to help the incumbent politician, such a contention has credibility.

The *ISLM* framework also has been used to analyze the appropriateness of Bank of Canada operating procedures. While interest rate targets can be shown to be more consistent with stable economic activity when the *LM* curve is unstable, a money supply target helps ensure greater stability when the (12)_____ curve is unstable. Since neither targeting procedure outperforms the other in every situation, it becomes an empirical question as to which curve is more stable and under which conditions. Thus it is not surprising that economists still debate over the appropriate targeting procedure the Bank should employ.

Another debate has centred around the slope of the *LM* curve. If the *LM* curve is very steep, approaching a vertical line, then an expansionary fiscal policy is likely to be an (13)_____ tool for expanding aggregate output since investment spending will be crowded out by the rising interest rates.

Finally, the *ISLM* model is useful in deriving the aggregate demand curve used in aggregate demand and supply analysis. Since aggregate demand and supply analysis is so powerful, this function of the *ISLM* model is especially important. A decline in the price level raises the real money supply, causing interest rates to fall and investment spending to rise. Simultaneous goods and money market equilibrium will correspond to higher levels of aggregate output as the price level falls, indicating that the aggregate demand curve slopes (14)_____ to the right.

The aggregate demand curve shifts in the same direction as a shift in the *IS* or *LM* curves. Increases in the money supply and government spending or decreases in taxes all cause the aggregate demand curve to shift to the (15)_____. We see in the next chapter that the aggregate demand and supply model provides a powerful framework for understanding recent economic events.

HELPFUL HINTS

Fiscal policy (changes in government spending and taxes) shifts the *IS* curve. Monetary policy (changes in the money supply) shifts the *LM* curve. In the long run, aggregate output returns to the natural rate level of output. If output is above the natural rate level, the price level rises, the real money supply declines, and the *LM* curve shifts left until aggregate output returns to the natural rate level of output. If output is below the natural rate level, the price level falls, the real money supply increases, and the *LM* curve shifts right until aggregate output returns to the natural rate level of output. Fiscal and monetary policies both shift the aggregate demand curve in the same direction. Expansionary policy shifts the aggregate demand curve to the right. Contractionary policy shifts the aggregate demand curve to the left.

EXERCISES

Practice Problems

1. Assume the economy is initially at the natural rate level of output (Y_n).
a. Show what happens in the short run to the interest rate and aggregate output when the Bank of Canada increases the money supply.

b. On the same graph you used to illustrate your answer to part *a,* show what will happen in the long run. Explain your result.

_____

_____

_____

c. Assume the economy is once again at the natural rate level of output (Y_n). Show what happens in the short run to the interest rate and aggregate output when government increases spending.

d. On the same graph you used to illustrate your answer to part *c,* show what will happen in the long run. Explain your result.

_____

_____

_____

_____

2. Complete the table by indicating whether each shift factor listed in the far left column shifts the *IS* or *LM* curve right (right), left (left) or not at all (no shift), and whether the resulting shift in *IS* or *LM* causes interest rates and aggregate output to rise (+), fall (−) or remain unchanged (0).

Shift factor	Direction of change	IS curve shifts…	LM curve shifts…	Effect on interest rate	Effect on aggregate output
Autonomous consumer expenditure	+				
Autonomous investment spending	–				
Government spending	+				
Taxes	+				
Net exports	–				
Money supply	–				
Autonomous money demand	–				

3. a. Suppose the *IS* curve is stable and the *LM* curve is unstable. In the graph below, Panel a, illustrate the effect on aggregate output of following an interest rate target. In Panel b, illustrate the effect on aggregate output of following a money supply target.

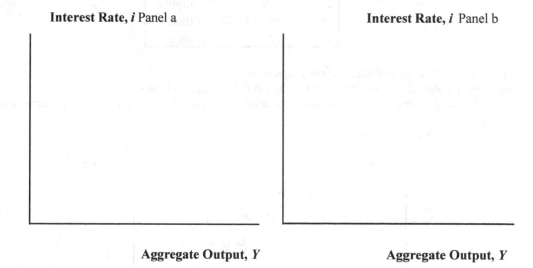

Interest Rate, *i* Panel a   **Interest Rate, *i*** Panel b

Aggregate Output, *Y*   **Aggregate Output, *Y***

b. Based on your analysis in part *a*, which type of policy would you recommend for an economy with a stable *IS* curve and an unstable *LM* curve? Why?

_____

_____

c. Suppose the *IS* curve is unstable, and the *LM* curve is stable. In Panel a on the next page, illustrate the effect on aggregate output of following an interest rate target. In Panel b illustrate the effect on aggregate output of following a money supply target.

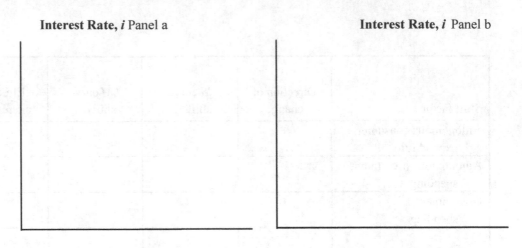

Interest Rate, *i* Panel a   **Interest Rate, *i*** Panel b

Aggregate Output, *Y*   **Aggregate Output, *Y***

d. Based on your analysis in part *c,* which type of policy would you recommend for an economy with an unstable *IS* curve and a stable *LM* curve? Why?

_____

_____

4. Consider the following data on interest rates, aggregate output, and the price level.

i	*P*	*Y*
2%	100	$1.0 trillion
7%	98	$1.5 trillion
4%	72	$1.8 trillion

a. Label both axes in Panel a of the graph below.
b. Use the data from the table to complete the *ISLM* graph in Panel a.
c. Use the data from the table to draw the aggregate demand curve in Panel b that corresponds to the *ISLM* graph in Panel a.
d. Label both axes in Panel b.

Panel a   Panel b

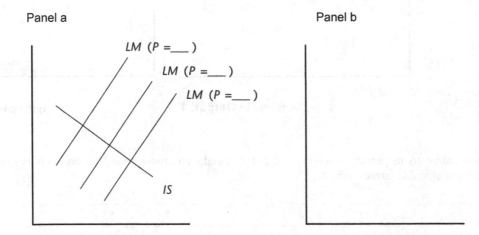

LM (P =___)

LM (P =___)

LM (P =___)

IS

Short-Answer Questions

1. List the factors that shift the *IS* curve.

_____

_____

2. List the factors that shift the *LM* curve.

_____

_____

3. Give an example of a change in investment spending that would cause a shift in the *IS* curve. Give an example of a change in investment spending that would cause a movement along the *IS* curve.

_____

_____

4. Give an example of a change in net exports that would cause a shift in the *IS* curve. Give an example of a change in net exports that would cause a movement along the *IS* curve.

_____

_____

5. Give an example of change in money demand that would cause a shift in the *LM* curve. Give an example of a change in money demand that would cause a movement along the *LM* curve.

_____

_____

Critical-Thinking Questions

Most of the analysis of fiscal and monetary policy in this chapter considers one type of policy at a time, holding the other type of policy constant. But in the real world, both monetary policy and fiscal policy are changing all of the time. Consider the combinations of monetary and fiscal policy listed in the table on the following page. Fill in the missing columns in the table by indicating whether the given combination of monetary and fiscal policy has a positive (+), negative (–), or ambiguous (?) impact on interest rates and aggregate output.

Fiscal Policy	Monetary Policy	Interest Rates	Aggregate Output
Expansionary	Expansionary	_____	_____
Contractionary	Contractionary	_____	_____
Expansionary	Contractionary	_____	_____
Contractionary	Expansionary	_____	_____

SELF-TEST

True-False Questions

Circle whether the following statements are true (T) or false (F).

T   F   1. An increase in the interest rate causes the *IS* curve to shift to the left, since investment spending will fall.

T   F   2. If businesses should suddenly become "bearish" (pessimistic) about the future profitability of investment, aggregate output will fall, all else constant. This is shown as a leftward shift of the *IS* curve.

T   F   3. Financial innovation—by increasing the liquidity of financial assets—has enabled some people to reduce their demand for money. The decline in the demand for money has the effect of shifting the *LM* curve to the left.

T   F   4. An expansion of the money supply will lead to lower interest rates and an increase in investment spending as people attempt to rid themselves of excess money balances.

T   F   5. The condition known as complete crowding out occurs when the demand for money is insensitive to the interest rate.

T   F   6. The effect of an open market purchase is to shift the *LM* curve to the left.

T   F   7. Assume that money demand is very unstable and the *IS* curve is stable. Such knowledge makes the case for monetary targeting stronger, since the *IS* curve will be stable relative to the *LM* curve.

T   F   8. A decline in taxes causes the aggregate demand curve to shift to the left.

T   F   9. Monetary policy changes have no effect on the aggregate demand curve, since it is only factors that shift the *IS* curve which affect aggregate demand.

T   F   10. High unemployment leads the Bank of Canada to expand the money supply. Such a policy will shift both the *LM* and aggregate demand curves to the right.

T   F   11. Aggregate output and interest rates are negatively related to government spending and positively related to taxes.

T   F   12. The less interest-sensitive money demand is, the more effective monetary policy is, relative to fiscal policy.

T   F   13. If the *IS* curve is more unstable than the *LM* curve, a money supply target is preferred.

T   F   14. Any factor that shifts the *IS* curve shifts the aggregate demand curve in the same direction.

T   F   15. If the *LM* curve is more unstable than the *IS* curve, an interest rate target is preferred.

Multiple-Choice Questions

Circle the appropriate answer.

1. Which of the following causes the *IS* curve to shift to the left?
    a. Increase in taxes.
    b. Increase in government spending.
    c. Increase in the money supply.
    d. All of the above.
    e. Only (b) and (c) of the above.

2. An increase in government spending causes both interest rates and aggregate output to increase. In the *ISLM* framework, this is represented by a _____ shift of the _____ curve.

    a. leftward; *LM*

    b. rightward; *LM*

    c. leftward; *IS*

    d. rightward; *IS*

3. In the early 1930s there was a significant contraction in the money supply. In the *ISLM* framework, such a contraction is illustrated as a _____ shift of the _____ curve.

    a. rightward; *IS*

    b. rightward; *LM*

    c. leftward; *IS*

    d. leftward; *LM*

4. In 1981, President Reagan in the United States was able to get through Congress a fiscal package containing a tax cut and increased federal expenditures. Such a policy shifts the _____ curve to the _____.

    a. *LM*; left

    b. *IS*; right

    c. *LM*; right

    d. *IS*; left

5. Assume that an economy suffers a recession in spite of an expansionary monetary policy. The *ISLM* framework suggests that even if the *LM* curve shifts to the right, the level of aggregate output might fall if the

    a. *IS* curve shifts to the right.

    b. investment function shifts to the right.

    c. *IS* curve shifts to the left.

    d. taxes are cut.

6. Suppose that the economy is suffering from both high interest rates and high unemployment. Viewed from an *ISLM* framework, we can conclude that _____ policy has been too _____.

    a. fiscal; expansionary

    b. monetary; expansionary

    c. monetary; contractionary

    d. fiscal; contractionary

7. Assume that econometric studies indicate that the demand for money is highly sensitive to interest rate changes. Such evidence would tend to support the belief that

    a. fiscal policy has no aggregate output effects.

    b. fiscal policy is effective in increasing output.

    c. monetary policy is effective in increasing output.

    d. none of the above is true.

8. Investment spending in the country Curtonia is highly unstable, making the *IS* curve very unstable relative to the *LM* curve. Given the nature of the economy, the Central Bank of Curtonia will want to target the

    a. money supply.

    b. interest rate.

    c. exchange rate.

    d. bank rate.

    e. monetary base.

9. The aggregate demand curve slopes downward to the right, since
    a. a decline in the price level raises the real money supply, lowering interest rates.
    b. a decline in the price level raises the real money supply, causing output to fall.
    c. an increase in the price level raises the real money supply, causing output to rise.
    d. none of the above occurs.

10. A Bank of Canada purchase of government securities will shift the aggregate demand curve in which direction?
    a. Right.
    b. Left.
    c. A Bank of Canada purchase of securities does not shift the aggregate demand curve.
    d. All of the above are a possible result of an expansion in the money supply.

11. Assume that the Bank of Canada pursues a policy of pegging the interest rate. If government policymakers _____ government spending, the Bank will be forced to _____ the money supply to keep interest rates from _____.
    a. decrease; decrease; rising
    b. decrease; increase; falling
    c. increase; increase; rising
    d. increase; decrease; rising

12. Within the *ISLM* framework an expansionary fiscal policy causes a(n) _____ in aggregate output and causes interest rates to _____.
    a. increase; fall
    b. increase; rise
    c. decrease; fall
    d. decrease; rise

13. Interest rates in Canada rose over the period 1965 through 1966. Since this coincided with the Vietnam War buildup, we can assume that the _____ curve shifted to the _____.
    a. *LM*; left
    b. *LM*; right
    c. *IS*; left
    d. *IS*; right

14. The _____ responsive is money demand to the interest rate, the _____ effective is _____ policy.
    a. more; more; fiscal
    b. more; less; fiscal
    c. less; more; fiscal
    d. less; less; monetary

15. A _____ in the price level, *ceteris paribus*, will mean _____ interest rates and thus a _____ level of investment.
    a. rise; higher; higher
    b. rise; lower; higher
    c. decline; higher; lower
    d. decline; lower; higher

16. Fiscal policy that moves the budget toward a larger surplus will _____ aggregate output and _____ interest rates.
    a. lower; raise
    b. raise; raise
    c. lower; lower
    d. raise; lower

17. After being elected in 2000, President Bush in the United States reduced taxes, which helped to move the federal government budget from a surplus to a deficit. The *ISLM* framework predicts that the effect was to
    a. shift the *LM* curve to the left.
    b. shift the *IS* curve to the left.
    c. raise aggregate output and lower interest rates.
    d. only (a) and (b) of the above.
    e. none of the above occur.

18. Which of the following has the same effect on the *LM* curve, all else the same, as does a decrease in the money supply?
    a. An increase in the interest rate.
    b. An increase in autonomous consumption expenditures.
    c. An increase in money demand.
    d. An increase in taxes.
    e. None of the above.

19. If investment spending is relatively insensitive to the interest rate, then the _____ curve is relatively _____ and monetary policy is relatively less effective than fiscal policy.
    a. *IS*; flat
    b. *IS*; steep
    c. *LM*; flat
    d. *LM*; steep

20. When the central bank reduces the money supply
    a. the interest rate rises in order to induce people to hold less money.
    b. the interest rate rises and investment spending declines.
    c. aggregate output rises as investment spending declines.
    d. only (a) and (b) of the above.
    e. only (a) and (c) of the above.

21. If the *LM* curve is relatively flat because money demand is relatively interest-sensitive, then a given reduction in taxes will lead to a _____ increase in aggregate output and a _____ increase in the interest rate.
    a. larger; smaller
    b. smaller; larger
    c. smaller; smaller
    d. larger; larger

22. If complete crowding out occurs, then
    a. an increase in the money supply will not decrease the interest rate.
    b. an increase in government spending will not increase the interest rate.
    c. a decrease in the money supply will not decrease aggregate output.
    d. an increase in government spending will not increase aggregate output.

23. If money demand is unstable, then the *LM* curve will not be stable. In this case, the best monetary policy for minimizing output fluctuations is
    a. a money supply target.
    b. an increase in the money supply.
    c. a reduction in government spending.
    d. an interest rate target.

24. The fact that changes in the money supply will not affect output and the interest rate in the long run, known as long-run monetary neutrality, results because
    a. the inflation rate is permanently changed when the money supply changes.
    b. the price level changes and leaves real money balances constant in the long run.
    c. complete crowding out prevents any effect on aggregate output.
    d. none of the above occur.

25. Which of the following will shift the aggregate demand curve to the left?
    a. An increase in the money supply.
    b. A reduction in investment spending.
    c. An increase in government spending.
    d. A reduction in taxes.
    e. None of the above.

26. Other things being equal, if the price level increases, then the _____ curve shifts to the _____.
    a. *LM*; right
    b. *LM*; left
    c. *IS*; right
    d. *IS*; left

27. In the long-run *ISLM* model, when the level of output _____ the natural rate level, the price level _____, which shifts the *LM* curve to the _____ until output returns to the natural rate level.
    a. exceeds; rises; right
    b. exceeds; rises; left
    c. remains below; falls; left
    d. remains below; rises; right

28. An increase in net exports will shift the _____ curve to the _____.
    a. *LM*; right
    b. *LM*; left
    c. *IS*; right
    d. *IS*; left

29. An increase in the volatility of bond returns would _____ the quantity of demanded money and this will shift the _____ curve to the _____.
    a. increase; *LM*; left
    b. decrease; *LM*; right
    c. increase; *IS*; left
    d. decrease; *IS*; left

30. A contractionary fiscal policy shifts the _____ curve to the _____, and the aggregate demand (*AD*) curve shifts to the _____.
    a. *LM*; left; right
    b. *LM*; left; left
    c. *IS*; left; right
    d. *IS*; left; left

CHAPTER 24

Aggregate Demand and Supply Analysis

CHAPTER SYNOPSIS/COMPLETIONS

This chapter develops and applies the tools of aggregate demand and aggregate supply analysis. Those tools are used to illustrate the effects of changes in the money supply, government spending and taxes, animal spirits, and supply shocks on output and the price level.

We construct the aggregate demand and aggregate supply model by first examining the individual curves. The aggregate demand curve describes the relationship between the (1)_____ level and the quantity of aggregate output demanded. The monetarists derive the aggregate demand curve from the quantity theory of money. Holding the money supply and velocity constant, an increase in the price level reduces the quantity of aggregate output demanded. A falling price level implies an increase in the quantity of aggregate output demanded. Keynesians argue that a falling price level—because it causes the real (2)_____ _____ to increase which in turn lowers interest rates—causes both investment spending and the quantity of aggregate output demanded to (3)_____. Both explanations are consistent with a downward sloping aggregate demand curve.

Though both monetarists and Keynesians agree that the aggregate demand curve is downward sloping, they hold different views about the factors that cause the aggregate demand curve to shift. Monetarists contend that changes in the (4)_____ supply are the primary source of changes in aggregate demand. An increase in the money supply shifts the aggregate demand curve to the (5)_____, while a decrease in the money supply shifts it to the left.

Keynesians do not dispute that a change in the money supply shifts aggregate demand, but they regard changes in fiscal policy and autonomous expenditure as additional factors that shift the aggregate demand curve. For example, Keynesians believe that increased government expenditures or a cut in taxes will shift the aggregate demand curve to the (6)_____, while a decrease in government expenditures or a tax increase shifts the aggregate demand curve to the left.

The aggregate supply curve is upward sloping, illustrating that an increase in the price level will lead to an increase in the quantity of output supplied, all else constant. Explaining why the aggregate supply curve slopes upward is fairly straightforward. Since the costs of many inputs (factors of production) tend to be (7)_____ in the short run, an increase in the price of the output will mean greater profits, encouraging firms to (8)_____ production, increasing the quantity of aggregate output supplied.

Note, however, that this increase in output cannot last. Eventually workers will demand higher wages, and resource suppliers will demand higher prices. As factor prices (9)_____, the aggregate supply curve shifts in, causing aggregate output supplied to fall back to its original level.

Combining the aggregate supply and the aggregate demand curves allows one to consider the effects on the price level and aggregate output when one of the factors affecting either aggregate demand or aggregate supply changes. For example, an increase in the money supply shifts the aggregate demand curve to the right. This implies that an increase in the money supply will cause both (10)_____ _____ and the price level to increase in the short run. In the long run, the (11)_____ _____ curve will shift in as workers demand higher nominal wages to compensate for the increase in prices. Since the aggregate supply curve will shift when unemployment and aggregate output differ from their natural rate levels, the long-run equilibrium will coincide with the natural rate level of output.

Therefore, changes in either monetary or fiscal policies can have only temporary effects on unemployment and aggregate output. In the long run, monetary and fiscal expansions can do nothing more than raise the (12)_____ _____. This concept is illustrated by the long-run aggregate supply curve, a vertical line passing through the natural rate of aggregate output.

The aggregate supply curve will shift inward not only as workers come to expect higher inflation, but when negative supply (13)_____ hit the economy (as in the 1970s when OPEC dramatically increased the price of oil) or when workers push for higher real wages. Unfortunately, the economy experiences both rising prices and falling aggregate output in the short run, an outcome referred to as (14)_____. Eventually, the aggregate supply curve will shift outward returning the economy to the natural rate of output.

The aggregate demand and supply analysis indicates that aggregate output and unemployment can deviate from their natural-rate levels for two reasons: shifts in aggregate demand and shifts in aggregate supply. Whether these shifts cause aggregate output to rise or fall, the change will be temporary. Factor prices eventually adjust, moving the economy back to the vertical long-run aggregate supply curve. In the long run, shifts in aggregate demand merely change the price level, and shifts in short-run aggregate supply have no permanent effects.

HELPFUL HINTS

The key to understanding the aggregate demand and supply model is to understand that there are two types of equilibrium. Equilibrium means a position of rest. The short-run equilibrium is a position of temporary rest. Short-run equilibrium is where the aggregate supply curve intersects the aggregate demand curve. This intersection can occur below, at, or above the long-run aggregate supply curve, which is the vertical line at the natural rate level of output. When this equilibrium occurs below (to the left of) the natural rate level of output, slack in the labour market will push wages down and cause the aggregate supply curve to shift downward and to the right until it intersects the long-run aggregate supply curve at the natural rate level of output. When the short-run equilibrium is above (to the right) of the natural rate level of output, tightness in the labour market will push wages up and cause the aggregate supply curve to shift upward and to the left until it intersects the long-run aggregate supply curve at the natural rate level of output. When the short-run aggregate supply curve intersects the aggregate demand curve at the long-run aggregate supply curve, the economy is in long-run equilibrium and there is no tendency for the economy to move from that position unless some "shock" causes either the aggregate supply curve or the aggregate demand curve to shift.

EXERCISES

Practice Problems

1. Suppose aggregate output is measured in trillions of dollars with the price level in 1996 having a value of 1.0. Further suppose that velocity is 3, and the money supply is $2 trillion.
a. Use the information given above along with modern quantity theory of money to calculate the values of aggregate output that correspond to each of the following price levels:

P	Y	P	Y
0.5		1.5	
1		2	

b.   Use the values you generated in part *a* to plot the aggregate demand curve on Figure 24.1.

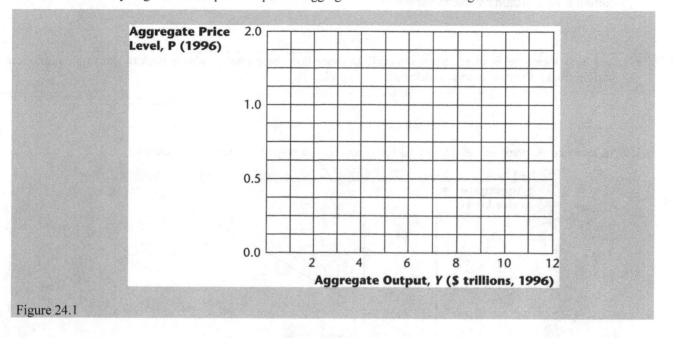

Figure 24.1

c.   Now assume that the money supply decreases to $1 trillion. Generate the new corresponding values of output in the chart below and plot them on Figure 24.1.

P	Y	P	Y
0.5		1.5	
1		2	

2.   Use the Figure 24.2 to answer parts *a* and *b*.

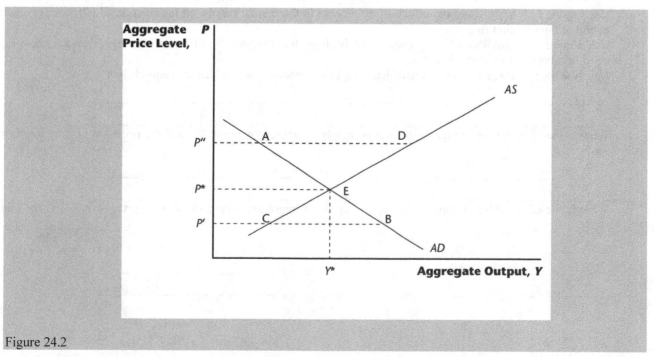

Figure 24.2

a.   At which price level is there excess supply? Describe how the economy adjusts back to short-run equilibrium starting from a situation of excess supply.

_____

b.   At which price level is there excess demand? Describe how the economy adjusts back to short-run equilibrium starting from a situation of excess demand.

_____

_____

3.   Suppose the economy is initially in long-run equilibrium at point 1 as shown in Figure 24.3.

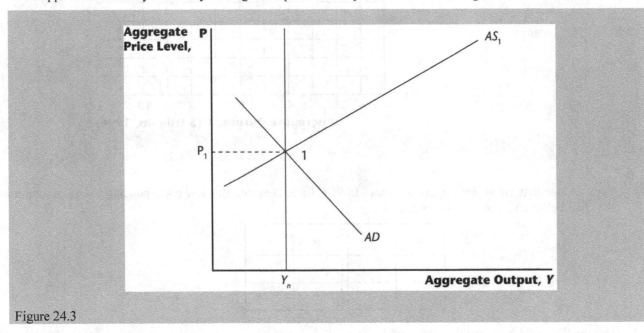

Figure 24.3

a.   Use Figure 24.3 to illustrate the effect of an increase in the money supply on the price level (P) and aggregate output (Y) in the short run.

b.   Use Figure 24.3 to illustrate the adjustment back to the long-run equilibrium starting from the short-run equilibrium you illustrated for part *a*.

c.   Describe the self-correcting mechanism that brings the economy back to long-run equilibrium.

_____

_____

d.   What is the effect of the change in the money supply on aggregate output (Y) and the price level (P) in the short run?

_____

_____

e.   What is the effect of the change in the money supply on aggregate output (Y) and the price level (P) in the long run?

_____

_____

_____

4. Suppose the economy is initially in long-run equilibrium at point 1 as shown in Figure 24.4.

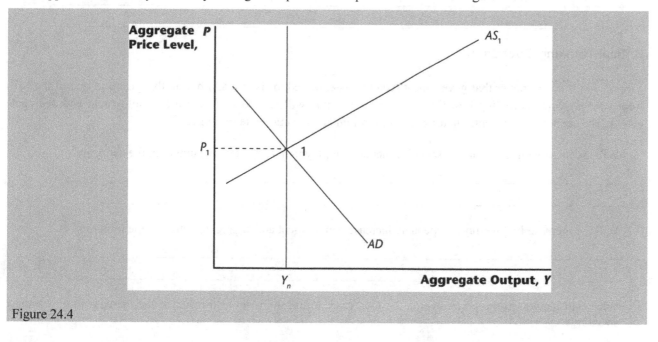

Figure 24.4

a. Use Figure 24.4 to illustrate the effect of a supply shock such as a reduction in the availability of oil on the price level (P) and aggregate output (Y) in the short run.
b. Use Figure 24.4 to illustrate the adjustment back to the long-run equilibrium starting from the short-run equilibrium you illustrated for part (a). Describe the adjustment process back to the long-run equilibrium.

_____

_____

Short-Answer Questions

1. According to the component parts approach to deriving aggregate demand, why does the aggregate demand curve slope downward?

_____

_____

2. According to the component parts approach to deriving aggregate demand, what factors cause the aggregate demand curve to shift?

_____

_____

3. According to the quantity theory of money approach to deriving aggregate demand, how does a decrease in the price level lead to an increase in the aggregate quantity demanded?

_____

_____

4. Explain why the aggregate supply curve slopes upward in the short run.

_____

_____

5.   Contrast the views of Keynesian and monetarist economists on the speed of the self-correcting mechanism.

_____

_____

Critical-Thinking Questions

You read in the newspaper that government spending is expected to rise by $30 billion this year and one of the MPs from your province is touting how this increase in spending will lead to an increase in employment and aggregate output. The economy is currently in long-run equilibrium at the natural rate of output.

1.   Will the increase in government spending increase employment and aggregate output in the short run?

_____

_____

2.   Will the increase in government spending increase employment and aggregate output in the long run?

_____

_____

3.   What will happen to the price level in the long run and the short run as a result of the increase in government spending?

_____

_____

4.   Now assume that the economy is below the natural rate level of output and your MP is a follower of Keynes. What policy action, if any, would your MP likely favour? Why?

_____

_____

5.   Now assume that the economy is below the natural rate level of output and your MP is a follower of Milton Freidman. What policy action, if any, would your MP likely favour? Why?

_____

_____

SELF-TEST

True-False Questions

Circle whether the following statements are true (T) or false (F).

T   F   1.   Monetarists argue that a change in the money supply is the primary factor causing aggregate demand to shift.

T   F   2.   Income velocity is defined as the value of nominal gross national product divided by the money supply.

T   F   3.   Milton Friedman argues that changes in the money supply affect output almost immediately as if it were injected directly into the bloodstream of the economy.

T   F   4.   Along a given aggregate supply curve, input prices are assumed to be fixed.

T   F   5.   If workers come to expect higher inflation, the aggregate supply curve will shift out to reflect the expectation of lower real wages.

T F 6. Persistently high unemployment is likely to force wage concessions by workers, resulting in an eventual outward shift in the aggregate supply curve.

T F 7. Suppose that the economy is currently producing an aggregate output above the natural level of aggregate output. We can expect price reductions in the future as firms lower prices to sell the excess output.

T F 8. Aggregate demand and supply analysis indicates that, if adverse weather causes major crop failures throughout Canada, aggregate output will fall and the price level will rise.

T F 9. In 1970 both inflation and unemployment increased. Such a condition is called "stagflation."

T F 10. Monetarists, unlike Keynesians, believe that wages and prices adjust very slowly over time.

T F 11. Since prices and wages take time to adjust to their long-run level, the aggregate supply curve in the short run differs from the aggregate supply curve in the long run.

T F 12. According to the quantity theory of money, changes in aggregate spending are determined primarily by changes in government spending.

T F 13. The amount of aggregate output supplied at any given price level goes to the natural rate level of output in the long run, so that the long-run aggregate supply curve is a vertical line at the natural rate of output.

T F 14. A rise in the expected price level causes the aggregate supply curve to shift to the right.

T F 15. When aggregate output is above the natural level of output, the aggregate supply curve shifts to the right; when aggregate output is below the natural rate level of output, the aggregate supply curve shifts to the left.

Multiple-Choice Questions

Circle the appropriate answer.

1. Keynesians and monetarists have different views regarding the factors that cause the aggregate demand curve to shift. This difference is best explained by which of the following statements?

   a. Monetarists place greater emphasis on the importance of money yet believe that fiscal actions can shift the aggregate demand curve, while Keynesians contend that money has no effect on aggregate demand.

   b. Keynesians believe that only fiscal policy can affect aggregate demand, while monetarists believe that fiscal policy is ineffective in altering the level of aggregate demand.

   c. Keynesians contend that both fiscal and monetary policy actions influence the level of aggregate demand, while monetarists claim that monetary policy is far more important than fiscal policy in affecting the level of aggregate demand.

   d. Keynesians place more significance on monetary actions than on fiscal actions, while monetarists believe that neither monetary nor fiscal actions influence the level of aggregate demand.

2. In Keynesian analysis, if investment is unresponsive to changes in the interest rate, the aggregate demand curve will be

   a. downward sloping.

   b. horizontal.

   c. downward sloping if consumer expenditures are sensitive to the interest rate.

   d. none of the above.

3. The upward slope of the short-run aggregate supply curve reflects the belief that

   a. factor prices are more flexible than output prices.

   b. output prices are more flexible than factor prices.

   c. factor prices are fixed in the long run.

   d. factor prices are completely flexible even in the short run.

4. Which of the following factors cause the aggregate supply curve to shift?

    a. Changes in the tightness of the labour market.

    b. Changes in expectations of inflation.

    c. Supply shocks such as commodity price changes.

    d. Attempts by workers to push up their real wages.

    e. All of the above.

5. The aggregate demand and supply analysis suggests that the economy has a self-correcting mechanism which ensures that aggregate output and unemployment will move toward their natural-rate levels. However, Keynesians contend that this mechanism

    a. is unacceptably slow due to the stickiness of wages.

    b. cannot be improved on, even though the adjustment process is slow.

    c. while slow, can be improved through activist policy.

    d. does both (a) and (b) of the above.

    e. does both (a) and (c) of the above.

6. If the economy experiences a period of both a rising price level and rising unemployment, one can reasonably infer

    a. that the aggregate demand curve has shifted to the right.

    b. that the aggregate demand curve has shifted to the left.

    c. that the aggregate supply curve has shifted out.

    d. that the aggregate supply curve has shifted in.

7. Which of the following statements accurately describes the difference between monetarists and Keynesians?

    a. Monetarists believe that crowding out can be a major problem reducing the effectiveness of fiscal policy, while Keynesians contend that crowding out will not be complete.

    b. Keynesians regard wage stickiness as a factor that prevents quick adjustment back to the natural rate of unemployment, while monetarists believe that wages are sufficiently flexible to ensure relatively quick adjustment.

    c. Monetarists do not see a need for activist policies, while Keynesians argue that activist policies can prove highly beneficial.

    d. All of the above.

    e. Only (a) and (c) accurately represent differences between monetarists and Keynesians.

8. The long-run aggregate supply curve is a vertical line running through

    a. the natural rate of output.

    b. the natural-rate price level.

    c. the natural rate of unemployment.

    d. none of the above.

9. Which of the following statements is not one commonly associated with Keynesian analysis?

    a. "The economy is inherently unstable, and failure to take corrective action now could mean prolonged unemployment."

    b. "It would be foolish to tie the hands of government policymakers and prevent them from responding to a negative supply shock."

    c. "Wages and prices, while not perfectly flexible, do respond quickly, and in the correct direction, to economic disturbances."

    d. "Crowding out is unlikely to be a problem in the current economic recovery."

10. If policymakers accommodate supply shocks by increasing the money supply, unemployment will return to its natural level sooner, but
    a. even Keynesians, in general, will oppose such a policy.
    b. the price level will increase in the long run.
    c. prices will take much longer in returning to their original level.
    d. none of the above will occur.

11. Keynesians contend that at a _____ price level the real quantity of money _____, _____ higher spending.
    a. lower; expands; encouraging
    b. lower; expands; discouraging
    c. lower; contracts; discouraging
    d. higher; expands; encouraging
    e. higher; expands; discouraging

12. OPEC oil price increases or fruit crop freezes are referred to as _____ price shocks and cause the aggregate _____ curve to shift _____.
    a. negative; demand; inward
    b. negative; demand; outward
    c. negative; supply; inward
    d. positive; supply; inward
    e. positive; supply; outward

13. The aggregate demand and supply framework indicates that in the long run the ultimate effect of a _____ in the money supply is an increase in _____.
    a. fall; aggregate output
    b. fall; the price level
    c. rise; aggregate output
    d. rise; the price level

14. _____ tend to question the effectiveness of _____ policy in shifting aggregate _____, since they believe that crowding out of investment will be nearly complete.
    a. Keynesians; fiscal; demand
    b. Keynesians; monetary; demand
    c. Monetarists; monetary; demand
    d. Monetarists; fiscal; demand
    e. Keynesians; monetary; supply

15. The _____ supply shock from declining oil prices in 1986 did not produce the business cycle boom that some had predicted, in part because a _____ in net exports that year caused a weakening in aggregate _____.
    a. negative; decline; demand
    b. negative; rise; supply
    c. negative; decline; supply
    d. positive; rise; supply
    e. positive; decline; demand

16. Which of the following explains why monetarists believe that the demand curve is downward sloping?
    a. The quantity theory of money shows that as the money supply rises, aggregate output rises.
    b. The quantity theory of money shows that for a fixed money supply and velocity, as the price level rises, aggregate real output falls.
    c. Since the velocity of money is fixed, changes in the money supply lead to changes in aggregate spending.
    d. All of the above.

17. If Italian goods became more popular around the world, and if Italian net exports grow, then
    a. Italy's aggregate demand curve will shift inward to the left.
    b. Italy's aggregate demand curve will shift outward to the right.
    c. Italy's aggregate supply curve will shift outward to the right.
    d. Italy's aggregate supply curve will shift inward to the left.

18. To Keynes, an important influence on business cycle fluctuations is _____, which is described as waves of optimism and pessimism.
    a. crowding out
    b. stagflation
    c. the velocity of money
    d. animal spirits
    e. hysteresis

19. If complete crowding out occurs, then as government spending increases,
    a. private spending falls by the same amount.
    b. the aggregate demand curve is unaffected.
    c. the aggregate supply curve shifts outward to the right.
    d. all of the above.
    e. only (a) and (b) of the above.

20. If _____ is above the short run equilibrium, then there is excess _____ and the price level will fall until it reaches its equilibrium level.
    a. aggregate output; demand
    b. aggregate output; equilibrium
    c. the price level; supply
    d. the price level; crowding out

21. The natural rate of unemployment
    a. is the rate of unemployment to which the economy tends toward in the long run.
    b. occurs when there is zero unemployment.
    c. is estimated to be around 10% by most economists.
    d. rises when output is above the natural level of output.

22. The self-correcting mechanism predicts that if aggregate output is initially above the natural level of output, then in the long run _____ will rise and the _____ curve will shift inward to the left.
    a. the price level; aggregate demand
    b. the natural rate of unemployment; aggregate supply
    c. the real wage; aggregate supply
    d. aggregate output; aggregate demand

23. According to _____, the self-correcting mechanism works very quickly and there is no need for government policy to restore output to its natural rate level.
    a. activists
    b. passivists
    c. nonactivists
    d. Keynesians

24. If the price level rises and aggregate output rises, then which of the following is the most likely cause?

   a. An increase in investment spending.

   b. A rise in household income taxes.

   c. A rise in the expected inflation rate.

   d. A positive supply shock.

   e. A negative supply shock.

25. If the natural rate of unemployment experiences hysteresis, then recent _____ unemployment will _____ the natural rate of unemployment and lower the natural rate level of output.

   a. high; lower

   b. high; raise

   c. low; lower

   d. low; raise

26. A decrease in the availability of raw materials is called a

   a. negative demand shock.

   b. positive demand shock.

   c. negative supply shock.

   d. positive supply shock.

27. The initial effect of a _____ shift in the aggregate _____ curve is a rise in the price level and a rise in aggregate output, while the ultimate effect is only a rise in the price level.

   a. leftward; supply

   b. leftward; demand

   c. rightward; supply

   d. rightward; demand

28. An increase in price level, holding the nominal quantity of money constant, leads to _____ interest rates and in turn to a _____ level of the quantity of aggregate output demanded.

   a. higher; lower

   b. lower; lower

   c. higher; higher

   d. lower; higher

29. _____, _____, and _____ will shift the aggregate demand curve to the right.

   a. An increase in G; an increase in T; an increase in NX

   b. An increase in G; an increase in T; a decrease in NX

   c. An increase in C; an increase in I; a decrease in T

   d. An increase in price level; an increase in G; a decrease in T

30. According to real business cycle theory, _____ and _____ are the major driving forces behind short-run fluctuations in the business cycle.

   a. technological shocks; sticky wages

   b. sticky wages; sticky prices

   c. supply shocks; technological shocks

   d. shocks to tastes; technological shocks

CHAPTER 25

Transmission Mechanisms of Monetary Policy: The Evidence

CHAPTER SYNOPSIS/COMPLETIONS

This chapter examines the connection between monetary policy and economic activity, focusing on the debate between the (1)_____ and the Keynesians over the years since the Great Depression, and illustrates how the accumulation of evidence has led to greater consensus regarding the importance of monetary policy on economic activity. Although views have converged, differences still exist, primarily because monetarists and Keynesians prefer different types of (2)_____.

Monetarists regard monetary policy's effect on economic activity as diverse and constantly changing; thus they prefer to model the impact of money supply changes directly. Evidence indicating a high correlation between changes in money growth and fluctuations in economic activity is referred to as (3)_____ _____ evidence. reduced-form evidence merely indicates the existence of a relationship; it does not describe how monetary policy affects economic activity.

Keynesians tend to be skeptical of reduced-form evidence, preferring to model the channels by which monetary policy affects the economy. Keynesian models are constructed using a system of equations, each equation describing part of the monetary transmission mechanism. These models are called (4)_____ models because they attempt to describe the relationships among the various segments of the economy; that is, they attempt to describe how the pieces of the structure fit together.

The structural model approach has three major advantages over the reduced-form approach:

1. Structural models allow us to evaluate each segment separately for its plausibility. This investigation improves our understanding of monetary policy's effect on economic activity.
2. Our improved understanding of the economy's workings may mean more accurate economic (5)_____.
3. Our ability to predict the consequences of institutional change may be improved from the knowledge of economic relationships provided by structural model evidence.

One disadvantage of the structural model approach is that it must be correctly (6)_____ or it will tend to give poor predictions. For example, suppose that a change in money growth causes stock prices to change, which in turn causes consumer expenditures to change. If this transmission mechanism is not part of the model, then the model will provide inaccurate results. In weighing the advantages and disadvantages, monetarists conclude that reduced-form models give more reliable results.

Although less sensitive to the correct specification, reduced-form models can prove to be misleading. Since reduced-form models focus on correlations, they may imply that movements in one variable cause the movements in another when causality actually runs in the other direction or is nonexistent. (7)_____
_____ refers to the condition where influence runs in the direction opposite that hypothesized. If two variables are highly correlated, it is possible that an independent (8)_____ factor influences the behaviour of both variables in a way that gives the appearance that one influences the other.

Early Keynesian models were poorly specified, leading to results indicating that monetary policy had little effect on economic activity. Had the early Keynesians specified relationships in terms of (9)_____ interest rates, rather than nominal interest rates, they would have been less likely to conclude that monetary policy does not matter.

In the early 1960s, the monetarists presented evidence indicating that monetary policy had never been more contractionary than during the Great Depression. The implication was that monetary policy mattered a great deal in determining aggregate economic activity. Milton Friedman and other monetarists emphasized three types of evidence when making their case about the importance of monetary growth: timing evidence, (10)_____
evidence, and historical evidence. Of the three types of evidence, most economists find (11)_____ evidence to be the most supportive of monetarist theory.

The impact of the monetarist attack on early Keynesian models led to improvements in these models to account for more channels of monetary influence on aggregate economic activity. Initial efforts extended the traditional interest-rate channel to account for changes in *consumer durable expenditure*. An important feature of the interest-rate mechanism is its emphasis on *real* rather than the nominal interest rate as the rate that influences business and consumer decisions. Because it is the real interest rate that affects spending, monetary policy can stimulate spending even when the nominal interest rate drops to zero. An expansionary monetary policy will raise the expected (12)_____ _____ and hence expected inflation, thereby lowering the real interest rate.

In addition to the interest-rate transmission mechanism, monetary policy can affect spending through asset prices (primarily foreign exchange and equities) other than interest rates and through asymmetric information effects on credit markets (the so-called *credit view*). For example, an expansionary monetary policy, because it lowers the real interest rate, causes the domestic currency to depreciate, which stimulates net exports and gross domestic product. Tobin's *q* theory indicates that (13)_____ (or equity) prices can have an important effect on investment spending. Under this monetary channel, increasing stock prices stimulate investment as firms discover that the cost of replacement capital declines relative to the market value of business firms.

According to the credit view, an expansionary monetary policy increases bank reserves and deposits, increasing the volume of bank loans available to borrowers who do not have access to credit markets to finance their spending. In addition to this bank lending channel, monetary policy may influence spending through the balance sheet channel. An expansionary monetary policy raises the net (14)_____ of firms (improves their balance sheets), reducing adverse selection and moral hazard problems, increasing the willingness of banks to extend loans to these firms.

Other credit channels include the cash flow channel, the unanticipated price level channel, and household liquidity effects. Expansionary monetary policy lowers nominal interest rates, reducing interest payments and thereby increasing (15)_____ _____. Because banks know that borrowers' improved liquidity reduces adverse selection and moral hazard problems, lending increases. Similarly, expansionary monetary policy raises the price level, lowering the real value of firms' liabilities. This improvement in firms' balance sheets reduces adverse selection and moral hazard problems, thereby increasing banks' willingness to lend. The view that unanticipated movements in the price level have important effects on aggregate demand is a key feature of the *debt-deflation* view of the Great Depression. Because households' interest payments, cash flow, liquidity, and real value of assets and liabilities are affected by changes in interest rates and the price level, monetary policy influences consumer spending too.

These three monetary transmission mechanisms indicate that changes in monetary policy can have a significant effect on aggregate demand. Research findings from the Great Depression support the economic significance of these monetary channels.

Although not all issues about monetary policy have been fully resolved, four lessons for monetary policy can be drawn from this chapter. First, changes in short-term nominal interest rates do not provide clear signals about monetary policy. Second, changes in prices of assets other than short-term debt instruments contain information about monetary policy. Third, fears about a liquidity trap are likely unfounded, as monetary policy can be effective in reviving a weak economy even when short-term interest rates are quite low. Fourth, price level stability is an important goal for monetary policy.

HELPFUL HINTS

The early reduced-form evidence suggested that changes in money were related to changes in aggregate economic activity. The early structural model evidence suggested that the link between changes in money and the economy was weak. These conflicting pieces of evidence led economists to search for additional channels through which money affects the economy. Economists have identified several additional channels.

EXERCISES

Practice Problems

1. For each of the following statements, indicate whether reduced-form evidence or structural model evidence is being presented by writing in the space provided an *R* for reduced-form evidence or an *S* for structural model evidence.
    ____a.   An increase in the money supply is followed by an increase in aggregate output.
    ____b.   Happy people earn higher incomes.
    ____c.   Drinking one ounce of alcohol per day appears to reduce cholesterol levels in the bloodstream, reducing the likelihood of coronary heart disease and heart attack.
    ____d.   A reduction in the money supply causes the volume of loans to fall, which causes investment to fall as banks ration credit. This in turn causes aggregate output to fall.
    ____e.   Medical research has found that men who take one aspirin per day following a heart attack significantly reduce the probability of a second heart attack.
    ____f.   An increase in the money supply causes interest rates to fall, which causes an increase in consumer durable expenditures and an increase in aggregate output.
    ____g.   An increase in the price of oil is followed by a reduction in aggregate output.
    ____h.   An increase in the money supply leads to an increase in stock prices, a rise in Tobin's *q,* and an increase in investment spending by firms.

2. Describe the reverse causation story for each of the following statements.
    a.   Increased police patrolling leads to higher crime rates.
    b.   Happier people earn more income.
    c.   A decrease in the money supply leads to a decline in aggregate output.
    d.   Drinking coffee causes heart attacks.
    e.   Going to the hospital increases the chance of death.
    f.   Children who read do better in school.

3.
    a.   What three pieces of evidence led early Keynesian economists to believe that monetary policy was ineffective?

    _____

    _____

    b.   Was early Keynesian evidence structural model evidence or reduced-form evidence?

    _____

    _____

c. What three types of evidence did early monetarists present that showed a strong effect of money on economic activity?

_____

_____

_____

d. Was the early monetarist evidence structural model evidence or reduced-form evidence?

_____

e. What are the three objections to the Friedman–Meiselman evidence on the importance of money for economic activity?

_____

f. Where do Keynesians currently stand on the debate over the importance of money for economic activity?

_____

_____

4. Consider the following hypothetical data on the supply of money and aggregate output. Assume that the direction of causation runs from output to money in this hypothetical economy.

a. Calculate the rate of money growth for years 2 through 5 to complete the table.

Year	Output, Y	Money Supply, M	Rate of Money Supply Growth, $\Delta M/M$
1	510	90	_____
2	525	100	_____
3	550	125	_____
4	550	125	_____
5	510	90	_____
6	510	90	_____
7	525	100	_____

b. Plot the three data series Y, M and $\Delta M/M$ onto Figures 25.1, 25.2, and 25.3 below; label the peaks and troughs for each data series.

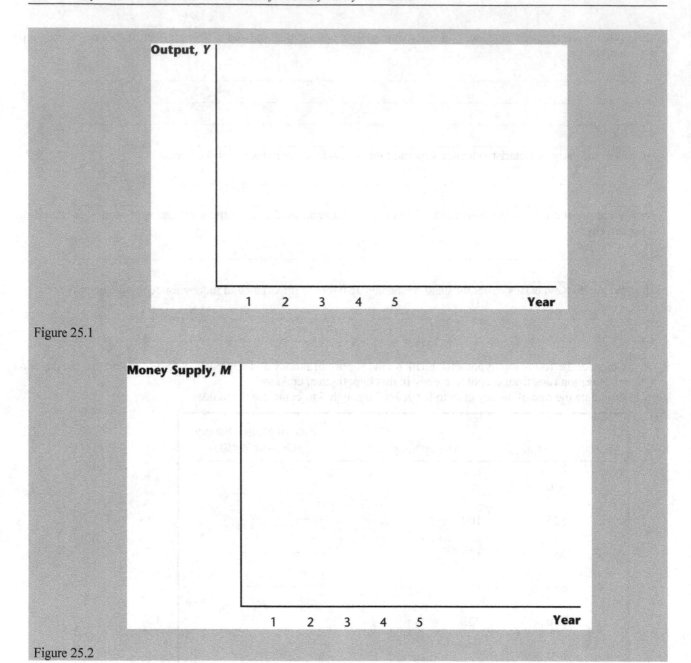

Figure 25.1

Figure 25.2

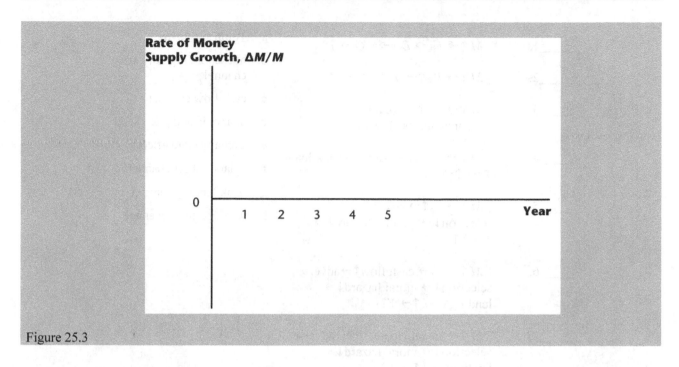

Figure 25.3

c. What is the principle of *post hoc, ergo propter hoc,* and what does it imply about the direction of causation between the rate of money supply growth and aggregate output in Figures 25.1 and 25.3?

_____

_____

d. Explain why timing evidence can be a dangerous tool for deciding on the direction of causation.

_____

_____

5. The traditional interest rate channel of monetary policy can be characterized by the following schematic

$$M \uparrow \rightarrow i_r \downarrow \rightarrow I \uparrow \rightarrow Y \uparrow$$

In the chart on the next page, match the names of the transmission mechanisms on the right with their schematic depictions on the left.

_____1. $M \uparrow \rightarrow i_r \downarrow \rightarrow E \downarrow \rightarrow NX \uparrow \rightarrow Y \uparrow$

_____2. $M \uparrow \rightarrow P_S \uparrow \rightarrow q \uparrow \rightarrow I \uparrow \rightarrow Y \uparrow$

_____3. $M \uparrow \rightarrow P_S \uparrow \rightarrow$ wealth $\uparrow \rightarrow$ consumption $\uparrow \rightarrow Y \uparrow$

_____4. $M \uparrow \rightarrow$ bank deposits $\uparrow \rightarrow$ bank loans $\uparrow \rightarrow I \uparrow \rightarrow Y \uparrow$

_____5. $M \uparrow \rightarrow P_S \uparrow \rightarrow$ adverse selection $\downarrow \rightarrow$ moral hazard $\downarrow \rightarrow I \uparrow \rightarrow Y \uparrow$

_____6. $M \uparrow \rightarrow i \downarrow \rightarrow$ cash flow $\uparrow \rightarrow$ adverse selection $\downarrow \rightarrow$ moral hazard $\downarrow \rightarrow$ lending $\uparrow \rightarrow I \uparrow \rightarrow Y \uparrow$

_____7. $M \uparrow \rightarrow$ unanticipated $P \uparrow \rightarrow$ adverse selection $\downarrow \rightarrow$ moral hazard $\downarrow \rightarrow$ lending $\uparrow \rightarrow I \uparrow \rightarrow Y \uparrow$

_____8. $M \uparrow \rightarrow P_S \uparrow \rightarrow$ value of financial assets $\uparrow \rightarrow$ likelihood of financial distress $\downarrow \rightarrow$ consumer durable and housing expenditure $\uparrow \rightarrow Y \uparrow$

a. Tobin's q theory

b. household liquidity effect channel

c. cash flow channel

d. unanticipated price level

e. exchange rate effect

f. balance sheet channel

g. bank lending channel

h. wealth effects channel

Short-Answer Questions

1. What are the advantages of structural model evidence?

_____

_____

2. What is the main disadvantage of structural model evidence?

_____

_____

3. What is the main advantage of reduced-form evidence?

_____

_____

4. Explain how monetary policy can stimulate the economy, even if nominal interest rates hit a floor of zero during a deflationary episode.

_____

_____

5. What does real business cycle theory imply about the direction of causation between monetary policy on the economy?

_____

_____

Critical-Thinking Questions

Suppose you are hired as an economic adviser to the Central Bank of Causation (a fictitious country). The head of the central bank shows you a graph indicating that the growth rate of money rises about three months before aggregate output rises and falls about three months before aggregate output falls.

1. Explain to the head of the central bank why it would be dangerous to base monetary policy decisions on the evidence presented in this graph.

_____

_____

_____

2. Suppose after careful research you have discovered that the direction of causation runs from money to aggregate output. The economy of Causation has just entered a recession in which the nominal interest rate is near zero and there is deflation. What policy would you recommend to bring the economy out of recession?

_____

_____

_____

3. Suppose after implementing the policy you described in your answer to Question 2, the economy experienced a subprime financial crisis like the one that hit the U.S. economy in the summer of 2007. Explain to the head of the central bank why the policy you recommended to bring the economy out of recession will likely result in a slow recovery.

_____

_____

_____

_____

SELF-TEST

True-False Questions

Circle whether the following statements are true (T) or false (F).

T   F   1. Reduced-form evidence examines whether one variable has an effect on another by looking at a sequence of steps and describing the process at each step so that the channels of influence can be better understood.

T   F   2. One advantage of the structural model approach is that it can give us a better understanding of how money influences economic activity.

T   F   3. Correlation does not necessarily imply causation.

T   F   4. Though nominal interest rates fell during the Great Depression to extremely low levels, real interest rates rose.

T   F   5.   Historical evidence that has focused on the effects of exogenous changes in the money supply indicates that changes in aggregate output are related to changes in money growth.

T   F   6.   Keynesians argue that while banks may tend to ration credit in response to "tight" monetary policy, such credit rationing has no effect on economic activity.

T   F   7.   Friedman and Schwartz argue that money growth affects output with "long and variable lags."

T   F   8.   Though Tobin's q theory provides a good explanation for the economic recovery that started in late 1982, it is inconsistent with the events of the Great Depression.

T   F   9.   Assume that the stock market index falls by over 500 points in one week and remains at this level long enough that people adjust their expectations downward regarding the average level of the stock market index. One should expect this event to affect the level of consumption.

T   F   10.   Economic theory suggests that the stock market crash of 1929 depressed consumer expenditures due to the loss of wealth and the increase in financial distress.

T   F   11.   By using structural model evidence, monetarists believe that monetary policy is very important to economic fluctuations.

T   F   12.   A weak link between nominal interest rates and investment indicates that there is no strong link between real interest rates and investment.

T   F   13.   Monetary policy can be highly effective in reviving a weak economy even if the short-term interest rate is already near zero.

T   F   14.   Early empirical studies found a strong linkage between movements in nominal interest rates and investment spending.

T   F   15.   Monetary policy is ineffective in economies with deflation and short-term interest rates near zero.

Multiple-Choice Questions

Circle the appropriate answer.

1.   Monetarists prefer reduced-form models because they believe that
    a.   reverse causation is never a problem.
    b.   structural models may understate money's effect on economic activity.
    c.   money supply changes are always exogenous.
    d.   each of the above is true.

2.   Scientists tend to be skeptical of reduced-form evidence because
    a.   the finding of a high correlation between two variables does not always imply that changes in one cause changes in the other.
    b.   reduced-form evidence may not account for all the channels of influence.
    c.   it fails to add insight to the process that leads movements in one variable to cause movements in another.
    d.   if the model is poorly specified it can lead to poor predictions about the future behaviour of the variable of interest.
    e.   of both (a) and (c) of the above.

3.   Monetarist evidence in which declines in money growth are followed by recessions provides the strongest support for their position that monetary policy matters.
    a.   Statistical
    b.   Historical
    c.   Timing
    d.   Structural

4. Early Keynesians tended to dismiss the importance of monetary policy due to their findings that
   a. indicated the absence of a link between movements in nominal interest rates and investment spending.
   b. interest rates had fallen during the Great Depression.
   c. surveys of businessmen revealed that market interest rates had no effect on their decisions of how much to invest in new physical capital.
   d. all of the above are true.

5. Monetarists contend that reduced-form evidence provides valid proof that monetary policy affects economic activity when it can be shown that the change in the money supply
   a. is an endogenous event.
   b. is an exogenous event.
   c. preceded the change in economic activity.
   d. was expected.

6. What were the monetarists' main conclusions from the early reduced-form evidence?
   a. One had to be careful to distinguish between real and nominal magnitudes.
   b. The early Keynesian models were incorrectly specified because they accounted for too few channels of monetary influence.
   c. Monetarists' models showed that fiscal policies had little or no effect on economic activity.
   d. Both (a) and (b) are correct.
   e. Both (b) and (c) are correct.

7. The availability hypothesis suggests that in periods characterized by "tight" money, banks may
   a. stop making any loans.
   b. continue to make loans, but only at much higher interest rates.
   c. ration credit rather than significantly raise interest rates.
   d. make available more loans to businesses with which they have had no previous dealings.

8. Because of asymmetric information problems in credit markets, monetary policy may affect economic activity through the balance sheet channel, which holds that an increase in money supply
   a. raises equity prices, which lowers the cost of new capital relative to the market value of firms, thereby increasing investment spending.
   b. raises the net worth of firms, decreasing adverse selection and moral hazard problems, thereby increasing banks' willingness to lend to finance investment spending.
   c. raises the level of bank reserves, deposits, and the quantity of bank loans available, which raises the spending by those individuals who do not have access to credit markets.
   d. does none of the above.

9. Assume that a contractionary monetary policy lowers the price level by more than anticipated, raising the real value of consumer debt. New Keynesian structural models suggest that a contractionary monetary policy is channelled into lower consumer expenditure through which of the following effects?
   a. Bank lending channel.
   b. Tobin's q.
   c. Traditional interest-rate effect.
   d. Household liquidity effect.

10. The household liquidity effect suggests that higher stock prices lead to increased consumer expenditures because consumers

    a. feel more secure about their financial position.

    b. will want to sell their stocks and spend the proceeds before stock prices go back down.

    c. believe that they will receive higher wages in the near future because companies are now more profitable.

    d. believe none of the above.

11. _____ prefer to emphasize _____ model evidence because they believe that _____ models do not add insight into how monetary policy affects the economy.

    a. Keynesians; structural; reduced-form

    b. Keynesians; reduced-form; structural

    c. Monetarists; structural; reduced-form

    d. Monetarists; reduced-form; structural

12. Monetarists claim that simple _____ models, because they may ignore important transmission mechanisms, tend to _____ the importance of monetary policy's effect on the economy.

    a. structural; overstate

    b. reduced-form; overstate

    c. structural; understate

    d. reduced-form; understate

13. Because they believed that _____ policy was _____, early Keynesians stressed the importance of _____ policy.

    a. fiscal; ineffective; monetary

    b. monetary; ineffective; fiscal

    c. monetary; potent; monetary

    d. fiscal; too potent; monetary

14. Economic theory suggests that _____ interest rates are a _____ important determinant than _____ interest rates in explaining the behaviour of investment spending.

    a. nominal; more; real

    b. real; less; nominal

    c. real; more; nominal

    d. market; more; real

    e. real; less; market

15. Which of the following accurately describes the current state of the monetarist-Keynesian debate on monetary policy and economic activity?

    a. Keynesians still insist that monetary policy is not an important source of business cycle fluctuations.

    b. Although Keynesians now agree that monetary policy matters, they do not believe that it is all that matters.

    c. There is now general agreement among Keynesians that fiscal policy is indeed an extremely important source of business cycle fluctuations.

    d. Only (a) and (c) of the above.

16. Suppose that a structural model specifies that X influences Z and that Y influences Z. In which of the following is the structural model appropriate for determining the influence of X on Z?

    a. X influences Y.

    b. X does not influence Y.

    c. X influences W and W influences Z.

    d. In none of the above is the structural model appropriate.

17. The statement "correlation does not imply causation" means that if two variables are correlated, then
    a. they cannot cause a third variable.
    b. they always cause a third variable.
    c. one variable causes the other, but it is not known which direction causality runs.
    d. one variable may or may not cause the other.

18. If one event happens before a second event, then this supports the assertion that the first event caused the second event
    a. as long as the first event was an endogenous event.
    b. as long as the first event was an exogenous event.
    c. as long as reverse causality exists.
    d. as long as the first event occurred after the second event.
    e. none of the above.

19. Even if the _____ interest rate is zero, the _____ interest rate can still be lowered by expansionary monetary policy as long as _____ is increased.
    a. real; nominal; government spending
    b. real; nominal; expected inflation
    c. nominal; real, expected inflation
    d. real; nominal; the money supply

20. Tobin's q theory predicts that as the money supply increases
    a. the price of stocks will rise.
    b. the ratio of firm market value to capital replacement cost will fall.
    c. investment goods are relatively expensive and firms will reduce investment spending.
    d. only (a) and (b) of the above.
    e. only (b) and (c) of the above.

21. According to the lifecycle hypothesis of consumption, consumption will _____ when the money supply falls, since the value of stocks and housing is _____ and consumer lifetime resources are _____.
    a. increase; higher; higher
    b. increase; lower; lower
    c. decrease; lower; higher
    d. decrease; higher; higher

22. The bank lending channel suggests that monetary policy will have a larger influence on spending by _____ firms, since _____ firms have _____ access to credit through stocks and bonds.
    a. small; large; greater
    b. small; large; less
    c. large; small; greater
    d. large; small; less

23. The cash flow monetary transmission channel suggests that as the _____ interest rate falls, firms' cash flow and _____ increase, which _____ adverse selection and moral hazard problems.
    a. real; liquidity; increases
    b. real; stock price; decreases
    c. real; liquidity; decreases
    d. nominal; liquidity; decreases
    e. nominal; stock price; increases

24. When the price level rises unexpectedly, firms' debt burdens _____ and net worth increases. The effect is to _____ adverse selection and moral hazard problems, which results in increased lending.

    a. increase; increase

    b. increase; decrease

    c. decrease; increase

    d. decrease; decrease

25. Credit channels are likely to be important monetary transmission mechanisms because

    a. asymmetric information, which forms the core of credit channel theory, does a good job of explaining financial market institutions.

    b. small firms, which are more likely to be credit-constrained, appear to be most affected by monetary policy.

    c. credit market imperfections appear to influence firms' expenditure decisions.

    d. all of the above.

    e. only (b) and (c) of the above.

26. If a high correlation of variable A and variable B misleadingly suggests that controlling variable A would help to control the level of variable B, then it is likely that

    a. changes in variable B affect changes in variable A on account of reverse causation.

    b. variable A and variable B are both affected by some other factor.

    c. either (a) or (b) of the above are possible.

    d. none of the above.

27. An increase in stock prices _____ the net worth of firms and _____ investment spending because of the reduction in moral hazard.

    a. lowers; lowers

    b. raises; lowers

    c. lowers; raises

    d. raises; raises

28. Which of the following is the key element in monetarists' discussions of why actual economies were not stuck in a liquidity trap during the Great Depression?

    a. Rational expectations.

    b. The fact that the real interest rate rather than nominal rate affects spending.

    c. Sticky prices.

    d. The fact that money does not matter at all.

29. Which of the following is true?

    a. Monetary policy is not effective if short-run interest rates are close to zero.

    b. Monetary policy is effective even if short-run interest rates are close to zero.

    c. Monetary policy is effective only if this policy is anticipated.

    d. None of the above.

30. In which of the following cases do stock prices transmit the effect of monetary policy to GDP?

    a. Traditional interest rate effects, household liquidity effects.

    b. Tobin's *q* theory, wealth effects.

    c. Exchange rate effects, bank lending channel.

    d. both (a) and (b) of the above.

CHAPTER **26**

Money and Inflation

CHAPTER SYNOPSIS/COMPLETIONS

Inflation is caused by high growth rates of the money supply. This chapter applies aggregate demand and supply analysis to show that inflationary monetary policy is an offshoot of large government deficits or policies aimed at hitting high-employment targets.

The German experience from 1921 to 1923 illustrates a classical scenario of (1)_____. The unwillingness of German government officials to raise taxes and their inability to borrow an amount sufficient to finance huge budget deficits left money creation as the only available means of financing government expenditures. This scenario has been repeated many times, for example, in Argentina and Brazil in the 1980s. In both instances, massive government budget deficits initiated rapid expansions in the money supply, which in turn led to rapidly accelerating rates of inflation.

While these episodes, along with others, confirm that sustained inflation can only occur if there is a continually increasing money supply, a variety of sources are actually responsible for the inflationary monetary policies of many countries. Budget deficits, concerns over unemployment, negative supply shocks, union wage pushes, and concerns over interest rates often lead to inflationary monetary expansions.

Economists are in general agreement that inflation is always and everywhere a (2) "_____ phenomenon." Evidence from both historical and recent inflationary episodes confirms the proposition that sustained inflation results from excessive monetary expansion.

The consensus must appear at first to be highly unusual, given that much of the two previous chapters has been devoted to the disagreements between monetarists and Keynesians. The apparent paradox is solved by the precise way in which economists define inflation. A one-shot (or one-time) increase in the price level is simply not defined as inflation by economists. Only when the price level is continually rising do economists consider such episodes to be inflationary.

Keynesians, unlike monetarists, believe that one-shot tax cuts or government-spending boosts are likely to raise aggregate demand, and thus the price level, but they contend that any effect on inflation will be merely (3)_____. In their view, fiscal actions are incapable of generating sustained price increases. Thus monetarists and Keynesians agree that rapid money growth is both a sufficient and necessary condition explaining inflation.

Regarding negative supply shocks, economists are again in general agreement that it is only through monetary (4)_____ that such shocks prove inflationary. In the absence of an increase in money growth, the price level would rise, but it would not continue to do so.

One must naturally wonder why, if it is well understood, inflation continues to plague so many countries to this day. Examination of the Canadian experience suggests that governments pursue many goals, some of which are not (5)_____ with price stability. Specifically, federal government efforts designed to reduce unemployment in the 1960s proved incompatible with the goal of general price stability. In the 1970s, a series of negative (6)_____ _____ compounded the problem by pressuring government policymakers toward accommodation in order to prevent high rates of unemployment.

Higher wage demands by workers can lead to inflation if policymakers fear that such demands will cause rising unemployment. Additionally, the government may set its (7)_____ target too low, causing overexpansion and inflation.

Large government budget deficits are another possible source of excessive money growth. Politicians are extremely reluctant to cut government expenditures and raise taxes because such actions are often politically unpopular. Thus the political process is likely to generate a bias toward large budget deficits and inflation.

Economists often find it difficult to distinguish between demand-pull and (8)_____ _____ inflation. Both types of inflation result when money growth becomes excessive. At first glance, one distinguishes between the two by looking at the behaviour of employment. Demand-pull inflation is associated with high employment, and cost-push inflation is associated with (9)_____ employment. Once inflation is underway, however, demand-pull inflations may exhibit cost-push tendencies as workers demand higher wages in expectation of higher inflation.

The government budget (10)_____ indicates that an increase in the government budget deficit must lead to an increase in the sum of the monetary base and outstanding government bonds held by the public. If the government pays for additional spending with higher taxes, the deficit does not increase and the monetary base does not change. Should the government run a deficit, it must issue bonds to pay for the additional spending. If individuals buy these newly issued bonds, there will be no change in the monetary base. When the public purchases the bonds, the government spends the proceeds, returning the funds to the public. Hence, the government sale of bonds to the public has no effect on the monetary base.

Deficit financing through central bank security purchases, however, leads to an increase in the monetary base. This method of deficit financing is often referred to as "printing money" because high-powered money is created in the process. The action is probably better referred to as *monetizing the debt* because the money supply increases as a result of the increase in government debt.

An examination of inflation in Canada from 1960 through 1980 dismisses the importance of budget deficits in explaining rapid money growth. It appears that the concern over unemployment led to over-expansionary policies which kept unemployment low over the period 1965 to 1973. In the latter half of the 1970s, inflation resembles the (11)_____ _____ variety as unemployment rose to a level that exceeded the natural rate level.

The debate over the appropriateness of activist stabilization policy has important implications for anti-inflationary policies. Monetarists argue against the use of activist policy to reduce unemployment. They believe the effort is fruitless because any reduction in unemployment will be merely temporary, and it may hinder anti-inflationary efforts. Monetarists hold that the economy is inherently (12)_____, as wages are sufficiently flexible so that deviations from the natural rate of output are quickly reversed. Further, monetarists contend that even in those instances where adjustment tends to be relatively slow, activist policies are not likely to improve circumstances. In their view, policy responses are ineffectual, or even harmful, due to the long (13)_____ _____ that plague government decision making. For this reason, monetarists tend to support monetary rules that limit the discretion of policymakers.

Keynesians are optimistic about the effectiveness of (14)_____ policies. They believe that available evidence indicates that wages and prices are sticky, implying prolonged deviations from the natural rate of output and unemployment. Therefore, they contend that government fiscal or monetary actions are required to restore the economy to full employment. Unlike the monetarists, Keynesians contend that fiscal policy actions will be effective and dismiss the possibility of complete crowding out.

The phenomenon of "stagflation" in the latter half of the 1970s focused greater attention on the importance of expectations. People had come to expect that macroeconomic policies would always be accommodating; thus, when policymakers announced intentions of fighting inflation, few people believed them. Following this experience, economists in greater numbers began to question the desirability of activist policy. Some economists argued that nonaccommodating policy would yield better inflation performance with no more unemployment. Importantly, policy must be (15)_____, which means that the public must expect that policymakers will carry out their promises. Although this conclusion is not universally accepted, the recognition of the importance expectations play in economics has led to a new field of macroeconomics which is presented in Chapter 27.

HELPFUL HINTS

A leftward shift in aggregate supply or a rightward shift in aggregate demand will cause the price level to rise. But persistent inflation is not a one-time increase in the price level—it is a continuous increase in the price level. Therefore, when we look for causes of persistent inflation, we must look for factors that can lead to either a persistent rightward shift in aggregate demand or a persistent leftward shift in aggregate supply. The only factor that is capable of generating persistent shifts is persistent increases in the money supply, which shifts the aggregate demand curve. A rise in the budget deficit, an increase in wages, and negative supply shocks all lead to a rise in the price level. These shift factors will only lead to persistent inflation if they cause the Fed to initiate a persistent increase in the supply of money.

EXERCISES

Practice Problems

1. a. What caused hyperinflation in Germany after World War I?

    _____

    _____

    b. Why did the German government pursue the policy you described in your answer to part *a*?

    _____

    _____

    c. How does the evidence you described in your answers to parts *a* and *b* rule out the possibility of reverse causation?

    _____

    _____

2. Suppose the economy is initially in equilibrium at point 1 in Figure 26.1, where aggregate output is equal to the natural rate level of output (Y_n).
a. Use Figure 26.1 to demonstrate the effect of a one-shot permanent increase in government expenditures.

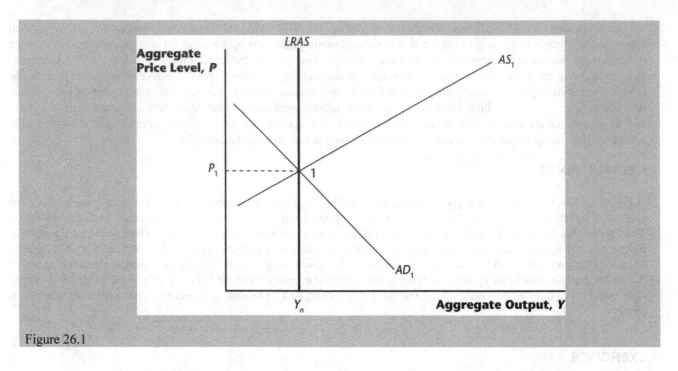

Figure 26.1

b. Did the one-shot permanent increase in government expenditures cause persistent inflation? Why or why not?

_____

_____

c. Use Figure 26.2 to demonstrate the effect of a negative supply shock.

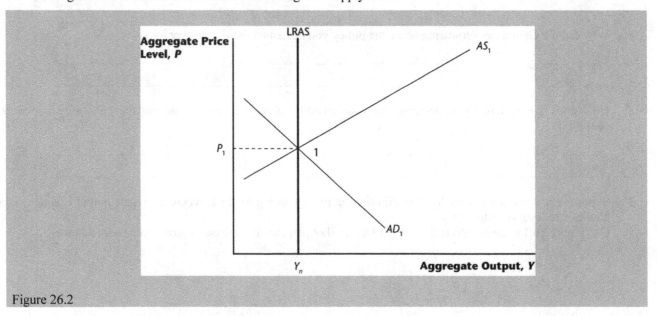

Figure 26.2

d. Did the negative supply shock cause persistent inflation? Why or why not?

_____

_____

3.   Suppose the economy is initially in equilibrium at point 1 in Figure 26.3 where aggregate output is equal to the natural rate level of output (Y_n).

a.   Now suppose that workers decide to seek higher wages because they expect inflation to be high. Use Figure 26.3 to show what happens to aggregate output and the price level as a result of an increase in wages.

b.   Use Figure 26.3 to show what advocates of discretionary policy with a high employment target would do if this situation developed.

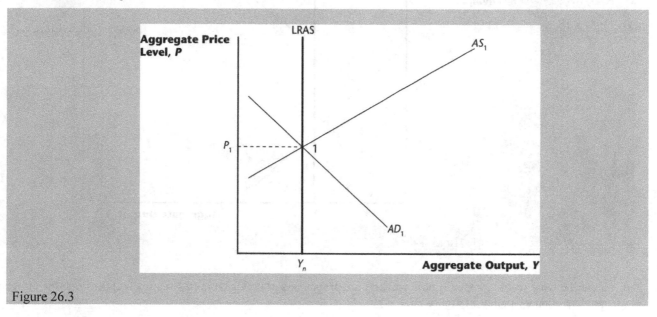

Figure 26.3

c.   Did the increase in wages and the resulting accommodating policy cause persistent inflation? Why or why not?

_____

_____

d.   Under what circumstances would an increase in wages lead to persistent inflation?

_____

_____

4.   Suppose that government spending is $500 billion, tax revenue is $300 billion, and the change in government bonds held by the public is $150 billion.

a.   Calculate the government budget deficit and the change in the monetary base.

_____

_____

b.   Explain why your calculation in part *a* does not imply that the Bank of Canada can simply print money to finance the government budget deficit.

_____

_____

c.   Under what circumstances are government budget deficits inflationary?

_____

_____

5. Suppose that policymakers are faced with the situation depicted in Figure 26.4 where the economy has moved below the natural rate level of output.

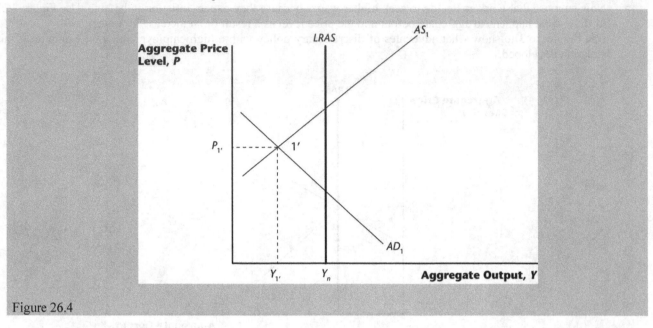

Figure 26.4

a. Describe what would happen if policymakers are proponents of nondiscretionary policy and illustrate the effect of nondiscretionary policy in Figure 26.4.

_____

_____

b. Describe what would happen if policymakers are advocates of discretionary policy and illustrate the effect of discretionary policy in Figure 26.4. Assume that the discretionary policy takes effect before wages and prices have time to adjust.

_____

_____

c. Describe what would happen if policymakers are advocates of discretionary policy and illustrate the effect of discretionary policy in Figure 26.4. Assume that the discretionary policy takes effect after wages and prices have time to adjust.

_____

_____

d. Under what circumstances would discretionary be preferable? Why?

_____

_____

e. Under what circumstances would a nondiscretionary policy be preferable? Why?

_____

_____

Short-Answer Questions

1. What is the difference between a one-time increase in the price level and persistent inflation?

_____

_____

2. Why is it not possible for continual increases in government spending or continual tax cuts to cause persistent inflation?

_____

_____

3. What causes persistent high inflation?

_____

_____

4. Under what circumstances will the pursuit of an employment target by policymakers lead to persistent inflation?

_____

_____

5. How would you distinguish between cost-push and demand-pull inflation by looking at the unemployment rate?

_____

_____

Critical-Thinking Questions

The popular press is often incorrect or misleading about its description of inflation and its description of the causes of persistent inflation. Below are three examples of newspaper headlines. For each example, state what is incorrect and/or misleading.

1. "Increasing Oil Prices Caused Inflation to Rise Last Month"

_____

_____

2. "The Government Tries to Reign in Spending Fearing That Deficits Will Cause Inflation"

_____

_____

3. "Unions Push For Higher Wages, Policymakers Fear Rising Inflation"

_____

_____

SELF-TEST

True-False Questions

Circle whether the following statements are true (T) or false (F).

T   F   1.   If inflation is defined as a continuous rise in the price level, then it is true that inflation can be eliminated by reducing the growth rate of the money supply to a low level.

T   F   2.   Keynesians disagree with the monetarists' proposition that inflation is a monetary phenomenon. That is, Keynesians believe that inflation can occur even when money growth has not been excessive.

T   F   3.   Any shift to the right in *AD*, regardless of its cause, will generate a higher inflation.

T   F   4.   The price level may rise in any one month due to factors unrelated to changes in the money supply. Thus one can conclude that continual price-level increases need not be related to changes in the money supply.

T   F   5.   Keynesians argue that factors other than a continually increasing money supply may lead to sustained inflation.

T   F   6.   Sustained inflation occurs when unions successfully push up wages, even if the monetary authorities refuse to accommodate the higher wages by expanding the money supply.

T   F   7.   Inflation, according to one view, is the side effect of government efforts to cure high unemployment.

T   F   8.   At first glance, one would expect falling unemployment to be associated with demand-pull inflation.

T   F   9.   Huge government budget deficits have been the initiating source of inflationary monetary policies in every instance of hyperinflation.

T   F   10. An examination of the period from 1960 through 1980 suggests that large government deficits are to blame for the inflationary monetary policies of this period.

T   F   11. Accommodating policy refers to an activist policy with a low inflation target.

T   F   12. Studies have shown that the welfare cost of inflation in Canada is much higher than in the U.S.

T   F   13. Cost–push inflation is a monetary phenomenon because it cannot occur without the monetary authorities pursuing an accommodating policy of a higher rate of money growth.

T   F   14. Supply-side phenomena cannot be the source of high inflation.

T   F   15. In all episodes of hyperinflation, huge government budget deficits are the ultimate reason for high money growth and persistent high inflation.

Multiple-Choice Questions

Circle the appropriate answer.

1. A continual increase in the money supply, according to Keynesian analysis, will cause

    a. the price level to increase, but have no lasting effect on the inflation rate.

    b. the price level to fall.

    c. inflation.

    d. output to increase and will have no effect on either the price level or inflation.

    e. none of the above.

2. Monetarists believe that a continually rising price level _____ due to factors other than growth in the money supply.

    a. may be

    b. is never

    c. is sometimes

    d. is always

3. In general, most economists believe that inflation can only occur if

    a. government spending increases.

    b. strong labour unions demand higher wages.

    c. negative supply shocks continuously hit the economy.

    d. the money supply is continually expanded.

4. Monetarists emphasize the importance of a constant money growth rate rule more than the balanced-budget amendment or restrictions on union power because

    a. they tend to regard excessive money growth as the cause of inflation.

    b. while they do not believe that excessive money growth is the cause of inflation, they do believe that it is related to excessive government expenditures.

    c. while they regard unions as the source of inflation, they know that they are too powerful politically to deal with.

    d. of each of the above.

5. Analysis of hyperinflationary episodes indicates that the rapid money growth leading to the inflation results when

    a. governments finance massive budget deficits by printing money.

    b. central banks attempt to peg interest rates.

    c. government taxes become too excessive.

    d. central banks lower reserve requirements too much.

6. A one-shot increase in government spending will have what effect on the inflation rate, according to the Keynesian analysis?

    a. Permanent increase.

    b. Temporary increase.

    c. Temporary decrease.

    d. No effect.

7. Assume workers know that government policymakers, because unemployment is politically unpopular, always accommodate wage increases by expanding the money supply. What type of inflation is likely to result if workers demand higher wages not fearing a rise in unemployment?

    a. Demand-pull inflation.

    b. Hyperinflation.

    c. Cost-push inflation.

    d. Demand-shock inflation.

8. If an economist were interested in testing whether federal budget deficits had been the source of excessive money growth for a particular country during the time period 1900–1930, she would be interested in the behaviour of

    a. inflation.

    b. the money-supply-to-monetary-base ratio.

    c. interest rates.

    d. the government-debt-to-GDP ratio.

9. When the government sets an unemployment target that is unrealistically low without realizing it, what is the likely result?

    a. Inflation.

    b. An unemployment rate that may actually drop below the natural rate for a period of time.

    c. Excessive money growth.

    d. All of the above.

10. Governments are likely to lose credibility in fighting inflation when
    a. government budget deficits remain high.
    b. government policymakers continue to accommodate wage demands and negative supply shocks.
    c. the commitment to high employment is viewed as government's number-one goal for political reasons.
    d. all of the above are true.

11. The German hyperinflation of the 1920s supports the proposition that excessive money growth leads to higher prices, and not the other way around, since the increase in money growth appears to have been
    a. unintentional.
    b. intentional.
    c. exogenous.
    d. endogenous.

12. A common element of hyperinflationary episodes discussed in the text is government unwillingness to
    a. finance expenditures by raising taxes.
    b. increase expenditures.
    c. finance expenditures by printing money.
    d. finance transfer payments by printing money.

13. Which of the following statements is true?
    a. The price level may rise in any one month due to factors unrelated to changes in the money supply. Thus one can conclude that continual price-level increases need not be related to changes in the money supply.
    b. Within the aggregate demand and supply framework, a continually increasing money supply has the effect of continually shifting the aggregate demand curve to the right.
    c. Keynesians argue that factors other than a continually increasing money supply may lead to sustained inflation.
    d. Sustained inflation occurs when unions successfully push up wages, even if the monetary authorities refuse to accommodate the higher wages by expanding the money supply.

14. Workers will have greater incentives to push for higher wages when government policymakers place greater concern on _____ than _____ and are thus _____ likely to adopt accommodative policies.
    a. inflation; unemployment; less
    b. inflation; unemployment; more
    c. unemployment; inflation; less
    d. unemployment; inflation; more

15. Which of the following statements is true?
    a. Cost-push inflation is not a monetary phenomenon.
    b. At first glance, one would expect rising unemployment to be associated with demand-pull inflation.
    c. Huge government budget deficits have been the initiating source of inflationary monetary policies in every instance of hyperinflation.
    d. Large government deficits are to blame for the inflationary monetary policies of the 1970s in Canada.

16. Economists such as Robert Barro hold the view that deficits
    a. cause the monetary base to decrease.
    b. cause the monetary base to increase.
    c. have no effect on the monetary base.
    d. are inflationary even when financed by tax hikes.

17. The reason that Keynesians do not believe that fiscal policy alone can lead to a continually rising price level is that
    a. fiscal and monetary policies will cancel each other out in the long run.
    b. the self-correcting mechanism will lower the inflation rate in the long run.
    c. there is a limit to how much taxes can be reduced or how much the government can spend.
    d. all of the above.
    e. only (b) and (c) of the above.

18. If energy prices rise tremendously, then which of the following is true?
    a. The aggregate supply curve will shift inward to the left in the short run.
    b. The aggregate supply curve will shift inward to the left in the long run after the self-correcting mechanism begins.
    c. The aggregate demand curve will shift inward to the left in the short run.
    d. The aggregate demand curve will shift outward to the right in the long run after the self-correcting mechanism begins.

19. Demand-pull inflation
    a. may be the result of a high money growth rate.
    b. results from the aggregate demand curve shifting outward to the right.
    c. can eventually trigger cost-push inflation if inflation expectations rise.
    d. will usually be accompanied by unemployment rates below the natural rate of unemployment.
    e. All of the above.

20. How can a government pay for a budget deficit?
    a. Lower taxes.
    b. Borrow by issuing government bonds.
    c. Decrease the monetary base.
    d. Increase government expenditures.

21. When government spending is paid for by monetizing the debt,
    a. the Bank of Canada pays for items with new currency.
    b. the central bank sells bonds to pay for items.
    c. the monetary base is reduced and the amount of government bonds held by the public is increased.
    d. the monetary base is increased and the amount of government bonds held by the public is reduced.
    e. none of the above.

22. Proponents of the theory of Ricardian equivalence believe that when the government runs a deficit,
    a. the demand for bonds increases.
    b. household saving decreases.
    c. the interest rate rises.
    d. only (a) and (b) of the above.
    e. only (a) and (c) of the above.

23. The length of time that passes before policymakers can correctly interpret economic data is known as the _____ lag.
    a. data
    b. recognition
    c. legislative
    d. implementation
    e. effectiveness

24. The case for an activist policy is made stronger if
    a. the political process takes longer to pass economic policy.
    b. it takes less time for the impact of policy to be felt.
    c. worker expectations regarding policy are unimportant when wages are negotiated.
    d. only (a) and (b) of the above.
    e. only (b) and (c) of the above.

25. Policy _____ tend to recommend the use of policy _____.
    a. activists; rules
    b. activists; lags
    c. nonactivists; rules
    d. nonactivists; discretion
    e. nonactivisits; expectations

26. A one-time increase in wages due to a successful wage push by labour unions causes
    a. continual inflation.
    b. a one-time increase in the price level.
    c. a one-time increase in real output.
    d. both (b) and (c) of the above.

27. Chronic government budget deficits will lead to inflation if
    a. they are financed by government sales of bonds to the public.
    b. they are financed by government sales of bonds to the central bank.
    c. they are financed by government sales of bonds to commercial banks.
    d. any of the above occurs.

28. A deficit can be the source of a sustained inflation only if it is _____ and if the government finances it by _____.
    a. temporary; issuing bonds to the public
    b. temporary; creating money
    c. persistent; creating money
    d. persistent; issuing bonds to the public

29. Inflation is defined as
    a. a rise in prices.
    b. a rapid rise in prices.
    c. a continuing and rapid rise in the price of necessary goods.
    d. a sustained increase in the general level of prices.

30. _____ happens when the amount of goods and services people are willing and able to buy goes up, leading to an increase in prices.
    a. Demand-pull inflation
    b. Demand-push inflation
    c. Cost-pull inflation
    d. Cost-push inflation

CHAPTER 27

Rational Expectations: Implications for Policy

CHAPTER SYNOPSIS/COMPLETIONS

In previous chapters you learned how government policy could, in principle, be used to steer output toward full employment. But in practice (especially during the 1960s and 1970s) discretionary policies have not been successful. The theory of rational expectations was developed in the 1970s and 1980s to examine why discretionary policies performed so poorly. This chapter examines the analysis behind the rational expectations revolution. The existence of rational expectations makes discretionary policies less likely to be successful and raises the issue of credibility as an important element affecting policy outcomes.

In his famous paper, "Econometric Policy Evaluation: A Critique," Robert Lucas argues that stabilization policies formulated on the basis of conventional econometric models will fail to stabilize the economy since (1)_____ about policy will alter the intended effects. Lucas argues that while conventional econometric models may be useful for forecasting economic activity, they cannot be used to evaluate the potential impact of particular policies on the economy. The short-run forecasting ability of these models provides no evidence of the accuracy to be expected from simulations of hypothetical policy alternatives.

To understand Lucas's argument, one needs to recognize that conventional econometric models contain equations that describe the relationships between hundreds of variables. These relationships (parameters), estimated using past data, are assumed to remain (2)_____. Lucas contends that such models will likely provide misleading results about the effects of a policy change (say, a monetary expansion); the actual effects are likely to be different than predicted because the change in policy will mean that the way expectations are formed will change, causing the real-world relationships (parameters) to change. Thus the effects of a particular policy depend heavily on the public's expectations about the policy.

Two schools of rational expectations economists have formed: the new classical and the new Keynesian schools. (3)_____ _____ rational expectationists contend that anticipated macroeconomic policies have no effect on aggregate output and employment. This conclusion rests on the assumption that all wages and prices are completely (4)_____ with respect to expected changes in the price level. For example, if policymakers are known to act in certain systematic ways, the public will come to anticipate policy changes, causing the aggregate (5)_____ curve to shift. People will respond to expected expansionary macropolicies by raising wages and factor prices. The aggregate demand curve shifts out, but the aggregate supply curve shifts in, neutralizing the impact on aggregate output. The (6)_____ _____ rises, but output remains unchanged at the natural-rate level.

Policymakers can affect the level of aggregate output and employment in the new classical rational expectations model only through policy surprises. Unanticipated policies will cause the aggregate demand curve to shift while leaving the aggregate supply curve unchanged, resulting in a change in the price level and aggregate output. Only unanticipated macropolicies can affect the level of output in the new classical model; anticipated policies cannot affect the level of output. This conclusion is referred to as the policy (7)_____ _____.
The proposition depends critically on two assumptions: rational expectations and perfect wage and price flexibility.

Many economists find the assumption of wage and price flexibility unacceptable. They note that the prevalence of long-term labour and supply contracts create (8)_____, which prevent wages and prices from fully responding to expected changes in the price level.

New Keynesians argue that the existence of long-term labour contracts—both explicit and implicit—leads to wage and price stickiness. In contrast to the new classical school, the assumption of rational expectations does not imply that (9)_____ policies are ineffectual in altering the level of aggregate output. The public may understand the consequences of a newly announced macropolicy yet be unable to fully respond in the face of contracted fixities.

(10)_____ _____ agree that unanticipated policies are more effective than anticipated policies in changing the level of aggregate output. Anticipated policies are effective in altering the level of aggregate output, but unanticipated policies have a larger impact. The new Keynesians suggest that activist stabilization policies can be used to affect the level of output in the economy, but policymakers must be cognizant of the Lucas (11)_____ _____. In other words, since expectations affect the outcome of policies, making predictions about a proposed policy's effects is more difficult than is implied by the traditional model.

New classical economists are less optimistic. They contend that (12)_____ macropolicies can only be counterproductive. Activist policies are likely to be destabilizing and inflationary.

A significant implication of rational expectations is that anti-inflationary policies can achieve their goal at a lower cost if these policies are viewed as (13)_____ by the public. The traditional model suggests that fighting inflation will be quite costly in terms of lost output and higher unemployment. Arthur Okun's rule of thumb indicates that a reduction of one point in the inflation rate requires a four percent loss in a year's GNP, a staggering cost for such a small gain. Recall that Okun's rule of thumb holds in a world where anti-inflation policies are not viewed as credible. To the extent that such policies foster credibility, fighting inflation will be less costly.

Evidence indicates that credible policies do reduce the adverse consequences of anti-inflationary policies. Actions designed to reduce government (14)_____ _____ appear to be particularly important in this regard. It appears that anti-inflationary policies that do not address budget-deficit problems may be viewed with little credibility and prove to be relatively costly. Some economists contend that recessions in Great Britain and the United States in the early 1980s were more severe because deficit issues went unresolved. Although this conclusion is controversial, it indicates the importance expectations play in economic theory.

HELPFUL HINTS

According to the theory of rational expectations, it is important to distinguish between anticipated and unanticipated policy. New classical and new Keynesian models both assume that people form expectations rationally but differ on the speed at which wages and prices can adjust to changes in expectations. New classical models assume the adjustment is immediate. New Keynesian models assume the adjustment takes time. As a result, new classical models predict that anticipated policy has no affect on aggregate output. New Keynesian models predict that anticipated policy does have some affect on aggregate output. Both new Keynesian and new classical models agree that establishing credibility is important for minimizing the output cost of reducing inflation.

EXERCISES

Practice Problems

1. Suppose your roommate studies late in the library each night, returning to your room after you have gone to bed and turned out the light. In an effort not to disturb you, he leaves the light off but ends up bumping into things in the dark and making so much noise that you wake up anyway. Fortunately your roommate is fairly quick about it, and after 5 minutes or so he is usually in bed. In an effort to remedy this situation, you decide to leave the light on

to reduce the noise. Your experiment fails. Not only does your roommate still make noise, but seeing that the light is on, he makes noise for 10 minutes instead of 5 minutes.

a.   How does your experiment with your dorm light relate to the Lucas critique?

_____

b.   How does your experiment with your dorm light relate to policymakers' ability to predict the effect of a change in policy on the economy?

_____

_____

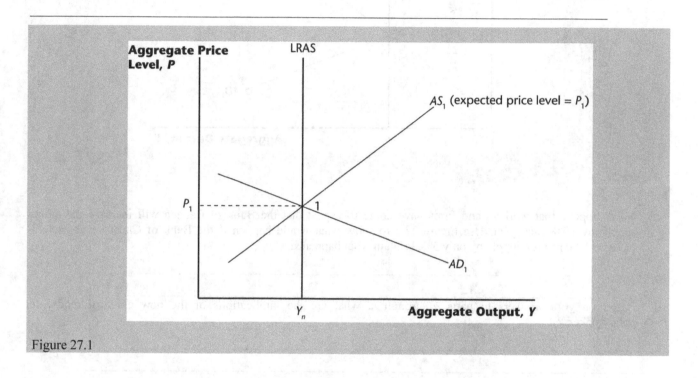

Figure 27.1

2.

a.   Use Figure 27.1 to show the effect of an unanticipated increase in the money supply in the new classical model. Explain what happened.

_____

b.   Use Figure 27.1 to show the effect of an anticipated increase in the money supply in the new classical model. Explain what happened.

_____

_____

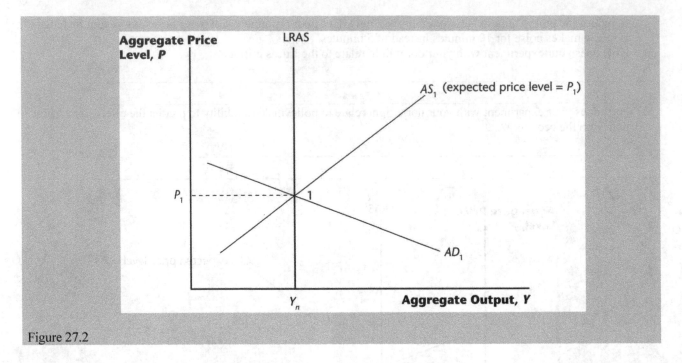

Figure 27.2

c. Now suppose that workers and firms have come to expect that the Bank of Canada will increase the money supply by 10% each year. Use Figure 27.2 to show what would happen if the Bank of Canada unexpectedly increased the money supply by only 5%. Explain what happened.

_____

_____

d. Based on your answers to parts *a* through *c*, what are the implications of the new classical model for policymakers?

_____

_____

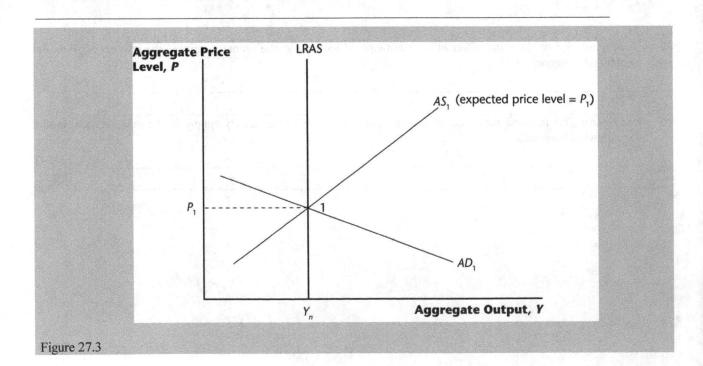

Figure 27.3

3.

a. Use Figure 27.3 to show the effect of an unanticipated increase in the money supply in the new Keynesian model. Explain what happened.

_____

b. Use Figure 27.3 to show the effect of an anticipated increase in the money supply in the new Keynesian model. Explain what happened.

_____

c. What are the implications of the new Keynesian model for policymakers?

_____

Short-Answer Questions

1. Suppose that temporary increases in the budget deficit in the past have not caused interest rates to rise. Explain why it would be dangerous to infer that a permanent increase in the budget deficit will not cause interest rates to rise.

_____

2. According to the new classical model, how can an increase in the money supply lead to a reduction in aggregate output?

_____

3. In the new classical model, only unanticipated policy changes have an effect on the business cycle. Does it follow that the Bank of Canada should randomly change policy so that people don't catch on to what it is doing? Explain.

_____

4. Why are wages and prices sticky?

_____

5. The new Keynesian model predicts that anticipated policy has an effect on output. Does it follow that policymakers should pursue discretionary policy? Explain.

_____

Critical-Thinking Questions

The policy recommendations of the three models presented in this chapter are sometimes contradictory. Suppose you are an economic advisor to the prime minister. The inflation rate is currently 10%, and the president asks you for recommendations to bring the inflation rate down to 5% without causing excessive unemployment.

1. What policy would you recommend based on the new classical model? Explain.

    _____

    _____

2. What policy would you recommend based on the new Keynesian model? Explain.

    _____

    _____

3. Of course the prime minister wants just one recommendation. What is the common element in both the new classical and new Keynesian models that you would recommend as part of any policy to reduce inflation? Explain.

    _____

    _____

    _____

    _____

SELF-TEST

True-False Questions

Circle whether the following statements are true (T) or false (F).

T   F   1. Robert Lucas, in his famous critique, argued that econometric model simulations provide no useful information with which to evaluate the effects of alternative economic policies.

T   F   2. A monetary acceleration may have different effects in 2004 than in 2005 if the public's expectations about the policy are different in those two years.

T   F   3. The new classical economists argue that neither anticipated nor unanticipated policies affect the level of unemployment.

T   F   4. The new classical economists argue that only unanticipated increases in the money supply can affect the general level of prices.

T   F   5. While an expansionary monetary policy can never lead to a decline in output in the traditional model, such a result is possible in the new classical model.

T   F   6. Anticipated policies have no effect on aggregate output or the rate of unemployment in the New Keynesian model.

T   F   7. The expansion of aggregate output will be smaller for an anticipated policy than for an unanticipated policy in the nonclassical rational expectations model.

T   F   8. It is the existence of rigidities such as sticky wages and prices, not adaptive expectations, that explains why anticipated policies can affect output in the new Keynesian model.

T   F   9. If expectations about policy are formed adaptively, then anticipated policies will actually have greater output effects than unanticipated policies.

T   F   10. If expectations are formed rationally, and prices and wages are completely flexible, then the best anti-inflation policy is likely to consist of a gradual reduction in the money supply over a period of several years.

T   F   11. Anticipated and unanticipated policies have an identical effect in the traditional models.

T   F   12. Expectation formation will change when the behaviour of forecasted variables changes.

T F   13. The new classical model suggests that an expansionary monetary policy can lead to an increase in aggregate output if the public expects an even more expansionary policy than the one actually implemented.

T F   14. Unlike the new classical model, in the new Keynesian model, the anticipated policy does have an effect on aggregate output.

T F   15. The new classical macroeconomic model demonstrates that aggregate output does not increase as a result of unanticipated expansionary policy.

Multiple-Choice Questions

Circle the appropriate answer.

1. Robert Lucas argues that using an econometric model that has been constructed on the basis of past data
    a. may be appropriate for short-run forecasting, but is inappropriate for evaluating alternative policies.
    b. may be appropriate for alternative policies, but is not appropriate for evaluating short-run forecasting.
    c. is appropriate for both short-run forecasting and policy evaluation.
    d. is not appropriate for either short-run forecasting or policy evaluation.

2. An anticipated expansion in the money supply will have no effect on aggregate output in which model?
    a. New Keynesian model.
    b. Traditional model.
    c. New classical rational expectations model.
    d. All of the above models.

3. In which of the following models does an anticipated increase in money growth affect the price level?
    a. Traditional model.
    b. New classical model.
    c. New Keynesian model.
    d. All of the above models.

4. The new Keynesian model indicates that anticipated policies affect aggregate output because of rigidities resulting from
    a. long-term contracts.
    b. adaptive expectations.
    c. the reluctance of some firms to alter prices and wages frequently, creating what can be considered implicit contracts.
    d. All of the above.
    e. Only (a) and (c) of the above.

5. The traditional model is distinguished from both the new classical and the new Keynesian model by the following:
    a. The traditional model assumes that expectations are formed adaptively, that is, on past behaviour of the relevant variable.
    b. The traditional model does not distinguish between anticipated and unanticipated policies.
    c. The traditional model assumes that the price level remains fixed.
    d. Both (b) and (c) of the above.
    e. Both (a) and (b) of the above.

6. Assume that the economy is characterized by sticky wages and prices, and rational expectations. If the Bank of Canada wishes to reduce unemployment by expanding the money supply, how will the announcement of such a policy influence the policy's effectiveness?

    a. The announcement eliminates the policy's effectiveness.

    b. The announcement diminishes the policy's effectiveness.

    c. The announcement has no effect on the policy's effectiveness.

    d. The announcement enhances the magnitude of the policy's effectiveness.

7. Kristin argues at a meeting of the Governing Council that the Bank of Canada should vote to quickly lower the overnight rate in an attempt to return the economy to full employment. One can infer from her argument that Kristin is

    a. either a new classical or a traditional economist.

    b. either a new classical or a new Keynesian economist.

    c. definitely not a new classical economist.

    d. definitely not a new Keynesian economist.

8. If people form rational expectations, an anti-inflation policy will be more successful if it

    a. is credible.

    b. comes as a surprise.

    c. is unanticipated.

    d. does all of the above.

9. At a meeting of the central bank's policy-making committee, Meghan argues that any decision regarding a contractionary monetary policy should be postponed until the legislative body votes on a deficit-reduction package currently before it. Meghan seems to be implying that

    a. an anti-inflationary policy would make more sense if people saw evidence of lower deficits.

    b. an anti-inflationary policy might be too costly in terms of lost output if such a policy was not believed to be credible.

    c. both (a) and (b) of the above are possible.

    d. neither (a) nor (b) of the above are a concern.

10. Assume that irrefutable evidence proves that while anticipated monetary expansions cause aggregate output to expand, unanticipated monetary expansions proved more potent than anticipated policies. What economic model would the evidence support?

    a. New classical model.

    b. New Keynesian model.

    c. Traditional model.

    d. Uninformed median-voter model.

11. _____ policies have no effect on aggregate output or the rate of unemployment in the _____ model.

    a. anticipated; new Keynesian

    b. unanticipated; new Keynesian

    c. anticipated; new classical

    d. unanticipated; new classical

12. The expansion of aggregate output will be _____ for an _____ policy than for an _____ policy in the _____ model.

    a. smaller; unanticipated; anticipated; new classical

    b. smaller; anticipated; unanticipated; new classical

    c. smaller; unanticipated; anticipated; new Keynesian

    d. smaller; anticipated; unanticipated; new Keynesian

    e. larger; anticipated; unanticipated; new Keynesian

13. It is the existence of rigidities such as sticky wages and prices, not adaptive expectations, that explains why _____ policies can affect output in the _____ model.

    a. unanticipated; new classical

    b. anticipated; new classical

    c. unanticipated; new Keynesian

    d. anticipated; new Keynesian

14. According to _____ economists, policymakers' attempts to stabilize the economy will be ineffective and may even make conditions worse.

    a. new classical

    b. new Keynesian

    c. Keynesian

    d. activist

15. If the government _____ budget deficits, an anti-inflationary policy is _____ likely to be regarded as credible.

    a. reduces; less

    b. reduces; more

    c. increases; more

    d. eliminates; less

16. Econometric models

    a. are ones in which the public is assumed to have rational expectations.

    b. are estimated using data and statistics.

    c. can be used to forecast future economic conditions.

    d. are no longer used by economists.

    e. only (b) and (c) of the above.

17. Suppose that a new professor is teaching a course for the first time and that students try to guess which questions will be on the midterm examination. Students display rational expectations most clearly if they base their guess on

    a. midterm examinations from previous semesters.

    b. suggestions from friends at other universities.

    c. the midterm review session taught by the professor.

    d. advice from students who took the class last semester.

    e. all of the above.

18. In the new classical model, policy that is designed to increase output will be successful if

    a. the price level rises less than anticipated.

    b. the price level rises more than anticipated.

    c. the price level rises exactly as anticipated.

    d. the price level does not rise.

    e. either (a) or (c) of the above.

19. The policy ineffectiveness proposition states that policy will have no effect on _____ as long as policy is anticipated, people have rational expectations, and _____.

    a. prices; prices and wages are sticky

    b. prices; prices and wages are fully flexible

    c. output; prices and wages are sticky

    d. output; prices and wages are fully flexible

20. Suppose that the central bank decides to lower the rate of inflation by lowering the growth rate of the money supply. If the inflation rate actually increases, then which of the following is a possible explanation?
    a. The central bank lowered the growth rate of the money supply more than was expected by the public.
    b. The public did not believe that the central bank would lower the price level, and the central bank did not lower the growth rate of the money supply.
    c. The public believed that the central bank would lower the price level, but the central bank did not lower the growth rate of the money supply.
    d. Only (a) and (b) of the above.
    e. Only (b) and (c) of the above.

21. In the new Keynesian model, if the central bank credibly announces that it will fight inflation, and if the public has rational expectations, then
    a. output will fall and the price level will fall.
    b. output will rise and the price level will fall.
    c. output will fall but it is impossible to determine what will happen to the price level.
    d. it is impossible to determine what will happen to output, but the price level will fall.

22. In the new Keynesian model, if the public has rational expectations, then anticipated policy will generally lead to _____ changes in output and _____ changes in the price level as compared to unanticipated policy.
    a. larger; larger
    b. smaller; larger
    c. larger; smaller
    d. smaller; smaller

23. Despite the fact that only unanticipated policy affects output in the new classical model, why is it not recommended that policymakers attempt to continually "fool" the public with unanticipated policy?
    a. Policymakers will have a difficult time knowing what public expectations are, and as a result the effect of policy on output will be unknown.
    b. It is impossible to continually fool the public by changing policy frequently.
    c. Unanticipated policy will not change the price level and therefore is inconsistent with reducing inflation.
    d. All of the above.

24. In which model of the economy can inflation be reduced with the least cost in terms of lost output by using a "cold turkey" approach?
    a. The traditional model.
    b. The new Keynesian model.
    c. The new classical model.
    d. The Keynesian model.

25. A _____ anti-inflation policy may be more costly than a _____ approach since it may be more difficult to be credibly implemented.
    a. "cold turkey"; rational
    b. traditional; rational
    c. gradual; "cold turkey"
    d. gradual; flexible

26. Eric the economist tells his students that all anticipated policy has no effect on aggregate output. You can probably infer that he is a
    a. Keynesian economist.
    b. Monetarist.
    c. Proponent of activist policies.
    d. New classical economist.

27. If long-term contracts create wage and price rigidities, then an anticipated monetary policy expansion will cause
    a. aggregate output to increase in the short run.
    b. the price level to rise.
    c. a permanent increase in aggregate output.
    d. both (a) and (b) of the above to occur.
    e. both (b) and (c) of the above to occur.

28. When an expansionary policy by the Bank of Canada is _____ and the expectations are rational, the output and price will increase. However, when this policy is _____, the output level remains unchanged and the price level _____.
    a. anticipated; unanticipated; goes up
    b. anticipated; unanticipated; goes down
    c. unanticipated; anticipated; goes up
    d. unanticipated; anticipated; goes down

29. According to the new classical model, an expansionary policy can lead to a decline in aggregate output if _____.
    a. the expectations are adaptive
    b. prices are sticky
    c. the public expects an even more expansionary policy than the one actually implemented
    d. both (a) and (b) above

30. According to traditional models, in response to an unanticipated anti-inflation policy, the output level _____ and credibility _____ important.
    a. increases; is
    b. increases; is not
    c. decreases; is not
    d. decreases; is

ANSWERS

CHAPTER 1

Chapter Synopsis/Completions

1. financial markets
2. securities
3. assets
4. bonds
5. interest rate
6. common stock
7. financial intermediaries
8. financial crises
9. banks
10. e-finance
11. money
12. business cycle
13. aggregate output
14. recessions
15. unemployment rate
16. aggregate price level
17. inflation rate
18. inflation
19. monetary theory
20. monetary policy
21. central bank
22. Bank of Canada (the Bank)
23. fiscal policy
24. budget deficit
25. budget surplus
26. foreign exchange market
27. foreign exchange rate
28. appreciation
29. depreciation

Practice Problems

1.
a. The foreign exchange market, because that is where dollars can be exchanged for euros.
b. The bond market, because that is where firms sell debt securities, known as bonds, to borrow large sums of money for capital construction.
c. The stock market, because that is where firms sell ownership shares of the company, known as common stock.

2.
a. The Bank of Canada
b. Quickly, because the growth rate of the money supply and the rate of inflation have a positive association.
c. Reduce the growth rate of the money supply, because a lower growth rate of the money supply is associated with a lower inflation rate.
d. Often, but not always, a reduction in the growth rate of money leads to a reduction in aggregate output (recession) and a corresponding increase in the unemployment rate.

3.

1.	B	2.	S
3.	F	4.	S
5.	F		

4.

1.	A	2.	A
3.	D	4.	D
5.	A	6.	D

Short-Answer Questions

1. Ford would like a weak Canadian dollar (the dollar buys less foreign currency or foreign currency buys more dollars). This makes Fords appear cheap to Americans, and they buy more.
2. You would like a strong dollar (the dollar buys a large amount of foreign currency). This makes your European trip cost less in terms of dollars.
3. The bond market.
4. Around 2008, because the value of the dollar hit its peak. Thus, Canadian goods were very expensive in terms of foreign currencies.
5. Institutions that borrow from one group and lend to another are financial intermediaries. Banks accept deposits (borrow from depositors) and lend those funds to loan customers. Insurance companies collect premiums (borrow from their insured customers) and lend those funds to loan customers (usually corporations).
6. Trust and mortgage loan companies, and credit unions and *caisses populaires*.
7. Money growth decreased, output is decreasing, and it is likely that unemployment is rising, inflation is decreasing, and long-term bond rates are falling.
8. Money and interest rates. The Bank of Canada (or simply the Bank).
9. Yes, pawnbrokers are financial intermediaries since they bring savers (the pawnbroker) and spenders (the borrower) together. Just like banks, the borrower leaves collateral for the loan, the conditions of the loan are written, and interest is charged. However, interest rates and collateral requirements are often higher than what is available through banks.
10. One would expect a fall in prices and economic output. This is in fact what happened. In 1929, real GDP was $52 billion (in 1986 dollars) and the GDP deflator was 11.9. By 1933, real GDP declined by 30% to $36 billion and the deflator by 18% to 9.7.

Critical-Thinking Questions

1. No. It is true that all recession since the beginning of the twentieth century have been preceded by a reduction in the growth rate of money. However, sometimes a reduction in the growth rate of money is not followed by a recession, making recessions hard to predict.
2. Yes. When output falls, unemployment usually rises, making it more difficult to find a job.
3. Inflation will go down in the future because inflation rates and growth rates of the money supply have a positive association.

Self-Test

True-False Questions

1.	F	2.	T
3.	F	4.	T
5.	T	6.	T
7.	F	8.	F
9.	T	10.	F
11.	T	12.	F
13.	T	14.	T
15.	F		

Multiple-Choice Questions

1.	b	2.	c
3.	a	4.	d
5.	b	6.	b
7.	a	8.	c
9.	d	10.	a
11.	b	12.	c
13.	c	14.	d
15.	d	16.	d
17.	a	18.	c
19.	b	20.	b
21.	a	22.	b
23.	b	24.	c
25.	a	26.	d
27.	a	28.	c
29.	c	30.	c

CHAPTER 2

Chapter Synopsis/Completions

1.	financial intermediaries	2.	financial markets
3.	equity markets	4.	exchanges
5.	over-the-counter	6.	capital markets
7.	maturity	8.	dividends
9.	primary markets	10.	investment banks
11.	secondary markets	12.	dealers
13.	money market	14.	liquid
15.	risk	16.	overnight rate
17.	municipal bonds	18.	foreign bonds
19.	eurobonds	20.	eurodollars
21.	risk sharing	22.	adverse selection
23.	moral hazard	24.	transaction costs
25.	economies of scale	26.	asset transformation
27.	financial panic		

Practice Problems

1. a. Indirect finance

    b. Direct finance

    c. Indirect finance

    d. Indirect finance

    e. Direct finance

    f. Direct finance

    g. Direct finance

    h. Indirect finance

2. a. debt, secondary, over-the-counter (all bonds are sold OTC), money

    b. equity, secondary, over-the-counter (Microsoft is traded on NASDAQ, an OTC market), capital

    c. equity, primary, no exchange or OTC market is involved yet, capital

    d.   debt, secondary, over-the-counter, capital

    e.   equity, secondary, exchange (Ford is traded on the NYSE), capital

3. a.   A collapse of financial intermediaries because the providers of funds doubt the health of the intermediaries and pull their funds out of both sound and unsound institutions.

    b.   *Restrictions on entry*: The government provides a charter only to upstanding, well-capitalized individuals.
       Disclosure: Intermediaries are subject to stringent reporting requirements.
       Restrictions on assets and activities: There are limits on the riskiness of the assets held by intermediaries.
       Deposit insurance: People suffer less of a financial loss when a depository institution fails.
       Limits on competition: Branching restrictions limit competition that was believed to cause failures.

4.

1.	a, c, d, e, g	2. c, d
3.	e	4. a, c, d
5.	a, c, d	6. g
7.	b, f	

5.

1.	Government of Canada treasury bills	2. Certificates of deposit
3.	Commercial paper	4. Banker's acceptances
5.	Repurchase agreements	6. Overnight funds

Short-Answer Questions

1. With direct finance, borrowers acquire funds directly from lenders by selling them securities. With indirect finance, a financial intermediary stands between the lender and borrower and helps transfer the funds from one to the other.

2. A debt security is for borrowing while an equity security is for ownership. The primary market is where new issues are sold, and the secondary market is where existing issues are resold. An exchange is centralized while an OTC market is decentralized and linked by computers. The money market is for short-term debt, and the capital market is for long-term funds.

3. Government of Canada treasury bills, because they are the most actively traded security and have no default risk. Corporate stocks. Corporate bonds.

4. Equity holders are residual claimants, so in the event of a bankruptcy, they receive funds only after all of the debt holders have been paid. Short-term debt securities have smaller fluctuations in prices than long-term securities do. Therefore, short-term bonds have the least risk.

5. Foreign bonds are sold in a foreign country and denominated in that country's currency. Eurobonds are denominated in a currency other than the currency of the country in which it is sold. There is no relationship between a Eurobond and the euro. That is, Eurobonds are not denominated in euros.

6. Moral hazard. Moral hazard is the risk that the borrower will engage in activities that are immoral from the lender's point of view. In this case, the borrower is using the money in a riskier manner than was agreed to in the loan contract.

7. They have lower transactions costs due to economies of scale. They provide risk sharing. They reduce the problems associated with asymmetric information by screening and monitoring borrowers.

8. Chartered banks, trust and mortgage loan companies, and credit unions and caisses populaires. Deposits are the main liability. Chartered banks are the largest.

9. Money market mutual funds. Since they buy such safe and liquid instruments with the funds they have acquired, they are able to allow shareholders to write cheques against the value of their share holdings.

10. Chartered banks, trust and mortgage loan companies, and credit unions and caisses populaires. The CDIC provides insurance of up to $100 000 for each depositor at a bank, examines the books of insured banks, and imposes restrictions on assets that banks can hold.

Critical-Thinking Questions

1. The transaction costs would be prohibitive because it would be expensive to pay a lawyer to write a loan contract that would be used only once. It would be risky because you would be putting all of your eggs in one basket by lending all of your money to one person. Finally, you are unlikely to know how to avoid the problems of asymmetric information. There could be adverse selection in that risky borrowers desire to borrow. There could be moral hazard in that the borrower may take the loan money and use it to gamble instead of buying a car.

2. Banks make many similar loans, so they pay the lawyer only once for a contract that can be used many times. Banks make a variety of different loans whose returns do not always move together, which reduces their risk on the group of loans. Banks know how to screen and monitor loan customers to reduce adverse selection and moral hazard.

Self-Test

True-False Questions

1.	T	2.	T
3.	T	4.	F
5.	T	6.	F
7.	T	8.	T
9.	F	10.	T
11.	F	12.	T
13.	F	14.	T
15.	F		

Multiple-Choice Questions

1.	c	2.	c
3.	a	4.	b
5.	d	6.	e
7.	c	8.	e
9.	b	10.	c
11.	e	12.	d
13.	c	14.	b
15.	b	16.	d
17.	b	18.	d
19.	c	20.	d
21.	c	22.	a
23.	c	24.	b
25.	b	26.	d
27.	d	28.	a
29.	b	30.	c

CHAPTER 3

Chapter Synopsis/Completions

1.	wealth	2.	income
3.	medium of exchange	4.	store of value
5.	liquidity	6.	payments system
7.	commodity money	8.	currency
9.	fiat money	10.	E-money
11.	e-cash	12.	monetary aggregates

13. unit of account

Practice Problems

1. a. medium of exchange
    b. store of value
    c. unit of account
    d. unit of account
    e. medium of exchange
    f. store of value
    g. unit of account
    h. medium of exchange

2. a. apples/orange, apples/pear, apples/banana, oranges/pear, oranges/banana, pears/banana.
        $[n(n-1)]/2 = (4 \times 3)/2 = 12/2 = 6$.
    b. dollars/apple, dollars/orange, dollars/pear, dollars/banana. Four.
    c. The system with money needs fewer prices so transactions costs are lower. The difference in transactions costs increases as the economy expands because the number of prices needed in a barter economy explodes as the number of goods increases.

3. a. fiat money
    b. commodity money
    c. electronic payment
    d. commodity money
    e. cheques
    f. e-money
    g. fiat money
    h. e-money (stored-value card)

4.

Number of Goods	Number of Prices in a Barter Economy	Number of Prices in a Money Economy
5	10	5
25	300	25
50	1225	50
500	124,750	500
5000	12,497,500	5000

5. When dollars cease to function as money, they will become near worthless pieces of paper, and you don't want to be stuck holding dollars when they become worthless. Therefore, you spend your dollars today, rather than tomorrow, because no one will accept dollars tomorrow. If you expect dollars to become worthless next week, you still want to spend them today, because others will do the same. Since no one wants to be stuck holding the dollars on the day that they become worthless, everyone tries to spend the dollars as soon as they believe that dollars will become worthless.

Short-Answer Questions

1. Income is a flow of earnings per unit of time. Wealth is a total collection of property that serves to store value. Money is the asset that is generally accepted in payment for goods or services. It is not necessarily true that people with high income or wealthy people have a great deal of money. Those with high income may spend it all, and wealthy people may hold their wealth in forms other than money.

2. System without money where goods and services are exchanged directly for other goods and services. Transaction cost is the time spent trying to exchange goods and services. Barter requires a "double coincidence of wants" and an enormous number of prices to establish relative values.
3. It must be easily standardized, widely accepted, easily divisible, easy to carry, and it must not deteriorate quickly.
4. Money is perfectly liquid because it is a medium of exchange. Other assets involve transaction costs when converting them into a medium of exchange.
5. Advantages are that cheques increase efficiency since some payments cancel each other out. Cheques can be written for large amounts, there is little loss from theft, and cheques provide a receipt. Some problems are that it takes time to get cheques from one place to another so you do not have access to your money immediately when you deposit a cheque, and cheques are expensive to process.
6. Currency, traveller's cheques, demand deposits, and other chequable deposits. All of the assets in M1 are a medium of exchange (perfectly liquid).
7. M2, because M2 includes all of M1 plus additional slightly less liquid assets.
8. Yes, because while the monetary aggregates tend to often move together, sometimes their growth rates diverge greatly.
9. The Bank of Canada must estimate deposits in small depository institutions because they report data infrequently, and because the adjustment of the data for seasonal variation is revised as more data become available.
10. Probably not. Since the monetary aggregates are substantially revised over time, the initially released data are not reliable.

Critical-Thinking Questions

1. Fiat money. It is money that is decreed by government as legal tender but it is not convertible into a particular precious metal.
2. It is lighter and, therefore, easier to transport. However, it will only be accepted if people trust that the authorities will not print too much of it, and that the paper money is difficult to counterfeit.
3. Commodity money, which is a precious metal or another valuable commodity. No. Modern money is fiat money and it is not redeemable in any particular precious metal.

Self-Test

True-False Questions

1.	T	2.	F
3.	F	4.	T
5.	F	6.	T
7.	T	8.	T
9.	T	10.	F
11.	F	12.	F
13.	T	14.	F
15.	F		

Multiple-Choice Questions

1.	d	2.	a
3.	b	4.	c
5	b	6.	c
7.	b	8.	b
9.	b	10.	a
11.	c	12.	c
13.	d	14.	d
15.	d	16.	b
17.	b	18.	b
19.	a	20.	c
21.	c	22.	d
23.	d	24.	a
25.	d	26.	b
27.	b	28.	c
29.	c	30.	b

CHAPTER 4

Chapter Synopsis/Completions

1. yield to maturity
2. present value
3. simple loan
4. coupon bond
5. discount bond
6. coupon rate
7. face value
8. consol
9. perpetuity
10. current yield
11. rate of return
12. interest rate risk
13. nominal interest rate
14. cash flows

Practice Problems

1. a. $\$1000/1.04 = \$961.54$

   b. $\$1000/1.08 = \$925.93$

   c. $\$1000/(1.04)^2 = \$924.56$

   d. The present value falls because a larger interest rate means that a value today would grow into a larger value in the future so a value in the future must be discounted to a greater degree to find its value today.

e.   The present value falls because a value today would grow larger if allowed to grow farther into the future so a value farther into the future must be discounted to a greater degree to find its value today.

2. a. $1018.52 = $1100/1 + i. Solve for i = $1100 − ($1018.52/$1018.52) = 0.08 = 8%. It would be below. If the price is above the face value (or par), then the yield to maturity must be below the coupon rate.

b. $965 = $100/(1 + i) + $100/(1 + i)^2 + $1000/(1 + i)^2 and solve for i. It would be above. If the price is below the face value (or par), then the yield to maturity must be above the coupon rate.

c. P = $100/1.07 + $1100/(1.07)^2 = $93.46 + $960.78 = $1054.24

d. P = $100/1.08 + $1100/(1.08)^2 = $92.59 + $943.07 + $1035.66

e.   The price of the bond falls. Bond prices and interest rates are negatively related.

f.   If i = 7%, P = $1100/1.07 = $1028.04. If i = 8%, P = $1100/1.08 = $1018.52. For the two year case, the price changes is $1054.24 − $1035.66 = $18.58. For the one-year case, the price change is $1028.04 − $1018.52 = $9.52. The longer to maturity, the greater is the change in the price of a bond from the same size change in the interest rate.

3. a.   15% − 13% = 2%

b.   12% − 9% = 3%

c.   10% − 9% = 1%

d.   5% − 1% = 4%

e. d above, because it generates the largest real interest rate.

f. c above, because it generates the smallest real interest rate.

4. a. $50/(1 i)

b. $50/(1 i)^2

c. $50 × (1 i)^2

d. $50 × (1 i)

5.

Price of the Discount Bond	Maturity	Yield on a Discount Basis	Yield to Maturity
$900	1 year (365 days)	11.1%	11.1%
$950	6 months (182 days)	10.56%	10.84%
$975	3 months (91 days)	10.28%	10.68%

Short-Answer Questions

1. $500 × 1.06 = $530.

$40/$500 = 0.08 = 8%

2. Fully amortized loan. Both require the borrower to make periodic payments to the lender until maturity. The payments on a fixed-payment loan are all the same size and each is part principal and interest. The payments on a coupon bond are each just interest payments and the last one at maturity is the principal.

3. Yearly coupon/face value. No, because the coupon and face value are fixed. Its price must be below par because the fixed coupons and principal are discounted to the present using a larger interest rate. In addition, the only way to make a bond with fixed coupons and par pay a higher yield to maturity is to have it sell for a lower price (a discount).

4. A coupon bond with no maturity. P = $70/0.07 = $1000. P = $70/0.14 = $500.

5. $i = C/P = \$70/\$700 = 0.10 = 10\%$. $i = C/P = \$70/\$700 = 0.10 = 10\%$. They are the same.

Critical-Thinking Questions

1.   No. Employing any positive interest rate, the present value of the lottery ticket is less than $30 000.

2. $\$10\ 000 + \$10\ 000/1.05 + \$10\ 000/(1.05)^2 = \$28\ 594.10$

3. $\$10\ 000 + \$10\ 000/1.08 + \$10\ 000/(1.08)^2 = \$27\ 832.65$

4.   5%. A smaller interest rate causes a present value to grow more slowly over time, and therefore a future sum would require a smaller discount when it is discounted back to the present

Self-Test

True-False Questions

1.	F	2.	F
3.	T	4.	T
5.	T	6.	F
7.	T	8.	F
9.	F	10.	F
11.	T	12.	T
13.	F	14.	F
15.	T		

Part B

1.	d	2.	a
3.	b	4.	c
5.	c	6.	b
7.	c	8.	b
9.	d	10.	c
11.	d	12.	e
13.	d	14.	c
15.	d	16.	c
17.	a	18.	a
19.	a	20.	b
21.	d	22.	d
23.	b	24.	c
25.	d	26.	d
27.	a	28.	b
29.	d	30.	c

CHAPTER 5

Chapter Synopsis/Completions

1.	expected return	2.	risk
3.	demand curve	4.	supply curve
5.	equilibrium	6.	wealth
7.	liquidity	8.	Fisher effect
9.	liquidity preference framework	10.	opportunity cost
11.	demand curve	12.	excess supply

13. asset market

Practice Problems

1. a.   increase, because your wealth has increased
    b.   decrease, because the relative liquidity of bonds has decreased
    c.   increase, because bonds are relatively less risky
    d.   increase, because bonds have relatively higher expected returns
    e.   decrease, because your wealth has decreased

2. a.

Price	Quantity demanded	Quantity supplied	Corresponding interest rate
$975	100	300	($1000 – $975)/$975 = 2.6%
$950	150	250	($1000 – $950)/$950 = 5.3%
$925	200	200	($1000 – $925)/$925 = 8.1%
$900	250	150	($1000 – $900)/$900 = 11.1%

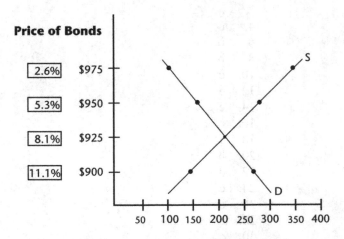

Price of Bonds

2.6%	$975
5.3%	$950
8.1%	$925
11.1%	$900

Quantity of Bonds

    b. $925, 8.1%, 200 billion dollars
    c.   At $950 (or an interest rate of 5.3%), the quantity demanded of bonds is $150 billion while the quantity supplied is $250 billion. The excess supply of bonds means that desired borrowing exceeds desired lending, causing the price of bonds to fall to $925 and the corresponding interest rate to rise to 8.1%.
    d. $950, 5.3%, 250 billion dollars.

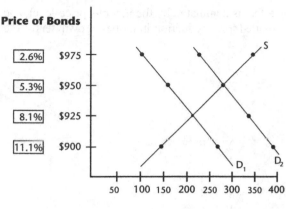

3. a. bond demand shifts right, price of bonds increases, interest rate falls

    b. bond demand shifts right, price of bonds increases, interest rate falls

    c. bond demand shifts left, price of bonds decreases, interest rate rises

    d. due to expected capital losses, expected returns on bonds falls so bond demand shifts left, price of bonds decreases, interest rate rises

    e. for each price of bonds, the real interest rate on bonds decreases, causing bond demand to shift left, bond supply to shift right, the price of bonds to fall, interest rates to rise

4. a. money demand shifts right, interest rates rise

    b. money demand shifts right, interest rates rise

    c. money supply shifts right, interest rates fall

Short-Answer Questions

1. Wealth, expected return relative to alternative assets, risk relative to alternative assets, and liquidity relative to alternative assets.

2. ($1000-$963)/$963 = 3.8%

3. The price of bonds is below equilibrium. An excess demand for bonds means that desired lending exceeds desired borrowing, the interest rate falls, and the price of bonds rises.

4. Lower interest rates in the future would mean higher bond prices in the future and an increase in expected returns on bonds purchased today, shifting bond demand to the right today. Bond prices rise and interest rates fall.

5. An increase in the expected profitability of investment opportunities, an increase in expected inflation, and an increase in the budget deficit.

6. For each price of bonds, the real interest rate on bonds increases, causing bond demand to shift right, bond supply to shift left, the price of bonds to rise, and interest rates to fall.

7. The Fisher effect.

8. Interest rates decrease. Liquidity effect.

Critical-Thinking Questions

1. Not necessarily. In the near term, if people are slow to adjust their expectations of inflation, then interest rates will first fall (liquidity effect). But in the longer run, the interest rate will rise to a point higher than the original interest rate (income, price-level, expected-inflation effects). If people adjust their inflationary expectation quickly, then the liquidity effect is overwhelmed by the expected-inflation effect even in the near term; interest rates rise in both the near term and long term.

2. The empirical evidence suggests that while there is a small short-term liquidity effect from a change in the

growth rate of money, in the long run the liquidity effect is dominated by the income, price-level, and expected-inflation effects. Therefore, after all effects are accounted for, a reduction in money growth tends to cause interest rates to decline.

Self-Test

True-False Questions

1.	T	2.	F
3.	T	4.	T
5.	F	6.	T
7.	F	8.	T
9.	T	10.	F
11.	F	12.	F
13.	T	14.	T
15.	T		

Multiple-Choice Questions

1.	b	2.	b
3.	a	4.	b
5.	b	6.	b
7.	c	8.	c
9.	a	10.	c
11.	e	12.	a
13.	b	14.	d
15.	a	16.	d
17.	a	18.	d
19.	d	20.	a
21.	d	22.	d
23.	d	24.	a
25.	d	26.	a
27.	c	28.	c
29.	b	30.	b

CHAPTER 6

Chapter Synopsis/Completions

1.	risk structure	2.	term structure
3.	default-free bonds	4.	risk premium
5.	credit-rating agencies	6.	liquidity
7.	risk premium	8.	yield curve
9.	inverted	10.	expectations
11.	segmented markets	12.	liquidity premium
13.	preferred habitat		

Practice Problems

1. a.   The demand for corporate bonds increases while the demand for default-free bonds decreases as funds move from Treasury bonds to corporate bonds.
   b.   The price increases and the interest rate decreases.
   c.   The price decreases and the interest rate increases.

d. The risk premium decreases because corporate bonds have less default risk.

2. a. The demand for corporate bonds shifts left and the demand for U.S. Treasury bonds shifts right. Interest rates increase on corporate bonds and interest rates fall on Treasury bonds, so the risk premium or spread increases.

b. The demand for corporate bonds shifts right and the demand for U.S. Treasury bonds shifts left. Interest rates decrease on corporate bonds and interest rates increase on Treasury bonds, so the risk premium or spread decreases.

c   The demand for BBB corporate bonds shifts left and the demand for AAA corporate bonds shifts right. This causes interest rate increase on BBB bonds and decrease on AAA bonds, causing the spread between BBB and AAA bonds to increase.

3. a. 1 year = 4%, 2 years = (4% + 5%)/2 = 4.5%, 3 years = (4% + 5% + 6%)/3 = 5%, 4 years = (4% + 5% + 6% + 7%)/4 = 5.5%.

b.

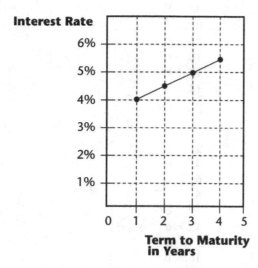

c. No. The expectations theory of the term structure can only explain an upward-sloping yield curve if short-term rates are expected to rise, but rates can't always be expected to rise.

d. 1 year = 4% – 4% = 0%, 2 year = 4.5% – 4% = 0.5%, 3 year = 5% – 4% = 1%, 4 year = 5.5% – 4% = 1.5%.

4.. In Figure 6A, the market is predicting that there will be a mild decline in short-term interest rates in the near future and an even steeper decline further out in the future. In Figure 6B the market is predicting that there will be a steep decline in short-term interest rates in the near future and a sharp increase further out in the future.

Short-Answer Questions

1. Risk of default, liquidity, and income tax treatment. An increase in the risk of default or a decrease in liquidity of a corporate bond causes the risk premium to increase. A decrease in the tax rate causes an increase in the interest rate on tax-exempt bonds (municipals), which can be considered an increase in the risk premium on municipals.

2. Moody's Investor Service and Standard and Poor's Corporation. They advise investors about the probability of default on corporate and municipal bonds. Investment-grade securities. Speculative-grade or junk bonds.

3. If long-term rates are an average of expected short-term rates, then an increase in short-term rates and expected future short-term rates will increase long-term rates too.

4. The theory argues that bonds of different maturities are not substitutes and people have a greater demand for short-term bonds than long-term bonds. Thus, the prices are higher on short-term bonds and their interest rates are lower.

Critical-Thinking Questions

1. 7%.
2. (6% + 7% + 8%)/3 = 7%.
3. The expected returns are the same.
4. The three one-year bonds are preferred. Other things the same, people prefer short-term securities. Thus, people require a liquidity premium (a higher interest rate) in order to be induced to hold longer-term bonds, and this three-year bond does not pay a liquidity premium.

Self-Test

True-False Questions

1.	F	2	T
3.	T	4.	F
5.	F	6.	T
7.	T	8.	F
9.	T	10.	F
11.	T	12.	F
13.	T	14.	T
15.	F		

Multiple-Choice Questions

1.	c	2.	c
3.	d	4.	a
5.	a	6.	d
7.	a	8.	a
9.	c	10.	c
11.	b	12.	e
13.	b	14.	d
15.	a	16.	b
17.	a	18.	c
19.	d	20.	c
21.	c	22.	d
23.	b	24.	a
25.	a	26.	b
27.	a	28.	c
29.	a	30.	d

CHAPTER 7

Chapter Synopsis/Completions

1.	rational expectations	2.	efficient market hypothesis.
3.	shareholders	4.	cash flows
5.	dividends	6.	generalized dividend model
7.	Gordon growth model	8.	adaptive expectations
9.	rational expectations	10.	optimal forecasts
11.	efficient market hypothesis	12.	unexploited profit opportunities
13.	arbitrage	14.	market fundamentals
15.	bubble	16.	behavioural finance
17.	short sales		

Practice Problems

1. a. $P = \$1/1.09 + \$17.50/1.09 = \$18.50/1.09 = \$16.97$

    b. $P = \$1/(9\% - 3\%) = \$1/0.06 = \$16.67$

    c. $P = \$1/(7\% - 3\%) = \$1/0.04 = \$25.00$

    d. $P = \$1/(7\% - 4\%) = \$1/0.03 = \$33.33$

    e. Interest rates on bonds would fall causing investors to accept lower returns in the stock market (k_e would fall). The economy would grow more quickly causing the growth rate of dividends to rise (g would rise). Stock prices would rise.

2. a. The price falls. Even though profits appear high, the stock price had fully reflected the greater expected profits, so this was bad news.

    b. The price stays the same (if no other events take place). Expectations were realized. The stock price had fully reflected the correct profits, so the announcement was not news.

    c. The price rises. It is not necessary that everyone in a financial market be well informed for unexploited profit opportunities to be eliminated. Smart money can move the market.

3. a. Long-term interest rates are likely to be unaffected. Since asset prices, and hence financial market yields, reflect currently available information, efficient markets theory suggests that the anticipated Bank of Canada action will not change long-term interest rates.

    b. Long-term interest rates might fall as people revise their expectations of inflation downward.

    c. Long-term interest rates are likely to rise as the excess demand for money leads to falling bond prices (see Chapter 6).

    d. When the Bank of Canada slows the growth of the money supply, predicting the interest-rate outcome requires some knowledge of people's expectations. While there is dispute as to whether or not unexpected money growth influences long-term interest rates, this example illustrates that expectations can play an important role in determining the effectiveness of monetary policy.

4. a. The price would decline to $85.47 ($100/1.17) after the opening.

    b. Microsoft's returns would be abnormally high, leading to an unexploited profit opportunity.

    c. This situation could not be maintained because in an efficient market, all unexploited profit opportunities will be eliminated.

Short-Answer Questions

1. Bill, because assets go to the person who values them the most. The price will exceed $15 and could range up to $20. The price is set by the one that values the asset the most, and that person will bid something greater than the next highest bidder.

2. More. The individual with superior information and certainty will discount the future cash flows at a lower interest rate, increasing the valuation of the stock.

3. No. If an event makes the average value of a random variable permanently larger, adaptive expectations will fail to fully adjust and will under-predict the variable, making forecast errors non-zero and predictable.

4. Yes. If an event makes the average value of a random variable permanently larger, rational expectations will fully reflect the new information, making forecast errors zero on average, and unpredictable.

5. Yes. Rational people may hold an asset whose price exceeds its fundamental value because they believe someone else will pay a higher price in the future.

6. Use a "buy and hold" strategy to generate an average market return at low cost.

Critical-Thinking Questions

1. No. If markets are efficient, the current price of the stock incorporates all available information. Since information about the storm is public, the price of the stock will already have risen before you can buy it.

2.   Yes. Since the information is not publicly available, it will not be incorporated into the price. You can buy at the low price and make abnormally high returns as the price appreciates.

3.   The price will rise, and the returns will return to the equilibrium return. Abnormally high returns cannot be maintained in the long run. The behaviour of smart money eliminates the unexploited profit opportunity.

Self-Test

True-False Questions

1.	F		2.	F
3.	T		4.	T
5.	T		6.	T
7.	F		8.	F
9.	F		10.	F
11.	F		12.	T
13.	F		14.	T
15.	F			

Multiple-Choice Questions

1.	c		2.	d
3.	d		4.	c
5.	c		6.	b
7.	c		8.	b
9.	a		10.	c
11.	c		12.	b
13.	d		14.	c
15.	d		16.	a
17.	b		18.	b
19.	c		20.	b
21.	a		22.	b
23.	d		24.	d
25.	d		26.	d
27.	d		28.	a
29.	c		30.	c

CHAPTER 8

Chapter Synopsis/Completions

1.	collateral		2.	secured debt
3.	restrictive covenants		4.	economies of scale
5.	liquidity services		6.	asymmetric information
7.	adverse selection		8.	moral hazard
9.	agency theory		10.	free-rider problem
11.	audits		12.	net worth
13.	principal-agent problem		14.	costly state verification
15.	venture capital		16.	incentive compatible
17.	economies of scope		18.	conflicts of interest
19.	spinning			

Practice Problems

1. a. Sellers know more about the quality of the product than buyers. Buyers must assume the product may be a lemon (low quality) and bid a low price. At that price, only low-quality products will be offered for sale. The market is too small and is inefficient.

    b. Private firms produce and sell information; government regulates firms, requiring them to increase information to lenders; lenders require borrowers to pledge collateral against a loan and have high net worth; financial intermediaries use their expertise to sort good firms from bad.

    c. No. The fact that financial intermediaries are larger than direct finance suggests that the adverse selection problems in direct finance have not been completely solved.

2. a. Managers act in their own interests instead of the interests of stockholders.

    b. Stockholders can produce information through audits and by monitoring management; governments can regulate to increase information to stockholders by requiring standardized accounting; funds can be supplied through debt contracts as opposed to equity contracts; financial intermediaries, such as venture capital firms, can monitor at a lower cost with no free-rider problem.

    c. No. The fact that financial intermediaries are larger than direct finance suggests that the principal-agent problems in direct finance have not been completely solved.

3. a. Adverse selection, moral hazard. Stocks suffer from the lemons problem and costly state verification so stocks are not the most important source of funding.

    b. Adverse selection. Stocks and bonds suffer from the lemons problem so they are not the most important source of funding.

    c. Transaction costs, adverse selection, moral hazard. Indirect finance reduces transaction costs for small lenders and efficiently collects information to reduce adverse selection and moral hazard, while avoiding the free-rider problem.

    d. Adverse selection, moral hazard. Banks make nontraded loans so the information they collect to reduce both adverse selection and moral hazard is less subject to the free-rider problem.

    e. Adverse selection, moral hazard. Governments regulate to increase information to lenders both before the loan and after.

    f. Adverse selection. More information is known about large, well-known companies, so they have access to direct finance.

    g. Adverse selection. Lenders select borrowers that provide collateral, which lowers the lender's risk.

    h. Moral hazard. Debt contracts require complicated restrictive covenants to lower moral hazard.

4.

a. 1. Sharp decline in the stock market.
    2. Unanticipated decline in the aggregate price level.
    3. Unanticipated depreciation of the domestic currency.
    4. A rise in interest rates that reduces cash flow.

b. 1. Sharp increases in interest rates.
    2. Asset market effects on balance sheets (steep stock market decline).
    3. An increase in financial market uncertainty.
    4. Problems in the banking sector.

5. When Bowie issues the bond, he receives funds today and promises to pay back the funds in ten years. The two asymmetric information problems are adverse selection and moral hazard. Adverse selection problems occur before Bowie issues the bonds, while moral hazard problems occur after the bonds are issued. Royalty sales from future albums are collateral and the value of collateral depends on the number and quality of future albums that Bowie records. However, once he raises the funds by issuing the bonds, the bond contract does not provide any incentive for Bowie to sell records. Therefore, a moral hazard problem exists if future album royalties are the collateral. This likely explains why the bondholders want past rather than future album royalty sales to serve as

collateral.

Short-Answer Questions

1. They take advantage of economies of scale by combining the funds of many small savers, and they gain expertise in carrying out repetitive transactions.

2. Due to the problems of adverse selection and moral hazard, lenders need costly information about borrowers. Individual lenders don't want to pay for gathering the information if they can use other's information for free, so little information is produced and too little is loaned.

3. Adverse selection is a problem before and moral hazard is a problem after a loan transaction. Adverse selection occurs when risky borrowers who have the most to gain are the ones who want to borrow. Moral hazard occurs when borrowers use the money they borrowed in a manner that lenders would consider undesirable.

4. Banks. Less important over time because information is getting easier to acquire, so direct finance should continue to grow.

5. Both. Both help banks select a borrower and both help make contracts incentive compatible because borrowers have more to lose.

6. The problem is smaller because debt holders receive a fixed payment of interest regardless of the performance of the firm while stockholders share in the profits.

Critical-Thinking Questions

1. The loan would have high transaction costs because a one-of-a-kind contract would have to be written. Your investment would not be diversified or liquid. It is a poor choice.

2. Your funds are so few and the denominations so large that you cannot buy a diversified portfolio. Transaction costs would be high due to brokerage fees. The funds would not be liquid. It is a poor choice.

3. Either choice would be diversified. Due to economies of scale and expertise of the intermediary, transaction costs are so low that the intermediary can offer liquidity services. Good choice.

Self-Test

True-False Questions

1.	F		2.	T
3.	T		4.	F
5.	T		6.	T
7.	F		8.	F
9.	F		10.	T
11.	T		12.	T
13.	T		14.	F
15.	T			

Multiple-Choice Questions

1.	c		2.	a
3.	a		4.	d
5.	d		6.	d
7.	a		8.	d
9.	d		10.	b
11.	b		12.	a
13.	b		14.	c
15.	d		16.	b
17.	d		18.	d
19.	a		20.	d
21.	a		22.	b
23.	d		24.	d
25.	d		26.	a
27.	b		28.	c
29.	d		30.	b

CHAPTER 9

Chapter Synopsis/Completions

1.	bank panic		2.	financial liberalization
3.	credit boom		4.	deleveraging
5.	asset-price bubble		6.	alt-A mortgages
7.	securitization		8.	mortgage-backed securities
9.	financial engineering		10.	structured credit products
11.	collateralized debt obligation		12.	speculative attack

Practice Problems

1. a. A decline in the stock market reduces the net worth of a borrowing firm, reducing the collateral pledged against the loan and increasing adverse selection and moral hazard.

    b. A decrease in the price level increases the real burden of a borrowing firm's debt (liabilities), reducing the net worth of a borrowing firm. As in *a* above, a firm has less to lose if it defaults on a loan, increasing adverse selection and moral hazard.

    c. A reduction in the value of the domestic currency raises the real burden of a borrowing firm's debt payments when the debt is denominated in a foreign currency, reducing the net worth of a borrowing firm. As in *a* above, a firm has less to lose if it defaults on a loan, increasing adverse selection and moral hazard.

d. When asset prices decline, firms write down (reduce) the value of the assets they own on their balance sheets. This reduces the net worth of the borrowing firm. As in *a* above, the firm has less to lose if it defaults on a loan, increasing adverse selection and moral hazard.

2. a. It is a process in which a substantial, unanticipated decline in the price level increases the burden of indebtedness.

b. It reduces economic activity because the reduction in the price level reduces the value of the borrowing firm's assets but not its liabilities, causing a deterioration in the firm's balance sheet. Adverse selection and moral hazard problems increase, lending contracts sharply, and aggregate economic activity remains depressed.

c. The Great Depression

d. Prices fell 25% during the Great Depression. The rate of unemployment was 25%.

3. a. It is a mortgage for borrowers with less-than-excellent credit records.

b. It is a standardized debt security back by mortgages.

c. The originator of the loan distributes the loan to the ultimate lender (investor), and thus the mortgage originator has little incentive to make sure that the mortgage is a good credit risk.

d. Mortgage originators loaned money to subprime borrowers, packaged the loans into mortgage-backed securities, and profitably sold them to investors around the world. So much easy credit entered the housing market that it drove housing prices above their fundamental values.

e. When the price of housing returns to the fundamental value, it causes many borrowers to default because they owe more on their homes than the home is worth. The defaults cause financial firms to become insolvent, reducing lending and economic activity.

4. a. Stage One. Adverse selection and moral hazard problems worsen.

b. Stage Two. A banking crisis develops as economic activity declines.

c. Debt deflation results as price levels decline, asymmetric information problems worsen, and economic activity declines further.

5. a. Factors that contributed to worsening conditions in the Canadian ABCP market in 2007were attributed to concerns about exposure to the U.S. subprime mortgage sector in the underlying assets. Investors in the ABCP market declined to roll over maturing notes.

b. The Bank of Canada indicated that it would not accept ABCP as collateral for loans to banks and that a solution from participants was expected.

c. The Montreal Accord was an agreement reached in August 2007 by the major market participants. Under the Accord investors agreed to a standstill period, mainly to allow for the restructuring of the frozen notes into long-term floating-rate notes.

Short-Answer Questions

1. Because an increase in adverse selection and moral hazard makes it difficult and more costly for lenders to find low-risk borrowers, lenders contract their lending, which reduces investment and economic activity.

2. Emerging market economies have weaker bank supervision and their banks lack expertise in screening and monitoring, so the lending boom is greater and the lending crash is greater. In addition, emerging market banks borrow abroad at higher interest rates, causing a greater crisis when their balance sheets deteriorate. The financial markets are less developed, so a banking crisis is even more harmful.

3. When the government runs a large deficit and private investors fear that the government will default on its debt, the government may force domestic banks to buy its debt. If the value of the debt decreases, it will reduce bank capital and bank lending will decrease.

4. A spike in interest rates causes an increase in adverse selection and moral hazard because only borrowers with risky projects are willing to borrow at the high rates. Bank lending decreases.

5. Banking crises. When the credit boom turns into a credit crash, the increase in defaults causes depositors to withdraw their funds from banks, causing a bank panic.

6. Financial liberalization or innovation creates a credit boom, which causes financial firms to take on excessive risk and also causes a bubble in asset prices. When the asset-price bubble pops, the credit boom turns into a credit crunch.

7. A government safety net increases adverse selection and moral hazard because it allows lenders to take on even more risk because borrowers feel secure that there is a government guarantee of the debt.

8. Mismanagement of financial innovation in the subprime residential mortgage market and a bursting of a housing price bubble were the sources of the recent subprime financial crisis.

Critical-Thinking Questions

1. It is an economy at an earlier stage of market development that has recently opened up to the flow of goods, services, and capital from the rest of the world

2. Severe fiscal imbalances caused the governments in Russia and Argentina to force domestic banks to buy their government debt, which later fell in value.

3. Mismanagement of financial innovation in the subprime residential mortgage market and a bursting of the resulting housing price bubble.

4. No. The sources are different so the solutions are different. Russia and Argentina needed to more closely balance the government's budget (raise taxes or cut government spending). The United States may need to regulate the markets for financial innovations such as mortgage-backed securities.

Self-Test

True-False Questions

1.	F	2.	F
3.	T	4.	T
5.	T	6.	F
7.	T	8.	F
9.	F	10.	F
11.	T	12.	T
13.	T	14.	F
15.	F		

Multiple-Choice Questions

1.	c	2.	d
3.	b	4.	a
5.	b	6.	d
7.	a	8.	d
9.	c	10.	c
11.	a	12.	b
13.	d	14.	c
15.	a	16.	c
17.	a	18.	b
19.	d	20.	c
21.	a	22.	b
23.	c	24.	d
25.	b	26.	d
27.	a	28.	a
29.	d	30.	b

CHAPTER 10

Chapter Synopsis/Completions

1. payoff
2. purchase and assumption
3. leverage ratio
4. Basel Accord
5. financial supervision
6. fair-value accounting
7. regulatory forbearance

Practice Problems

1. a. Chartering to prevent undesirables from controlling a bank—reduces adverse selection. Restrict asset holdings of banks—reduces moral hazard. Impose capital requirements on banks—reduces moral hazard. Examine banks—reduces moral hazard.

    b. Banks screening borrowers is similar to regulators chartering banks. Banks employing restrictive covenants preventing borrowers from investing in risky activities is similar to regulators restricting asset holdings of banks. Banks employing restrictive covenants requiring borrowers to have a minimum net worth is similar to regulators imposing capital requirements. Banks monitoring borrowers is similar to regulators examining banks.

2. a. The payoff method, and the purchase and assumption method. It uses the purchase and assumption method, which provides guarantees of repayment of large uninsured depositors and creditors of the insolvent bank.

    b. This avoids the financial disruption that could occur if depositors of a large bank lost their deposits.

    c. It increases the moral hazard problem because depositors have no incentive to monitor the bank, so the bank might take on even greater risk.

    d. There are more banks that are too big to fail, and there are conglomerate firms that may accidentally receive a safety net for their non-banking activities.

    e. The payoff method. With this method depositors and creditors may not get all of their money back and stockholders lose all of their money, so all participants have a greater incentive to monitor the bank's loans more closely.

3. a. Banks with deposit insurance are likely to take on greater risks than they otherwise would. This is the moral hazard problem.

    b. Deposit insurance attracts risk-prone entrepreneurs to the banking industry. This is the adverse selection problem.

    c. Deposit insurance reduces the incentives of depositors to monitor the riskiness of their banks' asset portfolios. This is the free-rider problem.

4. a. $100 000 will be insured (USD deposits and term deposits longer than five years are not insured).

    b. The CDIC will use the purchase and assumption method, whereby all of the failed bank's deposits will be taken over by a merger partner, effectively insuring all of the deposits.

    c. Because the failure of a very large bank makes it more likely that a major financial disruption will occur, bank regulators are naturally reluctant to allow a big bank to fail and cause losses to depositors.

Short-Answer Questions

1. Because depositors can't judge the quality of a bank's loans, depositors would be afraid to put their money in a bank, and they would withdraw it when an adverse shock hits the economy, causing a bank panic.

2. Adverse selection—risk-loving entrepreneurs may choose to enter banking. Moral hazard—banks take on excessive risk because depositors have no reason to monitor the bank.

3. To reduce moral hazard. The greater the capital-to-asset ratio (leverage ratio), the more the bank has to lose if it fails, and so it pursues less risky activities.

4. Capital adequacy, asset quality, management, earnings, liquidity, and sensitivity to market risk.

5. Competition may increase moral hazard because banks may try to maintain their profits by assuming greater risk. Restrictions reduced efficiency and raised charges to consumers.

Critical-Thinking Questions

1. Put the deposit in Risky Bank because your deposit is guaranteed regardless of whether the bank's loans turn out to be good or not.

2. Since there is such a high chance of the bank becoming insolvent, put your money in Safe Bank and accept the lower interest rate.

3. To avoid adverse selection, banks are chartered to make sure that excessively risky people and crooks are not allowed to control a bank. To avoid moral hazard, banks are supervised to make sure that they maintain significant capital and hold low-risk assets.

Self-Test

True-False Questions

1.	F	2.	F
3.	T	4.	T
5.	F	6.	F
7.	T	8.	T
9.	F	10.	F
11.	F	12.	F
13.	T	14.	T
15.	F		

Multiple-Choice Questions

1.	d	2.	c
3.	a	4.	c
5.	b	6.	d
7.	a	8.	b
9.	d	10.	c
11.	a	12.	d
13.	b	14.	b
15.	c	16.	d
17.	e	18.	c
19.	b	20.	d
21.	d	22.	e
23.	d	24.	a
25.	a	26.	b
27.	d	28.	d
29.	d	30.	b

CHAPTER 11

Chapter Synopsis/Completions

1. dual banking
2. state-branching
3. financial engineering
4. financial derivatives
5. ATM
6. deposit rate ceilings
7. Regulation Q
8. disintermediation
9 sweep accounts
10. branches
11. Schedule II banks
12. four-pillar approach
13. Bank Act Reform
14.bank holding companies

Practice Problems

1. a. Changes in demand conditions: interest rate volatility caused lenders to increase the demand for adjustable-rate mortgages and futures contracts.

    Changes in supply conditions: cost reductions from improvements in information technology increased the use of bank credit and debit cards, and electronic banking. It also allowed for expansion of junk bonds, commercial paper, and securitization.

    Avoidance of costly regulations: to avoid reserve requirements and Regulation Q, money market mutual funds and sweep accounts were created.

    b. $1000 × 0.08 × 0.10 = $8

    c. $1000 × 0.12 × 0.20 = $24

    d. The greater the interest rate and reserve requirement, the greater the opportunity cost of holding required reserves.

2. a. Decrease. More competition has made traditional banking less profitable.

    b. The elimination of Regulation Q caused banks to have to pay a competitive market rate for their deposits.

    c. Competition from junk bonds, securitization, and commercial paper have reduced the demand for bank loans and reduced profit on bank loans.

    d. Banks made riskier loans and pursued off-balance-sheet activities to earn fee income.

3. The junk bond market has allowed traditional borrowers to bypass banks, thereby reducing the income advantages banks once had on uses of funds.

4. a. Bank holding companies

    b. Automated teller machines (ATMs)

Short-Answer Questions

1. No. The Bank of Canada.

2. Banks supervised by the federal government operating side by side with banks supervised by the state governments. The federal government passes a law taxing state bank notes with the intention of eliminating state banks. State banks avoided the regulation, survived, and operate alongside national banks.

3. It set the maximum interest rate banks could pay on deposits. Repeal allowed banks to compete for deposits to reduce disintermediation, but it made the cost of funds rise to banks so they lost their cost advantage on their source of funds.

4. It has given less well-known and smaller companies the ability to bypass banks by gaining direct access to credit.

5. The rapid growth of international trade and multinational corporations, increased involvement of American banks in global investment banking, and the expansion of the Eurodollar market.

6. By opening branches overseas, creating Edge Act corporations, and opening international banking facilities (IBFs).

Critical-Thinking Questions

1. Canada has a few banks compared to the United States. This is due to the history of banking in Canada.

2. Ten banks each with 1000 offices would be more competitive because each bank customer would have a choice of ten banks rather than just one local bank.

3. Large banks are more efficient because they can take advantage of economies of scale and scope from advances in information technology. Large banks are better diversified so they have lower risk of failure.

4. No. The large number of banks is evidence of a lack of competition in the past due to branching restrictions. As banks compete, many will fail or be acquired by more efficient banks, reducing the number of banks.

5. No. Fewer banks with more branches is likely to offer the bank customer more choices, greater efficiency, and lower risk.

Self-Test

True-False Questions

1.	T	2.	T
3.	F	4.	T
5.	T	6.	T
7.	T	8.	T
9.	T	10.	T
11.	T	12.	F
13.	F	14.	T
15.	T		

Multiple-Choice Questions

1.	d	2.	d
3.	d	4.	a
5.	b	6.	c
7.	d	8.	d
9.	d	10.	a
11.	d	12.	d
13.	e	14.	e
15.	a	16.	a
17.	a	18.	b
19.	d	20.	c
21.	d	22.	c
23.	a	24.	a
25.	c	26.	d
27.	d	28.	c
29.	d	30.	c

CHAPTER 12

Chapter Synopsis/Completions

1. demutualization
2. individual life insurance
3. group life insurance
4. permanent life insurance
5. temporary life insurance
6. defined-contribution plan
7. defined-benefit plan
8. fully funded
9. underfunded
10. personal pension plans
11. underwriters
12. specialist
13. sovereign wealth funds
14. institutional investors
15. hedge funds
16. venture capital funds
17. capital buyout funds

Practice Problems

1. a. Life insurance companies sell policies that provide income if a person dies. Property and casualty companies pay for losses as a result of accidents, fire, or theft.
   b. In defined-contribution plans, benefits are determined by the contributions into the plan and their earnings. In defined-benefit plans, benefits are determined in advance.
   c. Fully funded plans are defined benefit plans where the contributions and earnings are sufficient to pay the defined benefits. In underfunded plans, the contributions and earnings are not sufficient.
   d. Private pension plans are voluntary employer-sponsored plans. Public pension plans are government-administered pension plans like the CPP.
   e. Investment banks assist in the initial sale of securities in the primary market. Securities dealers assist in the trading of securities in the secondary markets.
   f. Venture capital funds make investments in new startup businesses. Capital buyout funds make investments in established businesses.

Short-Answer Questions

1. People buy insurance policies to protect themselves against large financial losses hat can occur because of catastrophic events.
2. Reinsurance benefits insurance companies by reducing their risk exposure. Reinsurance allocates a portion of the risk to another company in exchange for a portion of the premium.
3. Insurance companies supply credit insurance by selling a derivative known as credit default swaps or by providing the insurance directly (monocline insurance).
4. Tax policies have impacted the asset growth of pension plans because contributions are tax-deductible.
5. Pension plans are also considered financial intermediaries because they provide income payments on retirement.

Critical-Thinking Questions

1. Government regulation and supervision failed to make sure that Fannie Mae and Freddie Mac did not take on excessive risk because their regulator (OFHEO) was weak with a limited ability to rein them in. Fannie and Freddie had string incentives to resist effective regulation and supervision because it would cut into their profits. They spent millions on lobbyists to manage their 'political risk'.
2. Fannie and Freddie carried out their mission to promote affordable housing by purchasing subprime and Alt-A mortgages.

3. The conflict of interest problem faced by those institutions was that they were supposed to serve two masters: As publicly traded corporations, they were expected to maximize profits for their shareholders, but as government agencies, they were obliged to work in the interests of the public.

Self-Test

True-False Questions

1.	T	2.	T
3.	F	4.	T
5.	F	6.	T
7.	F	8.	F
9.	T	10.	T
11.	T	12.	F
13.	F	14.	T
15.	T		

Multiple-Choice Questions

1.	a	2.	b
3.	d	4.	b.
5.	b	6.	d.
7.	c	8.	a
9.	c	10.	a
11.	d.	12.	c
13.	d	14.	b
15.	d	16.	c
17.	a	18.	a
19.	b	20.	c
21.	a	22.	a
23.	c	24.	d
25.	c	26.	d
27.	b	28.	c
29.	c	30.	a

CHAPTER 13

Chapter Synopsis/Completions

1.	balance sheet	2.	required reserve ratio
3.	reserve requirement	4.	liquidity management
5.	bank rate	6.	asset management
7.	liability management	8.	money centre banks
9.	capital adequacy management	10.	screen and monitor
11.	loan commitments	12.	collateral and compensating
13.	credit rationing	14.	gap analysis
15.	duration analysis	16.	off-balance-sheet
17.	loan sale		

Practice Problems

1.

a.

First Bank

Assets		Liabilities	
Reserves	$2000	Chequable deposits	$2000

b.

<table>
<tr><th colspan="2">First Bank</th><th colspan="2">Second Bank</th></tr>
<tr><th>Assets</th><th>Liabilities</th><th>Assets</th><th>Liabilities</th></tr>
<tr><td>Reserves $1000</td><td>Chequable $1000
deposits</td><td>Reserves $1000</td><td>Chequable $1000
deposits</td></tr>
</table>

c. Both banks end up with an increase of $1000 in reserves.

2.

a.

Assets		Liabilities	
Reserves	$19 million	Deposits	$94 million
Loans	$75 million	Bank capital	$10 million
Securities	$10 million		

No. The bank does not need to make any adjustment to its balance sheet because it initially is holding $25 million of reserves when desired reserves are only $20 million (20% of $100 million). Because of its initial holding of $5 million of excess reserves, when it suffers the deposit outflow of $6 million it can still satisfy its reserve requirements: Desired reserves are $18.8 million (20% of $94 million) while it has $19 million of reserves.

b.

Assets		Liabilities	
Reserves	$15 million	Deposits	$90 million
Loans	$75 million	Bank capital	$10 million
Securities	$10 million		

Yes. The bank must make an adjustment to its balance sheet because its desired reserves are $18 million (20% of $90 million), but it is only holding $15 million of reserves. It has a reserve deficiency of $3 million.

c. $3 million. As we see above, the bank has a reserve shortfall of $3 million, which it can acquire by selling the $3 million of securities.

d.

Assets		Liabilities	
Reserves	$18 million	Deposits	$90 million
Loans	$75 million	Bank capital	$10 million
Securities	$7 million		

e.

Assets		Liabilities	
Reserves	$15 million	Deposits	$80 million
Loans	$75 million	Bank capital	$10 million
Securities	$0 million		

The bank could fail. The desired reserves for the bank are $16 million (20% of $80 million), but it has $15 million of reserves. The proceeds from a distress sale of loans could result in a loss that exceeds bank capital, causing the bank to become insolvent.

3.

a.

Assets		Liabilities	
Reserves	$0	Deposits	$130
Loans	$130	Bank capital	$20
Securities	$20		

b. With a reserve ratio of 25%, the deposit outflow of $50 caused a total depletion of reserves. Therefore, the Bank of Cambridge did not have ample reserves to deal with the withdrawal.

c. Borrow reserves from other banks; sell securities; acquire reserves from the central bank; reduce loans.

d. Excess reserves are insurance against the costs associated with deposit outflows. The higher the costs associated with deposit outflows, the more excess reserves the bank will want to hold. Yet banks suffer losses from holding too much excess reserves because the opportunity cost of holding reserves is the interest income that could be accumulated from issuing loans.

4.

a. High Capital Bank: $60 million. Low Capital Bank: $40 million. High Capital Bank has a lower probability of becoming insolvent.

b. ROA for each = $6/$600 = 1%. ROE for High Capital Bank = $6/$60 = 10%. ROE for Low Capital Bank = $6/$40 = 15%. Low Capital Bank is more profitable.

c. There is a trade-off between profitability and safety. As a result, bank regulations impose bank capital requirements.

6.

a. $30 million – $50 million = – $20 million.

b. $0.02 \times -\$20$ million = – $400,000.

c. $-0.03 \times (-\$20$ million$) = \$600,000.$

d. Interest rates and profits are inversely related.

e. Change in value of assets = $-0.03 \times 4 \times \$100$ million = – $12 million.

Change in value of liabilities = $-0.03 \times 2 \times \$90$ million = – $5.4 million.

– $12 million – (– $5.4 million) = – $6.6 million.

Short-Answer Questions

1. Short-term government securities. They provide liquidity in case of deposit outflow and they earn interest while excess reserves do not.

2. Loans. Loans are riskier and less liquid than other bank assets.

3. $100. Reserves can be held as deposits at the Bank of Canada or as vault cash.

4. High return assets tend to be higher risk and less liquid.

5. The bank's reserves fall by $100.

Critical-Thinking Questions

1. The gap is defined as: rate-sensitive assets – rate-sensitive liabilities. Gap × change in interest rate = change in bank profits. Since banks tend to have more rate-sensitive liabilities than assets, the gap tends to be negative. Thus, an increase in interest rates reduces bank profits because the increase in interest a bank pays on its liabilities exceeds the increase in interest it receives on its assets

2. Duration is the average lifetime of a security's stream of payments. The percent change in market value of security = – percentage-point change in interest rate × duration in years. Since banks tend to have longer-term assets than liabilities, there is a greater reduction in the value of the assets than the liabilities in response to an increase in the interest rate. Thus, the net worth of a bank falls when interest rates rise.

Self-Test

True-False Questions

1.	F	2.	T
3.	F	4.	T
5.	F	6.	F
7.	F	8.	T
9.	T	10.	F
11.	T	12.	F
13.	F	14.	F
15.	F		

Multiple-Choice Questions

1.	d	2.	c
3.	d	4.	d
5.	d	6.	a
7.	d	8.	b
9.	c	10.	b
11.	a	12.	b
13.	a	14.	b
15.	d	16.	e
17.	d	18.	e
19.	a	20.	b
21.	c	22.	c
23.	b	24.	a
25.	b	26.	a
27.	d	28.	c
29.	c	30.	b

CHAPTER 14

Chapter Synopsis/Completions

1.	hedge	2.	short
3.	risk	4.	opposite
5.	standardized	6.	reduces

7. lowering   8. right
9. strike   10. European
11. sell   12. long

Practice Problems

1.

a. Futures are standardized contracts.
b. Futures can be bought and sold up until maturity .
c. Futures can be satisfied with any similar security.
d. Futures are marked to market daily.

2.

a. selling   b. short
c. default   d. arbitrage
e. standardized   f. reduce

3.

a. option   b. call
c. put   d. strike
e. European   f. American
g. swap

Short-Answer Questions

1. plain vanilla swap
    1. the interest rate on the payments that are being exchanged.
    2. the type of interest payments (variable or fixed-rate).
    3. the amount of notional principal.
    4. the time period over which the exchanges continue to be made.

2. 1. Allow financial institutions to convert fixed-rate assets into rate-sensitive assets without affecting the balance sheet.
    2. Can be written for very long horizons.

3. 1. Swap markets can suffer from a lack of liquidity.
    2. Swap contracts are subject to default risk.
    3. Swap markets require information about the counterparties.

Critical-Thinking Questions

Table 13.A Gain or Loss

	Price of Asset				
	$85 000	**$90 000**	**$95 000**	**$100 000**	**$105 000**
Part 1. Selling Canada bonds	−$10	−$5	$0	$5	$10
Part 2. Selling futures contract	$10	$5	$0	−$5	−$10
Part 3. Purchasing put option	$8	$3	−$2	−$2	−$2

Self-Test

True-False Questions

1.	F		2.	T
3.	T		4.	F
5.	T		6.	T
7.	F		8.	T
9.	T		10.	T
11.	F		12.	F
13.	F		14.	F
15.	T			

Multiple-Choice Questions

1.	d		2.	a
3.	c		4.	a
5.	c		6.	a
7.	d		8.	e
9.	a		10.	b
11.	a		12.	b
13.	c		14.	c
15.	a		16.	c
17.	c		18.	a
19.	c		20.	e
21.	b		22.	a
23.	e		24.	a
25.	e		26.	a
27.	b		28.	a
29.	c		30.	a

CHAPTER 15

Chapter Synopsis/Completions

1.	Board of Directors		2.	Governing Council
3.	Board of Governors		4.	New York
5.	interest		6.	bureaucratic
7.	independence		8.	inflationary
9.	undemocratic			

1.

1.	c	2.	a
3.	c	4.	b
5.	b	6.	b
7.	a	8.	c
9.	c		

2.

a.
1. Greater focus on long-run objectives.
2. Less pressure to finance deficits and less pressure to pursue inflationary policies.
3. More likely to pursue policies in the public interest even if politically unpopular.

b.
1. Greater accountability. If Bank of Canada policymakers make mistakes there is no way of voting them out, thus the system is undemocratic.
2. Coordination of fiscal and monetary policy would be easier.
3. Lack of evidence indicating that an independent Bank of Canada performs well.

Exercise 2

1.

a.
1. Bank note issue
2. Government debt and asset management services
3. Central banking services
4. Monetary policy

b.
1. Board of Governors
2. Federal Reserve Banks
3. Federal Open Market Committee
4. Federal Advisory Council
5. Member commercial banks

2. All national banks are required to be members of the Federal Reserve System. State banks can choose to be members.

3. The president can influence the Federal Reserve through his appointments to the Board of Governors. Congress can influence the Federal Reserve by passing legislation to make the Fed more accountable for its actions.

4. It increased the independence of the Bank of Japan by giving it more goal and instrument independence.

5. Countries with greater central bank independence do not have higher unemployment or greater output fluctuations.

Critical-Thinking Questions

1. Passage of this bill would reduce the Fed's goal independence. Current law does not require the Fed to pursue a specific inflation target. Passage of a bill requiring the Fed to pursue a specific inflation target would therefore reduce the Fed's goal independence but it would not affect the Fed's instrument independence because the Fed would still have the ability to use any instrument it deems appropriate to achieve the specified inflation goal.

2. This bill would make the Fed more like the ECB. The Maastricht Treaty currently specifies that the overriding, long-term goal of the ECB is price stability.

3. Passage of this bill would make it less likely that the Fed would pursue policies that would lead to a political business cycle because it would make Fed policy more transparent. Both elected officials and the public would be able to evaluate whether the Fed is meeting its goal for inflation. Under current law, the Fed does not have an explicitly stated goal for inflation and so elected officials and the public are less able to evaluate whether the Fed is pursuing policies that would lead to a political business cycle.

Self-Test

True-False Questions

1.	T		2.	F
3.	F		4.	T
5.	F		6.	T
7.	T		8.	F
9.	T		10.	T
11.	F		12.	F
13.	T		14.	T
15.	F			

Multiple-Choice Questions

1.	d		2.	c
3.	d		4.	c
5.	c		6.	b
7.	b		8.	c
9.	c		10.	d
11.	d		12.	a
13.	d		14.	e
15.	d		16.	c
17.	d		18.	a
19.	a		20.	d
21.	d		22.	d
23.	d		24.	c
25.	a		26.	c
27.	a		28.	c
29.	d		30.	a

CHAPTER 16

Chapter Synopsis/Completions

1. reserves
2. monetary base
3. open-market operations
4. bank rate
5. borrowed reserves
6. nonborrowed monetary base
7. high-powered money

Practice Problems

1. a

First Bank				The Bank of Canada			
Assets		**Liabilities**		**Assets**		**Liabilities**	
T-bills	+$100 000			T-bills	−$100 000	Reserves	−$100 000
Reserves	−$100 000						

Reserves in the banking system have fallen by $100 000.

b.

	First Bank				**The Bank of Canada**		
Assets		**Liabilities**		**Assets**		**Liabilities**	
Reserves	−$100 000	Advances	−$100 000	Advances	−$100 000	Reserves	−$100 000

Reserves in the banking system have again fallen by $100 000.

2.

a. The deposit liabilities of Bank A increase by $1000 and desired reserves increase by $200 (20 percent of $1000). Bank A can safely lend $800.

b. In the process of lending $800, chequable deposits of Bank A increase by $800. However, once the loan is deposited into Bank B, chequable deposits at Bank A fall by $800. Thus, chequable deposits at Bank A increase by $1000, which is the amount of the original deposit.

c.

Bank	Change in Deposits	Change in Loans	Change in Reserves
First Bank of Toronto	+$0.00	+$1000.00	+$0.00
A	+1000.00	+800.00	+200.00
B	+800.00	+640.00	+160.00
C	+640.00	+512.00	+128.00
D	+ 512.00	+409.60	+102.40
.	.	.	.
.	.	.	.
.	.	.	.
Total All Banks	+$5000.00	+$5000.00	+$1000.00

3. a. The simple deposit multiplier formula is $\Delta D = (1/r) \times \Delta R$.
   b. The $10 billion dollar sale of government bonds causes bank reserves to fall by $10 billion. This is partially offset by the $5 billion in advances that increase bank reserves by $5 billion. Thus on net, bank reserves fall by $5 billion.
   c. The change in chequable deposits is calculated by multiplying the $5 billion decline by 5 (−1/0.20). Chequable deposits fall by $25 billion in the simple model.

4. a. The bank will find itself with $5000 more reserves and a reduction in its holdings of securities of $5000.
   b. Its liabilities have increased by the additional $5000 of settlement balances. Its assets have now increased by the $5000 of additional securities it now holds.
   c. Reserves have increased by $5000, the amount of the open market purchase. With no change in currency circulation, the monetary base rises by $5000.

5.

a. $m = [1 + c]/[r + c]$

b. $c = \$280b/\$800b = 0.35$

   $m = 1.35/0.45 = 3$

c. $DR = r(D) = 0.10(800) = \$80\ b$

$R = DR + ER = \$120\text{ b}$

$MB = C + R = \$280 + \$120 = \$400\text{ b}$

d. $m = 1.35/0.43 = 3.139$

$M = \$400 \times 3.139 = \$1255.6\text{ b}$

e. $M = C + D$

$M = (c \times D) + D$

$M = (c + 1) \times D$

$M = 1.35 \times D$

$D = \$1255.6/1.35 = \$930.07\text{ b}$

$C = c \times D$

$C = 0.35 \times \$930.07 = \$325.52\text{ b}$

f. $DR = 0.08(930.07) = \$74.40\text{ b}$

$ER = \$120 - \$74.40 = \$45.6\text{ b}$

6.

a. $m = 1.4/0.5 = 2.8$

$M = m \times MB = 2.8 \times \$400 = \$1120\text{ b}$

b. $C + D = M$

$(0.04 \times D) + D = \$1120\text{ b}$

$1.4 \times D = \$1120\text{ b}$

$D = \$1120/1.4 = \$800\text{ b}$

$C = \$1120 - \$800 = \$320\text{ b}$

$DR = 0.1(800) = \$80\text{ b}$

$R = DR + ER = \$80\text{ b}$

c. $m = 1.4/0.56 = 2.5$

$M = 2.5 \times \$400 = \$1000\text{ b}$

$D = \$1000/1.4 = \$714.29\text{ b}$

$C = 0.4 \times \$714.29 = \$285.71\text{ b}$

$DR = 0.16(714.29) = \$114.29\text{ b}$

Short-Answer Questions

1. The three players in the money supply process are the central bank (the Bank of Canada), banks, and depositors. The Bank of Canada is the most important.

2. According to the simple deposit multiplier, $\Delta D = (1/r)\,\Delta R$, an open market purchase by the Bank of Canada will cause reserves to increase by $100. Assuming the required reserve deposit ratio is 10%, $\Delta D = (1/0.10)100 = \$1000$.

3.. An increase in the monetary base that arises from currency has no multiplier effect. An increase in the monetary base that arises from reserves does have a multiplier effect.

4. An increase in currency holdings causes both the money multiplier and the money supply to decline.

5. The Bank of Canada has precise control over the nonborrowed monetary base but it does not have precise control over borrowed reserves, which are determined by banks.

Critical-Thinking Questions

1. The multiplier would be 1.
2. Banks and depositors would play no role in the money supply process. Only the Bank of Canada would play a role in controlling the money supply under Friedman's proposal.
3. The Bank of Canada would have much more control over the money supply under Friedman's proposal because the multiplier would always be equal to 1.
4. Friedman's proposal would completely change how banks earn a profit. Banks currently earn a profit by loaning out a fraction of the funds they receive from depositors. Under Friedman's proposal, banks would have no excess funds to loan out because they would be required to hold 100% of the deposits on reserve. There would be no deposit creation by the banking system, and the money supply would essentially be set by the Bank of Canada. Banks would earn a profit by charging depositors a fee for holding their funds and providing cheque services. Banks would be more like the warehouse banks that existed in the Middle Ages simply to safeguard depositors' money.

Self-Test

True-False Questions

1. F	2. F
3. T	4. F
5. T	6. T
7. T	8. T
9. F	10. T
11. F	12. T
13. F	14. F
15. F	

Multiple-Choice Questions

1. c	2. b
3. d	4. c
5. e	6. d
7. c	8. e
9. a	10. a
11. b	12. b
13. d	14. d
15. b	16. d
17. d	18. d
19. c	20. c
21. b	22. d
23. a	24. c
25. b	26. c
27. a	28. c
29. d	30. c

CHAPTER 17

Chapter Synopsis/Completions

1. deposit shifting
2. advances
3. overnight interest rate
4. securities
5. dynamic
6. purchase
7. reverse repos
8. flexible

Practice Problems

1.

a. The Bank of Canada uses open market operations to target the overnight interest rate.

b. 1. Dynamic open market operations.
   2. Defensive open market operations.

c. 1. Open market operations occur at the initiative of the Bank of Canada.
   2. Open market operations can be used to any degree.
   3. Open market operations are easily reversed.
   4. Open market operations can be implemented quickly.

2.

a. 1. Standing liquidity facility loans.
   2. Last-resort lending.

b. Many deposits exceed the $100 000 limit that the CDIC promises to pay. Thus the lender of last resort prevents bank failures due to large depositor withdrawals. In addition, the CDIC contingency fund is limited and a wave of bank failures could seriously jeopardize the solvency of the system, leading to a severe financial panic that only a lender of last resort might prevent.

3.

a. Small changes in reserve requirements are too costly to administer, so it is too blunt a tool to be used effectively.

b. Raising reserve requirements can cause immediate liquidity problems for banks with small amounts of excess reserves.

Short-Answer Questions

1. The Bank of Canada uses open market operations to control the amount of nonborrowed reserves.

2. The main advantages of open market operations are that they occur at the initiative of the Bank of Canada, they are flexible and precise, they are easily reversed, and they can be implemented quickly.

3. The most important advantage of advances is that it allows the Bank of Canada to play the role of lender of last resort. The main disadvantage is that the Bank of Canada does not completely control the quantity of advances since borrowing at the bank rate is initiated by banks.

4. The Eurosystem's equivalent to the Bank of Canada's discount rate is called the marginal lending rate.

Critical-Thinking Questions

The Bank of Canada currently pays interest on reserves equal to $i_b - 0.50$ and advances are made at interest rate i_b. The overnight interest rate is limited to fluctuating between these two rates as illustrated below. If the demand for reserves rises from R^d to R^d_2, the overnight interest rate will be equal to i_b. If the demand for reserves falls from R^d to R^d_1, the overnight interest rate will fall to $i_b - 0.50$.

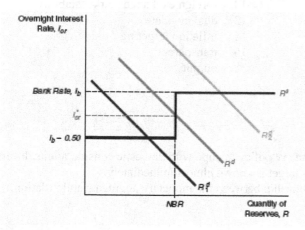

Self-Test

True-False Questions

1.	F	2.	F
3.	T	4.	F
5.	F	6.	T
7.	T	8.	T
9.	F	10.	T
11.	F	12.	F
13.	T	14.	T
15.	F		

Multiple-Choice Questions

1.	d	2.	a
3.	a	4.	c
5.	a	6.	c
7.	b	8.	c
9.	d	10.	c
11.	d	12.	c
13.	d	14.	e
15.	d	16.	d
17.	d	18.	e
19.	a	20.	b
21.	e	22.	b
23.	a	24.	a
25.	b	26.	a
27.	a	28.	d
29.	b	30.	b

CHAPTER 18

Chapter Synopsis/Completions

1.	nominal anchor	2.	time-inconsistency problem
3.	expansionary	4.	distrust
5.	high employment	6.	economic growth
7.	price stability	8.	interest rate stability

9. financial market stability
10. foreign exchange market stability
11. natural rate
12. dual mandate
13. domestic
14. inflation targeting
15. New Zealand
16. transparent
17. accountability
18. output
19. implicit

Practice Problems

1. a. It enables the central bank to adjust its monetary policy to cope with domestic considerations. Information on whether the central bank is achieving its target is known almost immediately.
   b. It works well only if there is a reliable relationship between the monetary aggregate and inflation.

2.
   a. 1. It enables monetary policy to focus on domestic considerations.
      2. Stability in the relationship between money and inflation is not crucial to its success.
      3. It's readily understood by the public and is highly transparent.
      4. It increases the accountability of the central bank.
      5. It appears to ameliorate the effects of inflationary shocks.
   b. 1. An inflation target does not send immediate signals to both the public and markets.
      2. It might impose a rigid rule on policymakers.
      3. Sole focus on the inflation rate could mean larger output fluctuations.
      4. It may lead to low growth in output and employment.

3.
   a. 1. It enables monetary policy to focus on domestic considerations.
      2. Stability in the relationship between money and inflation is not crucial to its success.
      3. It has had demonstrated success.
   b. 1. It has a lack of transparency.
      2. It is strongly dependent on the preferences, skills, and trustworthiness of the individuals at the central bank.
      3. It has some inconsistencies with democratic principles because the central bank is not highly accountable.

4.
   a. 1. Same graph as Figure 18-3.
      2. Same graph as Figure 18-4.

   b. Simultaneous usage of the two policy instruments is not possible. Graph a) tells us that targeting on reserve aggregates involves losing control of the interest rate. Graph b) tells us that interest-rate targeting leads to fluctuating quantity of reserve aggregates and the money supply. A central bank can therefore hit one or the other, but not both.

   c. Three criteria apply when choosing a policy instrument: The instrument must be observable and measurable, it must be controllable by the central bank, and it must have a predictable effect on the goals.

   d. Both interest rates and aggregates have observability and measurability problems, so it is not clear whether one should be preferred to the other. On the controllability criterion, a clear-cut case cannot be made that short-term interest rates are preferable to reserve aggregates since the central bank cannot set short-term real interest rates because it does not have control over expectation of inflation. On the predictability criterion, interest rates seem to be preferable to reserve aggregates. In recent years, most central banks have concluded that the link between interest rates and goals such as inflation is tighter than the link between aggregates and inflation. For this reason, central banks throughout the world now generally use short-term interest rates as their policy instruments.

   5.

   a. The Taylor rule has come up with an answer to suggest how the target for short term interest rates should be chosen. It indicates that the overnight interest rate should be equal to the inflation rate plus an "equilibrium" overnight rate, an inflation gap and an output gap.

b. $i_{or} = \pi + \bar{i}_{or} + \dfrac{1}{2}(\pi - \pi\,{}^*) + \dfrac{1}{2}(y - \bar{y})$

c. $i_{or} = 3\% + 5\% + \dfrac{1}{2}(5\% - 3\%) + \dfrac{1}{2}(2\%)$

$i_{or} = 10\%$

Short-Answer Questions

1. The Bundesbank's monetary targeting is best viewed as a mechanism for transparently communicating how monetary policy is being directed to achieve long-term inflation goals.

2. The three criteria that a central bank uses to choose a policy instrument are: (1) observability and measurability; (2) controllability; and (3) predictable effect on goals.

3. The overnight interest rate is determined by the demand and supply for reserves. The central bank controls the supply of reserves but the demand for reserves moves around in response to the reserve needs of banks. If the central bank targets the quantity of reserves, fluctuations in the demand for reserves will move the interest rate. If the central bank wishes to target the interest rate, it must be willing to move the supply of reserves to match movements in demand in order to keep the interest rate at its target.

4. An operating instrument is directly affected by the central bank's tools. An intermediate target is less directly affected by the central bank's tools but is more directly related to the goals of monetary policy.

5. The Bank of Canada is more likely to recognize a credit-driven asset price bubble while it is happening.

Critical-Thinking Questions

1. According to the Taylor rule, $i_{or}{}^* = 2 + 2 + 0.5 \times (2 - 2) + 0.5 \times 0 = 4$. If the economy is operating at potential and inflation is at its target of 2%, the Taylor rule calls for an overnight rate target ($i_{or}{}^*$) of 4%. This target rate for the nominal overnight rate implies a real overnight rate that is equal to 2% (real overnight rate equals nominal overnight funds rate – inflation). This would be neutral monetary policy because the real overnight rate implied by the Bank's target is equal to the equilibrium overnight rate. Under neutral monetary policy, monetary policy is neither stimulating or dampening GDP growth nor inflation.

2. According to the Taylor rule, $i_{or}{}^* = 2 + 1 + 0.5 \times (1{-}2) + 0.5 \times (-1) = 2$. If the economy is operating below potential and inflation is below its target of 2%, the Taylor rule calls for an overnight funds rate target ($i_{or}{}^*$) of 2%. This target rate for the nominal overnight rate implies a real overnight rate that is equal to 1%. This would be expansionary monetary policy because the real overnight rate implied by the Bank of Canada's target is less than the equilibrium overnight funds rate. Under expansionary monetary policy, GDP growth and inflation will tend to rise.

3. According to the Taylor rule, $i_{or}{}^* = 2 + 3 + 0.5 \times (3 - 2) + 0.5 \times (1) = 6$. If the economy is operating above potential and inflation is above its target of 2%, the Taylor rule calls for a overnight funds rate target ($i_{or}{}^*$) of 6%. This target rate for the nominal overnight funds rate implies a real overnight funds rate that is equal to 3%. This would be contractionary monetary policy because the real overnight funds rate implied by the Bank of Canada's target is greater than the equilibrium overnight funds rate. Under contractionary monetary policy, GDP growth and inflation will tend to fall.

Self-Test

True-False Questions

1.	T	2.	T
3.	T	4.	T
5.	F	6.	T
7.	F	8.	T

9.   T
11. T
13. F
15. F

10. F
12. T
14. T

Multiple-Choice Questions

1.   c
3.   e
5.   d
7.   d
9.   d
11. d
13. a
15. e
17. d
19. c
21. d
23. d
25. c
27. d
29. a

2.   d
4.   a
6.   e
8.   c
10. b
12. c
14. d
16. a
18. b
20. d
22. b
24. c
26. d
28. d
30. b

CHAPTER 19

Chapter Synopsis/Completions

1.   currency
3.   forward
5.   more
7.   depreciate
9.   tariffs
11. capital mobility
13. rise
15. appreciates

2.   deposits
4.   appreciated
6.   purchasing power parity
8.   traded
10. expected return
12. interest rate
14. appreciate
16. depreciate

Practice Problems

1.   a.   0.83
     b.   0.79
     c.   0.875

2.   a.   45 pesos per bushel.
     b.   11 pesos per dollar.
     c.   real exchange rate = 1.58

3.

Change in Factor	Response of the Exchange Rate
Domestic interest rate ↓	↓
Foreign interest rate ↓	↑
Domestic price level ↓	↑
Tariffs and quotas ↓	↓
Import demand ↓	↑
Export demand ↓	↓
Domestic productivity ↓	↓

4. a. A decrease in the domestic interest rate i^D causes the demand for dollar assets to shift left and the exchange rate to fall from E_1 to E_2.

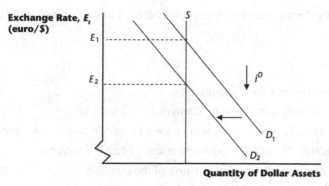

b. An increase in the foreign interest rate i^F causes the demand for dollar assets to shift left and the exchange rate to fall from E_1 to E_2.

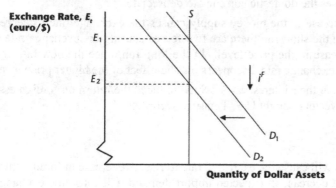

c. An increase in the expected future exchange rate E_{t+1} causes the demand for dollar assets to shift right and the exchange rate to rise from E_1 to E_2.

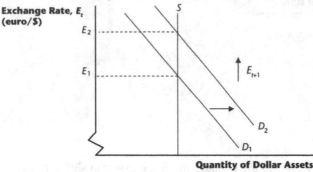

5. a. Be the same all over the world.
    b. The Canadian dollar should increase in value against other currencies because of an increase in the demand for domestic assets.

Short-Answer Questions

1. When the dollar depreciates, the price of imports (into the Canada) rises.
2. When the dollar depreciates, the quantity of imports demanded by Canadians will decline.
3. Both an increase in trade barriers and an increase in productivity will cause a country's currency to appreciate.
4. The demand for domestic assets is determined by the relative expected return of domestic assets.
5. A fall in the expected future exchange rate E^e_{t+1} will cause a depreciation of the currency.
6. When domestic real interest rates rise, the domestic currency appreciates.
7. When domestic interest rates rise due to an expected increase in inflation, the domestic currency depreciates.
8. A higher domestic money supply causes the domestic currency to depreciate.
9. Overshooting is when a one-time increase in the money supply causes the exchange rate to depreciate more in the short run than in the long run. In the short run there are two forces causing the exchange rate to depreciate: the increase in inflation and the increase in the price level. In the long run, once the new higher price level is reached, the effect of inflation on the exchange rate disappears but the effect of the higher price level remains.
10. Two reasons: Foreign central banks cut their interest rates, which reduced the return on foreign assets, and there was a "flight to quality" as foreign investors bought U.S. Treasury securities.

Critical-Thinking Questions

a. An increase in domestic interest rates will cause the exchange rate to rise. A decrease in foreign interest rates will cause the exchange rate to rise and a decrease in expected import demand will cause the exchange rate to rise. Since all three factors cause the exchange rate to rise, their combined effect is unambiguous.

b. An increase in the domestic price level will cause the exchange rate to fall. Quotas will cause the exchange rate to rise, and an expected rise in productivity will cause the exchange rate to rise as well. Since the impact of a rise in the domestic price level has the opposite effect as quotas and productivity, the overall effect of these changes is ambiguous.

c. An increase in export demand will cause the exchange rate to rise. A fall in the expected domestic price level will cause the exchange rate to rise and a fall in foreign interest rates will cause the exchange rate to rise as well. Since all three factors cause the exchange rate to rise, their combined effect is unambiguous.

Self-Test

True-False Questions

1.	T	2.	F
3.	F	4.	F
5.	T	6.	F
7.	T	8.	F
9.	T	10.	T
11.	T	12.	F
13.	T	14.	F
15.	F		

Multiple-Choice Questions

1.	f	2.	c
3.	c	4.	a
5.	b	6.	a.
7.	b	8.	d
9.	f	10.	d
11.	c	12.	a
13.	a	14.	d
15.	a	16.	c
17.	c	18.	a
19.	d	20.	b
21.	b	22.	a
23.	d	24.	c
25.	c	26.	b
27.	d	28.	d
29.	d	30.	b

CHAPTER 20

Chapter Synopsis/Completions

1.	dirty	2.	increase
3.	current account	4.	trade balance
5.	fixed	6.	reserve currency
7.	fixed	8.	devalue
9.	inflows	10.	exchange rate
11.	purchases	12.	increase
13.	contractionary	14.	increase
15.	depreciation		

Practice Problems

1. a. The T-account when the Bank of Canada buys $1 billion in foreign assets in exchange for $1 billion in currency:

Bank of Canada

Assets	Liabilities
Foreign assets (international reserves) +$1 billion	Currency in circulation +$1 billion

b.   The monetary base will increase by $1 billion as a result of this foreign exchange transaction.

c.   The T-account when the Bank of Canada buys $1 billion in foreign assets in exchange for $1 billion in deposits:

Bank of Canada

Assets	Liabilities
Foreign assets (international reserves) +$1 billion	Deposits with the The Bank of Canada (reserves) +$1 billion

d.   The monetary base will increase by $1 billion as a result of this foreign exchange transaction.

e.   The T-account when the Bank of Canada buys $1 billion in foreign assets in exchange for $1 billion in deposits, and then sells $1 billion in government bonds to sterilize the exchange rate intervention:

Bank of Canada

Assets	Liabilities
Foreign assets (international reserves) +$1 billion Government bonds −$1 billion	Monetary base (reserves) +$1 billion

f.   Sterilized exchange rate interventions leave the monetary base unchanged.

2.   a.   The long-run and short-run effects of an unsterilized sale of foreign assets.

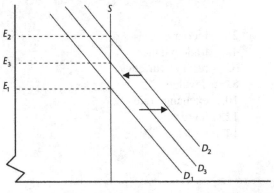

Quantity of Dollar Assets

b.   An unsterilized sale of foreign assets reduces the monetary base, which leads to a rise in the domestic interest rate in the short run and a decline in the domestic price level in the long run. The increase in the domestic interest rate and the decline in the domestic price level both act to push the exchange rate up (from E_1 to E_2) in the short run. In the long run, the interest rate returns to its original level but the price level remains at its lower level. Thus, the exchange rate depreciates part of the way back to its original level because the interest rate effect disappears but the price level effect remains.

c.   A sterilized intervention in the foreign exchange market leaves the monetary base unchanged and so the interest rate and price level remain unchanged as well. As a consequence, the demand for dollar assets remains unchanged and the exchange rate remains unchanged as shown on the next page.

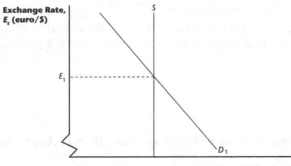

3.

a. An increase in the return on foreign assets will shift the demand curve for dollar assets to the left and the exchange rate will fall from E_1 to E_2.

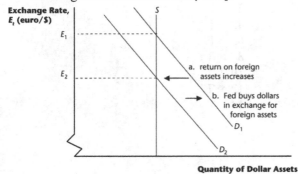

b. To keep the exchange rate at its original level (E_1) the Bank of Canada would buy dollars in exchange for foreign assets. This transaction would reduce the monetary base, which would cause the domestic interest rate to rise, which would in turn cause the exchange rate to rise back to E_1 as the demand for dollar assets shifts back to D_1.

4.

a. overvalued

b. The central bank would need to purchase domestic currency to keep the exchange rate fixed at par.

c. It would lose international reserves.

d. If currency traders fear that the central bank will run out of foreign assets, then they may mount a speculative attack on the currency.

e. A speculative attack on a country's currency will lead to a balance of payments deficit. The central bank will respond by raising interest rates.

f. The IMF may provide loans to the country in order to shore up its foreign reserves.

g. Countries may come to expect that the IMF will bail them out and as a result they may use macroeconomic policies that are more likely to lead to a balance of payments deficit.

Short-Answer Questions

1. In the case of a sterilized exchange rate intervention, the central bank offsets the intervention with an open market operation so that the monetary base remains unchanged. In the case of an unsterilized intervention, the central bank does not offset the intervention with an open market operation, and so the monetary base does change.

2. The current account balance includes everything that is included in the trade balance plus three additional categories of net receipts: investment income, service transactions, and unilateral transfers.

3. The net change in government international reserves = –$5 billion.

4. The anchor currency is the currency that other currencies are pegged to.

5. A dirty float (also called a managed float) is an exchange rate regime in which the central bank intervenes to keep the exchange rate within a certain range (rather than keeping the exchange rate fixed at a particular value).

Critical-Thinking Questions

1. Foreign clams on U.S. wealth are increasing.

2. U.S. claims on foreign wealth are decreasing.

3. At some point, America will have to pay back those claims on its wealth and that will make Americans poorer.

Self-Test

True-False Questions

1.	F	2.	F
3.	F	4.	F
5.	T	6.	F
7.	F	8.	T
9.	T	10.	T
11.	T	12.	T
13.	T	14.	F
15.	T		

Multiple-Choice Questions

1.	c	2.	b
3.	a	4.	d
5.	d	6.	c
7.	e	8.	c
9.	b	10.	a
11.	a	12.	b
13.	c	14.	a
15.	a	16.	a
17.	c	18.	a
19.	d	20.	d
21.	c	22.	c
23.	c	24.	a
25.	a	26.	d
27.	d	28.	c
29.	d	30.	a

CHAPTER 21

Chapter Synopsis/Completions

1.	velocity	2.	fixed
3.	exchange	4.	money
5.	flexible	6.	price level
7.	liquidity preference	8.	speculative
9.	decline	10.	negatively
11.	positive	12.	procyclical

Practice Problems

1. a. Velocity = 3
    b. The quantity of money = $5 trillion
    c. Velocity is constant.
    d. The price level will rise by 30%.
    e. The demand for money will be $10 trillion.
2. a. The price of bonds will rise as the interest rate falls back to normal.
    b. The return on bonds will increase.
    c. If interest rates are above normal, people will hold bonds instead of money because they will expect the interest rate to fall back to normal in the future, and as interest rates fall back to normal, the return on bonds will increase.
3. a. Average cash balances = $900
    b. Velocity = $1800 × 12/$900 = 24
    c. Average cash balances = $450
    d. Velocity = $1800 × 12/$450 = 48
    e. The cost of holding money is the forgone interest that you could earn by holding bonds. The benefit of holding money is that it reduces the transaction costs that you would have to incur by holding bonds. As the interest rate rose, the cost of holding money increased, and so you were willing to incur more transaction costs to hold bonds.
4. a. Freidman believed that changes in interest rates have little effect on the expected return on other assets relative to money, and as a result, money demand is insensitive to changes in the interest rate. In addition, Friedman believed that money demand is stable.
    b. According to Friedman, if the rate of return on assets other than money increases, the rate of return on money will increase as well. Even if money does not pay interest, banks compete to provide services to attract chequing account balances. These services might include convenient banking hours, free chequing, or a free toaster when you open up a chequing account.
    c. By substituting Friedman's money demand equation into the equation of exchange we get the following expression for the velocity of money: $V = Y/f(Y_P)$. In a business cycle expansion, permanent income (Y_P) rises by less than income (Y). As a result, Y rises by more than $f(Y_P)$ and V increases. The opposite happens in a business cycle contraction (Y falls by more than Y_P). Therefore V is procyclical— V rises in a business cycle expansion and falls in a business cycle contraction.

Short-Answer Questions

1. Irving Fisher reasoned that velocity is determined by the institutions in an economy that affect the way individuals conduct transactions, and those institutions evolve slowly over time. Therefore, velocity is roughly constant.
2. Classical economists believed that wages and prices were perfectly flexible, and as a result, the economy would remain at full employment.
3. No, velocity is not constant.
4. Keynes postulated three motives for holding money: the transactions motive, the precautionary motive, and the speculative motive. Keynes reasoned that the speculative motive is related to the interest rate.
5. Nominal money balances refers to the actual dollars that you hold. Real money balances equal the dollars you hold divided by the price level. Keynes reasoned that people desire to hold a certain amount of real money balances because real money balances measure how much a person can buy with their money. If prices in the economy double, the same nominal quantity of money will buy only half as many goods.
6. People hold precautionary money balances in order to make unexpected purchases. Precautionary money balances are positively related to income.

7. As interest rates rise, people will reduce their money holdings (because of the speculative motive) and therefore velocity will rise. Interest rates and velocity will be positively related.

8. Earlier in the text you learned that interest rates are procyclical. In a business cycle expansion, interest rates and velocity rise. In a business cycle contraction, interest rates and velocity fall. Velocity is procyclical.

9. James Tobin formulated a theory for why people hold money even when it pays no interest, but that theory relied on the fact that money is risk free. The fact that government securities are also risk free and at the same time do pay interest presents a challenge for this theory. Why do people hold money for speculative purposes when they could simply hold government securities?

10. Permanent income is expected average, long-run income. Permanent income has much smaller short-run fluctuations than current income.

Critical-Thinking Questions

1. a. The quantity theory of money implies that a 20% increase in the money supply will result in a 20% increase in nominal income, and if prices and wages are flexible, a 20% increase in the price level and no change in real output.

   b. If there is a liquidity trap, a 20% increase in the money supply will have no impact on real income, the price level, or nominal income.

   c. If the Keynesian liquidity preference function best describes money demand, but the interest sensitivity of money demand is somewhere between ultrasensitive and completely insensitive, then the increase in the money supply will lead to an increase in nominal income. However, the increase in nominal income will be something less than the 20% increase in the money supply because there is some interest sensitivity of money demand. Once again, the split between a change in real income and the price level depends on whether prices and wages are flexible.

   d. With Friedman's money demand function, the increase in the money supply causes interest rates in the economy to fall, which, according to Keynes, would make the demand for money rise. But in the Friedman theory, competition among banks would cause the return on money to fall along with market interest rates, and so people would not change their money demand in response to the decline in interest rates. As a result, the increase in the money supply would lead to a 20% increase in nominal income.

2. The Keynesian money demand function in part *c* best describes the real world. Neither extreme case (ultrasensitive or completely insensitive) are consistent with the data.

3. Since money demand is a function of interest rates, the Bank of Canada does not have precise control over nominal income. Nonetheless, the interest sensitivity of money demand also does not appear to be ultrasensitive, and so the Bank of Canada does have some, but not complete, influence over nominal income.

Self-Test

True-False Questions

1.	T	2.	T
3.	T	4.	F
5.	F	6.	T
7.	T	8.	F
9.	T	10.	T
11.	T	12.	F
13.	T	14.	T
15.	F		

Multiple-Choice Questions

1.	d	2.	a

3.	a	4.	d
5.	c	6.	b
7.	b	8.	b
9.	a	10.	b
11.	b	12.	a
13.	d	14.	a
15.	e	16.	c
17.	b	18.	c
19.	d	20.	e
21.	c	22.	c
23.	e	24.	b
25.	d	26.	d
27.	b	28.	d
29.	b	30.	b

CHAPTER 22

Chapter Synopsis/Completions

1.	aggregate demand	2.	investment spending
3.	income	4.	marginal propensity
5.	autonomous	6.	inventory investment
7.	planned	8.	multiplier
9.	employment	10.	*IS*
11.	higher	12.	income

Practice Problems

1. a.

Point in Figure 3	Disposable Income, Y_D	Consumer Expenditure, C	Change in Disposable Income, ΔY_D	Change in Consumer Expenditure, ΔC
E	0	300	–	–
F	200	460	200	160
G	400	620	200	160
H	800	940	400	320

b.

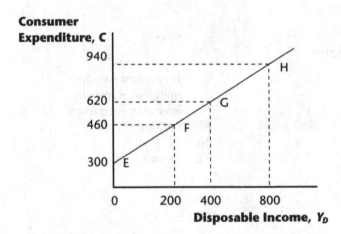

2. a. $Y^* = \$4000$ billion.
   b.

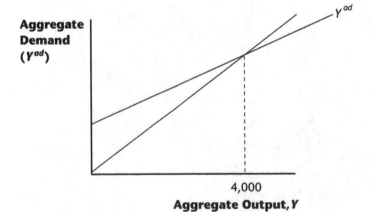

   c. $Y^* = \$3500$ billion.
   d. $\Delta Y/\Delta a = 1/(1-mpc) = 10$.
   e. $\Delta Y = [1/(1-mpc)]\,\Delta G = \$1000$ billion.
   f. $\Delta Y = -\$1000$ billion.

3.

a.

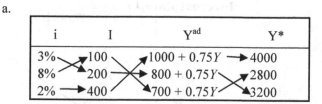

b.

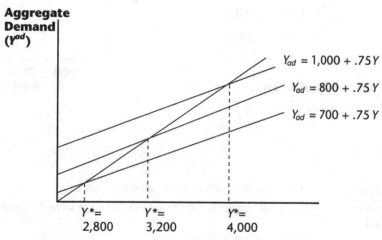

c. Use the numbers from part *a* to construct an *IS* curve.

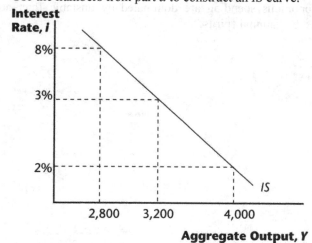

4.

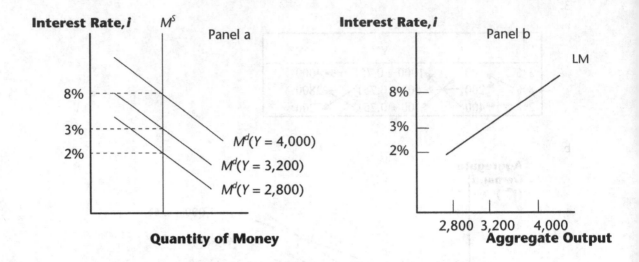

Short-Answer Questions

1. Consumer expenditure, planned investment spending, government spending, net exports.

2. In the Keynesian model, an increase in nominal output is the same as an increase in real output because the price level is assumed to be fixed.

3. $I^U = -50$, unplanned inventory investment is –50. Firms will respond by increasing production until the economy reaches equilibrium.

4. According to Keynes, changes in autonomous spending are dominated by unstable fluctuations in planned investment spending, which is influenced by "animal spirits."

5. $\Delta Y = [1/(1-mpc)]\ \Delta NX = -\$100$ billion.

Critical-Thinking Questions

1. $\Delta G = \$40$ billion

2. $\Delta T = -\$50$ billion

3. $\Delta G = \Delta T = \$200$ billion

Self-Test

True-False Questions

1.	T	2.	F
3.	T	4.	F
5.	F	6.	T
7.	T	8.	F
9.	T	10.	T
11.	T	12.	F
13.	T	14.	T
15.	T		

Multiple-Choice Questions

1.	d	2.	b
3.	a	4.	c
5.	b	6.	d
7.	a	8.	a
9.	b	10.	e
11.	a	12.	b
13.	a	14.	b
15.	c	16.	b
17.	c	18.	b
19.	d	20.	a
21.	b	22.	b
23.	d	24.	e
25.	d	26.	c
27.	a	28.	c
29.	d	30.	b

CHAPTER 23

Chapter Synopsis/Completions

1.	fiscal	2.	*IS*
3.	investment	4.	right
5.	*LM*	6.	excess
7.	income	8.	fall
9.	right	10.	rightward
11.	rise	12.	*IS*
13.	ineffective	14.	downward
15.	right		

Practice Problems

1. a. and b. The short-run (a) and long-run (b) effects of an increase in the money supply.

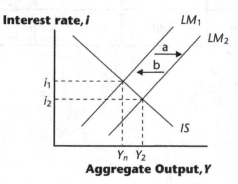

An increase in the money supply shifts the *LM* curve to the right in the short run (a). In the long run, the price level rises because aggregate output is above the natural rate level. As the price level rises, the real money supply falls causing the *LM* curve to shift back to LM_1 (b). In the long run, aggregate output returns to the natural rate level Y_n.

c. and d. The short-run (c) and long-run (d) effects of an increase in government spending.

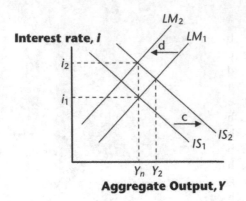

An increase in government spending shifts the *IS* curve to the right in the short run (c). In the long run the price level rises because the aggregate output is above the natural rate level. As the price level rises, the real money supply falls, causing the *LM* curve to shift left to LM_2 (d). In the long run, aggregate output returns to the natural rate level Y_n.

2.

Shift factor	Direction of change	*IS* curve shifts…	*LM* curve shifts…	Effect on interest rate	Effect on aggregate output
Autonomous consumer expenditure	+	right	no shift	+	+
Autonomous investment spending	−	left	no shift	−	−
Government spending	+	right	no shift	+	+
Taxes	+	left	no shift	−	−
Net exports	−	left	no shift	−	−
Money supply	−	no shift	left	+	−
Autonomous money demand	−	no shift	right	−	+

3. a.

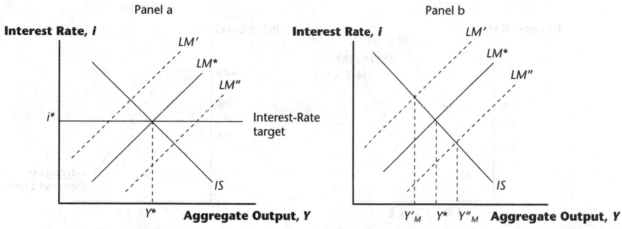

Panel a

Interest Rate, *i*

LM'

LM*

LM"

*i**

Interest-Rate target

IS

*Y**   **Aggregate Output, *Y***

Panel b

Interest Rate, *i*

LM'

LM*

LM"

IS

Y'_M Y^* Y''_M **Aggregate Output, *Y***

b. If the *LM* curve is unstable and the *IS* curve is stable (or more generally, if the *LM* curve is relatively more unstable than the *IS* curve), then a policy that targets the interest rate is preferred because it will keep aggregate output closer to *Y** as shown in Panel a above.

c.

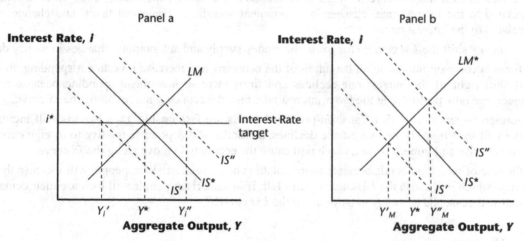

Panel a

Interest Rate, *i*

LM

*i**

Interest-Rate target

IS"

IS*

IS'

Y_i' Y^* Y_i''

Aggregate Output, *Y*

Panel b

Interest Rate, *i*

LM*

IS"

IS*

IS'

Y'_M Y^* Y''_M

Aggregate Output, *Y*

d. If the *IS* curve is unstable and the *LM* curve is stable (or more generally, if the *IS* curve is relatively more unstable than the *LM* curve), then a policy that targets the money supply is preferred because it will keep aggregate output closer to *Y** as shown in Panel b above.

4. a. through d.

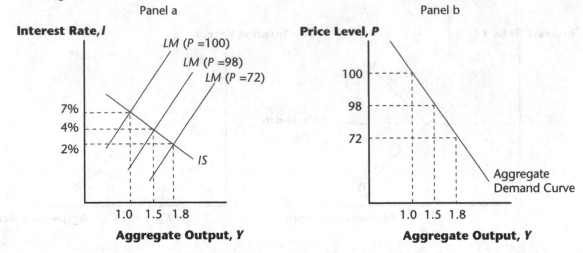

Panel a

Interest Rate, i

LM (P =100)
LM (P =98)
LM (P =72)

7%
4%
2%

IS

1.0 1.5 1.8

Aggregate Output, Y

Panel b

Price Level, P

100
98
72

Aggregate
Demand Curve

1.0 1.5 1.8

Aggregate Output, Y

Short-Answer Questions

1. Five factors shift the *IS* curve: changes in autonomous consumer expenditure, changes in investment spending unrelated to the interest rate, changes in government spending, changes in taxes, and changes in net exports unrelated to the interest rate.

2. Two factors shift the *LM* curve: changes in the money supply and autonomous changes in money demand.

3. If firms become optimistic about the future of the economy and increase investment spending, then the *IS* curve will shift right. If the interest rate declines and firms increase investment spending because new investment projects are now profitable at the lower interest rate, then the economy moves along the *IS* curve.

4. If foreign buyers decide that Canadian-produced goods are fashionable, then exports will increase and the *IS* curve will shift right. If the interest rate declines, the dollar will depreciate relative to foreign currencies causing exports to rise and imports to fall, which will cause the economy to move along the *IS* curve.

5. If the rate of return on bonds becomes more volatile and therefore riskier, people will increase their demand for money, which will cause the *LM* curve to shift left. If income rises, people will increase their demand for money, which will cause the economy to move along the *LM* curve.

Critical-Thinking Questions

Fiscal Policy	Monetary Policy	Interest Rates	Aggregate Output
Expansionary	Expansionary	?	+
Contractionary	Contractionary	?	-
Expansionary	Contractionary	+	?
Contractionary	Expansionary	-	?

Self-Test

True-False Questions

1.	F	2.	T
3.	F	4.	T
5.	T	6.	F
7.	F	8.	F
9.	F	10.	T
11.	F	12.	F
13.	T	14.	T
15.	T		

Multiple-Choice Questions

1.	a	2.	d
3.	d	4.	b
5.	c	6.	c
7.	b	8.	a
9.	a	10.	a
11.	c	12.	b
13.	d	14.	a
15.	d	16.	c
17.	e	18.	c
19.	b	20.	d
21.	a	22.	d
23.	d	24.	b
25.	b	26.	b
27.	b	28.	c
29.	a	30.	d

CHAPTER 24

Chapter Synopsis/Completions

1.	price	2.	money supply
3.	increase	4.	money
5.	right	6.	right
7.	fixed	8.	expand
9.	rise	10.	aggregate output
11.	aggregate supply	12.	price level
13.	shocks	14.	stagflation

Practice Problems

1. a.

P	Y
0.5	12
1	6
1.5	4
2	3

    b.   These points are plotted as *AD* (a) in the figure on the next page.

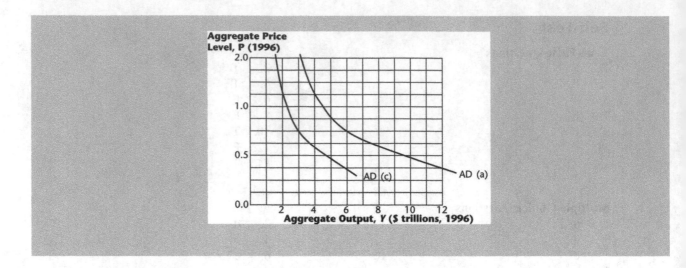

c.

P	Y
0.5	6
1	3
1.5	2
2	1.5

These points are plotted as *AD* (c) in the figure above.

2. a.   There is excess supply at P''. At P'' the quantity of aggregate output supplied at point D is greater than the quantity of output demanded at point A. Because people want to sell more goods and services than others want to buy, the prices of goods and services will fall and the aggregate price level will drop until equilibrium is reached at P^* (point E).

   b.   There is excess demand at P'. At P' the quantity of output demanded is greater than the quantity of output supplied. Because people want to buy more goods and services than others want to sell, the prices of goods and services will rise and the aggregate price level will rise until equilibrium is reached at P^* (point E).

3. a.   In the short run, an increase in the money supply will move the economy to 1' in Figure 24.6. The aggregate price level rises to $P_{1'}$ and aggregate output rises to $Y_{1'}$.

   b.   Eventually the aggregate supply curve shifts from AS_1 to AS_2 and the economy returns to long-run equilibrium at point 2 in the figure on the next page, where the aggregate price level is P_2 and aggregate output is Y_n.

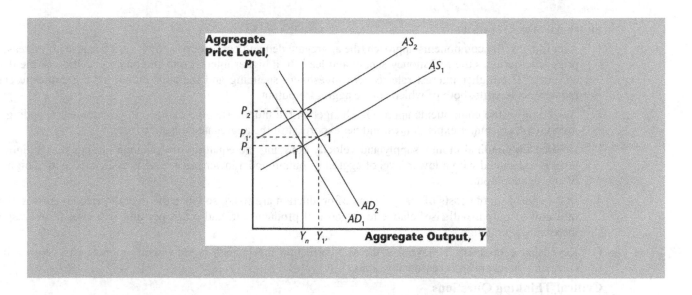

c. At point 1' output is $Y_{1'}$, which is above the natural rate level. Wages will rise eventually shifting the aggregate supply curve leftward to AS_2 where the economy finally comes to rest.

d. The initial short-run effect of the rightward shift in the aggregate demand curve is a rise in both the price level and output.

e. The ultimate long-run effect of the rightward shift in the aggregate demand curve is only a rise in the price level. In the long run, aggregate output remains unchanged at Y_n.

4. a. A reduction in the availability of oil causes the aggregate supply curve to shift left from AS_1 to AS_2 in the figure below. The economy initially moves from point 1 to point 2. The aggregate price level rises to P_2 and aggregate output falls to Y_2.

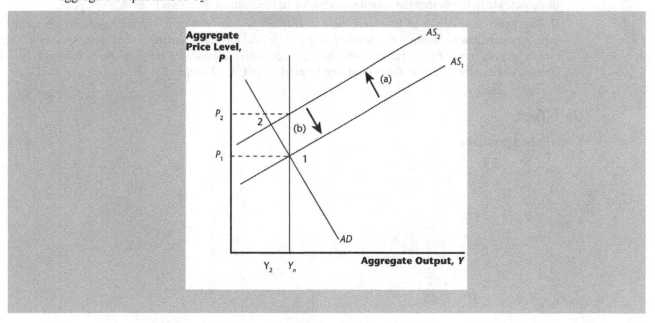

b. At point 2, output is below the natural rate level so wages fall and the aggregate supply curve shifts back to where it was initially at AS_1.

Short-Answer Questions

1. According to the components approach, the aggregate demand curve slopes downward because an increase in the price level reduces the real money supply and leads to a higher interest rate and an appreciation of the domestic currency. The higher interest rate reduces investment spending and the appreciation of the domestic currency reduces net exports, both of which reduce aggregate output.

2. According to the components approach, changes in the money supply, changes in government spending, taxes, investment, consumer expenditures, and net exports shift the aggregate demand curve.

3. Holding the nominal money supply and velocity constant, the equation of exchange implies that a higher price level is associated with a lower level of aggregate output and a lower price level is associated with a higher level of aggregate output.

4. In the short run, the costs of many factors of production are fixed, so when the overall price level rises, the price of a unit of output will rise relative to the cost of producing it, and profit per unit will rise. Firms respond by increasing production.

5. Keynesian economists believe that the self-correcting mechanism is slow while monetarists believe the self-correcting mechanism is reasonably rapid.

Critical-Thinking Questions

1. The increase in government spending will shift the aggregate demand curve to the right, which will cause employment and aggregate output to rise in the short run.

2. No. In the long run aggregate output returns to the natural rate level of output but at a higher price level.

3. The increase in government spending shifts the aggregate demand curve right and leads to an increase in the price level in the short run. In the long run, wages increase and the aggregate supply curve shifts left causing the price level to rise further.

4. If your MP is a follower of Keynes, he would likely favour an activist approach, which means that if the economy is below the natural rate level of output he would advocate boosting government spending, cutting taxes, or increasing the money supply in order to shift the aggregate demand curve back to the natural rate level of output. He believes that the automatic adjustment mechanism is relatively slow.

5. If your MP is a follower of Friedman, he would likely favour an nonactivist approach, which means that if the economy is below the natural rate level of output he would advocate leaving government spending, taxes, and the money supply unchanged. He believes that the automatic adjustment mechanism is relatively quick and the economy will adjust back to the natural rate level of output if left alone.

Self-Test

True-False Questions

1. T
2. T
3. F
4. T
5. F
6. T
7. F
8. T
9. T
10. F
11. T
12. T
13. F
14. T
15. F

Multiple-Choice Questions

1.	c	2.	c
3.	b	4.	e
5.	e	6.	d
7.	d	8.	a
9.	c	10.	b
11.	a	12.	c
13.	d	14.	d
15.	e	16.	b
17.	b	18.	d
19.	e	20.	c
21.	a	22.	c
23.	c	24.	a
25.	b	26.	c
27.	d	28.	a
29.	c	30.	d

CHAPTER 25

Chapter Synopsis/Completions

1.	monetarists	2.	evidence
3.	reduced-form	4.	structural
5.	forecasts	6.	specified
7.	reverse causation	8.	third
9.	real	10.	statistical
11.	historical	12.	price level
13.	stock	14.	worth
15.	cash flow		

Exercise 1

1.

R a.
R b.
S c.
S d.
R e.
S f.
R g.
S h.

2. a. More police are hired to patrol in areas where there is a high crime rate.

b. People who earn more income are happier.

c. A decline in aggregate output leads to a decline in the money supply.

d. People who are stressed and therefore prone to heart attacks drink more coffee.

e. People who are close to death go to the hospital.

f. Children who do well in school like to read.

3. a. (1) During the Great Depression, interest rates on U.S. Treasury securities fell to extremely low levels, suggesting that monetary policy was easy but aggregate output still contracted sharply. (2) Early empirical evidence found no link between nominal interest rates and investment spending. (3) Surveys of businesspeople revealed that investment decisions were not influenced by interest rates.

    b. Early Keynesian evidence was structural model evidence.

    c. (1) Timing evidence: The money supply tends to decline prior to the decline in aggregate output. (2) Statistical evidence: Changes in the quantity of money are correlated with changes in aggregate output. (3) Historical evidence: Historical episodes in which decreases in the money supply were clearly exogenous were followed by a decline in aggregate output.

    d. Early monetarist evidence was reduced-form evidence.

    e. (1) Reduced-form evidence is subject to the reverse-causation problem. (2) The Keynesian model was characterized too simplistically in the Friedman–Meiselman tests. (3) The Freidman–Meiselmen measure of autonomous expenditure might have been constructed poorly.

    f. Many Keynesians have shifted their views toward the monetarist position, but not all the way.

4. a.

Year	Output, Y	Money Supply, M	Rate of Money Supply Growth, $\Delta M/M$
1	510	90	–
2	525	100	11%
3	550	125	25%
4	550	125	0%
5	510	90	–28%
6	510	90	0
7	525	100	11%

    b.

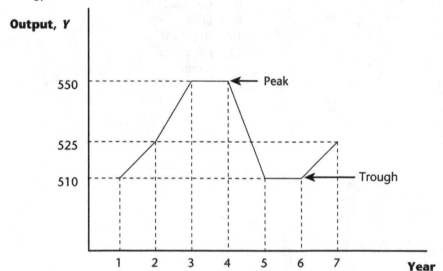

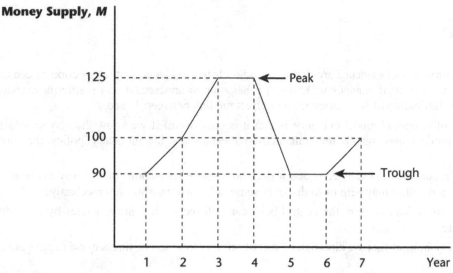

Money Supply, M

125 ← Peak

100

90 ← Trough

1 2 3 4 5 6 7   Year

Rate of Money Supply Growth, ΔM/M

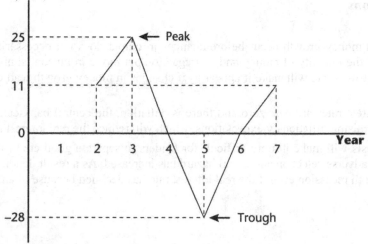

25 ← Peak

11

0   **Year**
   1 2 3 4 5 6 7

−28 ← Trough

c. The principle of *post hoc, ergo propter hoc* is that if event A occurs before event B, event A must have caused event B. The growth rate of money reaches a peak in period 3 and then turns downward in period 4. Aggregate output turns downward in period 5. The growth rate of the money supply reaches a trough in period 5 and then turns upward in period 6. Aggregate output turns upward in period 7. Thus, the growth rate of the money supply appears to "lead" aggregate output even though the money supply and aggregate output move up and down in unison.

d. As the above example illustrates, by comparing the growth rate of the money supply to aggregate output, we might incorrectly infer that money causes output even through (as was assumed) the direction of causation is the opposite.

5. <u>e</u> 1.   <u>a</u> 2.
    <u>h</u> 3.   <u>g</u> 4.
    <u>f</u> 5.   <u>c</u> 6.
    <u>d</u> 7.   <u>b</u> 8.

Short-Answer Questions

1. The advantages of structural model evidence are that it provides clearer evidence on the direction of causation; it is helpful in predicting the effect of changes in *M* on *Y*; it helps us to understand and predict how changes in institutions (such as the elimination of Regulation Q) will effect the link between *M* and *Y*.

2. The main disadvantage of structural model evidence is that it is only useful if we know the correct structure of the model. Structural models may ignore the transmission mechanisms for monetary policy that are most important.

3. The main advantage of reduced-form evidence is that it does not impose restrictions on the way monetary policy affects the economy. As a result, it may help us to discover some unknown transmission mechanisms.

4. If nominal interest rates hit a floor of zero, the central bank can still reduce real interest rates by committing to increase the inflation rate.

5. Real business cycle theory implies that the direction of causation runs from the business cycle (aggregate output) to money.

Critical-Thinking Questions

1. The fact that changes in money growth occur before changes in output does not necessarily imply that money causes output. In fact, if the quantity of money and aggregate output move in unison, simply by converting the quantity of money to a growth rate will make it appear as if changes in money growth lead changes in aggregate output.

2. Even when nominal interest rates are near zero and there is deflation, the central bank can stimulate aggregate output by committing to raising inflationary expectations, which will reduce the real interest rate.

3. A subprime financial crisis will make it more difficult for lenders to separate good credit risks from bad credit risks so the potential for adverse selection and moral hazard has increased. As a result, lending has slowed, which will slow the recovery from recession even if the real interest rate has declined because of an increase in expected inflation.

Self-Test

True-False Questions

1. F
2. T
3. T
4. T
5. T
6. F
7. T
8. F
9. T
10. T
11. F
12. F
13. T
14. F
15. F

Multiple-Choice Questions

1.	b	2.	e
3.	b	4.	d
5.	b	6.	d
7.	c	8.	b
9.	d	10.	a
11.	a	12.	c
13.	b	14.	c
15.	b	16.	b
17.	d	18.	b
19.	c	20.	a
21.	e	22.	a
23.	d	24.	d
25.	d	26.	c
27.	d	28.	b
29.	b	30.	b

CHAPTER 26

Chapter Synopsis/Completions

1.	hyperinflation	2.	monetary
3.	temporary	4.	accommodation
5.	compatible	6.	supply shocks
7.	unemployment	8.	cost-push
9.	low	10.	constraint
11.	cost-push	12.	stable
13.	time lags	14.	activist
15.	credible		

Practice Problems

1. a. Rapid money supply growth.

   b. The German government needed to make large reparation payments, and it was burdened by large reconstruction costs following World War I. It was politically unpopular to raise taxes and the amount of revenue needed exceeded the German government's capacity to borrow.

   c. The rapid money growth in Germany was clearly a response to exogenous events.

2. a. A one-shot permanent increase in government expenditures:

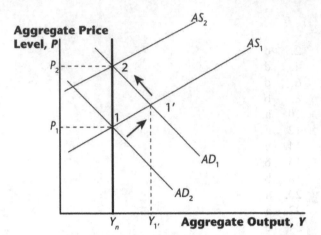

b. No, the one-shot permanent increase in government expenditures caused the price level to rise to P_2 but did not result in persistent inflation, which is a continuous rise in the price level.

c. A negative supply shock:

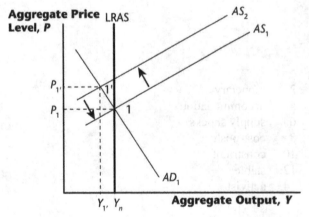

d. In response to the negative aggregate supply shock, the economy moves from 1 to 1' and then back to 1 again. A negative aggregate supply shock does not cause persistent inflation because it does not lead to a continuous increase in the price level.

3. a. The economy moves from 1 to 1'as wages rise.

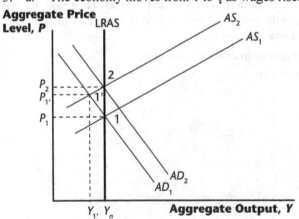

b. The economy moves from 1' to 2 as activist policymakers pursue policies to shift the aggregate demand curve to the right.

c. The increase in wages and the resulting discretionary policy did not cause persistent inflation because the price level stopped increasing after it reached P_2.

d. If workers continue to ask for higher wages and monetary policymakers continue to accommodate the decline in aggregate output by increasing the money supply, then persistent inflation will result.

4. a. DEF = $200 billion, ΔMB = $50 billion.

b. The change in the monetary base to finance the deficit is a two-step process. First Congress and the president (through the Treasury) issue bonds to finance the deficit. Then the Fed buys those bonds from the public, increasing the monetary base. In the United States as well as many other countries, the decision by the central bank to purchase bonds from the public (and therefore monetize the debt) is independent of the decision of Congress and the president to run a budget deficit.

c. A deficit can be the source of a persistent inflation only if it is persistent rather than temporary and if the government finances it by creating money rather than by issuing bonds to the public.

5. a. Under the nondiscretionary approach, policymakers would leave aggregate demand unchanged and wages and prices would adjust downward because the economy is below the natural rate level of output at 1'. As wages and prices adjust downward, the AS curve shifts to AS_2 and the economy returns to point 1.

b. Under a discretionary approach, policymakers would pursue policies to shift the aggregate demand curve to the right. If those policies take affect before wages and prices have time to adjust downward, the economy will move to point 2.

c. If discretionary policies take affect after wages and prices have adjusted downward, the economy will move to point 2'.

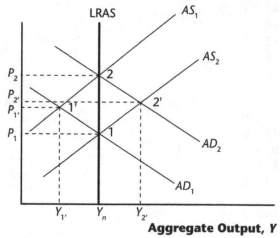

d. Discretionary policy is preferable if the wage and price adjustment process is extremely slow because it would keep the economy closer to the natural rate level of output Y_n.

e. Nondiscretionary policy is preferable if the wage and price adjustment process is rapid because discretionary policy in this situation would create excess volatility (aggregate output would swing from $Y_{1'}$ to $Y_{2'}$).

Short-Answer Questions

1. Persistent inflation occurs when changes in the price level are repeated for a substantial period of time.

2. Government spending cannot increase continually—there is a natural limit: government spending cannot exceed 100% of GDP. Similarly, taxes cannot be reduced indefinitely because eventually they would hit zero.

3. Persistent high money growth causes persistent high inflation.

4. When the employment target is too high, meaning that policymakers attempt to push unemployment below the natural rate, persistent inflation results.

5. With cost-push inflation, the unemployment rate is above the natural rate of unemployment. With demand-pull inflation, the unemployment rate is below the natural rate of unemployment.

Critical-Thinking Questions

1. "Increasing Oil Prices Caused Inflation to Rise Last Month": This headline incorrectly identifies a one-time increase in the price level (last month) as inflation. In addition, it also attributes inflation to a negative supply shock (the increase in oil prices), which is also incorrect since persistent inflation is caused by money growth.

2. "The Government Tries to Reign in Spending Fearing That Deficits Will Cause Inflation": This headline is misleading because deficits in and of themselves do not cause persistent inflation. If the deficits are persistent and the Bank of Canada monetizes the deficits, then persistent inflation can results. But it is not inevitable that deficits are inflationary.

3. "Unions Push for Higher Wages, Policymakers Fear Rising Inflation": Unions pushing for higher wages can lead to persistent higher inflation if the Bank of Canada follows an discretionary, accommodating policy, which sets up the expectations on the part of workers that their wage demands will always be met by an increase in the money supply. But again, it is important to distinguish between a one-shot increase in wages (which is not inflation) from a continual increase in wages that is accommodated by higher money growth (which is inflationary).

Self-Test

True-False Questions

1.	T	2.	F
3.	F	4.	F
5.	F	6.	F
7.	T	8.	T
9.	T	10.	F
11.	F	12.	F
13.	T	14.	T
15.	T		

Multiple-Choice Questions

1.	c	2.	b
3.	d	4.	a
5.	a	6.	b
7.	c	8.	d
9.	d	10.	d
11.	c	12.	a
13.	b	14.	d
15.	c	16.	c
17.	c	18.	a
19.	e	20.	b
21.	d	22.	a
23.	b	24.	e
25.	c	26.	b
27.	b	28.	c
29.	d	30.	a

CHAPTER 27

Chapter Synopsis/Completions

1.	expectations	2.	constant
3.	new classical	4.	flexible
5.	supply	6.	price level
7.	ineffectiveness proposition	8.	rigidities

9.   anticipated
11. policy critique
13. credible

10. New Keynesians
12. activist
14. budget deficits

Practice Problems

1.

a.   Your prediction was based on your past observations of what happened when the light was out. You assumed that when you turned the light on your roommate's behavior would not change—he would not make as much noise because he would not be bumping into things in the dark, but he also would not change the length of time he bumped around the room before going to bed. According to the Lucas critique, econometric models assume this same type of unchanging behaviour because they are based on past data. Your experiment failed because your roommate changed his behaviour by staying awake longer with the lights on.

b.   When policymakers use an econometric model to predict the outcome of a change in policy, they fail to take account of the fact that by changing policy, people will change their behaviour. The change in behaviour (staying awake longer with the lights on) invalidates the prediction based on past data.

2.

a.   In response to an unanticipated increase in the money supply, the economy will move from point 1 to 2' and output will rise to $Y_{2'}$. With an unanticipated increase in the money supply, the expected price level remains at P_1, so wages and prices remain unchanged and the economy moves along AS_1.

b.   In response to an anticipated increase in the money supply, the economy will move from point 1 to 2, and output will remain at Y_n. With an anticipated increase in the money supply, the expected price level increases along with the increase in the money supply and so the aggregate supply curve shifts left as the aggregate demand curve is shifting right.

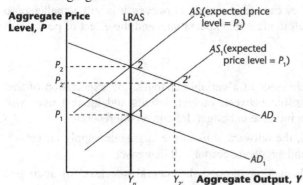

c.   If workers and firms expect the Fed to increase the money supply by 10%, then the aggregate demand curve to shift rightward to AD_2. If the Fed unexpectedly increases the money supply by only 5%, then aggregate demand will shift by less than expected (to $AD_{2'}$) but aggregate supply will still shift back to AS_2 based on an expected price level of P_2. Output will decrease to $Y_{2'}$.

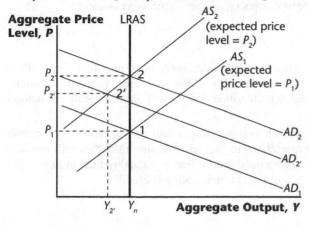

d. The policy recommendation that follows from the analysis in parts *a* through *c* is that policymakers should strive to minimize unanticipated changes in aggregate demand.

3.

a. In response to an unanticipated increase in the money supply, the economy will move from point 1 to point U and output will rise to Y_U. With an unanticipated increase in the money supply, the expected price level remains at P_1, so wages and prices remain unchanged, and the economy moves along AS_1.

b. In response to an anticipated increase in the money supply, the economy will move from point 1 to point A, and output will remain at Y_A. With an anticipated increase in the money supply, the expected price level increases along with the increase in the money supply, but prices and wages are sticky and do not fully adjust to the new expected price level, so the AS curve shifts leftward partially to AS_A.

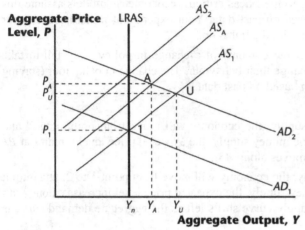

c. According to the analysis in parts *a* and *b*, anticipated policy can affect output. However, it is still a challenge to design policy to improve the economy because it is difficult to measure expectations and the effect of policy still depends on expectations in the new Keynesian model.

Short-Answer Questions

1. The Lucas econometric critique implies that when the behaviour of a variable changes, the expectation of that variable changes as well. Using past data on the relationship between budget deficits and interest rates will provide misleading predictions of the effect of a permanent increase in budget deficits on interest rates.

2. If the increase in the money supply is less than expected, the leftward shift in the aggregate supply curve will more than offset the rightward shift in aggregate demand and aggregate output will decrease.

3. No. Random policy changes would cause undesirable fluctuations around the natural rate level of aggregate output.

4. Wages and prices are sticky for three reasons: (1) long-term contracts, (2) reducing wages when demand declines may adversely affect worker productivity, and (3) changing prices is costly.

5. Not necessarily. Although discretionary policy has an effect on output according to the Keynesian model, the effect of discretionary policy is still difficult to predict (because expectations are difficult to measure).

Critical-Thinking Questions

1. Based on the new classical model, the policy recommendation is to immediately announce that the Bank of Canada will reduce money growth to achieve a reduction in inflation to 5%. If the announced reduction in money growth is credible (and the Bank of Canada follows through with the intended policy), inflation will fall without causing unemployment to rise.

2. A new Keynesian might recommend a more gradual approach because wages and prices are sticky, so even though workers and firms will immediately adjust their expectations to the new inflation rate, they will not fully adjust their wages and prices. The challenge of this policy recommendation is that a gradual reduction in inflation may compromise the ability of policymakers to convince the public that their policy is credible.

3. The common element of both theories is credibility. If the president decides to follow a gradual approach, he (or she) must overcome the fact that a gradual policy will tend to be less credible. If the president decides to follow a "cold turkey" approach, it is equally important that the policy is credible.

Self-Test

True-False Questions

1.	T	2.	T
3.	F	4.	F
5.	T	6.	F
7.	T	8.	T
9.	F	10.	F
11.	T	12.	T
13.	F	14.	T
15.	T		

Multiple-Choice Questions

1.	a	2.	c
3.	d	4.	e
5.	e	6.	b
7.	c	8.	a
9.	c	10.	b
11.	c	12.	d
13.	d	14.	a
15.	b	16.	e
17.	c	18.	b
19.	d	20.	e
21.	a	22.	b
23.	a	24.	c
25.	c	26.	d
27.	d	28.	a
29.	c	30.	c